DANGEROUS PROFESSORS

DANGEROUS PROFESSORS

ACADEMIC FREEDOM AND THE
NATIONAL SECURITY CAMPUS

❧

Malini Johar Schueller and Ashley Dawson, Editors

THE UNIVERSITY OF MICHIGAN PRESS
Ann Arbor

Copyright © by the University of Michigan 2009
All rights reserved
Published in the United States of America by
The University of Michigan Press
Manufactured in the United States of America
♾ Printed on acid-free paper

2012 2011 2010 2009   4 3 2 1

A CIP catalog record for this book is available from the British Library.

Library of Congress Cataloging-in-Publication Data

Dangerous professors : academic freedom and the national security
campus / Malini Johar Schueller and Ashley Dawson, editors.
    p.   cm.
    Includes index.
    ISBN-13: 978-0-472-07063-3 (cloth : alk. paper)
    ISBN-10: 0-472-07063-0 (cloth : alk. paper)
    ISBN-13: 978-0-472-05063-5 (pbk. : alk. paper)
    ISBN-10: 0-472-05063-X (pbk. : alk. paper)
    1. Academic freedom—United States.   2. Academic freedom—Case
studies.   I. Schueller, Malini Johar, 1957–   II. Dawson, Ashley, 1965–
LC72.2.D36   2009
378.1'21—dc22   2009014538

ACKNOWLEDGMENTS

Heartfelt thanks to the editors at the University of Michigan Press for their willingness to take on a project that touches on controversial issues, at a time when concern for the bottom line often encourages timidity among those who should be championing democracy on and beyond the campus.

We would also like to thank the anonymous readers for their insightful comments on how to improve the manuscript.

To our contributors, a big thank-you for your patience during the long journey to print.

We would like to thank Duke University Press for giving us permission to reprint the following essays:

Malini Johar Schueller, "Area Studies and Multicultural Imperialism: The Project of Decolonizing Knowledge," from *Social Text* 25.1 (2007), pp. 41–62.

Ashley Dawson, "The Crisis at Columbia: Academic Freedom, Area Studies, and Contingent Labor in the Contemporary Academy," from *Social Text* 25.1 (2007), pp. 63–84.

Malini Johar Schueller and Ashley Dawson, "Academic Labor at the Crossroads? An Interview with Andrew Ross," from *Social Text* 25.1 (2007), pp. 117–132.

Bill V. Mullen, "Blacklist Redux: W. E. B. Du Bois and the Price of Academic Freedom," from *Social Text* 25.1 (2007), pp. 85–104.

Vijay Prashad, "Teaching by Candlelight," from *Social Text* 25.1 (2007), pp. 105–116.

We would also like to thank Michigan State University for giving us permission to reprint Sophia McClennen, "E Pluribus Unum / Ex Uno Plura: Legislating and Deregulating American Studies post 9/11," *CR: The New Centennial Review* 8.1 (2008): 145–75.

Ashley would like to thank the City University of New York, whose generous sabbatical leave policies are in no small part responsible for the successful completion of this project. Of course, these policies are a result of the hard bargaining and solidarity of the Professional Staff Congress, which Ashley would also like to acknowledge. Both in New York and Florida, our academic home-grounds, concerted attempts by administrators to restructure the university and disempower faculty have made the completion of this project more compelling. The fortitude displayed by the members of the Graduate Student Organizing Committee during a brutally long strike against the ruthless administration of New York University, and the continuing efforts of the United Faculty of Florida to fight layoffs of faculty at the University of Florida, provided tremendous inspiration and a sense of real urgency during the long gestation of this manuscript.

CONTENTS

Case Studies

ᴧ

ACADEMIC FREEDOM

Contexts and Histories

cA

Ashley Dawson and Malini Johar Schueller

IN THE HEYDAY OF THE VIETNAM WAR, conservative critic Irving Kristol excoriated irresponsible university protestors for delivering "harangues on 'the power structure'" and for stooping to read "articles and reports from the foreign press on the American presence in Vietnam."[1] What elicited Kristol's ire was his sense that universities seemed to be providing spaces where alternatives to the dominant ideology could be articulated and contested. In the aftermath of 9/11, universities have come under virulent attack for the same reasons, creating a general climate of fear and intimidation. The firing and arrest of University of South Florida professor Sami Al-Arian, the dismissal of Ward Churchill for his refusal to recant his statements about 9/11, the sabotaging of Juan Cole's appointment in Middle Eastern history at Yale because of his criticism of U.S. foreign policy, and the 2007 derailment of tenure at De Paul University for renowned scholar Norman Finkelstein are only the most overt and obvious examples of administrators capitulating to government efforts to turn universities into ancillaries of the War on Terror.

Dangerous Professors takes these current threats to academic freedom as an opportunity to analyze the status of academic freedom today. By looking at the very idea of academic freedom in historical perspective, it also seeks to reexamine its underlying assumptions and limitations. The stakes in recent struggles over academic freedom are far higher than they might at first appear: this is not simply a tussle over some isolated professional protocol. Education and culture are vital components in the struggle for political power, and, as we discuss below, the Right has absorbed this lesson all too well. For most of the "American century," the battle over educational curricula and institutions was one of the key foci of the systematic and wildly successful organizing efforts of movement conservatives, and this has been particularly true in the last thirty years. These efforts are bearing fruit today not simply in the isolation and persecution of outspoken progressive intellectuals but in a wholesale assault on critical thinking and teaching in general. In tandem with these assaults, the corporatization of the university has produced a predominantly contingent labor force on campuses, thereby significantly eroding traditions of collective governance and institutional autonomy. At stake, then, is democracy on the college campus and beyond. After the attacks of September 11, 2001, for example, on-campus discussions that raised questions about the relationship between imperialism and terrorism or challenged the Bush administration's plans to export democracy to the Middle East by force of arms became the targets of severely jingoistic attacks.

We suggest that the contemporary moment reveals the limits of the professional, privatized, and privileged notion of academic freedom put forth in the past statements of professional bodies such as the American Association of University Professors (AAUP). As our contributors demonstrate, notions of academic freedom are mobilized today not just by critics of U.S. imperialism. They are also deployed by ardent nationalists intent on silencing dissent and by university administrators determined to squelch the organizing efforts of contingent university personnel. *Dangerous Professors* thus places recent high-profile attacks on individual dissidents within a broader context, contending that the casualization of academic labor is critical to the current transformation of universities into national security campuses. Recent interventions of the AAUP on behalf of contingent faculty are welcome steps toward fighting this trend.[2] It also demonstrates that academic corporatization, the curbing of dissent, and the imperial policies of the U.S. state are intimately linked.

In challenging the inequalities of the nascent national security campus, this volume emphasizes the need to expand our conceptions of democracy on campus beyond individualized and often exclusive conceptions of professional rights. Academic freedom is a necessary but insufficient condition for fostering effective critique. Against the narrow definitions of the concept articulated historically by professional bodies such as the AAUP, we thus seek to highlight an activist agenda for claiming the campus as a site for radical democracy, a critical public sphere that provides a bulwark against neoliberalism and imperialism. While campus democracy surely cannot achieve radical social and political change by itself, engaged teaching and research nevertheless have a vital role to play in maintaining a critical public sphere. Fresh definitions of academic freedom must take this expanded notion of campus democracy as their point of departure. In this project of reexamining the conditions for activist teaching and critical thinking, we take as our inspiration the work of Edward Said, who argued for the importance of the engaged intellectual and the central role of the humanities in critiquing orthodoxy and dogma.

THE STAKES OF ACADEMIC FREEDOM
❧

Although the current political attacks on academics must be decried as the policing of dissent, it is important to remember that the most influential guidelines about academic freedom in the American context have not only discussed the vital role of campus-based public intellectuals but also the appropriate limits of faculty expression. A key feature of the "1915 Declaration of Principles on Academic Freedom and Academic Tenure," Arthur O. Lovejoy and John Dewey's pioneering document on this subject, was the way it distinguished the university from a businesses venture and university teaching from private employment. Faculty members were not employees in the ordinary sense because "in the essentials of his [a faculty member's] professional activity his duty is to the wider public to which the institution itself is morally amenable."[3] The declaration charts the three components of academic freedom, "freedom of inquiry and research; freedom of teaching within the university or college; and freedom of extramural utterance and action."[4] In essence, the 1915 document seeks to delineate the special freedoms accruing from a commitment to the public good.

Yet the 1940 "Statement of Principles on Academic Freedom and Tenure," the most widely accepted document on academic freedom, articulates a tense relationship between the university and the nation, with the university being portrayed on the one hand as an active public sphere organization, a conduit for the nation's health, and an institution for social good and, on the other, a sphere of learning apart from the world. The document begins by linking universities to the society at large. Universities are "conducted for the common good and not to further the interests of either the individual teacher or the institution as a whole. The common good depends upon the free search for truth and its free exposition." Academic freedom, it argues, "is essential to these purposes."[5] It continues on, however, to define the rules of behavior that their professional role entails:

> College and university teachers are citizens, members of a learned profession, and officers of an educational institution. When they speak or write as citizens, they should be free from institutional censorship, but their special position in the community imposes special obligations. . . . Hence they should at all times be accurate, should exercise appropriate restraint, should show respect for the opinions of others, and should make every effort to indicate that they are not speaking for the institution.[6]

In aftermath of the civil rights struggles, and the major legal challenges to academic freedom that they inspired, a joint committee of the AAUP and the Association of American Colleges met to reevaluate the 1940 policy statement and adapt it to changing times. Their interpretive comments, adopted in 1970, reveal a willingness on the part of the AAUP to circumscribe the sphere of academic freedom. While vigorously maintaining the organization's commitment to free inquiry and controversial subject matter in the classroom, the 1970 statement underscores "the need for teachers to avoid persistently intruding material which has no relation to their subject."[7] While seemingly benign, such a statement is clearly a disincentive for interdisciplinarity and a curb on the potential of the humanities to engage with and change society.

Indeed Edward Said has argued that instead of a humanism legitimated by culture and the state that keeps the humanist in a restricted place, the humanist should engage with worldliness or the real historical world.[8] Said was particularly cynical about oppositional left criticism that despite its theoretical adherence to radicalism remained silent, for instance, on the question of human rights or that failed to distinguish between authoritarianism and totalitarianism.[9] For Said, humanism means "situating critique at the very heart of humanism, critique as a form of democratic freedom and as a continuous practice of questioning and of accumulating knowledge that is open to, rather than in denial of, the constituent historical realities of the post–Cold War world, its early colonial formation, and the frighteningly global reach of the last remaining superpower of today."[10] The role of the intellectual was not to be an ally of the state but rather to present alternatives to the narratives provided "on behalf of official memory and national identity and mission."[11] Said's notion of the humanist and the intellectual, that is, refuses the 1940 effort to compartmentalize the three components of academic freedom—freedom of research, teaching, and extramural utterance—and suggests that the extramural instead be reconceptualized as part of humanistic inquiry itself.

We mention these limits on the profession's dominant idea of academic freedom not to belittle the concept altogether but to point out ways in which professional self-policing can sabotage the more dynamic mission of the university for the purposes of mollifying corporations or donors, to whom the university is beholden, and the state, which commands from the university the task of ideological reproduction. Academic freedom defined as appropriate restraint can become a means of curbing dissent, particularly in highly charged periods such as wartime. It is this restraint that led the academic community to collaborate with McCarthyism by accepting the legitimacy of congressional committees and investigators intent on purging American universities of communists. For example, in a collective statement that they issued in 1953, a group of university presidents affirmed that the scholar's mission involved the "examination of unpopular ideas, of ideas considered abhorrent and even dangerous" and described the university as a unique, nonprofit structure that was different from a corporation. At the same time, they also stipulated that loyalty to the nation-state and free enterprise were essential to the university as well. Thus, they reasoned, membership in the Communist Party "extinguishes the right to a university position."[12]

CAMPUS RADICALISM AND THE
RIGHT-WING WAR ON EDUCATION
&

The efforts of the McCarthy era to establish individual and collective surveillance offer striking parallels to the strategies deployed in the culture wars of the 1990s and, more recently, during the War on Terror. Then as now, myriad well-funded and well-organized groups exploited public fears about national security to attack educational institutions.[13] The National Education Association, for example, has documented five hundred different organizations engaged in assaults on public education during the Mc-

Carthy period.[14] Perhaps the most prominent of these groups was Allen Zoll's National Council on American Education (NCAE), a highly influential organization devoted to capitalizing on fears concerning the impact of the supposedly immoral and socialistic mores indoctrinated in students by public school teachers. Distributing mass quantities of pamphlets with inflammatory titles such as *How Red Are the Schools?*, *They Want Your Children*, and *Awake, America, Awake, and Pray!*, Zoll's NCAE exploited allegations of "subversive" infiltration to strengthen the impact of local antitax and ultraconservative citizens' groups and to sway the outcomes of many local school board elections. Zoll's searing attacks on public education drew on a potent cocktail of anti-Keynesian laissez-faire ideology and exclusionary representations of U.S. identity as Christian, individualist, and capitalist. This toxic combination has only grown more powerful since Zoll's day, and now characterizes dominant segments of the conservative movement.[15] His strategy of using anti-Americanism to smear educators has been deployed once again to silence dissent during the War on Terror. The post-9/11 report of Lynne Cheney's American Council of Trustees and Alumni (ACTA), for example, castigated educators as the weak link in the U.S. war against terrorism and singled them out as a potential fifth column.[16]

However, it was not simply leaders of institutions who were vulnerable to the tactics of the scaremongers. The professional organizations and unions charged with protecting educators were equally affected by the pervasive atmosphere of fear that characterized the McCarthy era. Thus, although the National Educational Association (NEA), the world's largest organization of educators, moved quickly to create a defense committee, the National Commission for the Defense of Democracy Through Education, the organization ended up replicating some of the Right's central doctrines. In 1949, for example, NEA president Andrew Holt argued that teachers had a duty to inspire "our children with a love of democracy that will be inoculated against the false ideology of communism."[17] In addition, the organization refused to support the wave of teacher strikes that took place at midcentury, and although it did object frequently to loyalty oaths, it never advised teachers to refuse to sign them.[18]

Yet despite the purges of the 1950s and the massive increase in state funding of research following World War II, the U.S. university retained its relative autonomy as an organ of civil society, due in part to the broad institutionalization of tenure following the 1940 AAUP statement.[19] Thus teaching and research at universities also continued the mission of "searching for truth" and the avocation of professors to work for the "common good." One example will serve to make our point. William F. Buckley's rantings in *God and Man at Yale* about the advocacy of collectivism and Marxism by the Yale economics department faculty were at once a heartening endorsement of critical thinking and a chilling prognostication of the corporate pressures to which universities are increasingly subject. Buckley argued that the "faculty of Yale is morally and constitutionally responsible to the trustees of Yale, who are in turn responsible to the alumni, and thus duty bound to transmit to their students the wisdom, insight, and value judgments which in the trustees' opinion will enable the American citizen to make the optimum adjustment to the community and to the world."[20] John Chamberlain, in his introduction to Buckley's book, explicitly insists that knowledge production should be commodified: "Should the right to pursue the truth be constructed as a right to inculcate values that deny the value-judgments of the customer who is paying the bills of education? Must the customer, in the name of Academic Freedom, be compelled to take a product which he may consider defective?"[21] "Does Yale Corporation, which represents the education-buying customer, want any such thing?"[22] For evidence of the propagation of socialism, Buckley cites, for instance, his lecture notes from Professor Lindblom's economics course, in which Lindblom assaulted the concept of private property.[23] Buckley lamented that Yale, while being supported by Christian individualists, attempted to turn the children of these supporters into atheist socialists, in part through adherence to a Keynesian collectivism.[24]

As the emergence of community colleges increased minority enrollment and northern institutions began recruiting black students, campuses diversified. Radicalized by the Vietnam War, minority students such as those in the Third World Movement of 1968 articulated connections between imperialism abroad and the repression of people of color, the wretched of the earth, at home; among their demands were the employment of minority faculty as well as the creation of new programs such as ethnic studies and African American studies. Mass higher education, viewed as essential to economic competitiveness and national security, was generating levels of dissent conservatives have since attempted to curb. But while universities such as Stanford attempted to stifle dissidence by firing faculty like H. Bruce Franklin who dared to publicly proclaim the relationship between capitalist power, imperialism, and racism, entire fields of study such as American history (to take just one example) were thoroughly changed.[25] Revisionist historians such as William Appleman Williams gave legitimacy to the study of U.S. imperialism, while others pursued history from below. By the time Howard Zinn published *A People's History of the United States* in 1980, a wider public had been touched by this new history. In the next fifteen years, Zinn's book went through twenty-five printings and sold over four hundred thousand copies.[26] A similar reception was accorded to Edward Said's *Orientalism* (1978), which ushered in the field of postcolonial studies in the U.S. academy, provoking the enduring wrath of neoconservatives by making it impossible for Middle East studies to continue to provide an alibi for U.S. foreign policy.

The conservative reaction to this mounting politicization of academia was swift. In June 1969, recently elected president Richard Nixon delivered a speech at a public college in South Dakota in which he linked "drugs, crime, campus revolts, racial discord, [and] draft resistance" and lamented the loss of integrity in academia in the following terms: "We have long considered our colleges and universities citadels of freedom, where the rule of reason prevails. Now both the process of freedom and the rule of reason are under attack."[27] Despite Nixon's prominent role in the House Un-American Activities Committee hearings early in his career, the conservative counteroffensive against the campus movement did not follow the familiar inquisitorial script of the McCarthy era. Instead, the rightwing strategy for dealing with dissenting students and faculty was built on a memorandum penned by future Nixon Supreme Court nominee Lewis Powell. In an August 1971 letter entitled "Attack on American Free Enterprise System," Powell wrote to his friends at the National Chamber of Commerce to decry the liberal establishment's "appeasement" of anticapitalist sentiment on campuses around the United States.[28] It was high time, Powell argued, that business learned how to fight back against charismatic radicals such as Herbert Marcuse, whose influence was, in his opinion, corrupting an entire generation. Powell argued that the Chamber should begin its campaign by establishing a stable of social scientists whose work would articulate procorporate perspectives in the public sphere. In addition, the Chamber should aggressively insist on "equal time" for "independent scholars who do believe in the system" at campus speaking engagements. Finally, however, Powell conceded that the fundamental problem—the "imbalance of many [academic] faculties"—would take time to repair:

> Correcting this is indeed a long-range and difficult project. Yet, it should be taken as a part of an overall program. This would mean the

urging of the need for faculty balance upon university administrators and boards of trustees. The methods to be employed require careful thought, and the obvious pitfalls must be avoided. Improper pressure would be counterproductive. But the basic concepts of balance, fairness, and truth are difficult to resist, if properly presented to boards of trustees, by writing and speaking, and by appeals to alumni associations and groups. This is a long road and not one for the fainthearted.[29]

Powell's memorandum spread like wildfire through America's corporate boardrooms. Not only did it clearly identify a pivotal ideological struggle; it also advanced a sustainable strategy for changing campus culture, one that did not rely on the discredited tactics of government-sponsored witch-hunts that typified the McCarthy era. Rather than simply seeking to clamp down on wayward organizations such as the Modern Language Association (MLA), in other words, Powell advised the corporate elite to fund the work of intellectuals who would engage in what Gramsci called a war of position against critics of U.S. policies, both foreign and domestic, and of the capitalist world system in general.

Powell's memo has been plausibly credited with stimulating the foundation of such pivotal right-wing think tanks as the Heritage Foundation, the Manhattan Institute, the Cato Institute, and Accuracy in Academe, each of which has achieved dramatic success in swaying public policy over the last couple of decades while simultaneously producing research of dubious value.[30] From 1970 to 1996, the number of think tanks in the United States increased from fewer than sixty to more than three hundred.[31] And their numbers have grown at least ten times more since then.[32] Most importantly, conservative think tanks outnumber liberal think tanks by a ratio of roughly two to one and outspend them by more than three to one.[33] This should not of course be surprising given the strategic focus of the conservative foundations that support think tanks. As James S. Piereson, the executive director of the John M. Olin Foundation, put it, "The liberal foundations became too project oriented—they support projects but not institutions. They flip from project to project. . . . We, on the other hand, support institutions. We provide the infrastructure for institutions."[34]

Frank Chodorow's Intercollegiate Society for Individualists (ISI), renamed the Intercollegiate Studies Institute following his death in 1966, offers a particularly clear example of how the Right fosters its organic intellectuals and projects their voices using educational institutions. Today the

ISI administers the Collegiate Network (CN). With guidance from right-wing luminaries like William Bennett, the network offers financial and technical aid to editors and writers at scores of student publications at top universities around the country, including the *Dartmouth Review,* Princeton's *American Foreign Policy,* University of California—Berkeley's *California Patriot,* and the *Stanford Review.*[35] CN essentially offers young conservative intellectuals an alternative education and a gateway to future careers through annual journalistic training conferences, campus mentoring sessions, and summer and yearlong internships at leading national media outlets.[36]

The think tanks spawned by the Powell memorandum have deployed a remarkably consistent combination of neoliberal and neoconservative ideology across their thirty-year history. A key player early in this story was the Philanthropy Round Table, a consortium of conservative foundations organized in the late 1970s to coordinate donor efforts. This body was founded at Irving Kristol's Institute for Educational Affairs (IEA).[37] Kristol, of course, is one of the grandfathers of neoconservativism, active, as we noted at the outset of this introduction, in opposition to the social movements of the 1960s. Kristol's IEA, which identified promising young scholars, supported them with grants, and then helped them find work with activist organizations and publications, was funded by some of the biggest right-wing philanthropical groups, including the Olin, Scaife, and Smith Richardson foundations, as well as by corporations such as Coca-Cola, K-Mart, Mobil Oil, General Electric, and Dow Chemical.[38] Of course, these same foundations also went on to support more patently ideological organs of the Right such as the Project for a New American Century, the think tank that infamously laid out plans for a preemptive, unilateralist U.S. foreign policy during the Bush administration.

This funding overlap between organizations putatively devoted to educational issues and those devoted to more explicitly imperialist goals should not be particularly surprising given the consistent ideological emphasis of the major right-wing philanthropic foundations on free market capitalism and aggressive nationalism. As the Bradley Foundation website puts it, "The Lynde and Harry Bradley Foundation is likewise devoted to strengthening American democratic capitalism and the institutions, principles and values that sustain and nurture it. Its programs support limited, competent government; a dynamic marketplace for economic, intellectual, and cultural activity; and a vigorous defense at home and abroad of American ideas and institutions."[39] We should note that this ideological orthodoxy is also potently alluring to the increasingly powerful evangelical Protestant groups within the Right, with their neo-Victorian emphasis on the market as a divinely ordained mechanism for rewarding the virtuous and punishing the sinful and their frequently apocalyptic embrace of a thinly veiled racist war on Islam in the name of combating terrorism.[40]

Right-funded think tanks have also been the major source of post-9/11 attacks against academia. David Horowitz, for instance, is president and founder of the David Horowitz Freedom Center, formerly the Center for the Study of Popular Culture (CSPC), an organization that receives significant support from the Bradley Foundation, and which Horowitz has used to launch his attacks on the Left. In 2003, Horowitz founded Students for Academic Freedom (SAF), an organization using the discourse of freedom and diversity to suppress any critique of the neoconservative agenda and the War on Terror by policing classrooms, syllabi, and conferences in humanities departments. The conjunction of right-wing educational and political agenda is clear. Horowitz's major objective is to get states to pass an "Academic Bill of Rights," a bill that he contends is necessary given the liberal biases of university faculty. Modeled after and echoing phrases from AAUP documents on academic freedom, the Academic Bill of Rights attempts to restrict and regulate faculty expression and course content. Horowitz writes: "When I visited the political-science department at the University of Colorado at Denver this year, the office doors and bulletin boards were plastered with cartoons and statements ridiculing Republicans, and only Republicans. When I asked President Hoffman about that, she assured me that she would request that such partisan materials be removed and an appropriate educational environment restored."[41] Leaving aside the fact that Horowitz doesn't comment on the postings in business schools or medical schools, the problem is that "diversity" becomes an issue of political affiliation and education is straitjacketed as nationalism. Indeed, as Horowitz makes clear, he is bothered by "the role of the leftwing university in undermining American self-respect and self-confidence at a time when the nation was facing enemies who [are] deadly."[42]

What is most dangerous about Horowitz's agenda is the attempt to police faculty through Orwellian doublespeak under the guise of terms such as "pluralism, diversity, opportunity, critical intelligence, openness and fairness."[43] The Academic Bill of Rights, for instance, asserts that "reading lists in the humanities and social sciences should reflect the uncertainty and unsettled character of all human knowledge by providing dissenting sources and viewpoints where appropriate."[44] At first glance the statement simply appears as an endorsement of a Socratic methodology that has been central to the university classroom for decades. Clearly, a conception of academic freedom that denies the freedom to teach right-of-center perspectives on history, literature, or sociology has no place in the academy. Nor, more importantly, should a student's intellectual freedom to challenge any viewpoint, be it from the left or right, be gainsaid. But what proponents of the Academic Bill of Rights are proposing is a mandating and surveillance of course content that should, in principle, not be tolerated. The freedom to teach what one pleases in the classroom is central to the academy, even though, as Cary Nelson notes in his essay, the practice of such freedom is never absolute. It is crucial, however, that the status of a particular discipline not be determined for an instructor by an outside body. Right-wing organizations, unfortunately, have been quick to propose agendas for the teaching of particular disciplines. Thus the argument of the academic bill of rights about the unsettled nature of the humanities and social sciences is more than a validation of pluralism. While seemingly benign, such a position, as the AAUP notes, reduces all knowledge to uncertain opinion and suggests that all opinions are equally valid, thus negating the essential function of education.[45] In practice, this position has involved insidious policing: SAF urged its members to check if a conference on environmental issues included solely panelists who believed in global warming and encourages student vigilantism over liberal bias in all departments dealing with minority issues—women's studies, African American studies, Asian American Studies, and so on.[46] Horowitz also published a blacklist of 101 professors deemed dangerous, some because of their involvement in peace centers.[47] Most notoriously, under the pretext of "balance," the David Horowitz Freedom Center sponsored an "Islamo-Fascism Awareness Week" in October 2007 in which 114 college and university campuses participated. SAF, which distributes the booklet *Unpatriotic University,* now boasts 150 chapters in colleges and universities nationwide, and over a dozen legislatures have considered academic freedom legislation. Such campus vigilantism for patriotism—defined as unquestioning support for the state's policies in the Middle East—is also being vigorously promoted by Daniel Pipes, founder of Campus Watch, a project of the Middle East Forum that is committed to monitoring Middle East studies at universities.

Much of the vituperation about "bias" was channeled into attempts to monitor course content in Middle East and other area studies programs. In

2003, proponents of H.R. 3077, the International Studies in Higher Education Act, launched a vigorous campaign to make Title VI funding to area studies programs contingent upon the establishment of an "International Higher Education Advisory Board" comprised partly of appointed members from the Department of Homeland Security. The function of the board would be to "balance" readings considered anti-American (included under this rubric were all critiques of imperialism and colonialism, especially included those of Edward Said and anyone influenced by him) with those supporting U.S. foreign policy. Said's works continue to be targeted by the likes of Horowitz, Pipes, and a host of neoconservatives, in part, no doubt, because his entire career testified to the inseparability of pure and political knowledge and above all because his key work, *Orientalism,* questioned American claims of exceptionalism from empire by firmly locating the United States within the trajectory of Western colonial empires.[48] *Orientalism* also challenged the legitimacy of Orientalist social scientists whose expertise U.S. policymakers have relied upon and taken as truth in their dealings with areas as diverse as the Middle East and Vietnam. As Said stated in the 2003 preface to the twenty-fifth anniversary edition of *Orientalism,* the Iraq war, waged for world dominance and scarce resources, was "disguised for its true intent, hastened, and reasoned for by Orientalists who betrayed their calling as scholars. The major influences on George W. Bush's Pentagon and National Security Council were men such as Bernard Lewis and Fouad Ajami, experts of the Arab and Islamic world who helped the American hawks think about such preposterous phenomena as 'the Arab mind' and centuries-old Islamic decline that only American power could reverse."[49]

It is crucial here to recognize that Said's career stands as a challenge not only to neoconservative hostility to critique of the state but also to both neoconservative and neoliberal conceptions of the subject / the human. For Said it was imperative that his project be linked to his consciousness of being an "Oriental," of thinking about the self in Gramscian terms, as a product of historical processes.[50] For neoconservatives such as Horowitz and Pipes who argue ostensibly for diversity and balance, the self or subject is the raceless, classless subject of liberal humanism, and apart from historical processes, hence ostensibly "unbiased." This is also the subject of neoliberalism, answerable to the calls of the market alone; it is in the interest of advocates of neoliberalism to close off avenues where the marked historical subject can articulate alternatives to the free market or the state and nationalism. The two-pronged push to hire adjunct workers and to create more programs answerable to corporations either directly or indirectly through contracts from the Department of Homeland Security is a means of silencing people like Said who stand for curricular change and alternative intellectual practices. Perhaps the perfect embodiment of neocon politics and neoliberal economic agenda is Governor Jeb Bush, the first chancellor of the State Board of Education in Florida and also an active participant of ACTA.

Effectively, intellectual vigilantism has been trumped, although not replaced, by universities' managerial complicity with the state agenda and corporate concerns. What has taken place since 9/11, in other words, has been nothing short of a rebuilding of the national security campus. Thus, although H.R. 3077, the bill to regulate the postcolonial influence in area studies, was quashed after nationwide protests by academics, the Department of Homeland Security (DHS) has found better, more proactive measures to direct curriculum by funding centers and scholarships for financially strapped universities. Since 2003, DHS has offered 439 fellowships to students for homeland security research, and 227 schools offer degree or certificate programs in homeland security.[51] Such fellowships and Centers of Excellence, again created by DHS money, effectively redirect research at a time when federal funding of research and development (except for DHS, the Defense Department, and "terror"-related research at the National Institutes of Health) is at an all-time low.[52] Other components of the new national security campus include the Department of Defense's post-9/11 decision to enforce the 1995 Solomon Amendment that withdraws federal funds from universities that refuse to grant access to military recruiters; the provisions of the 2001 PATRIOT Act that increase government oversight of university education and research by expanding the definition of classified and sensitive information, restricting the movement and work of foreign-born students and scholars, and initiating surveillance of academic conferences and other research and teaching activities; the 2004 Intelligence Authorization Act and Intelligence Reform and Terrorism Prevention Act, which created the Pat Roberts Intelligence Scholars Program and the Intelligence Community Scholars Program respectively, both of which provide fellowships for students working for U.S. intelligence agencies; and, most recently, the National Defense Authorization Act of 2006, which establishes Science, Mathematics and Research for Transformation Scholarships for students who will work for the Department of Defense.[53] At the same time, budgetary crises are taken as opportunities to decrease the number of permanent faculty as well as reorganize priorities around national security. Witness the University of Florida's 2008 establishment of a grandiose center with a stated mission of fostering public leadership and addressing homeland security with the university's efforts a few months later to fire eleven tenure-track faculty in the humanities. Taken together, these measures demonstrate the sweeping institutional realignment of U.S. higher education with the bellicose policies of neoconservative unilateralist militarism and nationalism.

Dismayingly, professional organizations today are not only reacting in a defensive manner similar to NEA in the 1950s but have grown even less combative than their forerunners. Today, for example, prominent professional organizations and unions seem almost completely incapable of affecting the state and federal legislative agenda in any substantial way. The success of groups like Students for Academic Freedom in pushing for hearings concerning abuses of professorial power around the country by making charges that sound uncannily familiar to those aware of the red scares of the 1950s exemplifies how the very organizations that should be defending the right to free and critical inquiry today are failing to achieve their core mission. Our professional organizations should be moving to combat such hypernationalist gambits aggressively instead of simply issuing reactive statements such as the AAUP report "Freedom in the Classroom" (2007). This report, for instance, critiques right-wing surveillance tactics but fails to offer a proactive notion of freedom capable of promoting campus democracy, dissent, and anti-imperial critique.

Given contemporary moves to create national security campuses, the explicit alignment of education and imperialism that sparked works such as Said's *Orientalism* should be even more salient today than it was during the Vietnam era. Said's charge to the engaged intellectual to militate against orthodoxy is more urgent than ever, for we need to remember that, despite frequent genuflections to academic freedom on the part of administrators, scholars, and even policymakers, universities are now more rather than less complicit in corporate neoliberalism and bellicose neoconservativism than they were in the past. We hope this collection will play a role in fostering discussion of the changing conditions for effective defense of campus democracy. In their different ways, contributors to *Dangerous Professors* explore the means by which contemporary educators and intellectuals can challenge the new national security campus and the even more ubiquitous forms of insecurity and contingency that characterize academic capitalism.

OVERVIEW OF THE COLLECTION

✧

Although the War on Terror has made academic freedom a central concern in public discourse, only three books have explored this topic in the context of 9/11: Beshara Doumani's U.S.-based *Academic Freedom after 9/11* (Zone, 2006), Evan Gerstmann and Matthew Streb's *Academic Freedom at the Dawn of a New Century* (Stanford, 2006), and Robert O'Neil's *Academic Freedom in the Wired World* (Harvard, 2008). All three works examine general debates about academic freedom before going on to focus on specific areas of concern—Doumani on Middle East studies and languages, Gerstmann and Sterb on science, censorship, and academic freedom in a global context, and O'Neil on particular cases of academic freedom as well as the effect of new technologies on these considerations. *Dangerous Professors* is markedly different from these books in three ways. First, although it recognizes the attacks on the university since 9/11, unlike other works, this collection shows how ill-equipped prevailing ideas of academic freedom are to foster campus democracy; it focuses on the ways in which universities can offer resistance to empire. Second, while Doumani and O'Neill recognize the increasing corporatization of the university as one of the twin forces shaping campus life today (along with the attacks of 9/11 and the resulting atmosphere of fear), their books do not include a detailed examination of this conjunction, as does our collection. Third, ours is the only collection that offers crucial firsthand accounts from academics who have been persecuted because of their criticism of U.S. imperialism.

Dangerous Professors consists of four sections. The first section examines the complicated legal and theoretical underpinnings of contemporary concepts of academic freedom in historical context. The dangerous convergence of the Right's cultural project with that of academic capitalism is addressed in this section by the AAUP's current president, Cary Nelson. The loss of state funding throughout public higher education, Nelson argues, has led to an entrepreneurial administrative culture where the parameters of academic freedom (parameters set by senior administrators rather than faculty) are vulnerable to pressures from the well-funded organs of the Right. Simultaneously, the rise of careerism at the expense of collaboration among tenured faculty and an increasingly contingent labor force have created the conditions for flagrant violations of faculty rights. The post-Katrina firings of tenured faculty in New Orleans without reason, notice, or due process should serve as a chilling reminder of how, in the absence of legally binding contracts, administrators can use crises to rule by decree.

As Robert O'Neil argues in his contribution to the volume, the relationship between academic freedom and constitutional free speech has been the subject of considerable speculation and ample misinformation. Those who teach at state-supported campuses ostensibly enjoy both free speech and academic freedom, making a deeper understanding of the differences essential. But the problem with invoking the public employee speech test as the measure of a professor's freedom in extramural utterances, O'Neil argues, is that it turns out, ironically, to be both under- and overprotective. It affords too little protection because public employees' First Amendment rights may be limited on grounds that would be anathema to academic freedom. Meanwhile, government workers are permitted to make statements that almost certainly would demonstrate "unfitness to teach" on the part of professors in certain fields. Thus the beguiling parallel between academic freedom and freedom of speech, so appealing to the Colorado investigators of Ward Churchill, for example, turns out to be more of a trap than a boon to defenders of freedom of inquiry.

Finally, picking up the thread of ambiguity noted by the other contributors to this section, R. Radhakrishnan challenges the rhetoric of "bias" that is often hurled at exponents of controversial positions in today's anxiety-filled public sphere. For Radhakrishnan, notions of an "Archimedean," unbiased perspective are dangerous humbug. His essay underlines the implicit nationalism that lurks within unqualified notions of freedom at this historical moment, whether it be the project of democratizing the Middle East by force of arms or the (sometimes) subtler forms of ideological interpellation that mark the academy. As a result, Radhakrishnan argues, in the hypernationalist atmosphere of the War on Terror, proponents of academic freedom have been coerced into parsing themselves as antistate and antinational, while the state's agendas of national security and hyperpatriotism remain unmarked as ideology.

In the second section of *Dangerous Professors*, contributors place questions about the freedom to teach and research in historical context. Bill Mullen's discussion of W. E. B. Du Bois and African American education amplifies Radhakrishnan's theoretical points about the implicit nationalism of dominant versions of "freedom" by exploring the historical limits of the postwar promise of universal education. Through a reading of Du Bois's *The Education of Black People*, Mullen demonstrates how Du Bois came to see universalist education doctrines and conceptions of academic freedom based on free speech as constitutive elements of capitalist white supremacy, with working-class African Americans functioning as the originary "exclusion" of Western humanism. In claiming the *material* lives of African Americans as this exclusion, Mullen intends to underscore that invocations of academic freedom and free speech always disclose the socioeconomic locations of the places those values are proffered and defended. Mullen contends that reading Du Bois's own work on education provides a clear foreshadowing not only of Du Bois's own fate as an untenured radical in the American university—his partial exclusion from the American academy—but anticipates the reconsolidation of white supremacist, capitalist, racist and nationalist forces that constitute the "free speech" right wing on today's political U.S. spectrum.

Taking its cues from the same historical period, Stephen Leberstein's chapter argues that the post–Cold War world leaves us without our usual compass for locating attacks on academic freedom. Leberstein argues that today's threat to academic freedom is not simply a replay of McCarthyism, the prototype for which was arguably written in New York in a 1940 state legislative investigation into subversion in the public schools and colleges. An examination of that episode, known as the Rapp Coudert Committee investigation, shows how different earlier episodes of repression were from today's attempt to silence voices of dissent. Leberstein's essay compares the stakes and strategies of this earlier conflict with recent attacks on CUNY professors by groups like Lynne Cheney's Association of College Trustees and Alumni. By comparing these different assaults Leberstein seeks to chart viable strategies for defending public higher education and campus democracy today.

In her contribution, Malini Johar Schueller puts the current assault on Middle East studies, particularly the moves to curb the teaching of postcolonial theory via H.R. 3077, in historical perspective. She suggests that these attacks are a response to the decolonization of knowledge consequent upon worldwide independence movements of the 1960s, which in turn boosted racial struggles within the United States. With many on the right arguing for the United States to unequivocally don the mantle of empire after 9/11, anticolonial critiques quickly became suspect. She also demonstrates how the vituperative criticisms of Middle East studies scholars represents a frontal assault on civil rights and the culture of civil rights that brought in scholars from the Third World into the academy. For Schueller, the deployment of the language of multiculturalism is part of the state's attempt to subsume the racially marked subject into a nationalist narrative of pluralism and consensus useful for imperialism; what is distinct after 9/11, she argues further, is the state's use of insidious distinctions between the multicultural and the foreign. Schueller closes her essay by underlining the necessary correlation between institutional struggles for academic freedom and the broader project of decolonizing knowledge by seeing knowledge not as universal but as invested in questions of empire and race.

These arguments clearly remind us that the production of knowledge in the academy cannot be decoupled from questions of social justice (what the AAUP has called the "common good" and duty to the "wider public") and that the "search for truth" requires an engagement with political issues that questions the public/private, scholar/citizen divide. As Sophia McClennen argues in her essay on the assaults on American studies' current emphasis on a diverse and polyvalent nationhood, left-oriented defenses have been less than successful because they have been posed in terms of relativity rather than in terms of the "common good." Current attacks on American studies, that is, have created a context through which to reconsider the critical methods that ground the field, methods that McClennen describes as metaphorically linked to legislation/unification and deregulation/expansion and which she argues both replicate and respond to the ideology of the nation itself. Recent right-wing attacks advance a particular vision of the United States and the globe that is a direct outgrowth of Pax Americana, manifest destiny, the Cold War, and neoliberal globalization. As a means of tackling these contradictions, McClennen proposes a reinvigorated commitment to the ethical and political motives behind challenging the traditional idea of a unified nationhood.

Contributors to the third section of *Dangerous Professors* argue that the imposition of corporate models of knowledge production has necessarily entailed the widespread casualization of teaching within postsecondary education and thus endangered the building of a culture of campus democracy. Not only do such "flexible" faculty members lack many of the protections for academic freedom afforded by tenure, but they are seldom fully included in organs of collective bargaining or self-governance such as faculty unions and senates. When the number of contingent faculty increases, the ability of the faculty as a whole to direct its own affairs diminishes.[54] This section underlines the crucial but not always immediately apparent connections between increasing contingency and diminishing critique and democracy in U.S. higher education today, conditions that make universities vulnerable to becoming national security campuses.

As Vijay Prashad argues, now more than ever the academic Left cannot rely on institutional protection alone for its adversarial positions, but must instead engage in a broader campaign within the public sphere by seeking to remind citizens of the value of academia's (relative) autonomy. Prashad points to the history of attacks on academics who affiliated themselves with any form of collective action, suggesting that this history reflects a flawed liberal model of academic freedom based on critique that affirms the status quo rather than seeking systemic change. To overcome this tame if not supine tradition, the academic Left, Prashad argues, must defend itself through the social force of its ideas rather than appeals to the individual's right to free expression. Indeed, as the militant resuscitation of Lewis Powell's calls for "balance" by opportunistic post-9/11 neoconservative groups such as Students for Academic Freedom demonstrate, doctrines of free expression can be just as easily invoked by those seeking to curtail countersystemic research and teaching as by its proponents. While it would not do to impose too seamless a genealogy on contemporary assaults on academic freedom, neither should we ignore the place of contemporary calls for "balance" within a carefully formulated and slowly germinating political strategy.

When labor conflicts arise in a university workplace, the principle of academic freedom tends to be invoked by all parties. Taking the New York University strike of 2006–7 as a case study, Michael Palm and Susan Valentine's essay begins by asking whether battles over "academic freedom," in which opposing sides fight in its name, have transformed it into the proverbial empty signifier, the hollow stakes of discursive battles and cultural politics. Then, combining ethnography and analysis of the strike, Palm and Valentine's chapter attempts to redeem the notion of academic freedom by centering it on fights to win or retain academic labor rights. Managers of academic labor seek cover in the rhetoric of the ivory-tower ideal; for instance, NYU's antiunion administrators and spokespeople routinely complained that union grievances over teaching assignments violated not only management rights, but also the educational integrity of the institution. However, these same administrators' management policies shone a glaring light on academia as a workplace, rather than as a sanctuary removed from the demands of wage labor.

Taking the crisis over Columbia University's Middle East studies program as his focus, Ashley Dawson discusses the intimate connection between the corporatization of the university, hypernationalism, and the decline of academic freedom. As the internal structure of academia has changed, so its autonomy has declined and the impact of external political pressure has grown. Yet, faced with assaults by powerful corporate interests, educators have begun to strike back by emphasizing that it is they who are the true conservatives, intent on preserving access to higher learning by resisting tuition hikes, budget cuts, tax giveaways to the rich, and the assault on critical thought by neocon activists backed by wealthy private foundations. Dawson's essay tracks several organizing campaigns within the New York metropolitan area in which issues of pay equity and academic freedom converged. For Dawson, the only way to reassert the university's public role successfully is to challenge what French sociologist Pierre Bourdieu called the *doxa* or common sense of neoliberalism: that every sphere of social life should be subjected to the ruthless calculus of market-based efficiency.[35]

We conclude this section with an interview with Andrew Ross, who argues that academic institutions today are more vulnerable to political pressure because of their commercial ties than in the postwar heyday of the public university beholden to the state. The race to consolidate intellectual property (IP) claims and rights, Ross reminds us, has significantly reduced the freedoms of academics involved in commercially viable research. From the perspective of increasingly managed academic employees in general, the result of trends toward academic capitalism is systematic de-professionalization. Within such bleak conditions, Ross argues, the traditional academic ethos of disinterested freedom of inquiry is all the more necessary to academic managers not just to preserve the symbolic prestige of the institution but also to safeguard commonly available resources as free economic inputs. Drawing on his experiences as an organizer of Faculty Democracy at New York University, Ross points out that while academic freedom is a prime component of labor organizing in the academy, it can just as easily be an obstacle or a recipe for inaction when it is invoked as an a priori principle. Academic unionism has yet to face its "CIO moment," Ross underlines, when unions acquire the will to include all members of the workforce—full-time faculty, staff, contract teachers, adjuncts, and TAs. Only with such inclusive models will the university resist being a mouthpiece for the state.

The volume ends with firsthand accounts of struggles over academic freedom by high-profile critics of U.S. foreign and domestic policies. Aside from offering controversial intellectuals a chance to give their own version of the events that led to their pillorying in the mainstream U.S. press and their marginalization by image-conscious academic administrators, this section also provides advocates of campus democracy with an inside view of the strategies that both internal and external critics of dissenting voices on campus have used and the best ways to challenge them. Ward Churchill begins the section by exploring the gulf between the liberal assertions of freedom of inquiry coming from university administrators and trustees and the less than ideal reality that unfolded at the University of Colorado when such assertions were put to the test. Particularly noteworthy in Churchill's account is his documentation of the skill with which right-wing pressure groups such as Students for Academic Freedom were able to manipulate the mainstream media and, through the media, elected politicians. As Churchill shows in his essay, however, these tactics only served to strengthen the resolve of progressive student organizations on campuses around the United States. Thus, despite Churchill's eventual dismissal by the University of Colorado, his case suggests that progressive groups can have a strong impact both within and outside the walls of the campus if they organize successfully.

Like Ward Churchill, Robert Jensen focuses on a public scandal that erupted in response to his criticism of the hypernationalism that followed the attacks of September 11, 2001, when the president of the University of Texas singled Jensen out for criticism. What galls Jensen more than the president's attack and the campus campaigns of groups inspired by Students for Academic Freedom, however, is the failure of the faculty itself to mount any kind of coordinated campaign of opposition to such assaults. The committee charged with protecting academic freedom, for instance, did nothing to address the specific attack on Jensen, but simply reissued boilerplate language concerning academic freedom. For Jensen, these events suggest that the vast majority of academics are, like many other professionals, caught up in the small perquisites of their field, keeping their heads down by remaining immersed in their specialties. Jensen's essay offers a clarion call not simply for the politicization but also for the mobilization of the profession toward progressive, anti-imperialist ends.

We close this introduction by arguing that we need to resist the efforts of putative liberals such as Stanley Fish who see universities as bastions of neutrality and excoriate those who attempt to align the structure of universities to visions of social justice. Commenting on calls for divestment and the policing of workshops that supply sweatshirts to campuses, Fish writes, "It is the obligation of the investment managers to secure the best possible returns; it is not their obligation to secure political or economic justice. They may wish to do those things as private citizens or as members of an investment club, but as university officers their duty is to expand the endowment by any legal means available."[56] A clearer case of enlisting universities as agents for corporate exploitation can hardly be found. We therefore also reject Robert Post's argument that freedom of extramural expression be separated from the idea of academic freedom.[57] Against such moves to mollify the inquisitors, we need to remind ourselves that the production of knowledge in the academy cannot be decoupled from questions of social justice. In an eloquent injunction that questions what Andrew Ross aptly terms fundamentalism about academic freedom, Howard Zinn writes: "To me, academic freedom has always meant the right to insist that freedom be more than academic—that the university, because of its special claim to be a place for the pursuit of truth, be a place where we can challenge not only the ideas but the institutions, the practices of society, measuring them against millennia-old ideals of equality and justice."[58] Echoing the comments of many contributors to *Dangerous Professors,* Zinn rejects the injunction to stay in one's field and leave questions of politics, racial oppression, and class exploitation to others in the name of professionalism. Zinn instead urges social activism: "the theorist of radical change, who does not act in the real world of social combat is teaching, by example, the most sophisticated technique of safety."[59]

NOTES

1. Noam Chomsky, "The Responsibility of Intellectuals," *New York Review of Books,* February 23, 1967, http://www.chomsky.info/articles/19670223.htm, accessed February 20, 2008.

2. http://www.aaup.org/AAUP/pubsres/policydocs/contents/RIR.htm, accessed November 8, 2008.

3. American Association of University Professors, "1915 Declaration of Principles on Academic Freedom and Academic Tenure," in *Policy Documents and Reports,* 9th ed. (Washington, D.C.: American Association of University Professors, 2001), 294.

4. Ibid., 299.

5. "1940 Statement of Principles on Academic Freedom and Tenure, with 1970 Interpretive Comments," http://www.aaup.org/statements/Redbook/1940stat .html, accessed July 20, 2006.

6. Ibid.

7. Ibid.

8. Edward Said, *The World, the Text, and the Critic* (Cambridge: Harvard University Press, 1983), 175.

9. Ibid., 172.

10. Edward Said, *Humanism and Democratic Criticism* (New York: Columbia University Press, 2004), 47.

11. Ibid., 141.

12. "The Rights and Responsibilities of Universities and Their Faculties," a statement by the Association of American Universities, March 24, 1953, http://www.aau.edu/reports/RRofU.html, accessed July 20, 2006.

13. For a discussion of the manipulation of fear in relation to education since the release of *A Nation at Risk* in 1983, see Rick Ginsberg and Leif Frederick Lyche, "The Culture of Fear and the Politics of Education," *Educational Policy* 22.1 (2008): 10–27.

14. Stuart J. Foster and O. L. Davis Jr., "Conservative Battles for Public Education within America's Culture Wars: Poignant Lessons for Today from the Red Scare of the 1950s," *London Review of Education* 2.2 (July 2004): 127.

15. For a useful survey of the increasing impact of Christian fundamentalist groups on the contemporary Right, see Carl Davidson and Jerry Harris, "Globalization, Theocracy, and the New Fascism: The US Right's Rise to Power," *Race and Class* 47.3 (2006): 47–67.

16. Available online at http:/www.la.utexas.edu/-chenry/2001LynnCheneyjsgo 1ax.pdf. This statement was deleted from the revised February 2002 version of the report available on the ACTA website at http:/www.goacta.org/publications/ Reports/defciv.pdf. ACTA also posted on its website a list of 115 statements made by allegedly "un-American Professors."

17. Cited in Foster and Davis, "Conservative Battles," 131.

18. Ibid., 132.

19. The federal government contribution to university and college income changed from about 5 percent in 1946 to between 12 to 26 percent thereafter, settling down to about 15 percent in the 1980s. See R. C. Lewontin, "The Cold War and the Transformation of the Academy," in Noam Chomsky et al., *The Cold War and the University: Toward an Intellectual History of the Postwar Years* (New York: New Press, 1997), 24.

20. William F. Buckley Jr., *God and Man at Yale: The Superstitions of "Academic Freedom"* (South Bend, Ind.: Gateway Editions, 1977; orig. pub. 1951), lviii.

21. John Chamberlain, introduction to ibid., liv.

22. Ibid., lvi.

23. Buckley, *God and Man,* 91.

24. Ibid., lx, 88. As this account makes clear, Buckley's attacks on the Yale faculty were influenced by the rhetoric of forerunners such as Allen Zoll. Indeed, the young Buckley was the star protégé of Frank Chodorow, a colleague of Zoll's whose Intercollegiate Society for Individualists was one of the first organizations devoted to inculcating free market ideologies among college students. For a discussion of Buckley's links with ISI, see Katherine Demarrais, "'The Haves and the Have Mores': Fueling a Conservative Ideological War on Public Education (or Tracking the Money)," *Education Studies* 39.3 (2006): 217.

25. H. Bruce Franklin, *Vietnam and Other American Fantasies* (Amherst: University of Massachusetts Press, 2000), 2.

26. Howard Zinn, "The Politics of History in the Era of the Cold War: Repression and Resistance," in Chomsky et al., *Cold War and University,* 35–72.

27. Richard M. Nixon, speech delivered at General Beadle State College, Madison, South Dakota, June 3, 1969, in *Public Papers of the Presidents of the United States: Richard Nixon,* 1969 (Washington, D.C.: U.S. Government Printing Office, 1971), 429; quoted in Franklin, *Vietnam and Other Fantasies,* 126.

28. For an extensive discussion of Powell's memorandum, see David Hollinger, "Money and Academic Freedom a Half-Century after McCarthyism: Universities amid the Force Fields of Capital," in *Unfettered Expression: Freedom in American Intellectual Life,* ed. Peggie J. Hollingsworth (Ann Arbor: University of Michigan Press, 2000), 161–84.

29. The full text of the Powell memorandum is available at www.reclaim democracy.org/corporate_accountability/powell_memo_lewis.html, accessed November 8, 2008.

30. Even a very partial list of the influential publications sponsored by such groups is voluminous. They include, in chronological order, Allan Bloom, *The Closing of the American Mind: How Higher Education Has Failed Democracy and Impoverished the Souls of Today's Students* (1987); E. D. Hirsch, *Cultural Literacy: What Every American Needs to Know* (1987); Roger Kimball, *Tenured Radicals: How Politics Has Corrupted Our Higher Education* (1990); Dinesh D'Souza, *Illiberal Education: The Politics of Race and Sex on Campus* (1991); Arthur Schlesinger Jr., *The Disuniting of America: Reflections on a Multicultural Society* (1992); William Bennett, *The Devaluing of America: The Fight for Our Culture and Our Children* (1992); Richard Bernstein, *Dictatorship of Virtue: Multiculturalism and the Battle for America's Future* (1994); Lynne V. Cheney, *Telling the Truth: Why Our Culture and Our Country Have Stopped Making Sense and What We Can Do about It* (1995); Alan Charles Kors and Harvey A. Silvergate, *The Shadow University: The Betrayal of Liberty on America's Campuses* (1998); Gertrude Himmelfarb, *One Nation, Two Cultures* (1999).

31. Ginsberg and Lyche, "Culture of Fear," 19.

32. See the Foreign Policy Research Institute's listing of five thousand think tanks at http://fpri.org/research/thinktanks/, accessed November 8, 2008.

33. Ginsberg and Lyche, "Culture of Fear," 19.

34. Quoted in Demarrais, "Haves and Have Mores," 208. Liberal groups, it should be noted, have become far more aggressive in their efforts to establish think tanks capable of competing with those of the Right over the last decade.

35. Ibid., 221.

36. Ibid., 220.

37. On the IEA–Philanthropy Round Table link, see ibid., 205.

38. Ibid., 206.

39. The Lynde and Harry Bradley Foundation, www.bradleyfdn.org/pdfs/05WI grantsReduced.pdf, accessed November 8, 2008.

40. For an ideological map of the evangelical Right, see Davidson and Harris, "Globalization, Theocracy."

41. David Horowitz, "In Defense of Intellectual Diversity," *Chronicle of Higher Education,* February 13, 2004, http://chronicle.com/free/v50/i23/23b01201.htm, accessed February 20, 2008.

42. David Horowitz, "The Campus Blacklist," FrontPageMagazine.com, April 18, 2003; http://www.studentsforacademicfreedom.org/essays/blacklist.html, accessed November 7, 2008.

43. Academic Bill of Rights, http://www.studentsforacademicfreedom.org/abor.html, accessed November 7, 2008.

44. Ibid.

45. AAUP statement on Academic Bill of Rights, http://www.aaup.org/statements/SpchState/Statements/billofrights.html, accessed February 21, 2008.

46. Sara Dogan, *Students for Academic Freedom Handbook,* http://www.studentsforacademicfreedom.org, accessed November 8, 2008.

47. David Horowitz, *The Professors: The 101 Most Dangerous Academics in America* (Washington, D.C.: Regnery, 2006).

48. Edward Said, *Orientalism* (New York: Pantheon, 1978), 9.

49. Ibid.

50. Ibid., 25.

51. Michael Gould-Wartofsky, "Repress U," *The Nation,* January 10, 2008, http://www.thenation.com/doc/20080128/gould_wartofsky, accessed February 26, 2008.

52. See Steven Mikulan, "University of Fear: How the Department of Homeland Security Is Becoming a Big Man on Campus," *LA Weekly,* April 2–8, 2004, http://www.laweekly.com, accessed December 11, 2008.

53. Stuart Tannock, "To Keep American Number One: Confronting the Deep Nationalism of U.S. Higher Education," *Globalization, Societies, and Education* 5.2 (2007): 261.

54. For a representative discussion of academic capitalism's impact on faculty members, see David Noble, "Digital Diploma Mills," in *Steal This University: The Rise of the Corporate University and the Academic Labor Movement,* ed. Benjamin Johnson, Patrick Kavanagh, and Kevin Mattson (New York: Routledge, 2003), 33–48.

55. Pierre Bourdieu, *Firing Back: Against the Tyranny of the Market 2,* trans. Loïc Wacquant (New York: Verso, 2003), 80.

56. Stanley Fish, "Save the World on Your Own Time," *Chronicle of Higher Education,* January 23, 2003, http://chronicle.com/jobs/2003/01/2003012301c.html, accessed February 16, 2005.

57. Robert Post, "The Structure of Academic Freedom," in *Academic Freedom after September 11* (New York: Zone Books, 2006), 61–106.

58. Howard Zinn, *Academic Freedom: Collaboration and Resistance: The Twenty-Third T. B. Davie Memorial Lecture Delivered in the University of Cape Town on July 23, 1982* (University of Cape Town, 1982), 6.

59. Ibid., 16.

THEORIZING ACADEMIC FREEDOM:
ISSUES AND CONTENTIONS

ON WEAKENED GROUND

The AAUP and the Future of Academic Freedom

Cary Nelson

> Might not a teacher of nineteenth-century American litera-
> ture, taking up *Moby Dick,* a subject having nothing to do with
> the presidency, ask the class to consider whether any parallel
> between President George W. Bush and Captain Ahab could
> be pursued for insight into Melville's novel?
> —AAUP, "Freedom in the Classroom"

FOR DECADES ACADEMIC FREEDOM has seemed a relatively stable
feature of the psychology and practice of academic life. As of 2006, over
two hundred organizations had signed the 1940 "Statement on Academic
Freedom" issued by the American Association of University Professors
(AAUP). From the start, to be sure, there were inherent disparities between secular and religious institutions. Among schools chartered by different denominations, expectations about faculty speech and student intellectual freedom vary considerably, and those expectations have
themselves sometimes shifted substantially when church leaders, politics,
and doctrine changed. Wanting to maximize the academic freedom of faculty at religious institutions, the AAUP has worked hard to keep them on
board, emphasizing that doctrinal constraints need to be made explicit
and public, so that students and employees know what to expect. Not in-
frequently, however, religious institutions step over the line—as when
Brigham Young University fired a faculty member for publicly announcing

that she prayed to God the mother, rather than God the father—and the AAUP must launch a formal investigation. In religious institutions in many countries, of course, that delicate dance has no counterpart. There may simply be no credible equivalent of academic freedom for faculty and intellectual freedom for students. This history is worth recalling because religious intolerance now threatens academic freedom worldwide.

In this respect at least, academic freedom has always been an arena for cultural struggle, rather than an eternal verity perfectly embodied in every institution. Both for religious and secular institutions, the AAUP's very visible investigative reports on academic freedom and tenure—and its continuing need to censure a limited number of institutions—provides an evolving handbook of guidelines and markers for administrative behavior that crosses a line. Yet the means available to cross that line—and the cultural contexts in which the struggle for academic freedom is waged—evolve over time. And thus the meaning of academic freedom changes no matter how stable its official definition may seem. The most dramatic revelation about how much the status of academic freedom and shared governance can change overnight came with the educational aftermath of Hurricane Katrina. More about that at the end of this essay.

In two specific ways, academic freedom has been steadily put at risk over two generations. The first of these is embodied in a generational shift now in place for nearly four decades, during which AAUP membership declined from over 100,000 faculty members to about 44,000, the latter level having been maintained for a decade—until membership increased to 47,500 in 2008. The organization lost a considerable number of members during the heyday of faculty collective bargaining in the 1970s, when a number of faculties signed up to be represented by the American Federation of Teachers (AFT) or the National Education Association (NEA) and people let their AAUP memberships lapse. During that same period of time, in addition, the bulk of the AAUP's remaining membership began to shift to chapters engaged in collective bargaining under the AAUP banner. What we sometimes call American Civil Liberties Union (ACLU) style membership—represented by faculty who join purely on a principled basis—has drastically and disastrously declined, though unionized faculty in large, self-sufficient locals often see their national AAUP membership in terms of academic freedom and shared governance.

While it has been popular in some quarters to attribute the 1970s and 1980s membership decline to distaste for the AAUP's involvement in collective bargaining, another explanation is more likely. Faculty over the last several decades have become more career-oriented, more likely to be identified with their departments and their disciplines and less likely to be identified with either their institutions or the professoriat as a whole. Faculty thus focused on disciplinarity or their own advancement are less likely to join an organization altruistically devoted to the common good. What seems clear is that retiring AAUP members at non-collective-bargaining schools have not been replaced by sufficient numbers of young faculty joining the profession (and the AAUP) for the first time.

The consequence for academic freedom has been severe, if largely unnoticed—namely that many faculty who joined the profession over the last forty years have no knowledge of the history of academic freedom, little capacity to define or defend it, and little or no awareness of the mounting threats to its continued existence. Through one of my presidential initiatives, the AAUP started a program to correct this problem in the fall of 2007, sending twice-monthly educational emails about its history and current activities to nearly 400,000 faculty. Of course every new generation needs to be educated about its culture's ethical norms, just as each new member of a profession needs to be socialized to the profession's standards and values. Academia has now failed to perform that task for two generations. As a result, faculty are widely ignorant not only about academic freedom, but also about the practices of shared governance that assure academic freedom has an environment in which it can flourish. The AAUP increasingly receives complaints about academic freedom that have a distinctive shared-governance component.

Ignorance about the principles of academic freedom and their relation to good shared-governance practices has deepened alongside the other long-term trend eroding academic freedom. It has been largely invisible except to its victims—contingent faculty, part-time teachers and those hired full-time off the tenure track. The AAUP throughout its history has consistently asserted and reinforced the necessary bond between academic freedom and job security. Indeed Robert Post has emphasized that "the ideal of academic freedom was formulated precisely to transform basic American understandings of the employment relationship between faculty and their university or college."[1] If they can fire you tomorrow for what you say, you really do not have academic freedom, neither in the classroom, nor in print. After fighting reliance on part-time faculty for decades, the AAUP decided it was necessary to confront reality and win them a degree of job security and due process. Those aims are embodied in number 13 of our "Recommended Institutional Regulations," adopted in November 2006.

The reality we faced is this: the professoriate is now composed largely of part-time faculty who can in fact either be fired tomorrow or simply not rehired the next semester, often without stated cause or due process. From a profession characterized by a high degree of job security, we have become one characterized by complete insecurity of employment. Drastically underpaid, most part-time faculty who rely on their teaching for their whole financial support have no reserves and no capacity to sustain even brief job loss. Many practice elaborate self-censorship to avoid offending students, parents, or administrators. If you do not believe that, you should talk to contingent faculty who have agonized about removing potentially offensive readings from their syllabi for decades. Most tenured faculty, on the other hand, have remained willfully oblivious to this fundamental crisis in higher education's intellectual independence; they have preferred to look away and concentrate on their own careers. Meanwhile, increasing reliance on contingent faculty—they grew from roughly one-third of the teaching force in 1975 to nearly two-thirds now—has also undermined the faculty role in shared governance, even in such critical matters as designing the curriculum and hiring new colleagues.

In an ideal world, the tenured faculty would guard the rights of part-timers and vigorously defend their academic freedom. That does occasionally happen, but it is not the characteristic dynamic of academia's class system. Those with secure jobs have nonetheless themselves also paid a price for the fundamental disempowerment of large segments of their colleagues. For at least a decade the balance of power in higher education has begun to shift. While for nearly half a century power flowed outward from central administrations to departments, this pattern has been increasingly reversed, with centralized decision-making and top-down control now the norm throughout much of the United States.

The loss of public funding throughout higher education has led to an entrepreneurial administrative culture impatient with faculty resistance to profit-making ventures. Needless to say, part-timers have no role in these decisions and no real capacity to resist them. A fragmented tenured faculty meanwhile has no deep experience of solidarity to draw on and little collective experience of asserting its rights. The parameters of academic freedom are thus often set by senior administrators, rather than by faculty discussion and consensus. Emerging technologies are especially vulnerable to exclusion from the standards governing academic freedom in traditional domains. Thus senior administrators may simply deny faculty many freedoms in the use of email and university websites, despite clear AAUP policy statements on these matters.

All the patterns I have described so far share one central characteristic: they are fairly visible long-term trends susceptible to predictive analysis. If faculty want to marshal the resources to counter them, they can do so, assuming they recognize their historical situation and can learn to act collectively. But other forces—predominantly political—are also having a significant impact on academic freedom, and they are all fundamentally variable and unpredictable. As a result, the future of academic freedom is both uncertain and unstable. The faculty now stands on weakened ground, but its ultimate fate is neither set nor secure.

Perhaps the most widely publicized political affront to academic freedom is the multipronged assault on faculty speech in the classroom and on course syllabi. Heavily funded by individual conservative donors and by right-wing foundations alike, this ideologically coordinated effort embraces several organizations and a number of spokespersons who have gained national visibility through this campaign. There is, of course, no argument to be made against their right to promote their views, but that does not prevent those sympathetic to academic freedom from detailing how damaging this campaign may prove to be.

The American Council of Trustees and Alumni (ACTA), founded by Lynne Cheney and currently led by its president Anne Neal, has historically helped "train" college and university boards of trustees to distrust their progressive faculty and now engages in a broad campaign to smear both current faculty and a range of humanities disciplines. ACTA's published report "How Many Ward Churchills?" (May 2006) is its most indicative publication. The report argues that hundreds of courses across the country are designed to deliver the message "that the status quo, which is patriarchal, racist, hegemonic, and capitalist, must be 'interrogated' and 'critiqued' as a means of theorizing and facilitating a social transformation whose necessity and value are taken as a given."[2] In short, "indoctrination is replacing education."

Though ACTA does not trouble itself to draw the distinction, there is a difference between the assumptions listed in the first half of their prototype message and the activist appeal in the second. Many faculty convinced of the first set of claims are reluctant to embrace the agenda announced thereafter when they are teaching. ACTA is also satisfied with what is, in effect, a Google search for key terms. The appearance of words like *race, class, gender,* and *sexuality* in a syllabus is enough to prove a political agenda. To their credit, they do not lay the blame exclusively on individual leftist faculty. They find that a series of entire academic disciplines and specializations have been thoroughly corrupted by "the message." So their demand that these views be "balanced" by others is really a demand that disciplinary consensus be compensated for with extradisciplinary political perspectives. That counters the whole notion of professional training and expertise that underlies the AAUP's concept of academic freedom; it opens academic debate to any alternative point of view with political influence.

The litany of complaints about leftist biases—which are echoed by David Horowitz, another major player in the right-wing attack on higher education—includes a number of theses or conclusions that many of us consider to be important advances in our understanding of human culture. In a March 2007 debate with me—broadcast on C-SPAN2 on March 17 and 18—Horowitz complained about a University of Arizona syllabus that "assumes as an uncontroversial fact that 'gender is socially constructed.'" Horowitz insists students be informed there is disagreement about this matter. My guess is that virtually every instructor does in fact mention the opposing argument, the traditional claim that maleness and femaleness are fundamental, immutable categories. But I doubt that many contemporary humanities or social science faculty give equal time to the earlier view; they wouldn't consider it professionally responsible to do so.

There is widespread consensus in many fields that—whatever the spectrum of physical differences between men and women—the meaning of gender is socially constructed. Horowitz, on the other hand, as he argued in a May 19, 2008, debate with me in Eugene, Oregon, believes anatomical differences between the male and female brain mandate greater facility for men in fields like music and math. He goes on to claim that faculty who promote the theory of social construction typically say it is controlled by "a patriarchal ruling class that imposes passivity on women so that men can oppress them." But the theory of social construction is politically neutral; it would apply as well to a society dominated by women or to one where gender was politically irrelevant. Underlying the Neal/Horowitz position here is presumably the continuing conservative complaint about relativism, which the Right considers a left-wing plot, though that is hardly the case. The Right thinks relativism denies the existence of values. Instead relativism concludes they are a source of struggle, that they must be fought for because they are not guaranteed.

Horowitz also complains constantly that faculty teach in areas in which they do not have professional credentials and that this is part of the politicization of the academy. Professional credentials, for him, are the product of a doctoral education. But people acquire new areas of expertise throughout their careers. They do so by reading, talking, attending lectures, and thinking. My PhD is in English and American literature, but my publications include several books each about areas not part of my formal training, higher education and the Spanish Civil War. As a result, I have been asked to lecture about each topic both here and abroad. My refereed publications prove my expertise in these areas, but I might well have taught courses—without publishing—after wide reading. Horowitz has asked me to endorse some further mechanism to formalize faculty acquisition of new areas of expertise. I cannot imagine what he would have in mind. A written test? A review board? Neither he nor Neal has much understanding either of the life of the mind or the life of academic disciplines. The discipline I studied in the late 1960s in graduate school has precious little to do with the discipline I represent now. No faculty member in my graduate program would even have recognized the names of most of the American poets I've written about over the last twenty years. And while in graduate school I could not have named them myself.

Some years ago, when I applied to my university's Scholars' Travel Fund, administered by our Research Board, to attend the annual meeting of the Modern Language Association (MLA) to give an invited paper on the state of higher education, the fund's administrator refused the request and told me they would never again fund me to speak on higher education because I had no formal training in the subject. At the time, I had already published a number of books and essays on higher education. What's more, the invitation meant my disciplinary organization judged me qualified. In the amusing note I received from the Board, the administrator informed me I was an expert on the Spanish Civil War and on modern poetry, but not on higher education. How she confidently distinguished between two areas of knowledge acquired after the PhD—the Spanish Civil War and the politics of higher education—I cannot guess. In any case, the refusal was a genuinely unwarranted imposition of political opinion. She didn't like what I was saying about higher education and thought to silence me. It was also, more fundamentally, a violation of academic freedom. Although I was not an AAUP officer at the time, I called the national office and asked if they would take the case. They expressed some pleasure with the opportunity. My department head let the administrator know this, and she backed down. I'm not sure that I want her—or anyone else—running Horowitz's kangaroo court to judge more recently acquired scholarly expertise.

Horowitz repeatedly argues for some sort of mandated rough balance in the scholarly texts assigned to cover controversial issues. This would require not only an equal time provision but also elaborate mechanisms for oversight of course content. That would seriously constrain the ability of faculty to teach what they believe to be true and necessary. Students and faculty alike would lose the pedagogical benefit of an individual faculty member's passionate take on the discipline, his or her idiosyncratic set of interests and areas of expertise. We would lose much more in limiting academic freedom in this way than we could possibly gain.

The AAUP's statement on controversial speakers on campus has some relevance here. We reject demands that any particular event embody a "balance" between opposing positions. We reject the idea that a given group must invite speakers representing different points of view. And we certainly reject any notion that faculty should be required to represent points of view discredited by their disciplines. We believe balance is achieved over the long term by the full range of views students are exposed to in classes, public lectures, conversations, and through the media. All this is part of their education. Horowitz regularly cites global warming as a case where students may now only be exposed to one point of view. Apparently he never watches television. We trust our students to evaluate and accept or reject the opinions they encounter in the classroom and in the culture at large.

When I debated Horowitz in Washington, DC, a large banner was stretched across the stage: "TAKE POLITICS OUT OF THE CLASSROOM." This is an increasing focus of conservative critique and presents an extraordinary threat to academic freedom. When the AAUP clarified its 1940 statement on academic freedom and tenure in 1970, it advised professors to avoid the "persistent" intrusion of extraneous material into a class. I take "persistent" to refer to bringing outside material into the classroom so frequently that the ability to teach the course's advertised content is inhibited. Even then, I regard the warning as ethical and professional advice, not the logic for a regime of surveillance.

A complete prohibition on political speech not relevant to the subject would disable American pedagogy. Those teachers who found themselves teaching an 8:00 a.m. class on September 12, 2001—in the hours before campuses cancelled classes—probably found it necessary to discuss the attacks on New York's World Trade Center the day before. If teachers thought they could ignore the previous day's events, their students may have thought otherwise. Whether the class was on chemistry, home economics, or international politics, students might well have been "persistent" in bringing the subject up again later in the semester. There is room in many classes to devote a modest amount of time to topics not in the curriculum. Sometimes life gives us little choice. Academic freedom embraces such imperatives.

One of my good friends was devastated when a graduate student in the army reserves she was advising was called up for active duty and killed in Iraq. If she had chosen to talk about this to her students, I would consider it her right to do so. In the end it is the instructor's responsibility to decide what is or is not relevant to the moment in which he or she is teaching. Does that mean there are no abuses of academic freedom? Certainly there are, but academic departments are equipped to handle them, and departments tend to know the participants best.

There is a prevailing view in the academy that dispassionate, decathected argument serves us best. As Matthew Finkin has put it succinctly, pedagogical "freedom is accorded equally to dispassionate dissection and to committed partisanship."[3] Indeed, as Ernst Benjamin has argued, "open advocacy may better safeguard a student's right to form an independent judgment than the implicit bias inherent in the presumption that the faculty member's presentation is simply factual . . . advocacy not only need not lead to indoctrination but also is often the antidote."[4] When this bias spills over into an ideology devoted to neutrality and balance, we risk projecting the illusion that the public sphere is a reasonable and reliable space. The relentlessly reasonable classroom may reinforce confidence in the reasonableness of the nation-state in which it resides. Nonetheless, over forty years in higher education I have found that the overwhelming majority of faculty are reluctant to reveal their political views to their students. Yet I believe that students benefit from hearing committed advocacy from their professors. It helps them learn how to advocate for a position themselves. When the AAUP first addressed these issues in 1915, it had in mind a still significantly rural country and a much more impressionable student body. Neal and Horowitz would like to maintain that image of the infantalized student—vulnerable to faculty advocacy—because it is politically useful to them. But as successive waves of new media overtook the country—from radio to film to television to the Internet—the naive and unformed undergraduate largely disappeared. Today's students visit the city on television and in cyberspace before they leave the farm. They arrive well stocked with their own political opinions and ready to defend them. Good luck to any faculty members who think it will be easy to change their minds. Of course there remain differences in sophistication among students, and undergraduate juniors and seniors are less impressionable than freshmen. One might, therefore, have different personal teaching standards for political speech in beginning and advanced courses.

Fundamental to both Neal's and Horowitz's organized campaigns is an effort to confuse the public by eliminating any distinction between advocacy and indoctrination, despite a substantial scholarly history of efforts to differentiate between the two practices. Any faculty effort to advocate for a given position, they would have us believe, is an effort to indoctrinate students. Advocacy of course encompasses a vast range of rhetorical strategies, including strategies that summarize, compare, and contrast alternative positions. It is fundamental to the search for truth.

A number of the contributors to *Advocacy in the Classroom* (1996) and *The Future of Academic Freedom* (1996) make serious efforts to distinguish advocacy from indoctrination. Nadine Strossen, then president of the ACLU, argues that "advocacy is diametrically different from expression that is 'inculcating' or 'indoctrinating' . . . Advocacy is intended to open minds; inculcation is intended to close them."[5] As Louis Menand writes, "indoctrination isn't just bad pedagogy; it's bad advocacy."[6] Myles Brand, former president of Indiana University, acknowledges that there is "a gray area between strong advocacy and proselytizing" but emphasizes that "faculty members are expected to have a point of view; they are expected to advocate for a position."[7]

Yet defenses of advocacy—along with efforts to carve out some space for political remarks not connected with the course subject matter—are fundamentally inadequate unless they embrace the reasoning central to the AAUP's 2007 statement on the subject. For many political comments that Horowitz and other conservative critics would consider wholly unacceptable are fundamentally not irrelevant to the subject. A basic feature of human culture is that anything can be potentially connected with anything else; the capacity to make those connections is fundamental to human consciousness. Political commentary often derives from an instructor's efforts to draw analogies and comparisons between different bodies of knowledge and different historical periods. Thus the AAUP insists that instructors can reference contemporary political life to illuminate course subject matter—whatever academic discipline the course represents and whatever the catalog description and syllabus say. The answer to the question posed in my epigraph is thus emphatically "yes." A teacher of *Moby Dick* can, if he or she chooses, compare Ahab and George Bush as obsessional leaders or invite students to do so. What is perhaps most bizarre or unrealistic about the objections to a Bush/Ahab comparison is that the analogy is already out there, in circulation, not only in the popular press but also in Melville scholarship.

Analogies between a ship captain and a head of state are hardly incomprehensible. Is Iraq for Bush a contemporary incarnation of the white whale? Debates about presidential power are a staple of American history. It is perfectly valid for an instructor to deal not only with what a novel might have meant in its own time, but also what it may mean in ours. A literature class taking up such comparisons could help students understand the continuing vitality and relevance of the humanities.

We included the Bush/Ahab sentence because we recognized that people can easily sign on to a principle (the right to reference contemporary politics) without really confronting what it entails. Nonetheless, we knew the passage would draw fire. Indeed, I led with it in the press release that accompanied the report. We paired the Bush sentence with one about Bill Clinton, not because we had any illusions that "balance" was possible, but rather to make it clear political analogies are an equal opportunity realm. Views of Clinton's personal ethics, however, were not a hot topic of debate in 2007; the Bush sentence got all the attention. By far the most interesting discussion came in response to a Stanley Fish column in the *New York Times,* predictably a critique of our report. The online comments—over a hundred of them—demonstrated definitively what a rich conversation comparing and contrasting Bush and Ahab could do. People agreed, disagreed, and offered scores of alternative analogies. It was like an impromptu national classroom—witty, passionate, sardonic, inventive, instructive, outraged. Most importantly, it demonstrated the power of references to contemporary life as a way to engage people at their most articulate. I could offer no more persuasive evidence in support of "Freedom in the Classroom" than the III comments on Fish's essay.

When I debated Fish about politics in the classroom at the University of Illinois in October 2003, I described how I drew analogies in class between Vietnam era poetry and current events. The students had been assigned to read several antiwar poems before class. Then I read them aloud, substituting George Bush's name for Lyndon Johnson's and Iraqi place names for Vietnamese. Passages about the earlier president's Texas machismo, conveniently, did not require revision. Here is a brief example from Robert Duncan's poem "Up Rising." My substitutions are in brackets:

> Now Johnson [Bush] would go up to join the great simulacra of men,
> Hitler and Stalin, to work his fame
> with planes roaring out from Guam [Saudi Arabia] over Asia [Iraq] .
> . . . .
>> And men wake to see that they are used like things
>> spent in a great potlatch, this Texas barbecue
>> of Asia [Afghanistan], Africa [Europe], and
>> and all the Americas [the middle east] . . .
>> and the very glint of Satan's eyes from the pit of the hell
>> of America's unacknowledged, unrepented crimes that I
>> saw in Goldwater's [Cheney's] eyes
>> now shines from the eyes of the President
>> in the swollen head of the nation[8]

My first point was to demonstrate that, contrary to widespread disciplinary belief, topical poetry does not always age rapidly; it often remains applicable to subsequent events. The second point was to raise the question of whether Duncan's apocalyptic, mythic rendering of Vietnam had any purchase on our understanding of Iraq. I mentioned that I was opposed to the war, but I hardly needed to say more: Robert Duncan, Allen Ginsberg, Denise Levertov, Robert Bly, and Adrienne Rich did the work for me. Fish immediately responded, "If I were Cary's dean I would fire him!" I have the impression the AAUP would come to my defense.

Does that mean there are no excessively opinionated, overly politicized faculty in America, even in beginning courses? Certainly there are. Horowitz will now ritually bring some brainwashed waif to his public performances, trained to testify to recovered memory of instructional abuse. On-the-spot verification is hardly possible, but I assume a tiny minority of faculty behave themselves badly. Certainly, given that some faculty, like some people in all occupations, are less than sane, I expect that unacceptable behavior does occur. But there is no widespread, national, systemic problem and thus no necessity for a new reporting, surveillance, and punishment system. The AAUP does strongly endorse structures for students to seek redress for unfair grading, including politically based grading, but a system that would monitor political speech in the classroom would be repressive and destructive.

There are no doubt faculty who abuse their students politically, just as there are faculty who abuse their students sexually. At some point it becomes a discipline problem. Indeed, schools that cannot address the political mistreatment of students are most likely to be unable to deal with their sexual mistreatment either. Those institutions are typically poorly administered and thus dysfunctional in a whole series of areas. Horowitz prefers to isolate the issues he focuses on because that suits his political agenda, but the solution for an institution incompetently administered is a comprehensive overhaul, not a system to monitor political speech in the classroom.

After my debate with Horowitz, one of the attenders contacted me with a story: "In a course on the Arab-Israeli conflict, the academic had her students, as part of the course work, establish pen pal relations with Palestinians and only Palestinians, not Israeli Jews. This is an abuse and misuse of academic freedom. This, I hate to say, was not uncommon in all of the courses taught by this one professor, yet none of her courses were about the Arab perspective on the Middle East. Had those courses been on the latter topic, then I would say the course was as advertised. But this was not the case." I agree the course description should have been clear, including her precise expectations for student performance. If she penalizes students for taking opposing views, she should be sanctioned. Save for that, the pen pal exercise seems rather interesting. But should this instructor be required to present both sides of the issue? Would anyone trust her to do so? How exactly could she be reformed? Death threats? Cambodian-style reeducation camp? Salary cuts? What are the odds she could be convincingly evenhanded? Students would be better served by experiencing her convictions for what they are, it being hardly likely hers would be the only perspective they would encounter on campus or elsewhere in their lives.

It is true that many Jewish students who are sympathetic to Israel feel their views about the Mideast are unwelcome on campus; in the wake of September 11, many Arab students feel the same. Certainly there are Mideast studies programs—typically with faculty specialization spread across a number of area countries—where pro-Israeli sentiments are not kindly treated. On the other hand, there is a well-organized lobby for pro-Israeli opinion. Few people on either side of this issue seem ready to admit that pro-Palestinian political correctness and pro-Israeli opinion—wielded in different ways—compete constantly for student attention. A March 2007 report issued by the Israel on Campus Coalition implicitly suggests universities negotiate with outside "stakeholders" to reach consensus on how controversies over the Arab-Israeli conflict should be taught and represented on campus. Good luck. A number of world leaders have entered that terrain with minimal success. Campus groups should instead schedule speakers and seminars to assure their views are represented. A Ford Foundation "Difficult Dialogues" project at the University of California at Irvine may help us see how a more civil dialogue on the Middle East could be conducted. Meanwhile, we need to accept that many faculty with deep convictions about this subject will share them with students.

My own pedagogical ethic is somewhat different. Let me offer a crude but pointed definition of classroom academic freedom as I practice it. What academic freedom means to me is the opportunity to do as I please—within a complex system of ethical, moral, disciplinary, professional, and curricular constraints. Perhaps the second half of my definition demonstrates that none of us can actually do as we please; we cannot in fact even imagine what that would mean. I believe the individual faculty member must reflect on and negotiate this intersecting series of forces and discourses. The AAUP continues to offer advice on how to do so. My pedagogical ethic also means honoring my students' intellectual freedom, which means they are free to raise any subjects they wish and offer any opinions they can—with extra praise for disagreeing with me, since that makes my classes more interesting and trains them for future debate. I treat all their opinions with respect, because my professional and human values mandate that I do so. Students do not possess academic freedom because that implies disciplinary expertise and professional responsibility, which they do not yet have. But they need intellectual freedom. That's something the AAUP asserted clearly in its 1967 statement on student rights.

It is useful for faculty to let their colleagues know what their position is on political speech in the classroom and what their personal guidelines are. It is essentially a set of personal guidelines that Michael Bérubé offers when he suggests he would only advocate for specific legislation should it "materially and immediately affect the students" in his classroom, but that some subject matter would compel him to advocate "for one form of social organization over another."[9] The campus certainly needs to be a place where faculty can articulate, debate over, and advocate for a particular professional and pedagogical ethic. But that is quite different from succumbing to an impulse to impose any given pedagogy on one another, let alone ceding such authority either to administrators or to outside stakeholders. Academic freedom requires that faculty have wide latitude in conducting their classes.

Despite Horowitz's claims to the contrary, I believe American students do possess and exercise their intellectual freedom. His claim that Left faculty routinely deny this right has not been demonstrated. Horowitz's first effort to stigmatize progressive faculty involved efforts to get state-by-state "Academic Bill of Rights" legislation passed mandating political balance in faculty appointments. Ordinarily one does not learn about faculty members' politics during the appointment process, and it would be immensely destructive to interrogate people about them. It is true that faculty in some disciplines are more likely to be either Democratic or Republican, English being an example of the former, business being an example of the latter. But that hardly makes them campus radicals. The Yale English department fought the effort to organize graduate employees for collective bargaining with a vengeance, not exactly standard liberal behavior, though I expect most of these same faculty vote Democratic. Party identification clearly does not indicate what a person's campus politics will be like.

The legislative hearings aimed at considering Horowitz's Academic Bill of Rights in more than a dozen states were occasions for organized AAUP testimony, and Horowitz's efforts failed. The most extraordinary bill was one proposed in the Arizona state legislature, instituting a $500 fine for each verified instance of a faculty member making political comments in a classroom. Horowitz wrote the language but claims he intended it for K–12 education, not for colleges and universities. His decision to disavow the bill and deny responsibility bears comparison with a pilot dropping a bomb on a city from 10,000 feet and claiming he had no idea there were people there. The Arizona bill was fruit of the poisoned Horowitz tree. Where Horowitz has had some success is in getting universities to institute procedures for students to complain about political speech in the classroom and trigger investigations. Temple University and Penn State University both already had overly restrictive policies limiting classroom speech on the books. Penn State's policy (HR 64), on the books for some years, is especially bad:

The faculty member is entitled to freedom in the classroom in discussing his/her subject. The faculty member is, however, responsible for the maintenance of appropriate standards of scholarship and teaching ability. It is not the function of a faculty member in a democracy to indoctrinate his/her students with ready-made conclusions on controversial subjects. The faculty member is expected to train students to think for themselves, and to provide them access to those materials which they need if they are to think intelligently. Hence, in giving instruction upon controversial matters the faculty member is expected to be of a fair and judicial mind, and to set forth justly, without supersession or innuendo, the divergent opinions of other investigators. No faculty member may claim as a right the privilege of discussing in the classroom controversial topics outside his/her own field of study. The faculty member is normally bound not to take advantage of his/her position by introducing into the classroom provocative discussions of irrelevant subjects not within the field of his/her study.

Although the nonsexist language was added in the 1980s, the policy itself dates from the 1950s. It is thus McCarthy era rhetoric, taking passages from the 1915 AAUP statement out of context and ignoring subsequent clarifications. Like Horowitz, Penn State failed at the time to conceptualize the sense in which all teaching and research is fundamentally and deeply political. Humanities and social science teaching and research is more explicitly political—in dialogue with cultural values and norms that undergo continual change and are sites of struggle, articulated to assumptions about identity that are socially and politically constructed, engaged with social life and the public sphere and thus with the politics of culture, constrained and encouraged by discourses embedded in politics. Academic freedom entails the right to discuss all these relationships in any course whatsoever. Many of them are entangled with the political activities of state and national governments.

Both Horowitz and Penn State argue, in effect, that overt political remarks (and for Penn State, covert ones) can be strictly separated from the intricate web of connections between the academy and the politics of culture. I would disagree. The Penn State statement also illustrates the dangers of faculty at one institution—who lack sufficient background and historical knowledge—attempting to write nuanced policy. The AAUP's drafting process is infinitely more elaborate. What Penn State ended up with is nothing less than thought control. You are to remain even tempered at all times; avoid even "innuendo" of an opinion on controversial matters. While this might fall within the range of ethical advice, rather than enforceable regulation, it certainly could be brought to bear at time of con-tract renewal or tenure decisions and thus poses substantial risks to aca-demic freedom.

In 2006, however, in the wake of legislative hearings in Pennsylvania, both Penn State and Temple added reporting and investigative procedures for what students perceive as one-sided classroom advocacy. Having failed at getting legislators to act, Horowitz now disingenuously argues his real purpose all along was to get postsecondary institutions to reform them-selves. While the overwhelming majority of such complaints received may well be dismissed—because it is very difficult for people outside a class to judge context, because students are not likely to know what faculty will or will not find acceptable, and because the entire process will quickly be seen as invasive—once such procedures are activated they are likely to promote self-censorship. It also certainly gives Horowitz's allies a chance to harass selected faculty with multiple complaints. Moreover, it sets a bad prece-dent for group surveillance of and intrusion into the classroom, making raids on academic freedom culturally and institutionally acceptable.

Horowitz has made a major effort to personalize his campaign, to tell and retell the story of his conversion from Left to Right activist, since per-sonalizing his story helps him get free publicity, including a full page in *USA Today* in 2006. Lately, despite his own highly personal attacks on over a hundred individual faculty members, he has begun to protest that the Left attacks him, rather than dealing with the issues he raises. His feigned outrage bids fair to turn him into a new breed of attack dog—the pit bull that feels sorry for itself. These apparently contradictory tactics are actu-ally two sides of the same coin, designed to work together to distract us from focusing on the true nature of his enterprise—a well-funded collec-tive project of the Far Right. In the power dynamics of contemporary cul-ture, Horowitz is only a pawn in their game.

There is, however, one poignant element to the Horowitz conversion narrative. He habitually tells audiences his parents were communists but typically receives no reaction to this repeated revelation from conservative listeners. As it happens, the only people capable of understanding the rele-vant social and political history are the very people on the Left Horowitz vilifies. He has sold himself out to people who will never understand him.

The organized Right has successfully taken on a series of American in-stitutions. First they red-baited the judicial system: "Liberal judges are try-ing to reinterpret the constitution. Conservative judges just apply it." No doubt the founding fathers intended us to own assault rifles. Over time, the

United States Senate rolled over and handed the Right the federal judiciary. Then the Right red-baited the so-called liberal press. A component of that campaign was the attack on "liberal bias" on PBS television, a campaign Horowitz helped to orchestrate.[10] The press was then relentlessly accused of liberal bias, and it eventually went belly up and failed to do its job in the lead-up to the Iraq war. The Bush administration's claims about Iraq's weapons of mass destruction and its Al Queda connections went uninvestigated and uncontested. Bush, Cheney, and Powell got a free pass on every lie they wanted to tell the American people. Now higher education is being red-baited in the same way—with hyperbolic accusations of left-wing bias. The aim is the same: to housebreak yet another independent democratic institution. Anne Neal and David Horowitz are spokespersons for a cultural struggle over the heart and soul of American education.

We are now, to be sure, on the terrain of unpredictable cultural and political struggle. I would not, for example, pretend to predict the strategies the Right may employ in future efforts to limit academic freedom. The Bush administration was aggressive in barring scholars whose views were unwelcome from entering the United States, a particularly brutal and chilling aggression against the ability of American students and faculty members to participate in an international conversation. Both independently and in cooperation with the ACLU and other groups, the AAUP has been diligent in fighting these actions. Yet with the new administration, restrictions on foreign scholars could well be lifted. We cannot know.

The political and cultural climate for academic freedom—especially the level of public tolerance for political dissent on campus—could easily change; indeed it could change rapidly. In 2006 and 2007, growing public disenchantment with the Iraq war opened space for more dissent in all quarters of American life. Yet at least one plausible series of events has significant potential to curtail tolerance for the loyal opposition on campus. I refer to the possibility of a fresh series of terrorist attacks on American soil. It would not require anything so ambitious as we saw on September 11. A series of bombs placed in airplane cargo holds—even something so relatively low tech as a series of suicide bombings in public places— could be enough to fuel multiple repressive responses from Congress and the president. The nature of the response would depend, of course, on the nature of the aggression and the character of those in power, but some action would be almost inevitable. Campus criticism of such measures would not be welcomed in all communities. Imagine some version of Ward

Churchill's "little Eichmanns" remarks about a new series of American victims. Place them in the mouths of those vulnerable part-time faculty invoked at the opening of this essay, and one can see how the weakened institutional ground for academic freedom could lead to its curtailment where it is most vulnerable.

Could academic freedom—grounded as it is now in either an increasingly contingent labor force or a fragmented tenured professoriate—survive the perfect cultural and political storm? In a sense, the question has been unexpectedly asked and answered. The respect that the managerial class of administrators now widely in control of higher education has for faculty rights has been tested and demonstrated. The capacity of faculty to resist the perfect institutional storm has also been tested—and found wanting. Let me close, then, with an instructional riddle for higher education's new millennium. What would a university president do if all existing institutional restraints, all rules and regulations, all checks and balances structured into shared governance, all moral limits save those imposed by common law, were suddenly and decisively to be removed? Since this is a riddle for the new millennium, the president in question is not likely to be a philosopher-king. He or she is probably not among the most eloquent defenders of academic freedom on campus. He admires faculty who keep their mouths shut and bring in revenue, but he does not admire faculty who are the source of inconvenient ethical, political, and professional challenges. You do not look to such a president for intellectual leadership. You may live in fear that such a person would actually acquire a vision of the university's mission.

So how would such an administrator behave given complete freedom of operation? How would he restructure a college or university to meet popular and corporate interests if he could do so without any meaningful consultation? How would he treat dissident faculty in a political crisis? What if nineteenth-century-style, at-will faculty employment returned and swept aside faculty control not only over hiring but also over the curriculum and institutional mission?

Now, instead of a single corporate-style administrator given near absolute power, let's carve off a whole region of the United States. Say that a whole city separates itself from fifty years of shared governance and academic freedom. Say that the tenure system is tossed aside. Say that all human decency is abandoned. Say that administrators begin to lie in public without hesitation. Say that they rule by decree and that every university employee becomes expendable.

Unfortunately, in New Orleans a perfect educational storm was among Hurricane Katrina's after effects. Organized by a series of college presidents—at Tulane University, Loyola University, the University of New Orleans, Southern University at New Orleans, the Louisiana State University Health Sciences Center, and Xavier University—this educational hurricane swept aside academic freedom, shared governance, due process, and tenure. Everything I described in my worst-case scenario has already taken place. And it has established a precedent that other presidents will apply in comparable disasters—freak storms, earthquakes, fires, and terrorist attacks—or on a lesser scale in other reorganization projects. We have seen the future, and the faculty is not there.

In New Orleans, tenured faculty were fired with scant notice, no due process, no stated reasons, and no appeal save to the very administrators who terminated them. Some were told they'd had a couple of months notice. Others were told they had been taken off payroll and off health care the previous week. Departments and programs were closed down without appropriate review and without regard for shared governance or academic freedom. The schools used the excuse of Hurricane Katrina, but it is clear no level of emergency existed that required the elimination of due process. Loyola suffered losses of about $30 million, but its $300 million endowment remains intact.

Faculty senates in New Orleans voted against the actions, proposed alternatives, and in some cases offered votes of no confidence in the administration. Boards of trustees supported the presidents. The faculty were ignored. By then it was too late. One other key fact gives us all warning: most of these schools had excellent guarantees of academic freedom, governance procedures, due process regulations, and appropriate emergency guidelines on the books. All these rules and regulations—everything approved in the faculty handbooks, the senate rules, and governing statutes—were dismissed out of hand. One might say the levees shoring up academic freedom, shared governance, and tenure needed to be reinforced before the storm hit. The national AAUP published a detailed report on New Orleans in its May/June 2007 issue of *Academe.* Five administrations were censured in June 2007. As I write, we are in the midst of negotiating with them about reversing these actions. We have so far been successful with one of them.[11]

By the time the academic levees crumbled in New Orleans, it was too late for some proactive solutions, though I would have recommended returning to classes the following semester, earning a first salary check and then initiating job actions designed to close these universities down. It was certainly too late for the public institutions to organize rapidly for collective bargaining, a considerable challenge in Louisiana in any case. Nonetheless, the clearest lesson to be gleaned from New Orleans is this: the academic freedom defined in your faculty handbook may well mean nothing in the right context. Your written rules for tenure and due process may mean nothing, although the contractual status of faculty handbooks varies from state to state. That leaves faculty in many states with only one sure option: shared governance, due process, and tenure regulations need to be mirrored in legally enforceable contracts. You have to have a sound basis for taking the administration to court. It may well be that getting these regulations into signed contracts may be far more important than any salary or benefits a union can negotiate. A strong local AAUP chapter that can consistently speak truth to power and help educate the faculty is the first step.

In many states a faculty that is strong enough and sufficiently united can compel even a conservative administration to negotiate. That will require new faculty identities that embrace greater faculty solidarity and activism. We also need a broad, well-funded program to educate both faculty and the general public about the nature and value of academic freedom. For the university is now being subjected to sustained political, cultural, and economic assault. To deny that is to cede the future to corporatization and a form of higher education with little purchase on cultural critique. And it is to put academic freedom substantially at risk. It is not too late to act.

NOTES

1. Robert Post, "The Structure of Academic Freedom," in *Academic Freedom after September 11,* ed. Beshara Doumani (New York: Zone Books, 2006), 62.

2. ACTA's published report "How Many Ward Churchills?" (May 2006), 3.

3. Matthew Finkin, "The Tenure System," in *The Academic's Handbook,* ed. A. L. Deneef, C. D. Goodwin, and E. S. McCrate (Durham: Duke University Press, 1988), 88.

4. Ernst Benjamin, "Some Implications of the Faculty's Obligation to Encourage Student Academic Freedom for Faculty Advocacy in the Classroom," in *Advocacy in the Classroom: Problems and Possibilities,* ed. Patricia Meyer Spacks (New York: St. Martin's Press, 1996), 307, 311.

5. Nadine Strossen, "First Amendment and Civil Liberties Traditions of Academic Freedom," in Spacks, *Advocacy in the Classroom,* 73.

6. Louis Menand, "The Limits of Academic Freedom," in *The Future of Academic Freedom,* ed. Menand (Chicago: University of Chicago Press, 1996), 6.

7. Myles Brand, "The Professional Obligations of Classroom Teachers," in Spacks, *Advocacy in the Classroom,* 10–11.

8. Robert Duncan, *Bending the Bow* (New York: New Directions, 1968), 81–83.

9. Michael Bérubé, "Professional Advocates: When Is 'Advocacy' Part of One's Vocation," in Spacks, *Advocacy in the Classroom,* 189.

10. David Brock, *The Republican Noise Machine: Right Wing Media and How It Corrupts Democracy* (New York: Crown, 2004), 107.

11. See "Hurricane Katrina and New Orleans Universities," report of an AAUP Special Committee, *Academe: Bulletin of the American Association of University Professors,* May/June 2007, 59–126.

FREE SPEECH VERSUS ACADEMIC FREEDOM

᭡

Robert M. O'Neil

WARD CHURCHILL, THE OUTSPOKEN University of Colorado professor of ethnic studies, seems to have a rare capacity to provoke controversy—not only over what he says, but even over how society and his own institution should judge what he says. His name drew national attention and obloquy early in 2005 because of an essay he wrote and posted on a website soon after the September 11 attacks, in which he lauded the hijackers for having shown "the courage of their convictions," and referred to some of the victims who toiled in the World Trade Center as "Little Eichmanns." Disclosure of the essay's most inflammatory passages evoked intense controversy in Colorado. The governor urged all Coloradans to "denounce" Churchill's views, and strongly suggested that the errant professor should leave the Boulder faculty. Just before an emergency meeting of the university's regents, however, two lawyer members of that board made clear there would be no summary dismissal, if only because "the law requires a process to fire a professor" and that the institution would "face substantial legal liability" if they took immediate adverse action against Churchill.[1]

Instead, the university administration announced a very different response. Boulder campus chancellor Philip DiStefano pledged to launch an inquiry, aided by several deans and faculty members. Two central issues would form the focus of that inquiry. First, did Churchill's published statements and writings "exceed the boundaries of a public employee's constitutionally protected speech?" Second, was there evidence that Churchill had engaged in "research misconduct, teaching misconduct, or fraudulent misrepresentation" sufficient to "warrant further action by the University?" On the latter issue, a lengthy internal investigation resulted in dismissal charges for serious and extensive research misconduct, and led to a dismissal action by the board of regents.

It is the first question, however, that provides the theme of this chapter. Specifically, we should ask whether the chancellor posed (and proceeded to answer) the right question—or whether Churchill's volatile off-campus statements should properly have been judged by a different standard. In summary, we will find that the standard actually invoked in the Churchill inquiry turns out to be both underprotective and overprotective of the extramural speech of a tenured university professor. We then need to identify a proper standard to govern such sensitive (and mercifully rare) investigations.

Before the inquiry even began, Chancellor DiStefano had arguably cast the die that would shape the ensuing process. The day after Churchill's essay became public, the chancellor issued a brief but cogent statement. In this release, he made clear that the extreme statements of one member of his faculty, which he personally found "offensive" and which clearly did not reflect the values of the university, might turn out to be protected because the chancellor had to "support [Churchill's] right as an American citizen to hold and express his views, no matter how repugnant, as guaranteed by the First Amendment of the Constitution." The stated focus of the ensuing inquiry, launched a week later, differed in a subtle but important respect from the initial statement: the question that warranted closer scrutiny was whether Churchill's statements "exceed[ed] the bounds of a public employee's constitutionally protected speech." Some six weeks after launching the inquiry, Chancellor DiStefano submitted a report that, not surprisingly, absolved Churchill of dismissible behavior or expression on the basis of the widely publicized extramural statements. The whole issue of research misconduct remained for further study.[2]

After reviewing the "Little Eichmanns" essay and Churchill's several other controversial writings and lectures, Boulder's chancellor gave his view of the applicable First Amendment safeguards for public employee statements—that such expression enjoys protection "so long as their speech does not unduly disrupt the operation of the workplace or impede the performance of the speaker's duties." Despite the public outcry that Churchill's writings had prompted, the chancellor found that the outspoken professor had "continued in his faculty responsibilities and [that] the content of his speech has not disrupted the University's provision of services to its students or the ability of other faculty to perform their responsibilities." Accordingly, Churchill's "political expression" seemed to be "constitutionally protected against government sanction on the grounds of disruption, in spite of the damage it may have caused."

The only other possible basis for a formal sanction envisioned by the chancellor's report was the First Amendment's well-recognized exception for speech that incites "imminent lawless action" with a high probability that such action will occur. There had been no serious suggestion that Churchill's writings or speeches ever created such a "clear and present danger," and that was the end to the inquiry. Indeed, that was essentially the last word on the entire subject; subsequent analysis has focused almost entirely on Churchill's alleged research misconduct as a basis for possible dismissal or other sanction. What seems most puzzling is the pervasive scholarly indifference about the legal test that was actually applied to what may have been the most explosive extramural statements in the post–September 11 period. This chapter offers an opportunity to review this largely uncharted domain.

Although Professor Churchill was indeed a Colorado public employee, that fact by itself does not necessarily determine the appropriate standard by which to judge his speech. Indeed, a closer analysis of the status of public employee speech shows that such a standard, as applied to the extramural statements of a tenured university professor, turns out to be seriously underprotective. A brief review of the origins of the doctrine may be helpful. Until 1968, government workers were essentially at the mercy of the agencies for which they worked. Justice Oliver Wendell Holmes, then a Massachusetts state judge, once wrote that a New Bedford constable named McAuliffe, disciplined for speaking at a political rally, "may have a constitutional right to talk politics, but has no constitutional right to be a policeman."[3]

That rather callous view prevailed until, in the late 1960s, the Supreme Court first recognized a limited First Amendment protection for public employee speech. The case involved an Illinois public school teacher named Pickering who had been fired after writing to the local newspaper a letter that was highly critical of the school board's fiscal priorities. For the first time, the justices ruled that such speech (at least on a "matter of public concern") was presumptively protected, so long as it did not contain major falsehoods of which the speaker was (or reasonably should have been) aware.[4] Yet the doctrine thus announced, novel though it was in both free speech and public employment law, was fraught with exceptions.

These limitations turned out to be quite as important as the core of the safeguard that they qualified. For one, only speech that dealt with a "matter of public concern" could claim any such protection; expression of personal grievances, even though not couched as idiosyncratic complaints, still lay beyond the First Amendment. Not everyone in the civil service is protected even when airing "public concerns"; many government workers—especially at higher or executive levels—are viewed as working within the "kind of close working relationship" with a superior that imposes upon them a duty of loyalty and confidence of which a subordinate might be free.

Most important, the *Pickering* doctrine has from its inception been qualified by exceptions that seriously dilute its value to the outspoken public employee. The justices took care to note that Pickering's letter in no way "interfered with the regular operation of the schools," nor (as later cases refined this standard) did it "impair discipline by superiors or harmony among co-workers." Nor did the teacher's statement "discredit the [school system]" among those who were its clientele (such as parents and taxpayers). There was much more to *Pickering*'s limitations: In this seminal case, there was no evidence that writing the targeted letter took undue time away from the teacher's assigned responsibilities. Clearly its content was not of the sort that might be channeled into an established grievance channel. In these and other situations that were to be refined and explained through a host of post-*Pickering* public employee speech cases, it has become clear that civil servants are, to be sure, far better off than they were back in Officer McAuliffe's time, but are also far less protected as government workers than they would be as private citizens.

It is this contrast that creates grave doubt about the appropriateness of applying the *Pickering* standard to the speech of tenured faculty like Professor Churchill. Chancellor DiStefano, interestingly, did not cite *Pickering* among the several cases he invoked to define a public employee's speech rights. His report's brief analysis of legal principles contained no discussion of whether Churchill's essay touched a "matter of public concern" (though almost certainly it did so). Nor was there any mention of exceptions and qualifications save for this cursory reference—whether Churchill had "continued in his faculty responsibilities" and whether "the content of his speech . . . disrupted the University's provision of services to its students or the ability of other faculty to perform their responsibilities." A suitable answer to both inquiries settled the matter as far as the Boulder campus administration was concerned. And to be consistent with principles of academic freedom, that was undoubtedly the correct and proper disposition.

The problem for us is that a less benign university administration, proceeding from precisely the same premises as did Chancellor DiStefano, could reach starkly different results in a similar case. If, for example, there were any doubt whether such comments did touch upon a "matter of public concern"—the indispensable prerequisite for protection—a less sympathetic chancellor might have noted obvious differences between Pickering's laudable stated goal of informing fellow citizens and parents about school budget priorities, and on the other hand, Churchill's inflammatory rhetoric broadcast to a world still reeling from the terrorist attacks on the World Trade Center.

We might also consider the potential for an expansive reading of recognized *Pickering* qualifications when it comes to public employee speech that could be said to "disrupt or demoralize the agency" or "undermine client confidence in the agency." It does not require extravagant speculation to envision a hostile use of these *Pickering* exceptions by an administration bent on silencing a professor who is either a persistent critic or a constant embarrassment. Yet—and here is the rub—public employee speech doctrine, if it provides the appropriate template, would permit doing precisely that, even though the Colorado chancellor's report made no use of such limitations.

If the state of the law was somewhat precarious in early 2005, things have become substantially worse since that time. A year and a few months after the chancellor's report, the legal terrain changed markedly in a way that illustrates the frailty of using public employee speech as the sole standard of protection. At the end of its 2005–6 term, the Supreme Court profoundly altered the concept of "matter of public concern." In the case of a California prosecutor named Ceballos, who was disciplined after he protested departmental policies on the pretrial handling of evidence, the justices ruled that "public concern" no longer includes statements made about or within the scope of the speaker's job; "the First Amendment does not prohibit managerial discipline based on an employee's expressions made pursuant to official responsibilities."[5]

That ruling might portend profound and disturbing consequences for academic speech, as Justice David Souter noted in his dissent: "I have to hope," he cautioned, "that today's majority does not mean to imperil First Amendment protection of academic freedom in public colleges and universities, whose teachers necessarily speak and write 'pursuant to official duties.'" The majority seemed to acknowledge that Justice Souter might have a valid concern: "There is some argument that expression related to academic scholarship or classroom instruction implicates additional constitutional interests that are not fully accounted for by this Court's customary employee-speech jurisprudence." Nonetheless, following its consistent commitment to decide no more issues than are necessary to resolve the pending dispute, the justices saw no occasion here to determine "whether the analysis we conduct today would apply in the same manner to a case involving speech related to scholarship or teaching."

The *Ceballos* decision is troubling at three quite different levels. For one, if its narrowing of "matter of public concern" were now to be applied to professorial expression, it would have the perverse effect of virtually denying First Amendment protection to the academic expert, who typically speaks within his or her "official duties," while continuing to protect the dilettante or nonexpert, who would seem still free to speak with impunity on matters remote or distant from the speaker's scholarly specialty. While so bizarre a result almost certainly was not intended, it would seem to be unavoidable unless a later Supreme Court ruling were to follow the import of Justice Souter's dissent by creating some special exception for professors who speak boldly within their field of expertise.

That concern alone is worrisome enough. There are, however, two other ominous implications of the *Ceballos* ruling. If the meaning of so pivotal a concept as "public concern" can change as quickly and profoundly as the Supreme Court modified it in this case, then the doctrine of public employee speech seems to offer an even frailer source of support for the expression of university professors than previously appeared to be the case. Even more basic a concern is the risk of tying the scope of academic freedom—at least of free expression within the academic community—to so elusive a protective structure as the doctrine of public employee speech. While the general run of government workers, holding generally less sensitive positions, might be uneasy at having to guess how firmly and predictably the law protects their right to express unpopular views, university professors face a special and deeper risk.

Indeed, Chancellor DiStefano's report gave more than a hint of exactly such uncertainties and vagaries. Churchill chaired the Department of Ethnic Studies, in addition to his tenured faculty position. Immediately after the furor over the "Little Eichmanns" essay erupted, he resigned his administrative post, thus rendering moot what might well have been a contentious collateral issue. The chancellor's report noted that fact with an obvious sense of relief, adding an element of contrast: "[T]he outrage Professor Churchill has generated among state and federal elected officials, commentators and citizens across the country most likely would have warranted his removal as Chair of the Ethnic Studies Department had he not stepped down. However, his faculty position does not impose the same responsibilities to those external constituencies."

This is a rather startling suggestion, given the certainty with which the chancellor's review had found Churchill's faculty status to be protected. Under the doctrine of public employee speech, high-ranking administrators owe a duty of loyalty that would undoubtedly diminish their freedom to criticize the president or chancellor. But that was not remotely the case with Professor Churchill. Not only does a department chair seldom incur a fiduciary duty that constrains his freedom of speech, but the statements that drew public ire toward Churchill were hardly of the sort that any expectation of loyalty in a close-knit relationship would effectively constrain. And if the issue had genuinely been one of academic freedom (to which we shall turn shortly) there seems little doubt that a professor who holds an administrative appointment in addition to a tenured teaching position is less fully protected in the former role than in the latter—though not without some solicitude in both capacities.

Given this analysis, the only plausible speech-based distinction between Churchill as professor and Churchill as ethnic studies chair would reflect a belief that his job security was vulnerable to public indignation and outrage in one role but not the other. Logical though it may seem that faculty tenure ought to be more protective for an outspoken professor than the chairmanship of a small academic department, that result may not follow solely from applying the public employee speech doctrine—at least not without seriously undermining the value of that doctrine as a guarantor of faculty expression.

Accordingly, it is hard to avoid the conclusion that the standard applied in the initial Colorado inquiry was seriously underprotective of faculty expression, even though it happened in sensitive administrative hands to yield a quite acceptable result. If that were the only shortcoming, it would give one serious pause. Ironically, however, the public employee speech doctrine also turns out to be overprotective for reasons that did not complicate the first phase of the Churchill inquiry, but could not be avoided when the focus shifted to alleged research misconduct. Take the matter of misattribution or misappropriation of intellectual property, for starters.

Under the First Amendment, citizens are free to present as their own the writing or creative work of someone else up to the point of provable copyright infringement. In the academic community, however, the standard is far more rigorous. Much borrowing of someone else's creative work that would pass under the radar in business, government, or elsewhere is simply not acceptable under academic norms. As the Statement on Plagiarism of the American Association of University Professors cautions: "Within the academic world, where advancing knowledge remains the highest calling, scholars must give full and fair recognition to the contributors to that enterprise, both for the substance and for the formulation of their findings and interpretations."

Plagiarism, though not limited to the academic context, "has perhaps its most pernicious effect in that setting" because it is "the antithesis of the honest labor that characterizes true scholarship and without which mutual trust and respect among scholars is impossible." Certain norms that might be welcome but are seldom enforced elsewhere uniquely constrain those who write for academic outlets—for example, "scholars must make clear the respective contributions of colleagues on a collaborative project" and "professors . . . must exercise the greatest care not to appropriate a student's ideas, research or presentation to the professor's benefit." Indeed, when Chancellor DiStefano turned from Churchill's extramural statements to the integrity of his scholarship, such expectations appropriately came into play and formed the basis for the continuing part of the inquiry. Curiously, the inapplicability of public employee speech doctrine—which imposes no such special standards on the integrity of scholarship—received not even passing mention. It seemed clear beyond any need even to comment that much more is expected in this regard of a university professor than of an ordinary Colorado citizen.

In several other respects, the doctrine of public employee speech turns out to be overprotective as applied to faculty expression. The highly sensitive issue of sexual harassment offers a prime example. Purely verbal harassment—consisting solely of sexually offensive words or images—may seldom be made a target of legal sanctions in the industrial workplace or most other settings. But in the university classroom, special conditions and expectations arise. For years, two AAUP committees dueled over the appropriate standard, Committee A on Academic Freedom and Tenure taking a view sharply at variance with that of Committee W on the Status of Women. Finally in 1995 a joint subcommittee was created to craft a compromise that eventually drew nearly universal approbation.[6] Although making clear that in the academic setting "wide latitude is required for professional judgment in determining the appropriate content and presentation of academic material," the statement also recognizes that in the college classroom teachers owe a special duty to their students. Clearly, for example, a "sexual advance" or a "request for sexual favors" may constitute actionable harassment if it "implies that one's response might affect educational or personnel decisions that are subject to the influence of the person making the proposal." Even professorial speech of a sexual nature that lacks such inducement may be targeted if it is either "directed against another and is abusive or severely humiliating" or if such expression "is reasonably regarded as offensive and substantially impairs the academic or work opportunity of students, colleagues, or co-workers," adding that "if it takes place in the teaching context it must also be persistent, pervasive and not germane to the subject matter."

Quite apart from AAUP standards, several court cases have reviewed college students' complaints about alleged verbal harassment, occasioned by a professor's assignment of course material or classroom discussion that contains sexually explicit language and references. Not surprisingly, the results have varied widely, though courts have generally recognized the special obligation a professor owes to the students who seek to learn from the other side of the podium. In a closely related vein, the AAUP's most basic document, the 1940 Statement of Principles on Academic Freedom and Tenure, qualified its recognition of professors' "freedom in the classroom" with the caveat that "they should be careful not to introduce into their teaching controversial matter which has no relation to their subject." In these and other respects, the public employee speech standard fails fully to capture all the subtle but vital nuances of the academic relationship, and thus turns out to be curiously overprotective of certain dimensions of faculty speech.

One other AAUP-based exception has caused no end of trouble, and happily was not invoked in the Churchill inquiry. The basic 1940 Statement on Academic Freedom and Tenure urges that when professors "speak or write as citizens . . . their special position in the community imposes special obligations." Since "the public may judge their profession and their institution by their utterances . . . they should at all times be accurate, should exercise appropriate restraint, should show respect for the opinions of others, and should make every effort to indicate that they are not speaking for the institution." A later codicil stresses the importance of preserving a presumption in favor of free expression despite the seemingly constraining language. There have been several notable instances of outspoken faculty targeted for having failed to show the requisite responsibility in their extramural utterances—most notably, and unconscionably, the action of the University of California Board of Regents in dismissing Professor Angela Davis in the early 1970s. Institutions have in recent years been understandably reluctant to invoke the general provisions of this stated obligation, relying instead on more precise institutional (and occasionally AAUP) desiderata.

The most serious mismatch between academic and public employment norms comes to light in a very different area. Citizens are entirely free to hold and publish even the most outlandish views about such basic matters as which celestial bodies revolve around which (to recall Galileo's challenge) or how gravity operates. Most university professors are equally free to declare publicly their belief that the earth's surface is flat—however much such views may diminish their social standing or collegial esteem. But if the flat-earth advocate's academic field happens to be geology or geography, no university would be required to tolerate such demonstrably false and dangerous statements from a scholar who should know better—even though public employee speech standards would be completely protective. While AAUP policy has always avoided enumerating possible grounds of "cause" that might warrant the dismissal even of a tenured professor, it has always been clear that even the most senior scholar might forfeit that protection for a demonstrated "lack of fitness in . . . [his or her] professional capacity as a teacher or researcher." The expectations for a geographer or geologist are profoundly different in this regard from the academic community's standards for public utterances about the earth's surface from those in other fields.

Recent experience yields an example that may seem more plausible: Since 1976, Northwestern University engineering professor Arthur Butz has widely proclaimed his belief that the Holocaust never occurred. Most recently, in early 2006, he lauded statements to that effect by Iranian president Mahmoud Ahmadinejad, adding only his lament that "it was not a Western head of state." As it has done on many previous occasions, Northwestern's administration responded by distancing itself and the institution from Butz's "abhorrent" but "purely personal" views, and insisting that academic freedom protects even the utterances of such outrageous falsehoods. Only two conditions have ever been imposed—that Butz adequately perform his assigned duties as an engineering professor, and that he never intrude Holocaust denial into his classroom. He has scrupulously observed those limits, and remains seemingly beyond the reach of his many critics in Evanston and elsewhere.[7]

Suppose, however, that Butz' academic field were not engineering, but instead the study of modern European history. Surely by analogy to the flat-earth geologist or geographer, his university could insist that public Holocaust denial in such a case would evidence clear unfitness to continue as a member of the academic community—even though, as a citizen, one would enjoy complete impunity to utter such nonsense. Of course any effort to dismiss such an errant scholar would demand an elaborate procedure and ample proof, but so misguided and pernicious a historian could at least be the object of such a proceeding. One is tempted to extend the analogy to other mavericks—for example, a biologist who publicly insists that the Book of Genesis and not Darwin properly describes the origins of human life. Beyond those situations in which the misguided scholar's heresy is demonstrably false by any reasonable standard, the terrain becomes much rockier and the conclusion accordingly less certain. We need not for now go beyond the easy cases, which firmly establish one more respect in which the public employee speech standard may be overprotective of faculty expression.

It would not be quite fair to fault the Supreme Court's test as frontally as this comparison may imply. A footnote in the *Pickering* opinion did note that the case before the Court was not one "in which a teacher's public statements are so without foundation as to call into question his fitness to perform his duties in the classroom." So far, one might observe, the two doctrines seem to be in substantial accord. But there is more to the *Pickering* footnote: "In such a case, of course, the statements would merely be evidence of the teacher's general competence, or lack thereof, and not an independent basis for dismissal." Two obvious differences now emerge between the use of the term "fitness" in the AAUP standard and in the Supreme Court's public employee speech doctrine. For the *Pickering* Court, heretical or absurd statements by a public employee would provide no more than *evidence* of unfitness, whereas in the case of the flat-earth geographer or Holocaust-denying European historian, such persistent and public statements would *constitute unfitness per se,* regardless of other evidence, either extenuating or incriminating.

The other difference may be subtler, but is surely no less important: The Supreme Court's footnote reference to "fitness" seems to imply no relationship to any special expectations society may have about the speaker, but rather derives from general standards for the public sector. Thus the writer-teacher's field would seem irrelevant to the application of this standard; a math teacher who miscalculated budget data, or an English teacher who used atrocious grammar, or a historian who botched the origins of the school system, would seem to fare no better or worse when it came to "fitness" than would any other teacher—or perhaps for that matter any other civil servant. In the academic setting, by stark contrast, the speaker or writer's discipline makes all the difference; the philosopher or linguist or botanist can with total impunity espouse either flat-earth theory or Holocaust-denial, even though under a public-employee speech analysis the expectations of an academic specialty drive the entire process.

Two issues remain for brief inquiry: Could Professor Churchill have been deemed "unfit" on the basis of his public statements? And if public-employee speech is not the proper standard for judging the extramural utterances of such a polemical scholar, where should one find a more apposite guide? The first question is intriguing if only because the Colorado chancellor's inquiry did not even consider it, though it might well have done so. For a scholar whose field is ethnic studies to suggest that some victims who toiled in the World Trade Towers somehow deserved their horrible fate on September 11 may not evidence animus toward any ethnic group, but does seem tragically insensitive to the diverse workforce of lower Manhattan. But there is an easy answer to such a suggestion: A single outrageous outburst, even if it fell directly within a scholar's area of academic specialty, could never constitute the requisite evidence of "unfitness." The qualifying term *persistent* appears in several relevant AAUP policies, and must be implicit here as well.

A concurrent example offers a clearer illustration. Just as Churchill's offending essay surfaced, the chairman of religious studies at the University of Kansas, Paul Mirecki, proposed to offer a new course, Special Topics in Religion, Intelligent Design, Creationism and Other Religious Mythologies. Describing the course in an e-mail, Mirecki referred to religious conservatives in his state as "fundies," adding that the proposed course would be "a nice slap in their big fat face." When this statement came to light, Mirecki (like Churchill) at once relinquished his chairmanship and withdrew the course proposal. But his faculty status remained a target for many Kansas conservatives, despite the KU administration's firm support for his academic freedom as a tenured professor.[8]

Here, then, was a statement that fell directly within the speaker's academic specialty. Yet as clearly as with Churchill's intemperate postings, Mirecki's isolated quip about "fundies" could not possibly demonstrate the requisite degree of "unfitness" to trigger a valid dismissal proceeding. Indeed, even a modern European historian who in an unguarded moment expressed serious doubt about the Holocaust would appear to be a prime prospect for a collegial warning from a dean or chairman, but almost certainly not for any major threat to a continuing or tenured faculty appointment.

Finally, what policies should govern contentious and provocative faculty speech? Any action taken by a public institution should be no less protective than the *Pickering* standard, save to the extent that special and recognized academic norms warrant higher expectations on such matters as plagiarism, controversial material in the classroom, and demonstrably false statements at the core of one's discipline. Private institutions, though not constrained by First Amendment standards, should (and for the most part do) commit themselves to comparably protective standards in judging faculty speech. Any transgressions that are deemed to warrant a formal sanction on the university's part must be persistent and pervasive, thus permitting an occasional and even outrageous outburst by a Churchill or a Mirecki. Rigorous procedures are of course vital to any such proceeding, respecting not only the gravity of the substantive interests that are potentially affected, but also the centrality of due process in such matters.

NOTES

1. A more detailed discussion and analysis of the issues in the Ward Churchill case may be found in Robert M. O'Neil, "Limits of Freedom: The Ward Churchill Case," *Change*, September–October 2006, 34–41, www.carnegiefoundation.org/change/sub.asp?key=97&subkey=2016, accessed December 11, 2008. See also Robert M. O'Neil, *Academic Freedom in the Wired World: Political Extremism, Corporate Power, and the University* (Cambridge: Harvard University Press, 2008), 28–30, 43–44, 83–85.

2. In fact the University of Colorado administration eventually recommended, and the board of regents decreed, Professor Churchill's dismissal because of the discovery of grave research transgressions.

3. *McAuliffe v. Mayor and Board of Aldermen,* 155 Mass. 216, 29 N.E. 517 (1893).

4. *Pickering v. Board of Education,* 391 U.S. 563 (1968).

5. *Garcetti v. Ceballos,* 126 S. Ct. 1951 (2006).

6. American Association of University Professors, *Sexual Harassment: Suggested Policy and Procedures for Handling Complaints, in Policy Documents and Reports,* 9th ed. (Washington, D.C.: AAUP, 2001), online at www.aaup.org/AAUP/pubres/policy docs/sexharass.htm.

7. See O'Neil, *Academic Freedom,* 1–8.

8. See Chris Moon, "KU Prof. Resigns Top Post," *Topeka Capital-Journal,* December 8, 2005, A1.

ACADEMIC FREEDOM

What Is It About?

⚬

R. Radhakrishnan

IN THE YEAR 2003 I WAS A FULBRIGHT SCHOLAR in India, and
as an Indian-American academic living and functioning in India, I would
get regular messages from the U.S. State Department in the form of
alerts—red, green, yellow, and so on—with each color signifying the level
of danger I would be exposed to as an American citizen during my stay and
travels through India. These concerned bulletins were part of the global
and the utterly deterritorialized American war on terrorism. What I was
supposed to feel as a proper American citizen was gratitude for an
almighty and ubiquitous national power-knowledge mechanism protecting
me wherever I went, making me aware, by way of an exquisite calibration,
of danger and terror levels in different parts of India, and indeed, the rest
of the world. America cared for my freedom even as it advised me not to
travel to those wild and unfree places where terror was the norm and a barbaric hatred of America the rationale behind such a norm. Needless to say,
these communiqués made me feel quite the opposite: unfree, exploited,
and deeply critical and contemptuous of American paranoia. If anything,
it made me feel ashamed to be American. I should add to this scenario the
not insignificant detail that the American Consulate General's office and
the United States Information Service office in Chennai were in a state of
fierce embattlement, short of moats and drawbridges, and access to the

premises required Byzantine procedures of application and registration. It was in the name of my so-called self-protection from the nameless forces of terror that I felt most violated: my sense of being human alienated and outraged in the name of my American citizenship and sovereignty. My freedom as an American citizen was directly proportionate to the level of paranoia I was prepared to internalize in response to "the not-Us, the Them" who were out to get us just like that, for no reason at all. And what is most galling and scandalous in this entire calculus is the fact that "truths" and "perceptions" driven by American-nationalist paranoia claim the status of knowledge without contestation from other sources of knowledge and other perspectives on reality.

The point I want to make here is that access to freedom is based on a prior and ideologically tacit relationship between a certain normative and binding form of collectivity and a structure of individuality that is interpellated by the collective norm. In other words, the security meted out to me was not to me as a human being, but to me as an American citizen. It was Homeland Security as American security that is committed both to establishing Pax Americana on behalf of the entire world and to me as a faithfully "hailed" American. What if I said I wasn't American, or what if I foreswore my American citizenship? Or for that matter, what if I doubted the veracity of the alerts being thrown at me? This latter problem is what I would like to term the "instrumentation panel" problem. Let me explain. Imagine a situation where the instrumentation panel tells me that the gas tank is empty or that the automobile is overheated, but in fact neither of the cases is true. I can either believe in the procedural functionality of the panel absolutely and proceed to organize my behavior accordingly; or I could cultivate a critical attitude to the truths of the panel and keep myself open to other indicators of reality. Simply put, it is indeed highly likely that the instrumentation panel could be off the mark and not be in touch with reality. But here is the rub. In a controlled systemic environment where we as human subjects have been schooled and programmed to access reality exclusively by way of the reliability of the panel and its internal consistency, it has become virtually unthinkable that reality could be other than the readings we get on the panel screen. The panel screen in question here of course is nationalism. Indians turn to the Indian screen, Americans to the American screen, and so on. Our very perception of reality is thus posited on the a priori efficacy of the nationalist instrumentation panel: a panel that would have us believe that it is nothing but the site of objective and unbiased procedurality, whereas in fact, the so-called objective and unbiased procedures are fiercely coded to protect well-defined self-interests. The putative drive toward freedom is but a euphemism for the drive toward the protection of self-interest, at whatever cost. In fact, as American foreign policy has demonstrated over and over again, quite tirelessly, freedom is nothing but the demand and the fulfillment of the demand of American self-interest. Any interrogation—that is, any interrogation in any part of the world—of American self-interest is tantamount to a denial of freedom. The world would be better off to realize its freedom by way of a prior alignment with American self-interest, which in its dominance is nothing but global self-interest itself.

Whether it is the United States under George Bush or India under Indira Gandhi during the infamous Emergency months of the late 1970s, freedom has never been natural.[1] It has always been a regime dictated by ideological interests. The question then arises: how can a true freedom be at the beck and call of ideological motivation? The answer: by way of the naturalization of the ideology of nationalism. If somehow the freedom of the human being can be made to appear as a subset of the freedom of the citizen; and if furthermore, the citizen can be persuaded, in the name of her sovereignty as a national subject, to honor her country absolutely and acknowledge such a loyalty to her country as the first principle on which her freedom rests, it automatically follows that all exercises and practices on behalf of freedom and in opposition to the enemies of freedom have been successfully legitimated and usurped in the name of the nation. In other words, an ontological regime has been established: a regime that disallows an antagonistic or contradictory relationship between freedom and citizenship.[2] It is in the name of the citizen that freedom itself is baptized and recognized. It is easy to see how such a virulently ideological notion of freedom is open to easy manipulation by national leaders or CEOs such as President Bush who can bully citizens into abrogating and abusing their freedom as human beings so that they can be faithful to their freedom as loyal sovereign American subjects.[3] What such a totalizing interpellation preempts is the very notion of contradiction and contestation among "different freedoms." Having been totally interpellated by the ideology of citizen-freedom, the human subject is paralyzed and alienated from its right to choose among different freedoms, different dharmas. The national code of conduct or dharma becomes the only viable horizon under which freedom can be conceptualized, invoked, and practiced.

Why have I begun my essay on academic freedom with reference to the ideology and the politics of the nation-state? The reason is that, unfortunately but inevitably, the contemporary crisis of academic freedom (both in the abstract and with reference to specific instances) is most visible as a symptom on the body politic of the nation-state: in this case, the United States. All possible affirmative valences of academic freedom have been constrained, particularly after 9/11 and the consequent global war of America against terrorism, to take the form of "freedom from" state intervention, censorship, and punishment. The contents and directions of academic freedom, that is, whatever academic freedom is "about," its representative and representational burden, have been coerced into parsing themselves as antistate and antinational ideological manifestos, while, it goes without saying, the ideological burden of the state remains unmarked as ideology. Whether it be the Ward Churchill case, or the Finkelstein situation, or the generalized suspicion of postcolonial studies (and the stigmatization of Edward Said's work), or the criminalization of pro-Palestinian pedagogies in Middle Eastern Studies, or the blacklisting of the New Americanists who are questioning the role of the United States as global hegemon, it is the atmosphere of a carefully engineered national paranoia that has set the stage and the terms for the discussion of human freedom as American freedom.

Malini Johar Schueller begins her essay, in this collection, thus:

Security. Surveillance. Diversity. Balance. These have been the contradictory catchwords of the Right's attacks on academia since 9/11. Couched in the language of nationalism and advocating a hyperscopic regime of control through state and civil apparatuses, different right-wing organizations professing commitment to fairness and diversity have sought to regulate the work of postcolonialist Middle East studies scholars. Thus Daniel Pipes's website, Campus Watch, published dossiers on eight prominent professors of Middle East studies who demonstrated "bias" in their teaching and promoted anti-Americanism. The targeted eight were inundated with hate mail and death threats. Although Pipes removed the dossiers as a separate item after vigorous criticism from faculty nationwide, he continued Campus Watch's project of "Monitoring Middle East Studies on Campus." Each month, the website showcases a "Quote of the Month" that demonstrates the "terrorist" sympathies of a Middle East studies professor. The stated objective of Campus Watch is to redress the "intolerance of alternative views" within Middle East studies.

In the interview essay in this collection, Andrew Ross, in response to a question, has this to say:

> Because of the renewed interest in patriotism (both among boomer liberals as well as conservatives), my field, American studies, has been beset in all sorts of ways by charges of anti-Americanism. Not long after 9/11 (and during the anthrax scare) I remember receiving letters at NYU addressed to the "Department of Anti-American Studies." Around about the same time, Thomas Friedman recommended that Saudi Arabia establish more American studies programs in their universities, unconsciously invoking the sorry history of the field's Cold War manipulation by the state. Though I have no explicit evidence of this, I would imagine that overseas American studies programs are likely to be feeling some pressure from consulates and embassies to do their bit and support the State Department's flat-footed campaign to combat the worldwide rise of anti-Americanism.

Both these passages make it abundantly clear that the intervention of the State Department in academic governance and practice is neither coincidental nor epiphenomenal. If anything, the State Department has demonstrated, through the sheer power of its executive and administrative will, that its jurisdiction extends to all academic spaces. And vigilante groups like Campus Watch operate as para-state operations that arrogate to themselves the patriotic prerogative of monitoring academic sites as potential trouble sites of intellectual anti-Americanism. The question surely arises: which America or whose America? It cannot be forgotten that these measures of surveillance and punishment were undertaken precisely during times when the national consensus for Bush was dwindling, when the number of Americans who were protesting the slogan "not in our name" was rising by the very minute. The State Department's and the president's tactics of paranoia and control were nothing short of a "democratic coup" at the expense of the people: unilateral acts of executive power to secure and define America in a certain way, in abeyance of legislative and representative measures. Executive power had indeed become America, and a climate had been created where the questioning of America in the name of a different vision of America had been "lexicalized" in the official book of patriotism as "treason." Bush felt that America was slipping away by legitimate means; and he did all he could to clinch it by illegitimate means, through wiretapping, the suspension of civil rights, and violations of the

Constitution in the name of executive authority. Whether or not the Obama administration limits executive power, the importance of the State's periodic interventions into academia will remain.

It is time now to unpack terms like *America* and *American* both descriptively, and ideologically. Let us take a look at the designation *Department of American Studies.* What does the adjective *American* mean here, and what is its epistemological as well as methodological relationship to *Studies?* Clearly, the *American* in *American Studies* is not the same as the *American* in *American nation,* or *American foreign policy* or *American security or sovereignty.* In the term *American Studies,* America is as much the object of study, analysis, critique, and interpretation as it is a founding possibility. To think and constitute and reconstitute America self-reflexively as an object of knowledge has nothing to do with a tautological conservation of America.[4] The accountability of an American Studies professor is not to a natural and axiomatic America capable of endless identical repetitions of itself, but rather to America as an epistemological object. The purpose of an American Studies academician is to de- and reterritorialize America and not to canonize America uncritically with reference to American self-interest or American exceptionalism, or to invent itself perennially as American apologetics. It is indeed the mandate of the American Studies professor to examine whether in the deployment of the phrase *American Studies, America* functions dispassionately or as a form of naturalized "national bias." After all, isn't it commonplace to declare that academia has no place for bias, except of course we all are all complicitously aware that the proud and courageous declaration that academic freedom be free of all bias is indeed accompanied by a *sotto voce* murmur, an aside: "but for the national bias."

It is time now to take a closer, critical look at the politics as well as the epistemology of bias.[5] How is bias related, or not, to solidarity and accountability? It goes without saying that a human being who has decided to perform all her life as a professor of American Studies has a bias in favor of American Studies; but such a bias does not mean that the soul and mind of the American Studies professor have been thoroughly suborned and "prejudiced" by an uncritical and unconditional love of America. I would argue, quite to the contrary, that it is only on the basis of a fundamental conviction that "Academia knows no nationality" that the professor of American Studies can begin to fulfill her commitment to the field known as American Studies. In other words, the mandate of academic freedom is to make sure that processes of knowledge flow and take shape without fear of censorship. What is the difference between being an American plain and simple, and a practitioner of American Studies? Apart from the possibility that a professor of American Studies may not be an American at all, the real and critical difference is that it behooves the American Studies professor to "alienate" America from itself before America becomes the legitimate epistemological object of American Studies. The kind of academic, procedural, and methodological reflection, as well as the self-reflexivity, that is mandatory in the case of the American Studies professor is not at all binding for an American citizen who is under no obligation to be a self-reflexive American. In other words, the "becoming" of America as an epistemological object within academia ought not to be at the beck and call of an ideology of America that presumes to know itself in all its propriety and rectitude. When Andrew Ross receives mail, care of the Department of Anti-American Studies (analogous to the McCarthy years and the suspicion of un-American activities), the patriotic senders of the mail assume that they are in possession of a sacred handbook that already sets out definitively what is American and what is not. It is in the name of such a politically correct and preordained American orthodoxy that gung-ho patriots have been raising the issue of left didacticism on campuses and justifying Campus Watch and other measures of surveillance to make sure that "their America" remains the only thinkable America. To put it in terms that I have been using elsewhere in my writings, this attempt on the part of American zealots and chauvinists has been nothing but a monopolistic run on the very principle "in the name of" on which America is premised and performed.[6] It is their belief and assumption that their version of America is somehow not an interpretive version at all, but rather the truth itself of America as it has been, is, will be, and should be in fulfillment of its transhistorical essence.

What is most noteworthy in this ideological ploy of a defensive and paranoid Americanism is the ease with which these ideologues of American freedom invoke a discourse that is simultaneously national-territorial and transnational-deterritorialized. This is not really all that surprising, given how over generations and under different presidential leaderships, American domestic policy and foreign policy have worked in close complicity with the result that attempted assassinations of leaders of foreign countries have become an integral part of the celebration of freedom and democracy within American boundaries. It is in the context of the American formula hatched in hubris: America thinks; *ergo* the world exists (i.e., the objective reality of the world is nothing but its acquiescent responsiveness to American interests) that the world has become available to America as a series of strategic sites meant for intervention, control, and nation-building in alignment with American needs and ideological demands. Throughout the history of the national and now the unilateral superpower America, Vietnam, Korea, Cuba, Afghanistan, Iraq, Iran, and the Middle East have played strategic roles in the development of the American consensus on freedom and on America's definition of what a free world should like. It has always been in response to some perceived threat from some "other or the other" and the threat posed by such an Alterity that official slogans of American freedom have found their voice and register. Continuing along the same historical trajectory, it is now the fear of Islamic fanaticism and Middle Eastern terror (against which the state of Israel "stands in" as America's democratic proxy) that has become indispensable for the narrativization of American freedom.

Let me in this context look briefly (one of the essays in this collection does an excellent in-depth analysis of the situation) at the beleaguered situation of Middle Eastern Studies in Columbia University. The allegation by right-wing pro-Israeli Americanists has been that Middle Eastern Studies has become the hotbed for the advocacy of the Palestinian cause. The implication here of course is that advocacy on behalf of the Palestinian cause is ideologically virulent, whereas a Middle Eastern Studies pedagogy that is pro-Israeli is by definition decent, civilized, democratic, and antiterrorist. Needless to say, a pro-Israeli stance is the one favored and legitimated by U.S. foreign policy. Before I get into the question of the so-called need for a balanced presentation of the Middle East in Middle Eastern Studies, I would like to do a brief epistemological analysis of the topos known as Middle Eastern Studies at Columbia University. I would argue that primarily it is an academic-discursive space whose subject matter is the history and the happenings, synchronic and diachronic, that constitute the Middle East: also a space that happens to be in Columbia University, which happens to be in upper Manhattan in a city called New York in the United States. The fact that the physical location of the academic space happens to be in the United States does not render it a patriotic-national space, just as the reality that what happens in Palestine, and Iraq, and Iran has a vital bearing on American self-interest does not transform those areas into American colonies. The fact that the United States has a perspective on these areas does not make them an ontological product of the American point of view. These locations enjoy their own realities that have nothing to do with, and owe nothing to, America's self-interested perspective. Second, it is inevitable that the state of scholarship in Middle Eastern

Studies is polemically fraught and riven, as a reflection of realities on the ground in that part of the world. This is not to say that scholarship and pedagogy are free of polemics in other areas of scholarship that have to do with geopolitically peaceful and secure locations: it is just that the Middle East, like Ireland and Kashmir, is more blatantly and manifestly political than those other locations that are not symptomatic of the political in quite the same way. Third, the field of Middle Eastern Studies, like any other field of study, has the right to enjoy the experience of "its becoming toward a definitive being" without interference from any nation, state, or such sovereign intervention.

The historical fact that Middle Eastern Studies is the site of passionate and visceral contestations between Israeli and Palestinian perspectives should not make it an automatic target for surveillance and punishment. Fourth, it is inevitable that an academic domain such as Middle Eastern Studies will indeed reflect faithfully and symptomatically the divisiveness and the lack of consensus among its practitioners. This situation is no different than that of, say, a department of economics at a university where one-half of the faculty is uncompromising capitalists, and the other half is Marxists of various stripes. Just as some departments of economics, or political science, or literature, or sociology are right-wing and others left-oriented, here too, in the case of Middle Eastern Studies, some programs could be Zionist or pro-Israeli, and others, pro-Palestinian, pro-Islamic. Fifth, it cannot be the epistemological burden of a department to provide artificial closure or balance to a raging and ongoing conflict: such an administration of academic closure would constitute an egregious political violation of the academic freedom of the discipline to reflect the conflicts and disagreements that constitute its very being and rationale. Why doesn't the State Department insist that all departments of economics in the country be balanced by an "equal" number of Marxian economists? My point here is that the merits and the demerits of the Israeli position and the Palestinian cause need to weighed in their own terms, and coevally, with respect to each other. It is the United States' bias (based on its geopolitical self-interest in the area, in favor of the state of Israel and against Palestine) that acts as the brute force that normativizes and naturalizes pro-Israeli scholarship and pedagogical advocacy and criminalizes pro-Islamic and pro-Palestinian academic leanings. Take the factor of American self-interest out of the equation, and academic freedom can be made to mean something else altogether. To put it quite bluntly, it is the intervention of American foreign policy that decides which academic practices are free, and which not.[7]

Even if one were to honor the call for balance (more about the constitutive contradictions of such a call in just a little bit), the question is this: Who is calling for the balance and from what putative Archimedean point of view? Given the contested nature of the knowledges that we are talking about, and given the far from even turf on which these struggles are taking place, what does "balance" mean: balance leaning toward what forms of resolution or equilibration? To put it simply in the context of Middle Eastern Studies, why doesn't the State Department perceive the so-called flagrant pro-Islamic and pro-Palestinian pedagogies as a belated and desperate attempt to rectify an existing imbalance evident in America's double standards in its dealings with the Middle East? It is precisely because American foreign policy will not condemn the state of Israel as undemocratic in its brutalization of the Palestinian population that America is hated and reviled in Arab and Islamic countries. What is galling in this entire scenario is that the United States is indeed guilty of extreme and uncompromising partisanship on behalf of Israel, but it will not avow that its stance is one of partisanship. It would rather pretend that its official stance is a pure humanist, transpolitical, transhistorical, and transideological orientation in support of freedom. Let us take for example, the vilification of Edward Said's works, and the denial of aid to area studies programs that have been influenced by postcolonial thought. It would be far more honest for the State Department to announce and identify itself in ideological opposition to Said's *Orientalism* and thus join the battle as an interested party. But that is exactly what it will not do. What it does instead is to masquerade and depoliticize its ideological and counterrevolutionary position as one of disinterested neutrality, and merely calls for a rectification of the imbalance created by postcolonial ideological fervor.

The question that concerns me here is "bias." The major distinction between a capitalist/right-wing/liberal humanist understanding of the term *bias,* and a radical left-wing understanding is this. The former camp "always already" assumes and occupies a position of neutrality and objectivity and ordains that all bias is rampantly political and ideological. In other words, right-wing capitalist ideologues make the assumption that the reality base they speak from is devoid of historical conditioning or corruption and that objectivity and the status quo are one and the same. It is precisely because these ideologues naturalize objective reality in the name of the dominant discourse, that is, in the name of the world picture that has been secured by the historiography of the dominant discourse, that they confidently finger-point toward oppositions and resistances and taint them with the vicious burden of politics, partisanship, and ideological skewness. This is the reason why procapitalist positions are perceived as celebrations of reality itself, whereas resistances to capitalism are seen as ideological orientations: a capitalist will not admit to being an ideologue. There is a big difference between the right-wing disavowal of bias *tout court* and the radical negotiation with the politics as well as the inevitable epistemology of bias.

If the creation of knowledge is both for its own sake and in response to a constitutive accountability to the world out there; and if furthermore, knowledge making is both objective and at the same time a candid and self-reflexive avowal of the perspective that is engaged in the production, not the naturalization, of objectivity, then, the term *academic freedom* is subjected to a double accountability: to the production of free and objective knowledges, and to a thorough, rigorous, and self-reflexive examination of the perspectival, and in that sense biased, production of objective knowledges. Perhaps a word here is in order about what I mean by epistemological bias. To scholars like me working in the areas of critical theory, postcoloniality, and poststructuralism, it is a given (either by way of the work of Martin Heidegger, Hans-Georg Gadamer, Jacques Derrida, Karl Marx, Michel Foucault, or by way of the work of such powerful cognitive psychologists such as Mahzarin Banaji and others who have been attempting to recognize, qualify, and quantify ways in which "bias" enters all human thinking and cognition) that all knowledge production is interested and not disinterested, perspectival and not omniscient, partisan and not neutral, ideologically interpellated and not just natural. The implication is not that the reign of bias should rule rampant, but rather that, as Jacques Derrida would have it, the university should function as that profoundly subtle space where "thought should think itself," rather than absolve itself of the historical as well theoretical onus of self-reflexivity and self-problematization. If right-wing thought as well as left-wing ideas are equally ideological and biased, if both pro- and anticapitalist stances are derived through bias, if both pro-Israeli and pro-Palestinian platforms are orchestrated by preexisting interest and bias, then in that case, the function of the university is to stage the conflicts and contestations among clashing perspectives rather than call for balance and neutrality, as though balance and neutrality were panaceas, placebos, or ready-made remedies available across the academic counter. As I have already attempted to demonstrate, the very position that demands balance and neutrality can only be a position that is embroiled in the scene of conflict, and not an Archimedean point of objectivity. Balance and neutrality cannot be applied from without through a fiat or an edict. Here again, as I have tried to argue, the point of view that calls for stability and balance is in fact the point of view of American foreign and state policy that has already made up its mind about whose side it is on. To put it differently, the call is for a "dominant neutrality" and a "dominant stability."

The very mandate of academic knowledge production is to examine the mutually constitutive relationship between bias and freedom. How does bias articulate itself toward freedom, and how does freedom acknowledge its rootedness in the historicity of bias? How are the claims of one biased narrative to be evaluated with reference to the claims of another narrative in the absence of an a priori ground of transcendence? To put it in the context of Israel and Palestine, here is the unpalatable state of affairs. The Palestinian surge toward freedom has to take the necessary historical incarnation of "freedom from" Israeli occupation and control, whereas the Israeli search for freedom is embodied as "freedom from" Palestinian insurrection and terrorism. But clearly, there is and can be no moral and political equivalence between the two definitions of freedom for the simple reason that Israel is already a free national state that was created on the basis of a massive enforced Palestinian exodus, whereas the Palestinian search for freedom is still prenational. In this embattled encounter there is no room to entertain possibilities of freedom as such except by way of the oppositional perspectivisms of the parties embroiled in the struggle. In such a context, the academic formation known as Middle Eastern Studies cannot but be richly symptomatic of the discord and dissonance of realities on the ground. Why doesn't the U.S. government demand, in the name of academic freedom and balance, that pro-Israeli propaganda be toned down? We know that such a demand will never come about for the simple reason that in the name of balance and security and stability, the U.S. government has already made up its mind that the Israeli perspective is the right perspective. The reasoning that brings the U.S. government to such a conclusion is far from reasonable, objective, or disinterested. The reasons are, as any casual observer of American foreign policy will be aware, are those of American self-interest. Whether it be Afghanistan, or Iraq, or Iran, or El Salvador, or Nicaragua, American advocacy of freedom in the name of the world has been nothing but a congeries of opportunistic contradictions and unconscionable disavowals.

So who is guilty of politicizing academia? No one is. It is always already political and necessarily and unavoidably so. It is just that within the narrative of American capitalist-exceptionalist liberalism some perspectives on reality are not perceived as political at all, whereas other perspectives that are antagonistic to the American axis are identified as political, ideological, and "special interests." As we have already observed, the nation-state, in its own interests, has usurped the right to make the judgment call as to what is political and what is not, what is biased and unbalanced and what is not. It is also clear that the nation-state by virtue of its executive sovereignty can indulge in censorship and surveillance in the name of freedom. Take for example the case of the foreign or the international student in an American university. After 9/11, the Office of International Students/Scholars has been forced into complicity with the Department of Immigration and Naturalization Services with the result that the freedom of the international student is perennially under state surveillance. If this is not an outrageous violation of the freedom of a nonsubject, then what is? But again, as we have seen already, the cause of freedom has been subsumed by the war on terrorism. Under the aegis of a Pax Americana where you are "either with us or against us," freedom is all the more "ours" since it cannot be "theirs."

The basic question is not how the academic site should escape the mark of the political or depoliticize itself in the name of procedural neutrality, but rather, how should academia wear the mark of the political, but with a difference. The singularity about the academic site of knowledge production is that it is equipped to deal with politics in the name of epistemology, and to deal with epistemology in the name of politics, without synchronizing the two into one seamless temporality. Academic accountability is two-pronged: macrological and micrological, thematic and methodological, worldly and professional. Insofar as academia is in the world, and cannot but be anywhere else, its operations have to be "about" the world, that is, academia cannot, in the name of its internal autonomy, relinquish its obligation to represent and "speak" for the world. The critical immanent labor of academia has to relativize itself with reference to the material antecedence of the world. But here is the epistemological difference: the academic professional has the freedom to engage in a double session with the politics of representation, that is, engage in representation postrepresentationally. In other words, rather than seek definitive and official closure by way of the politics of representation, the academic intellectuals perform the task of representation open-endedly. The academic intellectual is obliged by her professional dharma to protect the truths of representation as performance from undue influence from representation as ideological orthodoxy. It behooves the academic intellectual to maintain with rigor the necessary lack of coincidence of political temporality with epistemological temporality. To put it in the context of the dharma of American Studies, the political truth of America can only be an ongoing, contradictory, and unpredictable function of the discovery of America as epistemological object by American Studies methodologies and performances. What I am invoking here in a concrete context is Foucault's memorable reminder to humanity, by way of his radical reading of Nietzsche, that the "subject" of knowledge has the obligation to perennially dissolve itself in processes of knowledge.[8]

The ultimate and the only mandate that academic performance has to honor is that of the decolonization of knowledge, knowledge as decolonization: a point that Malini Johar Schueller makes with telling clarity in her essay. As I conclude this essay, I would like to briefly unpack the theoretical as well historical implications of what it means to decolonize knowledge and to realize knowledge as decolonization. The first point to be made is that any decolonization of knowledge has to be a situated and perspectival decolonization, and not an unsituated or omniscient decolonization. Strange and hilarious as it may sound, it bears repeating that decolonization cannot be initiated from a colonial point of view. It has to be empowered from without as a war of maneuver, assuming that such a "without" is available, or engineered as a "war of position" from within the dominant discourse.[9] Nothing can be more scandalous or risible than the expectation that the project of decolonizing knowledge can be undertaken in the name of the global hegemon, that is, the United States and its unbridled exceptionalism as well as unilateralism. The fact of the matter is, and this claim would send shivers of anger and outrage down every patriotic American spine, that freedom has to be negotiated against the grain of American imperialism and its implicit exceptionalism.

In her elaboration of what she calls "multicultural imperialism," Malini Johar Schueller makes the following important diagnosis.

> Although the narration of the United States as an "empire for liberty" has a long-standing history going back to Jefferson, the post-9/11 narrative of exceptional (and exceptionally victimized) empire has been consistently coded as multicultural empire for liberty. Not only has this empire been continually narrated through the race and

gender diversity of the armed forces, but also through highly publicized calls for tolerance such as George W. Bush's characterization of the perpetrators of 9/11 as those belonging only to fringe groups of Islam and his broadcasts to the public, cautioning them not to target racial or religious groups. Yet while this pedagogical narrative of nation as empire is undoubtedly cast as one in service of all, a multicultural empire, the limits of nation are carefully policed through inevitably raced distinctions between the benign domestic multicultural and the sinister foreign. The resurgence of Orientalism post-9/11 has only heightened the discursive consensus through which "Arab," "Muslim," "Terrorist," and "anti-American" signify each other.

It is against this viciously manufactured discursive consensus that both the lay nonspecialist world and the world of academia have to come together: in the name of freedom, and in the name of diverse and heterogeneous knowledges with a will to resist American jingoism.

NOTES

1. For an anguished and historically situated rendition of the human condition as it is subjected to the violence of competing political regimes that naturalize terrorism in the name of freedom, see Maurice Merleau-Ponty, *Humanism and Terror: An Essay on the Communist Problem,* trans. John O'Neill (Boston: Beacon Press, 1969). Also see Etienne Balibar and Immanuel Wallerstein, *Race, Nation, Class: Ambiguous Identities,* trans. Chris Turner (London: Verso, 1991), for a thorough critique of the specious truth claims of nationalism, and Etienne Balibar, *Politics and the Other Scene,* trans. Christine Jones, James Swenson, and Chris Turner (London: Verso, 2002), for a rigorous reading of the formation of masses and collectivities in the context of wars and other such crises.

2. Judith Butler has been particularly convincing in her attempts to articulate meaningful connections between an ontological humanity and a humanity derived exclusively on the basis of national citizenship and sovereignty. See Butler, *Precarious Life: The Powers of Mourning and Violence* (London: Verso, 2004), *Giving an Account of Oneself* (New York: Fordham University Press, 2006), and *Excitable Speech: A Politics of the Performative* (New York: Routledge, 1997). For more on the relationship among freedom, the aesthetic, and the state, see the wide-ranging and influential collection *The Administration of Aesthetics: Censorship, Political Criticism, and the Public Sphere,* ed. Richard Burt (Minneapolis: University of Minnesota Press, 1994); and for an appreciative critique of Judith Butler's endeavor to gesture toward an ontological "we" against the grain of national-political jingoism, see my essay, "Grievable Life, Accountable Theory," *boundary 2* 35.1 (2008): 67–84.

3. See Sheldon Wolin, *The Presence of the Past: Essays on the State and the Constitu-*

tion (Baltimore: Johns Hopkins University Press, 1989), for an excoriating critique of America having run amok, in violation of democracy, as a megastate. See also my essay "When Is Democracy Political?" *boundary 2* 33.3 (2006): 103–22.

4. See Jacques Derrida, "The Principle of Reason: The University in the Eyes of Its Pupils," in *The Eyes of the University: Right to Philosophy 2,* trans. Jan Plug et al. (Stanford: Stanford University Press, 2004), 129–55, where he argues that the self-reflexive mandate of the critique produced in academia is "to think thought itself," and produce insights that are heterogeneous to the object of the critique.

5. It is Martin Heidegger who in the context of the existential hermeneutic of the *Dasein* enfranchised "pre-judice" as an essential component of knowledge production and insisted that the *Dasein* bravely enter and process itself through the hermeneutic circle and thereby realize circularity as a progressive epistemological procedure. Hans-Georg Gadamer, Heidegger's student, furthers this thought in his *Truth and Method,* 2nd ed., trans. revised by Joel Weinsheimer and Donald G. Marshal, and *Philosophical Hermeneutics,* trans. and ed. David E. Linge (Berkeley and Los Angeles: University of California Press, 1976). For a differently situated but an equally compelling accounting of "worldliness" between solidarity and critique, see Edward Said, *The World, the Text, and the Critic* (Cambridge: Harvard University Press, 1983).

6. For a range of critical engagements with the category of "in the name of," see my *History, the Human, and the World Between* (Durham: Duke University Press, 2008).

7. Louis Althusser's work on the Ideological State Apparatus remains as influential as now as it was when it was formulated a few decades ago.

8. See Michel Foucault, "Nietzsche, Genealogy, History," in *Language, Counter-memory, Practice: Selected Essays and Interviews,* ed. Donald Bouchard, trans. Donald Bouchard and Sherry Simon (Ithaca: Cornell University Press, 1977).

9. See Antonio Gramsci, *Selections from the Prison Notebooks,* ed. and trans. Quintin Hoare and Geoffrey Nowell Smith (New York: International Publishers, 1971), for succinct definitions of the wars of maneuver and position.

THE CULTURE WARS: FROM THE COLD WAR TO
NEOCON SURVEILLANCE

FRAGILE PROMISES

Academic Freedom at the City University of New York

Stephen Leberstein

AMONG THE SPECTACLES STAGED by modern American universities, the seemingly heartfelt proclamations of devotion to principles of academic freedom by trustees and administrators might reassure the faculty that they are secure in fulfilling their mission of pursuing the truth. College presidents, university chancellors, and even trustees from time to time pledge to honor the academic freedom of their faculty. This essay will explore how fragile those promises can be, demonstrating how attacks on public sector spending and institutions exploited fear and structural weaknesses in the universities to curb or silence dissent. Such promises are not new; they have been issued at other times of social turmoil and partisan politics, and this essay, a case study of the City University of New York, will try to put contemporary issues into historical perspective.

In late September 2001, a teach-in about the 9/11 terror attacks at the City College of New York led the next day to an inflammatory news story in the *New York Post* titled "CCNY Bashes America—Students, Profs Blame Attacks on U.S.," followed the day after by a stinging editorial denouncing both participants and the university's faculty and staff union, "the hard-left-wing, mired-in-the-'60s faculty union." "Anti-Americanism and anti-war sentiment raged yesterday during a 'teach-in' at City College," the *Post* reported; at a "forum sponsored by the professors' union, the Professional Staff Congress and nearly all the students who spoke had absorbed the lessons taught by their professors."[1]

The university chancellor, Matthew Goldstein, then issued a public statement condemning the professors who had "offered lame excuses to justify the September 11 terror attacks," and several trustees suggested that the professors were "seditious" and declared that "They have an invitation to take a hike." Neither Goldstein nor the trustees attended the teach-in; they based their statements solely on the account in the *Post*.[2] No official action was taken against the most visible participants, who received death threats as a result of the media reports.

Benno Schmidt, then the board of trustees vice chair, now its chair, only a week earlier had pronounced the university a safe haven for dissent:

> Academic freedom, freedom of inquiry in the search for truth, the freedom of thought to challenge and to speak one's mind, these are the matrix, the indispensable condition of any university worthy of the name. The City University of New York has a proud tradition of academic freedom. We will defend the academic freedom of our faculty and students as essential to the preservation of the University. That these are prized American values, as well as central to the academic mission, only makes their defense in times of crisis the more essential. (Adopted by the CUNY Board of Trustees, September 24, 2001)

How could these seemingly contradictory pronouncements be reconciled? In the absence of an answer to this question, it remained unclear how much protection Schmidt's proclamation would offer the faculty.

In a much earlier case at what were then known as New York City's municipal colleges, a similarly high-minded proclamation from the board's chair could not protect the faculty from their determined enemies. In 1938 Congressman Martin Dies (D-Tex.), chair of the fledgling House Committee on Un-American Activities, wanted information about Communists on the college faculties. Dies' suspicions were based on a complaint by Brooklyn College English professor Bernard Grebanier about what he regarded as the undue influence of the Communist Party at his college.

When Dies sought the help of Ordway Tead, chair of the city's Board of Higher Education, in ridding the municipal colleges of "subversives," Tead declared that the political affiliations of the faculty and staff were none of the board's business. "Our concern is with the scholarship and integrity of our faculties . . . [and] differences of opinion and attitude among faculty members are a wholesome sign of vitality, and as this is reflected in the teaching, it supplies students with a useful cross-section of the divergence of views in the community at large."[3]

Assurances of the faculty's academic freedom were quickly broken. These incidents spanning nearly seventy years show a pattern, of the promise and then betrayal, that has proven unfortunately consistent in its effect if different in detail.

The case of the municipal colleges—in 1938 there were only four colleges, Brooklyn, City, Hunter, and Queens, that later became the City University—will show how fragile such promises are in a politically charged environment, and when larger issues of structure, governance, unionization, and especially funding are at stake. As Marx had it, history repeats itself, the first time as tragedy, the second as farce.

During the Depression enrollment at the four municipal colleges mounted as unemployment soared. In order to accommodate burgeoning numbers of working-class youth, mostly the children of immigrants, the colleges crammed them into existing facilities and hired more of their own young alumni at low ranks to teach them. Many of the new faculty members resembled the students they taught in ethnicity and economic background. They lacked the protection of tenure until 1938, and were paid abysmally low salaries, just enough for "bed and bookcase," as one of them put it.[4]

Funding for the tuition-free colleges came from the city, and the hard times of the Depression set the stage for undermining board chairman Tead's promise. The left-led Teachers Union and its companion College Teachers Union, respectively American Federation of Teachers Locals 5 and 537, had come under fire from anti–New Deal conservatives. They were assailed for their effective lobbying to restore funding for schools and the public colleges, and also for championing such social justice issues as ridding school materials of racist books, integrating the faculty (and the faculty dining room) at City College, and support for a federal antilynching bill as well as higher pay, smaller classes, and the like.

Although Dies got nowhere, mounting right-wing pressure led to the creation of a state legislative investigating committee in 1940, the Rapp Coudert Committee, one of a number of "Little Dies Committees" around the country in that period.[5] The one in New York, however, was so effective that it set the pattern for anti-Communist purges for years to come.

The 1941 Rapp Coudert purge began largely outside the halls of the academy. While the reactionary president at City College, Frederick Robinson, had a long and very public history of conflict with progressive students and faculty, he was forced into retirement by 1938 as a result of Mayor LaGuardia's appointment of reform board members, several years before the state legislature authorized its investigation into subversive activities. The storm that followed drew most of its fury from forces outside the colleges.

Those the committee targeted had been active in union work, and the New York Teachers Union to which many belonged was militant as well as adept at lobbying City Hall and the state legislature to avert the worst effects of the budgetary axe. In the eyes of the Taxpayers Union of New York City, the anti-public-sector vigilantes of its day, the union was responsible for frustrating its agenda of slashing spending on public education, including higher education. Its president, Joseph Goldsmith, called for closing the City College and reducing the budget of the remaining colleges by $10 million.[6] When the legislature voted to investigate the schools, the Taxpayers Union was part of the chorus cheering it on.

It was no coincidence that the investigation began by subpoenaing all membership lists and other records of the New York Teachers Union, AFT Local 5, and of the New York College Teachers Union, AFT Local 537. Almost all of those ultimately dismissed or not reappointed had been active in the union, including thirteen activists whom Robinson had fired in the spring of 1936. Under pressure from labor and civil liberties groups, the board had reversed their dismissals by the start of that summer.

Similarly, the attempt to hire Bertrand Russell at City College in 1940 unleashed the ire of churchmen who regarded the philosopher as the devil of their day. Derided as "the god-less advocate of free love," Russell became in their eyes the emblem of much of what was wrong at the municipal colleges, where the faculty enjoyed new powers of self-governance as a result of the "democratization" plan of 1938. Preventing Russell's appointment at City College was the pretext for substituting external oversight for academic autonomy.

The investigating committee soon persuaded the city's Board of Higher Education to define teachers' political affiliation as a threat to national security, and to police its own faculty and staff in order to dismiss alleged Communists for refusing to name names. Before the U.S. entry into World War II in December 1941 brought the purges to a temporary halt, about fifty faculty and staff at City College had lost their jobs. None of them, however, was ever accused of misconduct in the classroom or in his scholarship. At the time, the committee said nothing about financing the woefully underfunded system of public education.

As a consequence, City College lost a generation of its most promising faculty members, including its only black professor. Even more important, the purge seriously narrowed the range of discourse on controversial issues. One of the informers was elevated to dean and served at the college through the mid-1970s. The risks of union and political activism could not have been a clearer lesson to those who remained.

In its 1942 report to the state legislature, the Rapp Coudert Committee's chief counsel, Paul Windels, stated that the real intent of the committee was to change the culture of the public colleges, to instill the instinct of self-censorship and self-policing in the academic community, "that amorphous section of the public referred to under the collective heading 'liberals' and 'intellectuals.'"[7] If that purge succeeded in its aim of ridding the public colleges of their troublemakers, it did so by substituting the judgment of politicians for the professional autonomy that is the indispensable mainstay of academic freedom.

As further evidence of how vulnerable to political reaction the faculty at City College had become, a politically active mathematics instructor, Lee Lorch, was fired in 1949. Lorch was active in the Tenants Committee to End Discrimination in Stuyvesant Town, the Metropolitan Life–owned complex built to house returned war veterans that refused to rent to African Americans. Lorch had gained some notoriety when he and his family invited a black family to share their own Stuyvesant Town apartment.

In response the NAACP called for an investigation of Lorch's dismissal, and the College Teachers Union was among the many groups that protested his firing. The American Jewish Committee also protested in the belief that Lorch was a victim of both anti-Semitism and racism. The committee charged that his firing "brings into disrepute our municipal college system and inevitably creates suspicion that religious considerations played a part in the college's action."[8]

Among those who protested Lorch's firing at a meeting of the Board of Higher Education was Justice Hubert T. Delaney of the Domestic Relations Court. Justice Delaney shed some light on the motives for the firing when he remarked that Lorch happened to be "vice president of a committee that got 3,500 signatures of tenants there [Stuyvesant Town] who were opposed to the exclusion of Negroes. I get pretty sick and tired of having a man called a Communist because he does a decent thing. I think we are giving Communists too much credit."[9]

Harry Wright, who became president of City College in 1941 and co-operated enthusiastically with the Rapp Coudert purge, commented when asked to explain Lorch's firing, "Sometimes in life we do things which you don't care to explain." Lorch taught math at Pennsylvania State University the year following his firing from City College and made his apartment at Stuyvesant Town available to a black family for the year. This led to his firing from the Pennsylvania university, too, an action a college spokesman explained by referring to Lorch's offer of his apartment to the black family as "extreme, illegal and immoral, and damaging to the public relations of the college."[10]

Lorch went on to teach at historically black colleges in the South and eventually at York University in Toronto. Last year, at age ninety-one, he received the annual award of the Mathematics Association of America for "distinguished contributions to mathematics and mathematics education," and is a member of the American Association for the Advancement of Science and of the Royal Society of Canada. After his firing from Penn State, the *New York Times* editorialized "that academic freedom is really imperiled if a professor is to be penalized because he takes a firm and positive stand against racial discrimination."[11]

Today's broken promises differ in kind and tenor from those of the earlier period, but they may be even more effective in curbing the independence of the faculty and sanitizing the discourse in colleges and in the public at large of ideas that unsettle those in power. As in the earlier period, the threat to academic freedom is rooted in the broader political context. While the earlier incidents grew out of the reaction to the New Deal, and probably a toxic mix of anti-Semitism and racism, today's stem from the rise of a neoliberal ideology and the eclipse of Keynesian economics, the reality of fundamentalist market policies with the consequent shifting boundary between the waning public sector and the engorged private sector.

At CUNY as across the nation, the faculty is becoming as stratified as it was in the 1930s. Less than half the nation's faculty are now tenured or on tenure-track lines, and more than half of all classes are taught by adjunct faculty, the most vulnerable.[12] A small number are "stars," Distinguished Professors in CUNY commanding salaries significantly greater than others and with teaching assignments much lower. The CUNY administration markets these stars in its subway advertising campaign, "Study With the Best," in which the photos of the top-tier faculty are shown in their classes and labs. This advertising campaign to "brand" CUNY fails to mention that most students don't have the chance to study with the stars when the majority of classes are taught by adjunct faculty.

The students are also increasingly stratified. Since remedial instruction at the university's four-year colleges was ended in 2000, and admission now depends on threshold scores on such standardized exams as the SAT or the ACT, those who might have been admitted to Brooklyn, City, Hunter, or Queens College, the system's more selective schools, are now sent to Language Immersion Institutes or the system's overcrowded, understaffed two-year colleges. Scores on these tests correlate with both family income and race, according to data from the test makers themselves, so the various strata are also beginning to reflect differences in race and economic status.[13] Some of the four-year schools now boast an Honors College, where top-scoring students pay no tuition, get free laptops, take honors classes separate from others, and get hundreds of dollars in passes to the city's cultural wonders.

The waning of New York's vaunted "social democracy" has meant steeply declining public support for the university.[14] Since the fiscal crisis of 1975–76, public funding for CUNY has consistently declined. In the last fifteen years alone, public funding has dropped 30 percent while tuition and fees have risen nearly 200 percent.[15] Student tuition now pays for nearly half the operating budget. The university now relies more and more on private support for new initiatives, and on the perennial effort to persuade city and state officials to maintain funding at last year's level. The decline in public support, always at risk in any case, has made university administrators ever more sensitive to what they regard as "bad news," and thus ever ready to eliminate its cause, as we shall see.

For example, at CUNY, academic freedom as "the fundamental matrix of the university" was quickly forgotten when an adjunct lecturer at York College, Mohammed Yousry, was indicted on terrorism charges in the spring 2002. Professor Yousry was supposedly suspended for his own well-being while external pressure built for his dismissal. An adjunct lecturer, however, Yousry lacked the protection of tenure, like the approximately 60 percent of U.S. faculty today who are contingent workers.

Professor Yousry was suspended in April 2002 and then summarily dismissed after his indictment along with Lynne Stewart, the attorney for Sheik Abdel Rahman, the convicted terrorist in the 1993 bombing of the World Trade Center, on charges of materially aiding terrorism.

Yousry's dismissal without any hearing took place before his trial even began in federal district court in New York. His guilt or innocence had not been determined when he was dismissed in 2002, although he has now been found guilty (essentially of fulfilling his professional duty as an Arabic-English translator appointed by the Justice Department).[16] At the time he was let go, there was no finding that his presence in the classroom posed any danger to himself, to his students and colleagues, or to the college, the standard for suspension pending a hearing as set forth in the AAUP's 1958 "Procedural Standards in Faculty Dismissal Proceedings."[17] In fact, his department chair invited him to return to his class to conclude the semester.

CUNY general counsel Frederick Shaffer, on the other hand, stated, in his reply to the AAUP's investigation report, that he chose to remove Yousry from the classroom because he was a "role model" for his students and his indictment was, after all, "a serious one." Shaffer's most revealing remark was that the university had acted "out of a concern that public confidence would suffer if Mr. Yousry were permitted to continue teaching at York College."[18] Shaffer argued that Yousry's dismissal did not harm his academic freedom since it was not based on his teaching or research. "Any reason, or no reason at all" was his explanation of why adjuncts might not be reappointed, so long, he said, as those reasons did not violate his academic freedom. As William Van Alstyne argued some time ago, however, such freedom cannot be secure where power can be used arbitrarily to act against persons by unaccountable standards and by procedurally deficient means.[19] In this case, Professor Yousry was not even notified that he was suspended, much less given any due process protection when he was dismissed.

If Yousry was removed for reasons other than his political affiliation or his speech, why then did the AAUP find that his academic freedom had been violated when Shaffer didn't? As an AAUP investigating committee wrote in an earlier case, "The profession's entire case for academic freedom is predicated upon the basic right to employ one's professional skills in practice, a right, in the case of the teaching profession, which is exercised not in private practice but through institutions. To deny a faculty member this opportunity without adequate cause . . . is to deny him his basic professional rights. . . . To inflict such injury without due process and, therefore, without demonstrated reason, destroys the academic character of the University."[20]

Shaffer argued that Yousry's academic freedom hadn't been violated because his firing had nothing to do with anything he said in the classroom, a stance characteristic of CUNY's approach to the issue of academic freedom. As power has increasingly been centralized in the upper reaches of the administration, decisions that would have been made by a departmental committee or a college governance body are now made solely by authority of the chancellor or the presidents. In this case, even the college president was unaware that Yousry had been banned from teaching at York College.[21]

For example, the chancellor issued a press release on October 17, 2005, proclaiming his commitment to academic freedom by endorsing the statement of the Global Colloquium of University Presidents.[22] Goldstein defined the terrain in two ways, both revealing of the administration's view of labor management relations in the academy. He said that academic freedom

> has been applied to various procedural demands by faculty unions. *Although a basic level of procedural fairness is necessary to protect academic freedom, it does not follow that colleges and universities must implement every demand for increased procedural safeguards, many of which have more to do with job security than to [sic] the right [of] free expression in teaching, research, writing or political activities.* I believe such matters are best dealt with through the process of collective bargaining. (Emphasis added)

If adjunct and contingent faculty are considered "at will" employees, as Shaffer did in the Yousry case, then under this standard they can be let go for "any reason or no reason at all," a situation in which they would have to rely on the kindness of strangers to protect their academic freedom. Unfortunately, the CUNY administration has refused to grant any additional procedural protections to adjunct faculty in bargaining negotiations.

The chancellor then goes on to say that in internal policy discussions administrators

> are often confronted with the need to participate in an ongoing debate . . . [and that] the University supports the right of administrators to take an opposing viewpoint [to that of the faculty], so long as their stance does not imply punitive action or retribution.

But when a senior administrator speaks out on university policy, he or she is usually speaking for the institution and doesn't have to rely on the protection of academic freedom, as would a faculty member voicing a dissenting view. Yet the chancellor claims the privilege of academic freedom for administrators when they are "confronted with the need to participate in an ongoing debate." Ordinary members of the university community might feel compelled to speak their minds as members of the faculty, or as citizens, claiming no authority as spokespersons for the institution.

But in speaking out on matters of institutional policy, administrators do speak with authority for their institutions. Unless an administrator specifically set aside his institutional authority in speaking out, his statement might well imply "punitive action or retribution" for those on the opposing side of the debate, the very outcome the chancellor claims he is committed to averting but one that many faculty members say they fear. While the chancellor was intent on including administrators under the umbrella of academic freedom in his statement at the Global Colloquium, he remained silent on the crucial issues of their disclaiming institutional authority when they speak, and of due process protection for faculty.

It was hardly coincidental that Goldstein chose to separate academic freedom, on the one hand, and union demands for "procedural fairness," which he dismisses, on the other. The strongest protection of the faculty's academic freedom is in enforceable collective bargaining agreements; union contracts generally provide due process procedures for those accused of misconduct and threatened with some form of sanction. But in the Yousry and other cases, such protection as we seem to enjoy has its limits. Contingent faculty members seldom enjoy such union protection, and none at CUNY. Further, after the 1980 Supreme Court decision denying Yeshiva University faculty the right to collective bargaining under the protection of the National Labor Relations (Wagner) Act, few private universities were unionized.[23]

Other cases at the City University show how vulnerable the faculty is to continuing violations of their academic freedom when more than half of all its classes are taught by part-time, or adjunct, faculty who do not have the protection of tenure.

One such case involved Susan Rosenberg, a well-regarded adjunct lecturer at John Jay College where she taught writing. Rosenberg had been hired in 2004 to teach a short course in a special program at Hamilton College in upstate New York, when her conviction and prison sentence for carrying concealed arms, and the implication that she was somehow involved in the 1981 Brinks Armored Car robbery in Rockland County, became known. Raucous public demonstrations organized by the Rockland County Emerald Society followed, and she withdrew from the Hamilton College course. Then at John Jay College of Criminal Justice, the new president, Jeremy Travis, banned her from ever teaching there again. Explaining his action, Travis said that police organizations had opposed her presence on the faculty and that he, as president, had to be conscious of the desires of the college's chief constituency.[24]

In another incident at Brooklyn College in 2006, after the Department of Sociology elected Professor Timothy Shortell as chair, the *New York Sun* ran an article attacking him for his personal beliefs about organized religion, views that appeared on a personal website completely unrelated to his duties at the college. Following this exposé, the college administration authorized an investigation into his fitness to serve as chair. Rather than suffer continued vilification and investigation, Professor Shortell withdrew his name. At the same time, Professor Priya Parmar, who teaches about theories of literacy in the School of Education at Brooklyn, was publicly attacked, again in the *New York Sun,* for her purported advocacy of Ebonics and accused of discriminating against students who didn't agree with her. None of the charges could be verified independently, and the students who accused her of bias turned out to have been disciplined for plagiarism. Fortunately, Professor Parmar was granted tenure this year.

It should not be so surprising that all of these recent incidents originated in groups outside the colleges. As the City University has taken on many corporate characteristics—with a chancellor and presidents who resemble CEOs, faculties with more contingent, part-time members than full-time members, a consumer culture reliant on marketing, and financing increasingly dependent on student tuition and private money—those in charge seem far more concerned with public relations than with the intellectual mission of the institution.

The growing corporate culture of the university has also led to a more banal kind of assault on academic freedom. Now it is not so rare to hear of a dean who orders a faculty member to change the grade of a student who complains to the college president or provost, as happened in 2007 at the Borough of Manhattan Community College and at City College. Or the administrator at Queensborough Community College who ordered a library faculty member to remove artifacts from an exhibit on Black History Month for fear that they might offend some group. Or yet another case at Medgar Evers College of a dean who ordered a faculty member to abandon a syllabus and texts he had long used, with departmental approval, and adopt her own. When he initially refused to comply, the dean had him physically removed from his class in front of his students.[25]

A more egregious case of how corporate culture intrudes into the university can be seen in the "sponsoring" of courses by public relations firms, a practice that deprives the faculty of their role in deciding what shall be taught and how. Such an incident at Hunter College came to light in March 2007, when it was reported that a trade association, the International Anticounterfeiting Coalition (IACC), sponsored a public relations course requiring students to mount an anticounterfeiting campaign on their campus as an assignment.[26] The trade group represents companies concerned about cheap knock-offs of their high-end products, like Chanel, Coach bags, Reebok, and others.

In this case, IACC paid Hunter College $10,000 to offer the course based on a package it provided, along with an IACC advisor to monitor the course.[27] When Professor Tim Portlock, the instructor, suggested introducing different perspectives on counterfeiting, the advisor reportedly said, "This is not why we're giving you $10,000." When Portlock argued for "alternate perspectives," the response was, "So, you think you're going to get some Senegalese guy to come unroll his mat for your students?"[28]

The object of the campaign resulting from the course was to convince students to shun fake luxury goods, like Coach bags, without letting anyone know the campaign itself was bogus. Similar IACC courses have been sponsored at other public colleges, including one at City College. Not coincidentally, Coach CEO Lew Frankfort, a Hunter alumnus, was awarded an honorary degree in May 2007 and then donated $1 million to the college.

No business likes bad publicity, and as colleges become more like businesses, they will try to burnish their "brand" and banish uncomfortable incidents that bring them unwanted attention. The increasing reliance on a contingent labor force for teaching makes it all the easier to cast aside those whose presence attracts bad publicity. At the same time, the lure of corporate support including contributions is evidently very attractive to senior administrators.

Today, of course, the issues that animated the Rapp Coudert Committee have changed, as we can see from these recent incidents. The Communist Party has largely lost its ability to strike fear into the hearts of Americans, but other demons are at hand. Scholars of the Middle East and, in particular those working on the Israeli-Palestinian conflict, are increasingly at risk of attack if they stray beyond the rigid boundaries of political orthodoxy.

A notorious example of the equation of dissent with sedition was the publication of a report titled *Defending Civilization: How Our Universities Are Failing America and What Can Be Done about It,* issued in 2002 by the American Council of Trustees and Alumni, cofounded by Lynne Cheney, wife of the vice president, and Senator Joseph Lieberman (I-Conn.). A number of CUNY faculty members were cited as examples of faculty who failed to "defend civilization."

Today's national campaign to police the nation's colleges and universities by the adoption of the so-called Academic Bill of Rights by governing boards, state legislatures, and Congress threatens academic freedom perhaps more fundamentally than the earlier Rapp Coudert purge did. Those advocating the new regimen, like David Horowitz, justify it on the grounds that the nation's liberal arts professors are mostly registered Democrats who routinely abuse their faculty prerogatives to indoctrinate their students.[29] Very little if any hard evidence of "indoctrination" has been presented so far, and at least one state, Pennsylvania, created a legislative investigating committee to look into the alleged problem but found none that could be substantiated.[30]

Horowitz nevertheless argued that faculties at many colleges are no longer capable of professional discipline on the grounds of faculty members' political affiliation, and he has created the Students for Academic Freedom project to solicit complaints of faculty bias against conservative students, suggesting that students have been victimized.[31]

A similar effort to protect students from putative discrimination at the hands of their professors became policy at the City University of New York in February 2007. The architect of the so-called Student Complaint Procedure was CUNY's general counsel, Frederick Shaffer, who was also at the center of the Yousry firing. He said that "the policy was for cases—and he estimated that there may be one or two a year—in which students feel a faculty member has been 'abusive' in class, generally in a dispute over political views."[32] Shaffer claimed, however, that the new policy would not violate academic freedom. A story in *Inside Higher Ed,* however, said that the CUNY policy "is very consistent with Horowitz's claim that there are categories of student complaints (he has tended to talk about political posturing in class) for which most colleges don't have a current policy."

CONCLUSION
❧

The risks to academic freedom today are great and threaten to undermine the social mission of the university that Arthur Lovejoy identified as its basis in 1915.[33] Ellen Schrecker, the nation's leading scholar on McCarthyism in the academy, sees the threat as more serious now than it was during the McCarthy period.[34] Horowitz and his followers would put political controls on the most critical educational functions of a university, including personnel decisions, curricula, and even teaching methods, all in the name of fostering "intellectual diversity," or for other, more banal purposes, including commercial ventures.

Although no repressive legislation has been adopted, the combination of partisan politics, continued attacks on public spending and on the public sector generally, the marketing of higher education, and changes in the structure of public universities, jeopardizes the ability of the faculty to carry out their jobs properly and thus to fulfill the university's social mission. Just as the purge that followed the Rapp Coudert investigation in 1941 showed how fragile the Board of Higher Education's promise of academic freedom was then, current circumstances show that today's pledges of allegiance to academic freedom offer little real comfort. Unlike the Rapp Coudert purge and the subsequent McCarthy and McCarran purges, this round of attacks on the academy may reach farther into the very core of its social purpose, even if fewer professors actually lose their jobs. As University of Chicago president Robert Maynard Hutchins remarked in 1951, "You don't have to fire many teachers to intimidate them all."[35] For Hutchins, the issue was not how many had been fired, but "how many think they might be, and for what reasons."

If college teachers choose to silence themselves to avert the harsh vilification of the academic police, then Paul Windels's goal in the Rapp Coudert investigation will have been achieved yet again for this generation of professors, those he termed that "amorphous section of the public referred to under the collective heading 'liberals' and 'intellectuals.'"

NOTES

1. "CCNY Bashes America—Students, Profs Blame Attacks on U.S.," *New York Post,* October 3, 2001, 3; "CCNY's Moral Myopia," *New York Post,* October 4, 2004, 32.

2. Robin Wilson, "CUNY Leaders Question Faculty Comments on Terror Attacks," *Chronicle of Higher Education,* October 19, 2001.

3. *New York Times,* August 24, 1938.

4. In June 1938, the Board of Higher Education adopted a plan to "democratize" the colleges, providing for tenure after three years' satisfactory service, and giving the faculty the right to elect department chairs, hire new colleagues, and decide personnel and curricular matters. "College Teachers of City Win Tenure," *New York Times,* June 21, 1938; Morris Schappes, interview by the author, September 20–21, 1981.

5. See Stephen Leberstein, "Purging the Profs: The Rapp Coudert Committee in New York," in *New Studies in the Politics and Culture of US Communism,* ed. Michael Brown et al. (New York: Monthly Review Press, 1993), for a fuller account of the committee's work.

6. Cited in Lawrence Chamberlain, *Loyalty and Legislative Action* (Ithaca, N.Y.: Cornell University Press, 1951), 162.

7. *Report of the Sub-committee Relative to the Public Educational System of the City of New York,* NYS Legislative Documents, 165th Session, 10 (1942), no. 48:22.

8. Dan North, "Math Association Honors Lee Lorch: Lifelong Fighter for Racial Justice," *Clarion,* April 2007, 6.

9. "Protests Voiced on Faculty Action," *New York Times,* June 9, 1949.

10. "Teacher Fighting Bias in Housing Faces Loss of Second College Job," *New York Times,* April 10, 1950.

11. "The Lorch Case," *New York Times,* April 11, 1950.

12. Monica Jacobe, "Contingent Faculty across the Disciplines," *Academe* 92.6 (2006): 43–49, see especially table, p. 46.

13. Commission on the Future of CUNY, "Remediation and Access: To Educate 'the Children of the Whole People,'" *Record of the Association of the Bar of the City of New York* 55.1 (2000), tables 6–9, pp. 123–24.

14. See Joshua Freeman, *Working Class New York: Life and Labor since World War II* (New York: New Press, 2000), chap. 15, esp. pp. 270–87.

15. Ashley Dawson and Penny Lewis, "New York: Academic Labor Town?" in *The University against Itself: The NYU Strike and the Future of the Academic Workplace,* ed. Monika Krause, Mary Nolan, Andrew Ross, and Michael Palm (Philadelphia: Temple University Press, 2008), 21–22.

16. For a fuller discussion of Yousry's connection to the case against Lynne Stewart, see Maya Hess, "Translation on Trial," *ATA Chronicle,* September 2003, www.atanet.org/chronicle/translation_on_trial.htm, accessed December 13, 2008.

17. AAUP, "1958 Statement on Procedural Standards in Faculty Dismissal Proceedings," in *Policy Documents & Reports,* 9th ed. (Washington, D.C., 2001), 11–20.

18. CUNY Response to AAUP Draft Report, August 20, 2004, in *Academe* 90.6 (2004): 23.

19. Quoted in Matthew Finkin, *The Case for Tenure* (Ithaca, N.Y.: Cornell University ILR Press, 1996).

20. Investigating Report, St. John's University, *AAUP Bulletin* 52 (1966): 12–19.

21. Jordan Kurland, Associate General Secretary, AAUP, to Russell Hotzler, President, York College, October 28, 2002; Kurland to Matthew Goldstein, Chancellor, CUNY, November 2002; and Hotzler to Kurland, December 18, 2002, all correspondence in possession of the author.

22. Matthew Goldstein, "Statement on Academic Freedom," October 17, 2005, www1.cuny.edu/forum/chancellor/?p=4, accessed April 24, 2008.

23. *NLRB v. Yeshiva University,* 444 U.S. 672 (1980). Ironically, the Court based its Yeshiva decision on the grounds that faculty members were part of management because they shared power in governing the university.

24. Jeremy Travis, President John Jay College, to Roger Bowen, General Secretary AAUP, December 20, 2004, in possession of author.

25. All of these incidents were reported to the Professional Staff Congress Academic Freedom Committee, which the author chairs.

26. "This Course Brought to You By . . . ," *Inside Higher Ed,* March 3, 2008, www.insidehighered.com/news/2008/03/03/hunter, accessed on March 5, 2008.

27. Tim Portlock, interview by the author, April 2, 2008.

28. Dania Rajendra, "Course Controversy at Hunter: Coach, Inc., pays $10,000 for Class," *Clarion,* April 2008, 5.

29. Horowitz's campaign is supposedly based on an unpublished study of the political affiliations of faculty by his Center for the Study of Popular Culture in California.

30. "Professors' Politics Draw Lawmakers into the Fray: Liberal Bias in Pennsylvania," *New York Times,* December 25, 2005.

31. Jennifer Jacobson, "What Makes David Run," *Chronicle of Higher Education,* May 6, 2005. Horowitz's idea for this project apparently came from a meeting with SUNY officials in 2002, including Edgar Egan, chair of the SUNY Board of Trustees, Candace de Russy, a trustee, and Peter Salins, SUNY provost, all worried about leftist indoctrination in the classroom.

32. *Inside Higher Ed,* January 18, 2007.

33. "Declaration of Principles on Academic Freedom and Academic Tenure," *AAUP Bulletin,* December 1915, 17–39.

34. Ellen Schrecker, "Worse than McCarthy," *Chronicle of Higher Education,* February 10, 2006, B20.

35. Robert Maynard Hutchins, "Afraid to Teach," *Look,* March 9, 1951, 2.

BLACKLIST REDUX

W. E. B. Du Bois and the Price of Academic Freedom

Bill V. Mullen

Speech . . . is never a value in and of itself but is always produced within the precincts of some assumed conception of the
good to which it must yield in the event of conflict. When the
pinch comes . . . and the institution (be it church, state or university) is confronted by behaviour subversive of its core rationale, it will respond by declaring "of course we mean not tolerated — — —, that we extirpate," not because an exception to a
general freedom has suddenly and contradictorily been announced, but because the freedom has never been general and
has always been understood against the background of an originary exclusion that gives it meaning.
　—Stanley Fish, *There's No Such Thing as Free Speech*

One could not be a calm, cool, and detached scientist while
Negroes were lynched, murdered, and starved.
　—W. E. B. Du Bois, *Dusk of Dawn*

IN "EXPOSING LIES OF THE AMERICAN LEFT," a 2003 interview
with Stephen Good and Rick Kozak, Daniel J. Flynn, executive director of
Accuracy in Academia, explained his impetus for helping to form the organization that has become—as readers of this volume know well—a flash-
point for attacks on a wide range of academic Leftists. In response to the
question from his interviewers "When did you first become aware of how

much the left hates America?" (a nod to Flynn's book *Why the Left Hates America*) Flynn explained that while he was a student at UMass Amherst in the 1990s "a series of demands were put forth by student activists" on campus. "They wanted the school to get rid of the Minuteman, a symbol of Revolutionary War patriotism, as the nickname of the sports teams, and they wanted to name the library in honor of W.E.B. Du Bois."[1] Flynn said he objected immediately to the nickname ban of a "racist, sexist white man with a gun" as "ridiculous," but that "discovering what was back of the Du Bois demand took a little investigation":

> Like most others, I thought Du Bois was some kind of early version of Martin Luther King, a civil-rights hero. I found that he was nothing of the sort. In fact, he disagreed with Martin Luther King on most of the tenets of the civil-rights movement. Du Bois apparently hated America, and he called Stalin a great, courageous man. He renounced his U.S. citizenship and moved to Kwame Nkrumah's Marxist hellhole in Ghana.[2]

Flynn also noted that given Du Bois's decision to join the Community Party, his reception of the Lenin Peace Prize, and the fact of a national holiday named in his honor in China, "The idea that an American university would honor W.E.B. Du Bois despite this record and at the height of the Cold War struck me as odd, if not bizarre."[3] Later in the interview, discussing "the roots of anti-Americanism" section of his book, including Communist Party activism, relativism, cultural Marxism, and multiculturalism, Flynn is asked, "Which of these do you think did the greatest damage and was most responsible?" Flynn opined that "the most lasting was that of the Communists. Even if we're talking about a movement that was at its apex 50 or 60 years ago, its impact is still being felt because of psychological conditioning. . . . The well-conditioned left knows how to respond to crisis anywhere in the world because it has been programmed to do so. The response is: America is at fault."[4]

One is struck first by the pregnant consistencies in this vision: it is always the "height" of the Cold War in Daniel Flynn's America; citadels of learning are bastions of civilization and free thought—until challenged by political heresy; the borders of the nation are always already under siege. Flynn's muscular articulation of delimited tolerance is also consistent with what Stanley Fish would characterize as the way of the liberal discursive world: "When the First Amendment is successfully invoked," writes Fish—

think in the above of Flynn's fierce safeguarding of the Minuteman mascot—"the result is not a victory for free speech in the face of a challenge from politics but a political victory won by the party that has managed to wrap its agenda in the mantle of free speech."[5] Now, to argue that groups like Accuracy in Academia or Free Speech adherents can claim some form of "victory" over the American Left, one would need corroborating evidence that free speech *has* successfully been deployed in its containment and suppression. My argument in this essay is that it has indeed won the larger exclusion of what we might call the total W. E. B. Du Bois from the ideological *site* of the university. I want to make this argument by proposing a convergence in our understanding of both "free speech" in the abstract and "academic freedom" in the local as mutually constitutive elements of higher education as a location for the production and replication of both capitalist (and ruling class) hegemony, on one hand, and attendant forms of racism that are both "officially" and unofficially marked. To this end, the subject of my essay is carefully chosen: it is the Historically Black College and University in the United States, its historical development and role in early twentieth-century America, and its analytical place within the evolution of Du Bois's own views on academic freedom, liberal humanism, and higher education. In particular, the essay will concentrate analysis on Du Bois's book *The Education of Black People.* The book is a collection of essays and lectures written across the course of his lifetime about the role and nature of the Historically Black College and University. The book demonstrates Du Bois's gradual and often contradictory development of an historical materialist methodology that demystified liberal humanism as, for lack of better words, the superstructure of American higher education. The essays demonstrate how Du Bois came to see universalist public education doctrine, and particularly its conceptions of free academic inquiry, as constitutive elements of capitalist white supremacy, and working-class African Americans quite literally as the originary "exclusion" of Western humanist discourse. In claiming the *material* lives of African Americans as this exclusion, I want to underscore that invocations of academic freedom and free speech always disclose the socioeconomic locations of the places those values are proffered and defended. Indeed implicit in Fish's conception of free speech, and in Du Bois's epigraphic insistence on the relationship of scholarship to social conditions of race, is the idea that *all* forms of public discourse carry the residue of social structures, and that social structures, like universities, are embodiments of abstract "values." Hence Du Bois's uneasy relationship to academia throughout this career, culminating in his forced resignation from Atlanta University in 1944, may be understood, I want to argue, as a metonymy of Du Bois's own free speech analytic. That is, reading Du Bois's own work on education provides a clear foreshadowing not only of his own fate as an untenured radical in the American university—his own partial exclusion from the American academy—but anticipates the reconsolidation of white supremacist, capitalist, racist, and nationalist forces that constitute the "free speech" right wing—or center wing, as it were—on today's political U.S. spectrum. That Du Bois himself should be a rarely acknowledged impetus and avatar to this movement, as I will also demonstrate here, is important for rethinking the merits of Stanley Fish's famous declaration, one to which I will return in conclusion to this essay: "There is no such thing as free speech, and it's a good thing." I will argue that Du Bois's academic career and analysis of the university provides both a cautionary tale and an exemplar of Fish's claim, while recommending how "free speech" advocates might best utilize their time in the service of truly transformative educational practices and structures to which Du Bois dedicated a good deal of his public life.

In January 1894 W. E. B. Du Bois submitted a petition to the faculty at Humboldt University in Berlin seeking to advance to his final examination for the Ph.D. in economics. Du Bois had completed three full semesters at Humboldt with support from the Slater Fund, an American philanthropic organization. His petition to advance came after completion of his Ph.D. thesis but prior to completion of the normally required triennium. The request was turned down. David Levering Lewis suggests that the rejection was primarily based upon a chemistry professor's objection to a student waiving three semesters of work.[6] Yet official minutes of the January 18 meeting offer a competing reason that would grow larger in Du Bois's memory and historical imagination. "The faculty is of the opinion that in the case of foreigners, whose education is significantly different from that usually to be found at German schools, a dispensation of having fulfilled the triennium should be granted only in quite special and exceptional cases and even then only when it is a matter of the last semester, and therefore rejects the petition of the student du [*sic*] Bois."[7]

Du Bois returned to Harvard, from which he famously graduated as the first black Ph.D. in economics. Yet some quarter century later the Berlin shunning was recast as the plot catalyst for his 1928 novel *Dark Princess.* Matthew Towns, a young African American physician-in-training, is denied the opportunity to complete his medical degree when training physicians refuse to allow him to complete his obstetrics requirements. Black physicians, he is cautioned, cannot be expected to deliver white babies. American racism here stands in for Teutonic academic formalism, a substitution hinted at when Towns leaves New York to travel to Berlin. There, he falls in with the Dark Princess, Kautilya, a Russian-trained radical helping to lead a cadre of Asian and African revolutionaries-in-exile in overthrow of their respective homeland regimes. While Matthew's medical school slight and the role of the university are never formally revisited in Matthew and the Princess's breathless conception of a New World Order, the two do postulate a theory of social knowledge based on their experiences working with and among train porters and box workers in the United States. Attempting to theorize the potential for an international episteme of what ails the laboring world, the Princess speculates in a letter to Matthew: "Brain and Brawn must unite in one body. . . . Workers unite, men cry, while in truth always thinkers who do not work have tried to unite workers who do not think. Only working thinkers can unite thinking workers."[8]

Du Bois's reconfiguration of the bureaucratic staging of academic exclusion, a mere provincial slight as he experienced it in 1894, magnified across the course of his life into an inordinately complex analysis of the limits of Western humanism and its discursive promise of universal education and academic freedom. The university rejection of Du Bois's "foreign" education in Berlin raised perforce, as evidenced in its retelling in *Dark Princess,* questions about the relationship of individual rights to public discourses of social equality; definitions of liberal subjectivity comprised by state apparatuses, especially the university, and the articulable limits of racism, class exploitation, and finally social revolution under capitalism. It is fitting, then, that these concerns became the dominant themes of *The Education of Black People.* Indeed the publication history of the book may be seen as an index to their interrelation. *Education* was first published in 1973, ten years after Du Bois's death. It includes seven essays on higher education originally selected by Du Bois and submitted in book manuscript form to William Couch, director of the University of North Carolina Press, in February or March 1940. At the time of his submission, Du Bois was chairman of the Department of Sociology of Atlanta University. The manuscript was originally submitted under the title "Seven Critiques of Negro Education, 1908–1938." According to Herbert Aptheker, editor of the 1973 published edition of the book, the manuscript began a round of review by Press readers who included Edgar W. Knight, professor of education at UNC and chairman of the Commission on Curricula Problems and Research of the Southern Association of Colleges and Secondary Schools; Howard W. Odum, professor of sociology at UNC; and Henry M. Wagstaff, UNC professor of history. On September 21, 1945, Couch wrote to Du Bois to report that the Press's Board of Governors had authorized publication "if the finance committee gave final approval."[9] Du Bois replied three days later, "I am quite willing to have you publish my book on the financial basis which you mention. I have never received much income from my books but on the other hand I do not think that any publisher has actually lost money. In any case the money consideration is the least thing I have in mind in writing."[10]

Yet the book was never published. Aptheker notes that except for a note on the "manuscript record" of UNC Press that reads "Ret'd to author 2-19-41," no record exists to explain the Press's decision not to publish. Intriguingly, Couch's original letter indicating board approval to publish included a caution that he doubted the book would do more than "pay for itself" and warned that the "European situation"—the recent outbreak of World War II—might upset plans for publication. UNC's argument that costs overruled publication bears somewhat closer scrutiny in light of both the *content* of the manuscript and what might be called the objective conditions of Du Bois's academic standing circa 1940. To address the latter first: the most popular narrative accounts of Du Bois's standing as head of the Department of Sociology at Atlanta University from 1934 until his forced resignation in 1944 hold that Du Bois returned to academe full time as a place of political refuge after his falling out with the NAACP over his increasingly Leftist political views. In this account, Du Bois's academic appointment, his success in launching *Phylon* at Atlanta University, and his significant scholarly output during this period—including publication of *Black Reconstruction* in 1935, *Black Folk Then and Now* (1939) and *Dusk of Dawn: An Essay toward an Autobiography of a Race Concept* (1940) bespeak a relative political and intellectual security afforded by academia—a shelter from the storm of his messy public break with the civil rights organization he founded. Yet the manuscript itself of "Seven Critiques of Negro Education," read as the elided texts or lacunae of Du Bois's *published* work of this period, discloses the precise limits and cost of what was publically speakable for Du Bois during a period of his life in which he formally committed himself to a Marxian point of view. Put another way, "Seven Critiques of Negro Education" discloses and anticipates sixty years of delimited ideological discourse in U.S. higher education, beginning with the Red

Scare purgings from American universities of the 1940s and 1950s, and extending to the current moment of new McCarthyism. That they do so by reference almost entirely to the role of Historically Black Colleges and Universities in the United States provides a structural ground for understanding the exclusionary logic thrust upon Du Bois himself.

As a starting point it is important to note that the essays in "Seven Critiques" were originally all commissioned speeches, mostly at Historically Black Colleges: one at Hampton and Howard, four at Fisk, and one to a New England fund-raising audience. In a preface written in 1940 and originally intended for publication with the book, Du Bois noted, "The spoken word is not usually an attractive form of literature shorn as it must be of its responsive living audience."[11] This bow to the oral tradition was also marked by Du Bois's insistence that publishing the texts of the speeches as they were delivered would provide "a sort of living record of reaction" that "would in a way tell more of what Negroes have been thinking concerning the development of their education especially in the colleges."[12] By choosing not to edit the speeches and merely to annotate them, Du Bois was signaling the situation of his talks as something like an unbounded space for the articulation of black thought. Yet the essays themselves are literally and figuratively bound up by and with the contradictions of that precarious assumption. Over and over, the essays say, the very site of black intellectual life is conscripted by its relationship to capitalism and white supremacy. "Academic freedom" becomes the disarticulated oxymoron emblematic of this contradiction.

In "The Hampton Idea," the book's first essay, delivered in 1906, Du Bois posits black education as a form of underreach represented by what he calls the "Hampton-Tuskegee idea of Negro education."[13] The speech followed on Du Bois's attendance at several summer conferences at Hampton that had struggled "in vain" with "the idea of knitting together in thought and statement the case of higher education and Industrial education."[14] Du Bois's initial frustrations with these efforts manifest themselves in his critique of Booker T. Washington and industrial education in *Souls of Black Folk*. In the summer of 1906, despite being "under a certain suspicion" after publishing that critique, Du Bois was invited to speak at what he described as a "smug Hampton."[15] The idealizing spirit with which Du Bois routinely addressed matters of race and culture early in his career manifests itself as a legacy of Western humanist thought to which Du Bois cannot reconcile the Hampton mission, characterized crudely in the speech: "there has come a distinct philosophy of education which makes the earning of a living the center and norm of human training and which moreover dogmatically asserts that the subject matter and methods of work peculiar to technical schools are the best for all education—that outside them there is properly no higher training."[16] Hampton, Du Bois avers, is the "center of this, as I regard it, educational heresy, and because with all the striking history of this school, the noble lives given to its upbuilding, and the peculiar efficiency of its present organization, there is always present a tone which, as it seems to me, contradicts and almost sneers at the wonderful ideals which founded this great school."[17] Interestingly, those "ideals" themselves are elided in the essay: Du Bois dropped from his speech these words from the original manuscript: "In Greece for instance the higher training became very largely aesthetics and literature suited to a nation of artists and philosophers, but leaving fatal gaps in the fuller human training. So too Rome trained her jurists and administrators in a way never since surpassed, but again failed in her larger and broader outlook."[18] This elision suggests Du Bois's uneasiness about the cultural restrictedness of a discourse of free inquiry that later essays would make much more explicit. In its place is a striving reorientation toward a black educational practice whose contours are barely knowable: "When now we have gained for our race training in modern industry, and for our national leaders, self-assertion through a higher training in life and thought and power, then we can move toward the goal. What is that goal? It is at present one great Ideal: the abolition of the color line; the treatment of all men according to their individual desert and not according to their race."[19]

These vague, concluding preachments gather a poignant meaning for this essay. The ironic Washingtonian rhetoric of "self-assertion," the "color line" shibboleth and the platitudinous embrace of liberal rights discourse in this Hampton address is more appropriately a euphemism for a problem Du Bois cannot truly confront or resolve, namely the material impossibility of Hampton, and by extension the Historically Black College and University, avoiding its parochial, subservient role in early industrial capitalism. Between 1906 and 1933, Du Bois attempted to wrestle this contradiction into tenable form. Indeed, Du Bois's early speeches often framed the material problematic of black education and Historically Black institutions—literally its economic absences—within a matrix of advocacy for unhindered academic inquiry offered as a compensatory gold standard of liberal humanist aspiration. The most pointed example from *The Education of Black People,* "Galileo Galilei," was an address delivered in 1908 at Fisk University. The address followed upon Fisk's successful development of a new Department of Applied Science with money furnished by the general education board and the Slater Fund, which had supported Du Bois's German studies. An associate professor of agriculture and associate professor of mechanical arts had been added to the faculty, as had new courses. Yet as Du Bois noted in prefatory remarks to his speech, "There was no way in which this proposed department could be regarded as the beginning of a technical or engineering school of college rank. At best it was a poor imitation of what Hampton and Tuskegee were struggling to do."[20] Du Bois's analysis of the situation, however, fell prey to a form of mystification embedded in his defense of free speech principles. The flailing efforts at industrial education at Fisk, he wrote, "seemed to many of the alumni and to me as a Surrender and a Lie."[21] "We were alarmed. We were fighting for academic life. We were striving for the survival of the Negro college in a day of starvation and ridicule."[22] The lie, in this case, was for Du Bois intellectual sin. Galileo's tortured public disawoval of heliocentrism was offered as a parable for black social degradation following from an abandonment of liberal humanism:

> A stubborn determination at this time on the part of the Negro race, to uphold its ideals, keep its standards, and unceasingly contend for its rights, means victory; and victory a great deal sooner that any of you imagine. But a course of self-abasement and surrender, of lowering of ideals and neglecting of opportunity—above all, a philosophy of lying in word or deed for the sake of conciliation or personal gain, means indefinite postponement of the true emancipation of the Negro race in America, for the simple reason that such a race is not fit to be freed.[23]

Du Bois here conflates academic free inquiry with the promise of fulfilled subjectivity, racial equality, and full participation in civil society. As in his Hampton address, humanist "rights" discourses envelop Du Bois's mission statement on black potentiality. Here we can register the starvation of such rhetoric in the material response to it: the president of Fisk resigned in the summer following his address; the Department of Applied Sciences was eliminated in 1909, and, in Du Bois's telling, contributions of white philanthropists to Fisk fell off precipitously. "Perhaps one cause of this was my speech," Du Bois forlornly wrote in appendage in 1940. I will return to assessment of the relationship between Du Bois's words and their impact a bit later, but note here that his 1908 Fisk address contains in miniature the contradiction regarding academic freedom with which I am interested: namely, that its invocation functions to elide or displace the material ground of academic inquiry as the dependent client of ruling-class hegemony. Du Bois's despairing afterword to this speech and his later retrospective commentaries to be discussed disclose a latent consciousness of this problematic: a residual humanist confidence that his life as a U.S. intellectual slowly crushed. Indeed the next selection in *The Education of Black People*, "The College-Bred Community," follows a pattern virtually identical to the Fisk address. The main difference was purpose and audience. Du Bois notes in his 1940 annotations to the lecture, "We had begun at Atlanta University the first systematic study of the American Negro made anywhere in the world; and yet Atlanta University was starving to death."[24] Thus he agreed to speak to "the white, rich, and well-born in Brookline, Massachusetts" of the "indispensable need of the college-bred man in the South."[25] Du Bois sets his agenda as "lifting the submerged mass of black people in the South . . . through the higher training of the talented few."[26] He also consolidates his vision of the benefits of separate Black education: "What the Negro needs, therefore, of the world and civilization, he must largely teach himself; what he learns of social organization and efficiency, he must learn from his own people."[27] This is the formula for "the COLLEGE-BRED COMMUNITY."[28] Thus northern philanthropy remains the staging ground of black exclusion, and Du Bois's "talented tenth" a metonymic idea for what ideally supersedes it: "those things which it must know if it is going to share modern civilization."[29]

One might now see plainly Du Bois's Talented Tenth conception as the profound idealization of material "exclusions" in black life understood both as the deferred promise of fully achieved civil rights and the "trickle down" inversion of economic want. This confidence in free *academic* inquiry may be measured in relation to free speech discourse in Du Bois's early addresses in two symmetrical ways. The first is through the Fish-eye lens: "people cling to First Amendment pieties," writes Fish, "because they do not wish to face what they correctly take to be the alternative. That alternative is politics, the realization . . . that decisions about what is and is not protected in the realm of expression will rest not on principle or firm doctrine but on the ability of some persons to interpret—recharacterize or rewrite—principle and doctrine in ways that lead to the protection of speech they want heard and the regulation of speech they want silenced."[30] Viewed this way, the failure of Du Bois's appeals may be weighed precisely to the extent to which they confirmed orthodoxy—what we might call hegemony. In the "Envoy" afterword to "The College-Bred Community," Du Bois laments, "To these and similar speeches of mine . . . there was some but not great response. Between 1910 and 1925 (arguably the peak years of the most vicious forms of Jim Crow) the case of college training for Negroes in the South became desperate."[31] Du Bois nearly manifests himself as the equivalent to the scholarship boy in Ellison's *Invisible Man,* mouthing myriad subtleties tantamount to a ventriloquist's call for "social responsibility." Yet the very final words of the envoy are in this light also telling: "I began to feel," writes Du Bois, "that one of the reasons that Atlanta University did not get funds was my presence and I therefore accepted a chance to change my scientific career to a career of propaganda in New York with the Nation [*sic*] Association for the Advancement of Colored People, as editor of the *Crisis.*"[32]

Du Bois's 1910 conversion might be understood as a turning point for his conception of academic freedom in the American University. Du Bois's move, that is, was a turning away from liberal humanism as a form of loyal opposition to a system that was more apparently than ever constraining and delimiting black economic and social relationships. I want to suggest that it was the shock of two events that enabled Du Bois to supersede this role: the first was the wreck of the global depression, and the second his reading of Marx. This turn is captured in "Education and Work" and subsequent addresses published in "Seven Critiques" written after 1929. These essays demonstrate a marked shift in Du Bois's rhetoric and analysis. Specifically, they offer analysis of American and African American higher education primarily as ideology. "Education and Work" was a commencement speech delivered at Howard University in 1930 at the invitation of Mordecai Johnson, university president. The essay reviews the dilemma of Negro education through the prism of a shattered world economy that exposes, Du Bois's argues, the limitations of all extant models of black higher education in the United States. Du Bois frames the problem as a rhetorical question he seeks provisionally to answer: "If it was doubtful as to how far the social and economic classes of any modern state could be essentially transformed and changed by popular education, how much more tremendous was the problem of educating a race whose ability to assimilate modern training was in grave question and whose place in the nature and the world, even granted they could be educated, was a matter of baffling social philosophy? Was the nation making an effort to parallel white civilization in the South with a black civilization? Or was it trying to displace the dominant white master class with new black masters or was it seeking the difficult but surely more reasonable and practical effort of furnishing a trained set of free black laborers who might carry on in place of the violently disrupted slave system?"[33] Du Bois has shifted the terrain of discussion notably from what might called matters of the ideal. While he acknowledges that "The chief thing that distinguished the American Negro group from the Negro groups in the West Indies, and in South America, and the mother group in Africa" is the "number of men that we have trained in modern education," on the other hand, "there cannot be the slightest doubt but that the Negro college, its teachers, students, and graduates, have not yet comprehended the age in which they live."[34] Du Bois writes,

> the tremendous organization of industry, commerce, capital, and credit which today forms a super-organization dominating and ruling the universe, subordinating to its ends government, democracy, religion, education, and social philosophy; and for the purpose of forcing into the places of power in this organization American black men either to guide or help reform it, either to increase its efficiency or make it a machine to improve our well-being, rather than the merciless mechanism which enslaves us; for this the Negro college has today neither program nor intelligent comprehension.[35]

It is worth noting here Du Bois's doubled use of "comprehension." It does not, as in earlier essays, signal something like classical learning, or the mind in contemplation, but rather is a model of social cognition capable of discerning power relations in general, and in particular the African American position without those power relations—of grasping something Marxists like to call totality. Changed, too, is Du Bois's language: "super-organization . . . merciless mechanism" now describe the social structure that encases black higher education. Not surprisingly, then, Du Bois writes, one of the most common educational products generated by black industrial education is what Frazier would famously call a "black bourgeoisie" straining and striving against both a glass ceiling—Du Bois calls it "a white-collar proletariat, depending for their support on an economic foundation which does not yet exist"—while drifting into a spiritual malaise one might call conditioned alienation: "The average negro undergraduate has swallowed hook, line and sinker, the dead bait of the white undergraduate, who, born in an industrial machine, does not have to think, and does not think."[36] A guarantor of this condition, Du Bois writes, is the Negro industrial school's neglect to teach what Du Bois calls "the most important part of modern industrial development: namely, the relation of the worker to modern industry and to the modern state."[37] The cause of that error is also clear for Du Bois: 'The Negro industrial school was the gift of capital and wealth. . . . How natural it was to look to white Capital and not to Labor for the emancipation of the black world—how natural and yet how insanely futile!"[38]

We would also be remiss not to note the echoes in "Education and Work" of Marx and Engels. The essay points back particularly to *The German Ideology* in two important respects: first, in the insistence upon the existence of ruling-class ideas and a ruling class "which has the means of material production at its disposal," and second, in the premise that ruling-class ideas depend upon a "division of labour" manifest particularly in "the division of mental and material labour."[39] Indeed if readers had missed the corrective thematic in *Dark Princess* two years earlier—"only working thinkers can unite thinking workers"—then it is pedantically and pedagogically spelled out in the final pages of "Education and Work" as "the ideals of Negro students and graduates." They are, in Du Bois's words:

(1) "A simple healthy life on limited income is the only responsible ideal of civilized folk"; (2) "The ideal of Work not idleness, not dawdling, but hard continuous effort at something worth doing"; (3) "Knowledge—not guesswork, not mere careless theory; not inherited dogma clung to because of fear and inertia and in spite of logic, but critically tested and laboriously gathered fact marshaled under scientific law and feeding rather than choking the glorious world of fancy and imagination of poetry and art, of beauty and deep culture" and (4) "Sacrifice . . . When I say sacrifice, I mean sacrifice. I mean a real and definite surrender of personal ease and satisfaction. I embellish with no theological fairy tales or a rewarding God or a milk and honey heaven . . . I am repeating the stark fact of survival of life and culture on this earth: Entbehren sollst du—sollst entbehren. [Thou shalt forego, shalt do without.]"[40]

It is a long way indeed from the Talented Tenth to "civilized folk," and an even longer way from the "gift" of black culture to each according to his ability, to each according to his needs. Yet still in the envoy appendage to the essay, Du Bois is self-critical of a kind of residual idealism still looking to name its object: "the speech lacked something," he wrote. "I was strong in exposition and criticism but weak in remedy. I was at this time in my social thought entering a wider and broader ocean, and I did not yet see clearly whither was I was sailing."[41]

Du Bois's next two speeches in 1933 and 1938 made that direction quite clear. "The Field and Function of the Negro College" was delivered at Fisk University on the forty-fifth anniversary of Du Bois's graduation from that place. It is a vexing, turbulent address, a striking example of the internal dialectical struggle between competing models of analysis in Du Bois's career up until World War II. The first section of the essay posits two differing but mutually informed models of the university: the first a "bush school" in West Africa offering education to members of Bantu, Yoruba, and Sudanese tribes dedicated to preserving the "stable culture" of ritual, initiation and self-development. The second is the Western university whose system is "culture for the cultured," exemplified by the British system. Yet a third model is Harvard or the University of Berlin of Du Bois's German sojourn, institutions whose initial plebeian or national mission had been broadened to include some selection of "masses" of men, including the occasional Negro like Du Bois. Now, writes Du Bois, "We are on the threshold of a new era." Encouraging readers to cast off "outworn ideals of wealth and servants and luxuries," Du Bois calls for African Americans "led by trained university men of broad vision" to work out "by economics and mathematics, by physics and chemistry, by history and sociology, exactly how and where he is to earn a living and how he is to establish a reasonable life in the Untied States or elsewhere." Yet the most important point of the essay is this: Du Bois's vision is tethered entirely to a destruction (we might say a deconstruction) of his earlier delimited valuation of liberal humanism. In its place, Du Bois opines:

> Only a universal system of learning, rooted in the will and condition of the masses and blossoming from that manure up toward the stars is worth the name. Once builded [*sic*] it can only grow as it brings down sunlight and star shine and impregnates the mud. The chief obstacle in this rich land endowed with every natural resource and with the abilities of a hundred different peoples—the chief and only obstacle to the coming of that kingdom of economic equality which is the only logical end of work, is the determination of the white world to keep the black world poor and make themselves rich. The disaster which this selfish and short-sighted policy has brought lies at

the bottom of this present depression, and too, its cure lies beside it. Your clear vision of a world without wealth, of capital without profit, of income based on work alone, is the path out not only for you but for all men.[42]

Du Bois's utopian rhetoric here is, in conventional historical materialist terms, still delimited by color: he lauds his own program in the next sentence as "against national unity and universal humanism" precisely because it accepts segregation as an immutable and irreversible given. Black hands and black hands left alone, Du Bois avers, can build a knowledge workers' paradise.

And yet· "The argument of the Howard speech did not seem to me to be altogether final," writes Du Bois in the 1940 envoy: "Something was missing and from that day I began to read and study Karl Marx. I began to understand my recent visit to Russia. I became interested in the New Deal and I wanted to supplement the liberalism of Charles Sumner with the new economic contribution of the twentieth century."[43] Several things need to be said retroactively about Du Bois's understanding of his place in the time of "The Field and Function." In 1933, he began teaching a course titled Karl Marx and the Negro at Atlanta University, and published an article of the same name in *Crisis*. The article is, like his Fisk address, a watershed moment in Du Bois's analysis of Western humanism. In it Du Bois, while withholding support for Communism, argues that Marxism offers the most salient means for analyzing the situation of both global capitalism and the place of African Americans within it. The essay recuperates Marx's arguments on slavery and the Civil War—excavating influences on black Reconstruction—to conclude that "It was a great loss to American Negroes that the great mind of Marx and his extraordinary insight into industrial conditions could not have been brought to bear at first hand upon the history of the American Negro between 1876 and the World War."[44] Thus Du Bois's next major address on higher education, the 1938 speech "The Revelation of Saint Orgne the Damned," delivered at Fisk on the fiftieth anniversary of his graduation, is an allegory deploying the history of black higher education as a vehicle for Du Bois's Communist conversion. Orgne, an anagram for *Negro*, begins the essay positing questions about the meaning of race and the future of his own soul. Du Bois imagines the Saint "as he stood on his Mount of Transfiguration, looking full at life as it is and not as it might be or haply as he would have it."[45] His answers come as a series of revelations or epiphanies on the physics and metaphysics of free speech and free thought. "It is the contradiction and paradox of this day," writes Du Bois, "as those who seek to choke and conventionalize art, restrict and censor thought and repress imagination are demanding for their shriveled selves, freedom in precisely those lines of human activity where control and regimentation are necessary; and necessary because upon this foundation is to be built the widest conceivable freedom in a realm infinitely larger and more meaningful than the realm of economic production and distribution of wealth. The less freedom we leave for business exploitation the greater freedom we shall have for expression of art."[46]

Freedom, Du Bois writes, is possible only "when poverty approaches abolition; when men no longer fear starvation and unemployment."[47]

> In such a world living begins; in such a world we will have freedom of thought and expression, and just as much freedom of action as maintenance of the necessary economic basis of life permits; that is, given three or six hours of work under rule and duress, we ought to be sure of at least eighteen hours of recreation, joy, and creation with a minimum of compulsion for anybody.[48]

Du Bois here elaborates "freedom" as, in a Marxian sense, freedom from exploitation. Freedom is here surplus to the processes of capitalism, literally outside and necessarily beyond its realm of productive forces, what Marx and Engels called in *The German Ideology* its "civil society":[49] "so far as the physical constitution of the universe is concerned, we must produce and consume goods in accordance with that which is inexorable, unmoved by sentiment or dream. But this realm of the physical world need be only the smaller part of life and above it is planning, emotion and dream; in the exercising of creative power; in building, painting and literature there is a chance for the free exercise of the human spirit, broad enough and lofty enough to satisfy every ambition of the human soul."[50] "Freedom" here is also linked to anticolonial struggles—"the rise of dark Japan and fall of darker Ethiopia"—and to the extirpation of war—"a whole world at war to commit twenty-six million murders."[51] In short, the major keynotes of the last third of Du Bois's life are predicated in "The Revelation" on the reconfiguration through real and discursive field of black higher education of all that has potentially been "excluded" from his field of vision by his prior purchase of putatively free thought. Put another way, Du Bois's revelation might be described in Fish's terms as a recognition of "politics" as the alternative to an idealized conception of free speech.

That "Seven Critiques" was a truly *political* book was also evident in the silencing that accompanied it: after UNC Press would not publish it, Reynal and Hitchcock refused the book in 1943—this at a time when Du Bois remained in good standing at Atlanta University and with the NAACP, a condition not long to last. In short, "Seven Critiques of Black Education" might be understood in the locus of his own career and, I want to argue now, in the discursive moment of "free speech" and "academic freedom" debate in the United States, as one of a number of originary "exclusions" against which the ahistoricized discussion of the terms takes place. Against this revised and more complete history, I want to reconsider in the final section of this essay the oft-noted fact that in the American academy the original exclusion has fundamentally been Communism, and demonstrate how malleable the case of Du Bois has been in servicing characterizations of dissent in the contemporary period.

In February 1942, in the interim between the rejection of *The Education of Black People* by UNC Press and Reynal and Hitchcock, and two years prior to his forced retirement from Atlanta University, the Atlanta field office of the FBI, as Mike Keen has reported, began an investigation of Du Bois "for possible subversive activities" after an informant reported that in a speech made in Japan Du Bois had spoken too favorably about Japanese military prowess. Additional FBI offices were brought in to conduct further research, which included a reading of excerpts from Du Bois's 1940 *Dusk of Dawn,* passages of which were excerpted and filed in field reports, including Du Bois's declaration that "KARL MARX was one of the greatest men of modern times and that he put his fingers squarely upon our difficulties when he said that economic foundations, the way in which which men earn their living, are the determining factors in the development of civilization and their basic patterns of culture"—a perfect gloss on Du Bois's 1938 speech at Fisk cited earlier.[52] Intriguingly, the FBI background check included an inquiry with the Harvard Club of Maryland as to whether Du Bois had been a member; the response, according to Keen, was "not only that Du Bois had never been a member, but that no Negro had ever been a member."[53]

Du Bois's file lay dormant until 1949, when it was reopened and he became the subject of intense FBI scrutiny resulting famously in the revocation of his passport in 1952. Needless to say by 1952 the United States had reached something truly like the "height of the Cold War." President James B. Conant and Du Bois's Harvard alma mater had by 1949 formulated a resolution adopted by the National Education Association that stated membership in the Communist Party "and the accompanying surrender of intellectual integrity, render an individual unfit to discharge the duties of a teacher in this country."[54] In 1953, the year after revocation of Du Bois's passport, the Association of American Universities stated that a university professor invoking the Fifth Amendment laid "upon his [*sic*] university an obligation to reexamine his qualifications for membership in its society."[55] Of course, to "reexamine qualifications for membership in society" is the impetus for Daniel Flynn's student activism at UMass, and the raison d'être of Accuracy in Academia. And while here the argument might be made that since Du Bois himself had extricated himself from the university system by 1944—and was neither a member of the CP at that time, nor a victim of a formal "purge"—we would be stretching our epistemic frame to link him to a McCarthyist assault on academic freedom. But as Flynn's brand of activism reminds us, and as McCarythyism taught us the first time around, exclusions themselves give substance to the presence of ideas. The fact that "Seven Critiques of Black Education" lay dormant until well after Du Bois's death signals this, as does Flynn's resurrection of a Du Bois unrecognizable except as a marker of the "meaning" of free speech for activists like Flynn. In short, the book and the writer remain, in the discourse and discussion of academic freedom, powerful exclusions that are indexes to the always already delimited condition of free speech in the United States.

Clearly, Daniel Flynn has not forgiven Du Bois his challenge to the necessary exclusions of academic freedom. Has the academy? With the exception of Herbert Aptheker, Gerald Horne, Manning Marable, and more recently Kate Baldwin, it is not a stretch to say that Du Bois's academic reputation still resides largely on the basis of its delicate and nervous excision of nearly fifty years of Marxian-influenced writing and political work.[56] As Aptheker himself has noted, this boycott has been periodically broken: in 1960, at the height of his exclusion, Du Bois was invited to address an audience at Johnson C. Smith University in Charlotte, North Carolina. His speech, "Whither Now and Why?" detailed his blacklisting, his legal battles, the transformative nature of his travels to Russia and China, assailed democratic process—"Half of the citizens of the United States do not even go to the polls"—and lamented, "If the Negro or white colleges are going to depend on the gifts of the rich for support they cannot teach the truth." "This impoverishment of the truth seekers can only be avoided," Du Bois concluded, "by eventually making the state bear the burden of education and this is socialism."[57]

The socialist imperative in Du Bois's reflections still awaits our undivided attention. Indeed, Du Bois's essays on higher education command consideration of the vital place of Marxist thought across the wide body of his work, his fairly unflinching dedication to the articulation of dissident ideas, and perhaps most importantly, for the current moment of this volume, the manner in which he swam consistently against the direction of delimited academic freedom.[58] In addition, Du Bois's essays on higher education, concentrated on the precarious and ever dependent financial and economic conditions of the Historically Black College and University, cogently anticipate the explosion of scholarship in the past twenty years dedicated to analysis of the "corporate university," the political economy of higher education, and the restrictions on academic freedom that can attend processes of privatization, state subsidy, and patronage. Indeed a retrospective reading of Du Bois's essays suggests that the Historically Black College and University and its perpetual dependencies on the aforementioned processes seems a harbinger of the condition so many "historically white" private and public universities find themselves in today. We might then be even less surprised that the ever-prescient Du Bois was at the ready to point out the implications of that condition for academic freedom and academic dissent.

Yet my final point in conjuring up the legacy of Du Bois's meditations on academic freedom, universal education, and free speech is really to worry this: if it is the putative academic *Right* that retains the greatest interest and public sway in speaking of the radical, the socialist, the Communist Du Bois, then we have conceded not just the rules of the game but the game itself. Organizations like AIA, to return to Stanley Fish's argument, have already accepted long ago the bargain that "there is no such thing as free speech"—it is their most hard-fought love object to assure that this remains so on terms of their own devising. It is the academic Left, I think, that continues to ride the hobby horse of wishful alternative. We should not. We should instead engage *not only* in debate over the terms of free speech but confront the dominant culture, the state, the university itself, on its own terms: the terms of politics. If we don't, we risk the powerful historical manipulations that continue to succor the ghosts and specters of an unspeakable, unspoken Du Bois that Daniel Flynn and friends continue to depend on for their victories.

NOTES

Stanley Fish, "There No Such Tings as Free Speech, and It's a Good Thing," in *There's No Such Thing as Free Speech and It's a Good Thing, Too* (New York: Oxford University Press, 1994), 104.

W. E. B. Du Bois, *Dusk of Dawn: An Essay Toward an Autobiography of a Race Concept* (New York: Schocken, 1968), 67.

1. Stephen Good and Rick Kozak, "Picture Profile: Exposing Lies of the American Left," Insight on the News, 2003, http://www.insightmag.com/media/paper441/news/2003/01/07, accessed March 20, 2005.

2. Ibid., 2.

3. Ibid., 2.

4. Ibid., 3.

5. Stanley Fish, *There's No Such Thing as Free Speech and It's a Good Thing, Too* (New York: Oxford University Press, 1994), 110.

6. David Levering Lewis, *W.E.B. Du Bois: The Fight for Equality and the American Century, 1919–1963* (New York: Henry Holt, 2000), 144.

7. Hamilton Beck, "W.E.B. Du Bois as a Study Abroad Student in Germany, 1892–1894," *Frontiers* 2 (1996): 1–25.

8. W. E. B. Du Bois, *Dark Princess: A Romance* (Jackson: University Press of Mississippi, 2000), 286.

9. Herbert Aptheker, introduction to W. E. B. Du Bois, *The Education of Black People: Ten Critiques, 1906–1960* (Amherst: University of Massachusetts Press, 1973), i–xxi.

10. Ibid., viii.

11. Du Bois, *Education of Black People*, 3.

12. Ibid.

13. Ibid., 5.

14. Ibid.

15. Ibid.

16. Ibid., 11.

17. Ibid., 11–12.

18. Ibid., 11.

19. Ibid., 15.

20. Ibid., 18.

21. Ibid.

22. Ibid.

23. Ibid., 29.

24. Ibid., 31.

25. Ibid.

26. Ibid., 32.

27. Ibid., 37.

28. Ibid., 38.

29. Ibid., 37.

30. Fish, *Free Speech*, 110.

31. Du Bois, *Education of Black People*, 40.

32. Ibid., 40.

33. Ibid., 63.
34. Ibid., 66.
35. Ibid.
36. Ibid., 67.
37. Ibid., 72.
38. Ibid., 72–73.
39. Ibid., 64, 65.
40. Ibid., 79–80.
41. Ibid., 82.
42. Ibid., 99.
43. Ibid., 102.
44. Ibid., 56.
45. Ibid., 103.
46. Ibid., 116.
47. Ibid.
48. Ibid.
49. Karl Marx and Frederick Engels, *The German Ideology,* ed. C.J. Arthur (New York: International Publishers, 2004), 57.
50. Ibid., 117.
51. Ibid., 125.
52. Mike Forrest Keen, *Stalking the Sociological Imagination: J. Edgar Hoover's FBI Surveillance of American Sociology* (Westport, Conn.: Greenwood Press, 1999), 15.
53. Ibid.
54. Herbert Shapiro, "Political Correctness and the American Historical Profession," http://www.hist.umontreal.ca/hst7000/ShapiroPC.htm, accessed April 8, 2005.
55. Ibid.
56. I have in mind these books that make central or at least important Du Bois's engagement with Marxism and Marxist thought as a crucial development in this thinking: virtually all of Herbert Aptheker's written and editorial work on Du Bois, including his meticulously annotated edition of *The Education of Black People;* Manning Marable's *Black Radical Democrat* (Boston: Twayne, 1986); Gerald Horne's *W.E.B. Du Bois and the Afro-American Response to the Cold War, 1944–1963* (Albany: SUNY Press, 1986); and Kate Baldwin's *Beyond the Color Line and the Iron Curtain: Reading Encounters between Black and Red, 1922–1963* (Durham, N.C.: Duke University Press, 2002).
57. Du Bois, *Education of Black People,* 157.
58. It is worth noting that Du Bois's academic career thrived outside the United States in inverse relation to its domestic blacklisting. Between 1952 and 1963 he received an honorary doctorate from the faculty of Humboldt University in East Germany and a similar degree from Charles University in the Czech Republic; he was a guest lecturer at Nkrumah's Ghana Academy of Learning and at Peking University in China. While his books were being removed from shelves in U.S. universities, they were being rapidly translated into Russian and Chinese. Meanwhile, Du Bois chose the official over unofficial exile under which he had lived in the 1950s, an exile also motivated, as Gerald Horne has noted, by the mechanics of academic freedom. Du Bois's Ghana exile was in part inspired by difficulties he encountered

raising foundation and university support in the United States for the publication of his proposed *Encyclopedia Africana* after joining the Communist Party in 1961. In Ghana, Du Bois elicited backing for publication of the book not only from Ghanian Convention People's Party chairman Kwame Nkrumah, but from scholars in France, Spain, and China as well as the London-based Committee of African Organizations, comprising the leading national liberation forces of Africa, including the South African National Congress.

AREA STUDIES AND MULTICULTURAL IMPERIALISM

The Project of Decolonizing Knowledge

Malini Johar Schueller

SECURITY. SURVEILLANCE. DIVERSITY. BALANCE. These have
been the contradictory catchwords of the Right's attacks on academia
since 9/11. Couched in the language of nationalism and advocating a hyperscopic regime of control through State and civil apparatuses, different
right-wing organizations professing commitment to fairness and diversity
have sought to regulate the work of postcolonialist Middle East Studies
scholars. Thus Daniel Pipes's website, Campus Watch, published dossiers
on eight prominent professors of Middle East Studies who demonstrated
"bias" in their teaching and promoted anti-Americanism. The targeted
eight were inundated with hate mail and death threats. Although Pipes removed the dossiers as a separate item after vigorous criticism from faculty
nationwide, he continued Campus Watch's project of "Monitoring Middle
East Studies on Campus." Each month, the website showcases a "Quote of
the Month" that demonstrates the "terrorist" sympathies of a Middle East
Studies professor. The stated objective of Campus Watch is to redress the
"intolerance of alternative views" within Middle East Studies.[1]

In September 2003, members of the U.S. House Subcommittee on Select Education approved H.R. 3077, the International Studies in Higher
Education Act, which authorized the creation of an advisory board, appointed by the secretary of the Department of Homeland Security, to

oversee the curricula of area studies centers that received funding from Title VI of the Higher Education Act of 1965. Curricula, it was stated, needed to better reflect the needs of national security.[2] Expert testimony for the act came from its tireless promoter, Stanley Kurtz, fellow at the conservative Hoover Institution and editor of *National Review.* Alarmed at the purported anti-Americanism of postcolonial theory–influenced Middle East Studies, Kurtz singled out the pernicious consequence of the writings of Edward Said and recommended federal oversight over these centers. His recommendations: balance and diversity.

Such a blacklisting of professors and State surveillance of academics, in addition to the mushrooming of faculty policing organizations such as Students for Academic Freedom (SAF), which boasts chapters in over 130 institutions, demonstrate a victory of the Right's attempt to contain resistance and discipline academia into becoming an ideological apparatus of the security state. Undoubtedly, such inroads into academia have precedents, most recently in McCarthyism. However, the current incursions into academia are markedly different in two striking ways: first, the Right's appropriation of the language of multiculturalism; and second, its concern not simply with the political affiliations and activities of academics as was typical of McCarthyism, but with the very paradigms of knowledge production such as postcolonial theory. I suggest that the current attack on area studies, particularly Middle East Studies, is a response to the decolonization of knowledge consequent upon worldwide independence movements of the 1960s, which boosted racial struggles within the country. Despite the use of the language of multiculturalism, the Right's offense is a frontal assault on civil rights and the culture of civil rights. In what follows, I will examine the different contexts of the debates surrounding area studies' legislation in order to understand the complex relationships between the university, political culture, the State, and the macronarratives of imperialism and decolonization. The deployment of the language of multiculturalism is part of the State's attempt to subsume the raced subject into a nationalist narrative of pluralism and consensus useful for imperialism; further, what is distinct after 9/11 is the State's use of insidious distinctions between the multicultural and the foreign.

The broad underpinnings of my argument are that academic practices within the U.S. university, particularly those of the humanities and social sciences, cannot be understood without their relationship to imperialism, which has structured the production of knowledge. Yet, if the university is an integral part of the modern world system, which, with the United States as center, continues today to perpetuate a neocolonial globalization, in tandem with a military style imperialism and a resurgence of Orientalism, it is also a changed scene of colonial difference where subaltern knowledges are gaining currency. Walter Mignolo describes a modern/colonial world system, a period extending from the fifteenth century to the global colonialism of the present, as one premised on the process of subalternizing all non-European knowledges. That process, he argues, began changing in the mid-twentieth century when centers and peripheries were no longer far apart and new forms of knowledge which had been subalternized and considered important only as objects of study began to emerge as "loci of enunciation."[3] Colonial difference, once "out there," away from the center, is now all over "in the peripheries of the center and in the centers of the periphery" and is the space where the coloniality of power is enacted and where "the restitution of subaltern knowledge is taking place."[4] The U.S. university, I contend, is such a space of colonial difference where the decolonizing of knowledge, indeed the subalternizing of European knowledge, has been occurring. It is this restitution of subaltern knowledges, the most powerful of which date to the period of worldwide decolonization in the 1960s, that the State, especially since 9/11, constituting itself as empire through sovereign (rather than disciplinary or governmental) power, is particularly eager to challenge and neutralize. The current relationship between subaltern knowledge and the State (along with its Rightist allies) cannot therefore be explained through narratives blind to colonial difference such as governmentality (Foucault), state of exception (Agamben), or for that matter corporatization/neoliberalism alone.[5] Indeed neoliberalism needs to be seen not simply as an economic but civilizational regime, separating ideas of individualism and free market democracy from collective (read: barbaric) and regulated State structures.

ACADEMIA AND THE STATE: THE CASE OF AREA STUDIES

↔

Despite what seems like a pernicious State encroachment into Middle East Studies as revealed in the now temporarily quashed H.R. 3077 (resurrected under H.R. 609, The College Access & Opportunity Act), area studies have always been associated with the interests of the nation. When the American Oriental Society, which we might see as a regional precursor of area studies, established itself in 1843, it clearly affiliated itself with missionary activity, long seen as a signifier of imperial power. John Pickering, in his opening address to the society, stressed the close relationship between the scholarly study of Oriental languages and literatures and missionary activity, deeming the former a "means of disseminating religious instruction," as befitting a major nation.[6] Thus area studies, in its guise as Oriental Studies, clearly saw itself as an arm of missionary imperialism, a trend that continued in the early twentieth century. K. S. Latourette, who helped establish East Asian Studies at Yale, authored *The Christian Missions in China* (1929), while A. C. Coolidge, who designed Slavic Studies at Yale, published *The United States as a World Power* (1908).[7]

By midcentury, the strategic national value of area studies seemed self-evident to scholars. The Committee on World Regions of the Social Science Research Council reported in 1943, for instance, that "The immediate need for social scientists who know the different regions of the world stands second only to the demand for military and naval officers familiar with the actual and potential combat zones."[8] In 1946 Army Specialized Training Programs for languages emerged at Princeton and the universities of Indiana, Michigan, and Pennsylvania. And in 1952, Hans Morgenthau would write in the *International Social Science Bulletin* that "area studies are frequently motivated by the recognition of America's predominant place in world affairs, which necessitates a knowledge of the world with which the United States must deal."[9] By the 1950s, area studies were being generously funded by the Rockefeller, Carnegie, and Ford foundations. Indeed, the most spectacular boost to area studies was engendered by Cold War politics. The launching of the first Sputnik in 1957 propelled Congress to pass the National Defense Education Act (NDEA) and under Title VI of NDEA, area studies centers were funded in universities, thus formalizing the material and political basis for the relationship between area studies and the State. By the early 1960s, eight of the Title VI centers had been framed to study the modern Middle East. The early leaders of Middle East Studies were no dissenters and saw their discipline as an armature of Anglo-American policy. As Philip Hitti, founder of the Program in Near Eastern Studies at Princeton argued, American universities were the most vital force for shaping Near East societies in their struggle against communism from the outside and feudalism from within.[10]

By the 1960s, area studies had been recruited to become the policy equivalent of what Said ascribed to Orientalism as a discursive formation: a means of disciplining and domination. The particular kind of disciplining envisioned by the State and often subscribed to by area studies practitioners was specifically colonial, hostile to independence movements in the Third World and popular socialist revolts in South America. The directives of Project Camelot, funded by the U.S. Army, and which sought to solicit social systems models for predicting and influencing social changes in developing countries, made this clear:

> The many programs of the U.S. Government directed toward this objective are often grouped under the sometimes misleading label of counterinsurgency (some pronounceable term standing for insurgency prophylaxis would be better). This places great importance on positive actions designed to reduce the sources of disaffection which often give rise to more conspicuous and violent activities disruptive in nature. The U.S. Army has an important mission in the positive and constructive aspects of nation building as well as a responsibility to assist friendly governments in dealing with active insurgency problems.[11]

Moves toward decolonization or popular movements against repressive right-wing regimes were viewed as hostile to U.S. interests; and under no circumstances could people's "sources of disaffection" be linked to the regimes themselves. Even though Project Camelot was canceled by the U.S. Congress after it aroused public protests in Chile, scholars expressed a variety of opinions on its goals.

While the goals of Project Camelot, often agreed to by area studies scholars, expressed the State's hostility toward worldwide decolonization, scholars of the Middle East were similarly skeptical of, if not hostile to, national liberation movements. Reflecting on the state of Middle East Studies in 1978, Edward Said located this colonial mind-set to the Orientalization of the Other endemic to the field. Middle East experts who advice policymakers, Said wrote:

> are imbued with Orientalism almost to a person. . . . The Orientalist now tries to see the Orient as an imitation West which, according to Bernard Lewis, can only improve itself when its nationalism "is prepared to come to terms with the West." If in the meantime the Arabs, the Muslims, or the Third and Fourth Worlds go unexpected ways after all, we will not be surprised to have an Orientalist tell us that this testifies to the incorrigibility of Orientals and therefore proves that they are not to be trusted.[12]

Most Middle East Studies scholars, like U.S. policymakers, could thus be counted on to have no sympathy for the cause of Palestinian sovereignty, which would always be associated with "terrorism."

Yet, to see area studies scholars as merely acquiescent to the imperatives of the State or to see State directives as successfully containing dissent is to problematically think of power as absolute. Elements of resistance constantly erupted from the very attempts to mandate area studies to serve the State. Indeed the requirement of the NDEA to have its scholarship recipients sign loyalty oaths and noncommunist affidavits stirred the ire of many academics who voted noncompliance with the order.[13] And perhaps, in what was the most subversive working of the Ford Foundation fellowships, which were based on an implicit acceptance of the United States as world hegemon, was the Africa grant given to Immanuel Wallerstein, who would subsequently produce his masterly treatises on imperialism as central to the capitalist world system. It is this decolonization of knowledge that the Right resisted all through the 1970s and most virulently since the overt attempts to suppress criticisms of the State since 9/11.

THIRD WORLD LIBERATION AND THE DECOLONIZATION OF KNOWLEDGE
ᐳ

It is worth recalling that what Mignolo calls the "restitution of subaltern knowledge" at the peripheries of the center was initiated in the United States most dramatically through racially disenfranchised students who sought both to extend the imperatives of civil rights into education and to link their struggles to those of Third World decolonization. The Third World Movement, which began in San Francisco State College in 1968, comprised African Americans, Latina/os, Asian Americans, and Native Americans, all of whom declared ghettos and barrios to be internal colonies of the United States and who modeled themselves after Third World liberation struggles. The founding of race-based academic programs, now loosely covered under the umbrella term *multiculturalism,* is directly attributable to the demands raised by these students. Similarly, the Black Panther Party grounded its demands in a critique of U.S. imperialism and saw the subjugation of African Americans as analogous to that of the Vietnamese under U.S. occupation. Indeed a major imperative of the Black Panther Party, one initiated by Huey Newton, was to educate the "colonized" African Americans about their rights within the laws of the nation, particularly their rights to protection from police harassment in the streets of Los Angeles. (The initiative was subsequently mandated through the 1966 Supreme Court decision on the Miranda warning, although obviously that did not end the racial profiling of African Americans.) The project of multicultural education thus emerged from a context of struggles over access to material resources and was tied to the inevitably linked goals of recognition and redistributive justice for the colonized within the United States. Multiculturalism implied affirmative action. The goal of race-based programs, developed as a result of demands by students of the Third World Movement, was to decenter Eurocentrism in the academy and bring to the fore race as a systemic form of oppression, legislated through the juridical apparatuses of the nation-state and normalized through different ideological apparatuses. The academy, particularly in the humanities, thus became a nexus through which civil rights, the decolonization of knowledge, and the critique of imperialism could powerfully intersect.

Nowhere, perhaps, was this synergy more powerfully apparent than in Middle East Studies, where the mapping of the Middle East had traditionally served to discipline the field to the imperatives of colonialism and imperialism. Methodologically, Orientalism and a chronopolitics that denied coevalness to the Other were accepted paradigms. Middle East cultures were seen as a rich storehouse of timeless wisdom from which the present had degenerated.[14] With the entry of social scientists into the arena following World War II, the U.S. version of developmentalism or modernization theory built upon Orientalist assumptions about Arab Muslim backwardness and added to it policy recommendations about how to enable Middle Eastern countries reduplicate Western societies. Paradigmatic of this line of scholarship was Daniel Lerner's *The Passing of Traditional Society: Modernizing the Middle East* (1958), which categorically stated, "What the West is . . . the Middle East seeks to become."[15] Well into the 1960s and continuing today, Orientalist scholars of the Middle East have downplayed the significance of imperialism, proclaiming, like Bernard Lewis, that "in the Middle East the impact of European imperialism was late, brief, and for the most part indirect."[16] As Stanley Kurtz, the major advocate of H.R. 3077, and Martin Kramer, who produced the antipostcolonial polemic *Ivory Towers on Sand,* argue, Said's *Orientalism* radicalized Middle East Studies and shook its colonial foundations. Analyses of imperialism's role in scholarship on the Middle East were legitimized, resulting in a stringent reevaluation of earlier scholarship and the production of works like Timothy Mitchell's *Colonizing Egypt* (1988) that turned the Orientalist mirror back on Europe.[17] By the mid-1990s, scholars like Ghassan Salame and Saad Eddin Ibrahim were challenging the social science experts of the seventies by emphasizing the diversity of Muslim societies and challenging the view of Islam as a degenerate force; yet others like Avi Shlaim were demonstrating the disastrous consequences of U.S. foreign policy in the Middle East.[18]

But while the impact of *Orientalism* on the field is undeniable, it was prepared for and, in a sense, anticipated by the critiques of Middle East Studies produced in the aftermath of the civil rights movement and the Vietnam War and which led to the formation of scholarly organizations critical of the complicity of Middle East with U.S. imperialism—the Middle East Research and Information Project (MERIP) in 1971 and the Alternative Middle East Studies Seminar (AMESS) in 1977. However, the impact of *Orientalism* might not have been as potent if it had not been for the changed composition of Middle East Studies scholars. And it is vital to emphasize that this change was an integral consequence of civil rights. The 1965 Immigration Act, which fundamentally deracialized new immigration, was championed by advocates of civil rights and was seen as an extension of the movement to end legal discrimination based on race; in the eyes of a rapidly decolonizing world, it was also seen as a step toward legitimizing U.S. Cold War claims to represent the "free" world.[19] Although cynical detractors of postcolonial theory have derided the supposed subaltern status of what they see as privileged Third World immigrant academics in the United States, there is little doubt that the migration of intellectuals from the periphery to the center or South to North, challenged the intellectual foundations of area studies that were predicated on colonial racial-cultural hierarchies.[20] What I am tracing here is not a simple identity politics (which the Bush administration was happy to exploit and the D'Souzas of the world happy to explode), but I am not throwing out the "politics"of race either.

Thus I see the attempted surveillance of area studies by the State and the continued intimidation of Middle East Studies faculty by the Right as, in one sense, responses to the gains of the civil rights era. Martin Kramer's *Ivory Towers on Sand,* touted by the neocons as an authoritative text on Middle East Studies, particularly suitable for the security state, is especially clear in its disapproval of both the global migration encouraged by the 1965 Immigration Act and of civil rights themselves. It is worth quoting Kramer at length here:

It [*Orientalism*] became a manifesto of affirmative action for Arab and Muslim scholars and established a negative predisposition toward American (and imported European) scholars. In 1971, only 3.2 percent of Middle East area specialists had been born in the region, and only 16.7 percent had the language and foreign-residence profiles coincident with a Middle Eastern background. "Our membership has changed over the years," announced MESA's president in 1992, "and possibly half is now of Middle Eastern heritage."

Referring to Said's assessment of MESA as that of "a metropolitan story of cultural opposition to Western domination," Kramer continues:

In fact, so total an "ideological transformation" in MESA (which even named Said an honorary fellow) would not have taken place had there not been a massive shift in the ethnic composition of Middle Eastern studies.[21]

Similarly, Norvell B. De Atkine and Daniel Pipes lament the "indigenization [that] has changed MESA from an American organization interested in the Middle East to a Middle Eastern one that happens to meet in the United States." "Scholars of the Middle East," they argue, "are . . . infected with 'county-itis'—identifying more with their subjects than with the United States."[22] While there is obviously a simplistic identity politics at play in the assumption that Americans (a category that clearly excludes Arab Americans) and Europeans are unaffected by the intellectual challenges of decolonization or by the same token that every Arab American or Arab living in the United States has revolutionary sympathies, it is the case that the shift in Middle Eastern Studies from Orientalism to anticolonialism, this decolonization of knowledge, was facilitated, as it was in literary studies, by the entrance into the academy of scholars of Third World origins.

However, Kramer's diatribe against the changes in intellectual paradigms is also clearly an argument against civil rights. For Kramer, the virtual invisibility of native scholars in the apartheid of Middle East area studies in the 1970s is no cause for alarm. Instead, the corrective two decades later when the ratio of native to nonnative scholars is even, becomes a case of egregious favoritism. The marginal gains of equal opportunity get viewed as carte blanche access. In the vein of Rightist diatribes on white male victimage (to which Susan Faludi in *Stiffed* became an unwitting contributor), Kramer views the entry of scholars of Middle Eastern heritage into MESA as a disenfranchisement of white scholars. Affirmative action becomes the oxymoronic reverse discrimination and, recalling earlier periods of immigration panic, "massive" hordes of Arabs create a brown peril for MESA. Of course, the question Kramer does not ask is why Arab scholars in the United States are scarcely represented in fields such as American Studies, Gender Studies, or British literature. Is the relatively strong representation in MESA symptomatic of a ghettoization wherein Arab scholars are *only* allowed entry into certain areas, whereas other areas are heavily policed and where entry might demand a certain kind of cultural capital? You are okay as an "Arab" but please don't try to teach Shakespeare. But Kramer would go further: you are welcome as long as you carry the accouterments of the "Arab" we understand, and we need only so many native informants.

If the decolonization and civil rights movements of the 1960s created an activist citizenry committed to the agenda of social and racial justice, and whose demands created social welfare programs designed to counter racial oppression, the Right's program since the Reagan years and continued thereafter in the arguments of the neocons has been to roll back the reforms of those years and declare the goals of those movements (economic redistribution and political representation) inimical to the national good. Witness George Bush's analysis of the L.A. riots as caused by welfare programs rather than racial disenfranchisement.[23] In the post-9/11 security state, activist citizenship has been declared not only unnational but a threat to the security of the nation. It is telling that Ann Coulter's 2003 invective against "liberal" policies is titled *Treason: Liberal Treachery from the Cold War to the War on Terrorism.* More recently, following Obama's election victory, Horowitz, in a direct mail letter, labeled MoveOn.org and ACORN as dangerous, anti-American organizations. The pedagogical narrative of nation is one of ostensible racial diversity and ideological consensus. This diversity, based on an ethnicity concept of race in which everyone is ethnic, equally positioned, and included in the national narrative, supports a neoconservative color-blindness that appropriates diversity while denying structural inequalities. The popular culture version of this phenomenon, one that resonates with the religious Right, is the Left Behind series, which conjoins doctrinal narrowness and unconditional support for U.S. imperialism with racial expansiveness.[24] This ideological consensus, refashioning Cold War national agendas for the present, is succinctly captured in the central proposition of the Project for a New American Century: "American leadership is good both for America and the world."[25] The twin imperatives of color-blind inclusion and American global power have coalesced into what I call a multicultural imperialism that seeks to regulate public discourse. Within this regulatory mechanism, radical, race-based multiculturalism, and critiques of imperialism, both legacies of the civil rights and decolonization movements, are deemed national security threats. The policing of area studies is thus twinned with an assault on the academic and cultural legacies of civil rights, which therefore necessitate a "war" on this culture. The resurgence of Orientalist discourse thus needs to be seen both as a means of legitimating the State's global imperial project as well as a means of normalizing colonial racial difference.

Kramer's *Ivory Towers in the Sand* leaves little doubt that the object of its attack is as much problems in Middle East Studies as the legacies of civil rights culture in the academy, particularly its association with decolonization movements. The receptivity of Middle East Studies to postcolonial theory, Kramer writes, is consequent upon the "surge of the student left into the faculty ranks [who] took over the institutions of Middle Eastern studies."[26] Similarly, the preface to the book singles out for attack scholars in the area, culpable for distorting Middle East Studies. Predictably, they are described as "infused with third worldist biases" and "caught up in the passion of its discredited causes. There is a widespread sympathy for Middle Eastern radicalism and an abiding suspicion of America's global role."[27]

In their attempts to affect legislation to monitor and control the activities of the academic Left, critics of Middle East Studies have been joined by numerous other conservative organizations dedicated to purging academia of Left influence. David Horowitz, who has been spearheading the Academic Bill of Rights, bemoans what he perceives as the preponderance of the Left in academia: "Marxists, socialists, post-modernists and other intellectual radicals—whose ideas of how societies work have been discredited by historical events . . . still dominate their academic fields."[28] He attributes Leftist influence to the unfortunate 1960s phenomenon of politicizing the undergraduate classroom. SAF, for instance, is clear about its policing of areas and programs developed as a result of sixties initiatives. Under the pretext of monitoring faculty who are particularly partisan in their teaching, the handbook for SAF specifies the programs targeted for maximum surveillance—"Cultural Studies, American Studies, English literature, Women's Studies, African-American (or Black) Studies, Chicano/Latino/Hispanic Studies, Lesbian/Gay/Bisexual/Transgender Studies, American-Indian Studies, and Asian-American Studies."[29] The targets of SAF are the race- and gender-based programs advocated by students of the Third World Movement as well as programs like Cultural Studies and American Studies that have been receptive to these areas.

THE MAKING OF MULTICULTURAL IMPERIALISM
ᕙ

It is crucial to recognize the current attempts to regulate academia, particularly in the humanities, as concerted attacks on civil rights culture and decolonization movements because in their efforts to mobilize right-wing support for the stifling of dissent, all conservative surveillance organizations—the advocates of H.R. 3077, Campus Watch, proponents for the Academic Bill of Rights, and SAF are strategically deploying the language of multicultural inclusion. The conservative agenda is presented as one of promoting balance, diversity, and tolerance in academia, and purging universities of "extremism" and "bias." Martin Kramer, who sounded the alarms about Middle East Studies shortly after 9/11, argued that the area "lack[s] a culture of tolerance for diversity in ideas and approaches."[30] Stanley Kurtz, the key expert witness for the consideration of H.R. 3077, and who cites Kramer as his sole authority, continued Kramer's strategy of advocating surveillance of Middle East Studies under the guise of ushering in openness. Despite the fact that *Orientalism* has been stringently critiqued by the president of MESA and other MESA scholars, even while it has had considerable influence, Kurtz buys wholesale Kramer's assertion that MESA members are uncritical Saidian ideologues.[31] Middle East Studies, he argues, needed to "balance" the readings of Said and his like-minded colleagues with readings from Orientalists like Bernard Lewis; university faculties need to be "balanced" among those who oppose and support U.S. foreign policy. He supports the "vigorous and open debate" and the importance of "divergent points of view" currently endangered through government funding of Title VI programs dominated by anti-Americanism.[32] Similarly, Campus Watch justifies its surveillance of Middle East Studies on the grounds that the monolithically Leftist bent of faculty in the area has resulted in a discipline that lacks intellectual diversity.[33]

Perhaps the most ardent user of the rhetoric of multiculturalism for silencing the academic Left is David Horowitz, whose article on monitoring faculty to the extent of screening the posting of political cartoons on office doors is titled "In Defense of Intellectual Diversity."[34] Touting the consistent lack of representation by conservatives on university campuses (significantly, Horowitz does not visit business or medical schools) and the intellectual intimidation perceived by conservative students, Horowitz has sought to mobilize these students to press for academic bill of rights on their campuses by appropriating the language of radical multiculturalism. Horowitz's candid admission is worth quoting at length:

> I encourage them [conservative students] to use the language that the left has deployed so effectively in behalf of its own agendas. Radical professors have created a "hostile learning environment" for conservative students. There is a lack of "intellectual diversity" on college faculties and in academic classrooms. The conservative viewpoint is "under-represented" in the curriculum and on its reading lists. The university should be an "inclusive" and intellectually "diverse" community.[35]

Horowitz's strategy is fascinating not only because of its illustration of classic Orwellian doublespeak, but also, more importantly because it demonstrates the contradictions of race and the problematic politics of multiculturalism in the public arena today. Clearly, Horowitz's injunctions to conservative students are based on an acknowledgment of the importance of civil rights agendas of the sixties such as diversity, representation, and inclusion. On the other hand, material initiatives such as affirmative action have been vociferously opposed by all conservatives. However, liberal multiculturalism is to be blamed as well. "Diversity," "representation," and "inclusion" are hollow without a rights-based commitment to spelling out why we need them, and such a commitment has been abandoned by many on the Left.

As Omi and Winant have argued, the movement away from the radical, rights-based conception of race in the 1960s to ethnicity theory in the 1970s and 1980s meant that issues of systemic racism were replaced by those of assimilation, based on the immigrant paradigm that argued that all immigrants, regardless of color, went through similar adaptation processes.[36] In practice, ethnicity theory had two consequences: (*a*) purely recreational forms of identity, such as German American, could be seen as analogous to identities subject to systemic racism, such as African American and Hispanic; (*b*) the immigration process could serve as a macronarrative for racial progress where history from 1865 onward could be represented as a triumphal march of assimilation and adaptation. Indeed the latter vision of multicultural progress has become so favored a narrative of nation that racism, segregation and exclusion are seen only as the purview of fringe groups such as neo-Nazis or the KKK. On the other hand, the continued systems of racial disenfranchisement, the hypersegregation of African Americans, for instance, from the erstwhile institutions of slavery and Jim Crow to contemporary versions such as the ghetto and the carceral,[37] are disrecognized as systemic racism both by neoconservatives who attempt to defund any initiatives toward social justice and by liberals who acclaim color-blind notions of justice. This severance of race from rights across a broad sociopolitical spectrum has made it possible for multiculturalism today to simply represent a politics of cultural recognition, without recognition of equal social reward or redistributive justice.[38]

This discourse of liberal multiculturalism has proven to be particularly amenable to conservative appropriation. As Satya Mohanty pointed out a decade ago, while claims for diversity and difference in the sixties had a political edge, they are now being used for conservative ends via a "state sponsored multiculturalism" that deflects attention from the material issues of race politics.[39] State-sponsored multiculturalism and militarist imperialism form an unholy alliance in what I have called a multicultural imperialism. Thus Stanley Kurtz's criticisms of Edward Said's theories as "biased" and "extreme" draw superficially on the language of multiculturalism in which all races are welcomed and where, implicitly, racism has no play—the talk show model of multiculturalism where critical race theorists and KKK members are given equal weight. Horowitz's rhetoric of balance and diversity draws upon a similar model. Indeed the marshaling of multiculturalism in the service of unilateral militaristic imperialism was perfected by the Bush administration, which paraded its united colors of empire (through a tokenism that suppressed exclusions and inequalities) in the figures of Condoleezza Rice, Alberto Gonzalez, Carlos Gutirrez, Alphonse Jackson, and Elaine Chao. Yet in the neocon clarion call for academic surveillance ostensibly to promote "diversity," the imperative for academic knowledge to support U.S. imperialism was clear. David Horowitz, for instance, passionately denounced the role of the "leftwing university" in "undermining American self-respect and self-confidence at a time when the nation was facing enemies who were deadly."[40] Indeed, Horowitz argues that the harboring of oppositional intellectuals in State-funded academic institutions is a public outrage. As evidence he cites the UCLA Senate's (April 2003) overwhelming condemnation of the invasion of Iraq after the United States had "liberated Iraq" and when 76 percent of the population supported the war.[41] The implication is that such institutions are obliged to be alibis for State policy and serve as unthinking reflectors of public opinion at its most jingoist. But if we are stuck in either liberal multiculturalism or a politics beyond race, we can't understand how the rhetoric of tolerance and imperialism coexist other than through bad faith, for instance, Martin Kramer's condemnation of the lack of "a culture of tolerance for diversity in ideas" in Middle East Studies and his recommendation that scholars articulate "that which is uniquely American in the American approach to the Middle East. The idea that the United States plays an essentially beneficent role in the world."[42] Nor can we understand George Bush's calls for tolerance of Islam generally while authorizing the Department of Homeland Security to arrest thousands of Arab Americans. Here Wendy Brown's analysis of tolerance as a civilizational discourse that always puts the West on the side of tolerance is useful.[43] It exemplifies the new vocabulary of contemporary multicultural imperialism. It is because "we" are tolerant, in contrast to others who are not, that there is a discursive consensus through which "Arab," "Muslim," "terrorist," and "anti-American" signify each other.

For the Arab community in the United States (Arab being monolithically constructed as Muslim, non-Israeli, and often illogically equated with being Middle Eastern), this has meant that these minorities have been positioned as Other/outside the imagined community of the tolerant nation whose interests, it is presumed, they threaten.[44] Whereas the question "Where are you from?" had always cast Asian Americans as foreign by interrogating their right to be "here," for Arab Americans since 9/11 there has been no question, but rather a stereotypical conviction: "I know where you're from and what you're like." Multicultural tolerance, in other words, meets its limits where it becomes "foreign" to tolerance and civilization and signifies being anti-American. It was therefore no contradiction for Bush to proclaim tolerance while simultaneously giving free rein to the FBI to interrogate and arrest thousands of Arab men, and inciting citizens to engage in racial profiling by encouraging them to report all "suspicious activity." No doubt, such an atmosphere legitimated the ultimate dismissal of Sami Al-Arian from his tenured faculty position at the University of South Florida.

Of course, not all foreignness signifies anti-Americanism—European immigrants and travelers are not racially profiled for terrorism—but any critique of U.S. imperialism is deemed, by the Right, a threat to the security of the nation and therefore viewed as unnational. (Postcolonial theory acquired this dubious distinction in the hearings for H.R. 3077.) At a certain level, the Left, through its critique of empire, intersects with the foreign in being cast as unnational.[45] The foreignness/unnationalness of both the Left and the Arab Middle Easterner go far to explain the monitoring of Middle East Studies and of the academic Left in general. As mentioned earlier, Martin Kramer's hostility to the "foreign" composition of scholars in MESA relies upon current associations of Middle Easterners with unnational foreignness. Stanley Kurtz's testimony for H.R. 3077, which relies on Kramer's argument about the pernicious and omnipresent influence of Edward Said and postcolonial theory on Middle East Studies, similarly draws upon the discursive consensus that marks both anti-imperial critique and an Arab lineage as foreign, in order to characterize Said as outside the imagined community of nation. Thus Said's role as journalist for the Egyptian weekly *Al-Ahram* and his excoriation of U.S. foreign policy therein, position him outside the nation both through the act of critique and through the circuit of "foreign" that the Egyptian weekly provokes. Said's foreignness is again at play in his by no means novel reading of the U.S. Constitution as raced. "He has belittled the reverence in which Americans hold the Constitution" by pointing out its "wealthy, white, slaveholding, Anglophilic" male authorship.[46] Kurtz's statement demonstrates the narrow bounds of nation imagined by the Right. Not only is Said marked as foreign in relation to the national symbolic, but national subjects are implicitly defined through their sacralization of, rather than their engagement with, nation-making documents. As illustrated by David Horowitz, the nation must be teleologically narrated as multicultural triumph. Explaining the success of a recent speech, Horowitz writes, "I reminded them how a white slave-owner named Thomas Jefferson put into the founding document of this nation the revolutionary idea that all men are created equal and how within a generation as a direct result of the efforts of England and America slavery had been abolished in the Western world."[47]

Key to this equal opportunity, multicultural imperialism is therefore not to raise questions about the endless "war on terror." This delegitimation of complex, critical thinking and the equation of dissent with terrorism was spelled out in George W. Bush's address to the nation: "Every nation in every region now has a decision to make: Either you are with us, or you are with the terrorists."[48] Bush's totalitarian Manichaeanism was echoed by conservatives such as Daniel Pipes promulgating academic surveillance. Thus Pipes's illustration of hating America includes suggesting that the Iraqi invasion was motivated by the nation's oil supply (Noam Chomsky) and that preemptive war was a return to the rule of the jungle

(Eric Foner).[49] No less opposed to intellectual debate was the November 2001 report of the American Council of Trustees and Alumni (ACTA) in which unacceptable speech by faculty included comments such as "Ignorance breeds hate," and "[T]here needs to be an understanding of why this kind of suicidal violence could be undertaken against our country."[50] In this prohibitive cultural milieu, Orientalism, as key cultural component to militaristic imperialism, witnessed a remarkable resurgence as a mechanism of control.

ORIENTALISM, DISCIPLINING, AND MIDDLE EAST STUDIES:
THE MUSLIMS ARE COMING
♣

The marshaling of the language of multiculturalism for the purposes of ensuring that Middle East Studies serves the ends of U.S. imperialism, rather than the decolonization imperatives of the 1960s, has been accompanied by a corresponding ratcheting up of discourses of Orientalism in the public arena. Based on a fundamental premise of racial-cultural difference between an enlightened West and backward Others, the discourse of Orientalism has been a bulwark to justifications of colonialism and imperialism. September 11, 2001, ushered in a virtual renaissance of Orientalist discourses in which empire was not only justifiable but necessary. Samuel Huntington's 1993 thesis about the post–Cold War world as an immutable "clash" between the universalist civilizations of the West and the rest or the West and Islam, based on a historical account that naturalizes wars as cultural clashes (without so much as a mention of imperialism and colonialism), and bolstered by arguments of colonial apologists like V. S. Naipaul and Bernard Lewis, received immediate political currency following 9/11.[51] Categories of colonial racial difference, never totally absent even during the Cold War, were given renewed legitimacy by the State. No less significant has been the broad coalition of Israel lobbyists and neocons who influence Congress and revile any attempt to understand the Palestinian cause.[52] There is little reason to believe that such influences will dwindle under Obama. Thus Middle East Studies scholars who have attempted to decolonize scholarship by seeking alternatives to the representation of Muslim Arabs either as creatures of unchanging timeless societies or irrationally crazed ones (especially those that seek nationalism/decolonization) find themselves particularly under fire.

Thus it is not surprising that Daniel Pipes, the founder of Campus

Watch, relies on the most overt of Orientalist categories—Muslim Arabs as subhuman and filthy—to serve racial difference. In an essay for *National Review* appropriately titled, "The Muslims are Coming! The Muslims are coming!" Pipes concurs with the religious Right in worrying about the influx of Muslims into the West, particularly because of the low birthrate in Western countries and the excessive fertility of Muslims. This Muslim peril, echoing late-nineteenth-century paranoias of the yellow peril, is diagnosed by Pipes as the major danger facing Western countries. Pipes writes, "In contrast to Westerners, who are not able even to maintain their present numbers . . . Muslims revel in some of the most robust birth rates in the world. . . . countries with large numbers of Muslims have a crude birth rate of 42 per thousand; by contrast, the developed countries have a crude birth rate of just 13 per thousand."[53] Needless to say, this rhetoric of sensible, restrained civilizations being overwhelmed by hordes of exorbitantly fertile Muslims has been used in the suppression of minorities worldwide, most recently by Hindu fundamentalists in India. Continuing his analysis of the consequences of Muslim immigration, Pipes writes, "Fears of a Muslim influx have more substance than the worry about jihad. West European societies are unprepared for the massive immigration of brown-skinned peoples cooking strange foods and not exactly maintaining Germanic standards of hygiene."[54] What might a decade ago have been castigated as a paranoid racist narrative of filth, pollution, and abjection was clearly viewed as significant multicultural scholarship by the Bush administration when Bush in 2003 nominated Pipes to be on the Board of Directors of the United States Institute of Peace. Despite massive opposition to Pipes's nomination, Bush made a recess appointment after the Senate adjourned for the summer, thus allowing Pipes to serve a partial term.[55] Colonial racial difference and Orientalism were thus legitimated as State policy even as multicultural tolerance was recruited to police academia.

And even as Bush was ostensibly differentiating good Iraqis from terrorists, tolerant Muslims from murderous fundamentalists, the neocons' favorite book about the Arabs in the months leading to the Iraqi invasion was Raphael Patai's *The Arab Mind,* first published in 1973. In its obsession with veiled women and its reduction of so diverse a geopolitical space as "the Arab world" to an undifferentiated, presocial sexual drive, Patai's book is consistent with Orientalist representations of the oversexed, irrational, traditional Arab male.[56] Patai argues, for instance, that resultant upon gender segregation and the veiling of women, sex became a "prime mental preoccupation in the Arab world."[57] However, despite the thorough condemnation of the book by scholars of Middle East Studies, it is used as the definitive text on "the Arabs" for the military. Republished in 2002, it now has an enthusiastic introduction by Norvell "Tex" De Atkine, head of Middle East Studies at Fort Bragg, who touts it as "essential reading." "At the institution where I teach military officers, *The Arab Mind* forms the basis of my cultural instruction."[58] A clearer statement about the imbrication of multicultural Orientalism, schooling, and foreign policy can hardly be found.[59]

Similarly, calls for the surveillance of Middle East Studies and analyses of the pernicious influence of postcolonial theory and its putative founder, Edward Said, have relied not only on Orientalism but also on a neo-Orientalist civilizational discourse of tolerance through the deployment of the terms *terrorism* and *fundamentalism*. Although, as Edward Said has pointed out, these categories generated out of the metropolitan centers of London and Washington became universally deployed, in the United States there has been a clear discursive consensus about what constitutes these categories, even as they lack definitional or logical clarity.[60] Thus terrorism is never used to designate homegrown groups like the KKK that have indeed fomented terror, or groups like the Michigan Militia who explicitly arm themselves against the State; abroad the term is almost never used in connection with right-wing Israeli groups who deliberately attack civilians. But Palestinians are routinely terrorists, particularly if they resist occupation. Similarly, fundamentalism signifies terrorism not when, say, antiabortion Christian fundamentalists intimidate women and murder physicians, but does so when a Muslim burns a U.S. flag.

The interpretation of the September 11 attacks as acts of terrorism against the values of tolerance and freedom, and which needs no further analyses, justified an endless "war against terror" that has included the preemptive invasion of Iraq. In such a scenario, September 11 signifies the vulnerability/insecurity of the homeland and the threat of terrorism. Stanley Kurtz's testimony on behalf of the surveillance of Middle East Studies, paradigmatic of similar calls for academic monitoring, artfully builds its argument upon these oppositions. Thus in his denunciation of the pernicious effects of postcolonial theory, Kurtz cites the assigning of writings by postcolonial intellectuals such as Tariq Ali and Arundhati Roy to K–12 teachers in order for them to understand the question "Why do they hate us?" Such readings, argues Kurtz, betray an "extreme animus to the United States," indicative of the "extremist political bias" of Title VI programs dominated by Said's postcolonial theory. As Kurtz easily slides from "extreme" to "extremism" in his characterization of Said, postcolonial theory, and Middle East Studies, all arguably directed against the nation, he evokes the specter of terrorism and the crazed Arab / Muslim / Middle Easterner without resort to conventional racism. Thus Said is deemed a terrorist not because he is "Arab," which would be "racist," but because he is extremist, presenting an immutable cultural difference of the likes propounded by Huntington. Of course, as Said himself had demonstrated, irrationality and extremism have long been used as euphemistic racial markers of a backward Arab world in contrast to a rational West.

Kurtz's testimony, in fact, repeats the narrative of nation most favored by the State since 9/11—a classic three-part Aristotelian drama with the actions of the terrorists disturbing the peace; the destruction of September 11 signifying national vulnerability and terrorist brutality; and the need for security apparatuses to protect the homeland. Invoked by the State as a justification of the invasion of Iraq, the tripartite drama also structures Kurtz's testimony. Thus the first part of the testimony is replete with references to "extremism" (used six times), which stands in for terrorism; the second evokes the tragedy of 9/11 (referred to nine times) and exhorts academic knowledge to serve State policy; and the third underlines the urgency of "security" (mentioned four times). Membership within the nation is thus constructed as the need for personal security acquired through loyalty to the figure of the president, who stands in for Father/Law providing the security of the symbolic. That this security can be acquired at the expense of the social justice network of social security, as argued by George W. Bush, is the paradoxical logic of fear that justifies imperialism and its discursive ally, Orientalism.

Given the enormous role of culture and knowledge production in the apparatus of imperialism, it is imperative that academics, particularly those involved in the analysis and understanding of culture, not only be vigilant of Rightist attempts to take over or contain public discourse but also of their own potential collusion in updated discourses of imperialism through the rhetoric of color-blind tolerance. Systematically defunded universities need not necessarily become allies of empire. Instead, they should strive to produce intellectuals whose role is "to present alternative narratives and other perspectives on history than those provided by combatants on behalf of official memory and national identity and mission."[61] At present, the best hope for these alternative narratives is a committed postcolonial perspective that takes seriously the brutal histories of colonialism and imperialism that continue to structure our lives.

NOTES

1. http://www.campus-watch.org/.

2. H.R. 3077: International Studies in Higher Education Act of 2003 (Introduced in House), http://thomas.loc.gov, accessed January 5, 2009.

3. Walter Mignolo, *Local Histories / Global Designs: Coloniality, Subaltern Knowledges, and Border Thinking* (New Jersey: Princeton University Press, 2000), 13.

4. Ibid., ix.

5. I am referring to Foucault's 1978 essay where he posits governmentality as the late capitalist way in which states operate. Governmentality operates through a diffuse set of strategies—policies, departments, institutions, discourses—that work to regulate bodies and reproduce subjects for the State. See "Governmentality," in *The Foucault Effect: Studies in Governmentality,* ed. Graham Burchell, Colin Gordon, and Peter Miller (Chicago: University of Chicago Press, 1991), 87–104. Agamben identifies the state of exception that allows modern states to engage in a legal civil war, thus silencing adversaries through a permanent state of emergency, as the established way contemporary societies have operated since the end of World War I. See Giorgio Agamben, *State of Exception,* trans. Kevin Attell (Chicago: University Of Chicago Press, 2005), 1–4.

6. John Pickering, "Address," April 7, 1843, *Journal of the American Oriental Society* 1 (1849): 2.

7. Cited in Vijay Prashad, "Confronting the Evangelical Imperialists: Mr Kurtz: the Horror, the Horror," *Counterpunch,* November 13, 2003, http://www.counterpunch.org/prashad11132003.html.

8. Cited in Immanuel Wallerstein, "The Unintended Consequences of Cold War Area Studies," in Noam Chomsky et al., *The Cold War and the University: Toward an Intellectual History of the Postwar Years* (New York: New Press, 1997), 195.

9. Hans J. Morgenthau, "Area Studies and the Study of International Relations," *International Social Science Bulletin* 4.4 (1952): 647–51, cited in Wallerstein, "Unintended Consequences," 208.

10. "Remarks by Dr Philip Hitti on His Near Eastern Mission," *Near East Colleges Quarterly* 10 (October 1946): 7.

11. Project Camelot, "Document Number 1," in *The Rise and Fall of Project Camelot,* ed. I. L. Horowitz (Cambridge: MIT Press, 1967), 48, cited in Wallerstein, "Unintended Consequences," 221.

12. Edward Said, *Orientalism* (New York: Vintage, 1978), 321.

13. Richard Ohmann, "English and the Cold War," in Chomsky et al., *Cold War and University,* 88.

14. For the importance of the denial of coevalness, see Johannes Fabian, *Time and the Other: How Anthropology Makes Its Object* (New York : Columbia 1983), 25.

15. Daniel Lerner, *The Passing of Traditional Society: Modernizing the Middle East* (New York: Free Press, 1958), 47; Lisa Hajjar and Steve Niva, "(Re)Made in the USA: Middle East Studies in the Global Era," *Middle East Report* 205 (October–December 1997), http://www.merip.org/mer/mer205/remade.htm, accessed July 30, 2006.

16. Bernard Lewis, *The Middle East and the West* (New York: Harper, 1968), 31, cited in Yahya Sadowski, "The New Orientalism and the Democracy Debate," *Middle East Report* 183 (July–Aug 1993): 20.

17. Hajjar and Niva, "(Re)Made in the USA."

18. Ghassan Salame, "Islam and the West," *Foreign Policy* 90 (Spring 1993): 22–37; Avi Shlaim, *War and Peace in the Middle East: A Critique of American Foreign Policy* (New York: Whittle Books in Association with Viking, 1994).

19. For an analysis of the relationship between civil rights and the contradictions of Cold War foreign policy, see Nikhil Pal Singh, "Culture/Wars: Recoding Empire in an Age of Democracy," *American Quarterly* 50.3 (1998): 471–522.

20. My argument about the effects of the migration of Third World scholars applies only to the humanities and social sciences and not to business or hard and applied sciences, where many faculty have willingly recruited themselves as agents of U.S. neoliberalism.

21. Martin Kramer, *Ivory Towers on Sand: The Failure of Middle Eastern Studies in America* (Washington, D.C.: Washington Institute for Near East Policy, 2001), 39.

22. Norvell B. DeAtkine and Daniel Pipes, "Middle Eastern Studies: What Went Wrong?" *Academic Questions* 9.1 (1995–96): 60, http://weblinks2.epnet.com, accessed July 29, 2006.

23. For an analysis of this shift see Michael Omi and Howard Winant, *Racial Formation in the United States: From the 1960s to the 1990s,* 2nd ed. (New York: Routledge, 1994), 146.

24. See Melani McAlister, "Left Behind and the Politics of Prophecy Talk," in *Exceptional State: Contemporary US Culture and Imperialism,* ed. Ashley Dawson and Malini Johar Schueller (Durham, N.C.: Duke University Press, 2007).

25. See http://www.newamericancentury.org.

26. Kramer, *Ivory Towers on Sand,* 121.

27. Fred S. Lafer and Michael Stein, preface to ibid., ix.

28. David Horowitz, "The Campus Blacklist," FrontPageMagazine.com, April 18, 2003, http://www.studentsforacademicfreedom.org/essays/blacklist.html, accessed November 16, 2008.

29. Sara Dogan, with Ryan Call and Lee Kaplan, *Students for Academic Freedom Handbook,* 31, http://www.studentsforacademicfreedom.org.

30. Kramer, *Ivory Towers on Sand,* 129.

31. Joel Beinin, "The New McCarthyism: Policing Thought about the Middle East," *Race and Class* 46.1 (2004): 106.

32. Statement of Stanley Kurtz, testimony before the Subcommittee on Select Education, Committee on Education and the Workforce, U.S. House of Representatives, June 19, 2003, http://edworkforce.house.gov/hearings/, accessed June 7, 2006.

33. Campus Watch: Monitoring Middle East Studies on Campus, http://www.campus-watch.org/about.php, accessed November 16, 2008.

34. David Horowitz, "In Defense of Intellectual Diversity," *Chronicle of Higher Education,* February 13, 2004, 612–1313.

35. Horowitz, "The Campus Blacklist."

36. Michael Omi and Howard Winant, *Racial Formation in the United States* (New York: Routledge, 1986), 12.

37. Loïc Wacquant, "From Slavery to Mass Incarceration," *New Left Review* 13 (February 2002): 55.

38. For analyses of what multicultural recognition should entail, see Charles

Taylor, "The Politics of Recognition." in *Multiculturalism: Examining the Politics of Recognition,* ed. Amy Gutman. (Princeton: Princeton University Press, 1994), 25–73. See also Nancy Fraser, "Social Justice in the Age of Identity Politics: Redistribution, Recognition and Participation," Tanner Lectures on Human Values, Stanford University, April 30–May 2, 1996.

39. Satya Mohanty, *Postmodernism, Objectivity, Multicultural Politics* (Ithaca, N.Y.: Cornell University Press, 1997), 17.

40. Horowitz, "The Campus Blacklist."

41. Ibid.

42. Kramer, *Ivory Towers on Sand,* 129.

43. Wendy Brown, *Regulating Aversion: Tolerance in the Age of Identity and Empire* (Princeton: Princeton University Press, 2006).

44. See Leti Volpp, "The Citizen and the Terrorist," on the new racial category of "Middle Eastern, Arab, or Muslim" constructed after 9/11 in *September 11 in History: A Watershed Moment?* ed. Mary L. Dudziak (Durham, N.C.: Duke University Press, 2003), 147–61.

45. Thus Howard Dean, critic of the Iraqi invasion since its inception, was cast in an ad by the conservative Club for Growth as somehow lacking Americanness and associated with signifiers of foreignness. Dean was advised to take his "tax-hiking, government expanding, latte-drinking, sushi-eating, Volvo driving, New York Times–reading, Hollywood loving, left-wing freak show back to Vermont where it belongs." George W. Bush, on the other hand, claimed cultural authenticity by casting himself as cowboy who in true western style promised the nation to "smoke out" Osama. Cited in Thomas Frank, *What's the Matter with Kansas: How Conservatives Won the Heart of America* (New York: Henry Holt, 2004), 17.

46. Statement of Stanley Kurtz.

47. Horowitz, "The Campus Blacklist."

48. "Address to a Joint Session of Congress and the American People," September 20, 2001. http://www.whitehouse.gov/news/releases, accessed January 5, 2009.

49. Daniel Pipes, "Profs Who Hate America," *New York Post,* November 12, 2002, http://www www.danielpipes.org/article/923, accessed January 5, 2009.

50. Cited in Beinin, "The New McCarthyism," 104.

51. See Samuel P. Huntington, "The Clash of Civilizations?" *Foreign Affairs,* Summer 1993, 40–41.

52. See John J. Mearsheimer and Stephen M. Walt, *The Israel Lobby and U.S. Foreign Policy* (New York: Farrar, Straus and Giroux, 2008).

53. Daniel Pipes, "The Muslims Are Coming! The Muslims Are Coming!" *National Review,* November 19, 1990, www.danielpipes.org/article/198, accessed November 16, 2008.

54. Ibid.

55. See Beinin, "The New McCarthyism," 110–11.

56. Said, *Orientalism,* 287. Indeed, in *Orientalism* Said critiqued Patai for his construction of the Oriental as fixed, stable, and in need of investigation (308–9).

57. Cited in Seymour M. Hersh, "The Gray Zone," *New Yorker,* May 24, 2004, 1, http://www.newyorker.com/printable/?fact/040524fa_fact, accessed November 16, 2008.

58. Cited in Brian Whitaker, "Its Best Use Is as a Doorstop," *Guardian Unlim-*

ited, May 24, 2004, http://www.guardian.co.uk/elsewhere/journalist/story/0,7792, 1223525,00.html, accessed November 16, 2008.

59. My discussion of Patai's book also appears in Dawson and Schueller, *Exceptional State.*

60. Said, *Culture and Imperialism* (New York: Knopf, 1993), 309–10. For an analysis of the discursive consensus about what constitutes terrorism, see Judith Butler, *Precarious Life: The Powers of Mourning and Violence* (London: Verso, 2004), 4–6.

61. Edward Said, *Humanism and Democratic Criticism* (New York: Columbia University Press, 2004), 141.

E PLURIBUS UNUM / EX UNO PLURA

Legislating and Deregulating
American Studies post 9/11

Sophia McClennen

> it will take you and your leaders
> forever
> and forever
> and forever
> it will take you forever
> to learn the word for peace
> —Ariel Dorfman

THE ADMINISTRATION OF GEORGE W. BUSH presented one of the most extreme examples of linguistic manipulation at the service of acquiring power in U.S. history. To cite merely a few of the most common tactics, the administration misrepresented, lied, obfuscated, named, renamed, refused to name, censored, and silenced.[1] Take, for example, the Abu Ghraib photo scandal, which demonstrated how the administration avoided words, resemanticized words, and renamed places in a strategic effort to use language to preserve and expand social control. Responding to the administration's deployment of linguistic exploitation, Susan Sontag wrote: "Words alter, words add, words subtract. . . . To refuse to call what took place in Abu Ghraib—and what has taken place elsewhere in Iraq and in Afghanistan and at Guantanamo Bay—by its true name, torture, is as outrageous as the refusal to call the Rwandan genocide a genocide."[2] Sontag highlighted Donald Rumsfeld's evasion of the word *torture,* but the refusal to link word and deed was not the only linguistic strategy used by the Bush White House. Shortly after the photos of torture were publicly circulating, Rumsfeld took a trip to Abu Ghraib. While there, he told soldiers, "I am a survivor" in response to calls for his resignation.[3] If Rumsfeld was a survivor, then what were the torture victims? What linguistic conditions made it possible to call Rumsfeld a "survivor" while denying the existence of the tortured prisoners? Consequently, not only did the administration refuse to name the torture as "torture," they also artfully began to reappropriate words that might have been used to describe the conditions at Abu Ghraib. Then the administration used another of its well-worn linguistic games: they renamed. While Rumsfeld was visiting the prison, a new complex on the Abu Ghraib grounds was christened "Camp Redemption."[4] Was there the hope that the name *Abu Ghraib,* along with all of its connotations of violence and abuse, would cease to circulate? Could the name *Camp Redemption* manage to redeem the administration and all of its supporters?

This act of renaming was not the first time that the Bush administration attempted to alter an unpleasant history in its favor, nor is it the first time that the U.S. government has deployed such a tactic. In fact, linguistic manipulation has been one of the prime weapons of dominant power transhistorically and transregionally. Sacvan Bercovitch, for instance, has traced the way that the Puritans sought a "rhetoric adequate to their sense of mission" by employing a "wholesale inversion of traditional hermeneutics."[5] That said, it seems clear that 9/11 created a convergence of events that facilitated an unprecedented assault on language, meaning, and critical thinking within the United States, an assault that has been waged with particular force in the realm of higher education. Stanley Kurtz, the conservative critic who has argued for government oversight of areas studies programs, connects the War on Terror with newfound opportunities for right-wing incursions into higher education policy: "The war has unquestionably brought a new level of scrutiny to our politically correct campuses. Once the initial years of the campus culture war had passed, the public decided that campus leftism was either beyond the reach of anyone who hoped to do something about it, or irrelevant. The war changed that."[6] Consequently, the War on Terror enabled a series of attacks on higher education, many of which focused on the teaching of America. This essay suggests that the post-9/11 assaults on American studies have created a context through which to reconsider the critical methods that ground the field, methods that I describe as metaphorically linked to legislation/unification and deregulation/expansion and that both replicate and respond to the ideology of the nation itself. After surveying the attacks on higher education, especially as they relate to American studies, I briefly analyze the critical history of the field in an effort to suggest strategies for challenging these threats.

The right-wing assaults on higher education post-9/11 are numerous, and they have been waged via a number of means including the right-wing media, the Internet, student and parent groups, and state and federal legislation. Taken together, these groups form what Vijay Prashad terms "an academic front of the Right."[7] In broad strokes, there have been a number of related attacks on "leftist," "liberal," or "anti-American" curricula and faculty that roughly break down into investigations and accusations regarding area studies, American studies, the political affiliations and critical perspectives of faculty, and student rights. Area studies has come under fire for anti-Americanism by groups like Campus Watch, via critics like Daniel Pipes, Martin Kramer, and Stanley Kurtz, attacks that culminated in federal legislation regarding the reappropriation of Title VI funds dedicated to foreign languages and cultures (H.R. 509, previously H.R. 3077). American studies has been the subject of a number of pamphlets authored by the American Council of Trustees and Alumni (ACTA). Led by the work of Lynne Cheney, Anne Neal, and Jerry Martin, ACTA has instigated a number of federal investigations into the patriotism of American studies, most notoriously in the post-9/11 report *Defending Civilization: How Our Universities Are Failing America and What Can Be Done about It,* the infamous text that charged that "colleges and university faculty have been the weak link in America's response" to terrorism.[8] David Horowitz, founder of Students for Academic Freedom and author of the Academic Bill of Rights, has attacked faculty diversity and teaching methods, claiming that universities are overwhelmingly dominated by the Left, that students are bullied into adopting leftist perspectives, and that classroom topics have become overly politicized at the expense of teaching a diversity of critical viewpoints. Horowitz runs a website that allows students to post complaints about their professors and includes a step-by-step guide for students and parents who want to start their own Students for Academic Freedom chapters. Twenty states at the time of this writing have considered versions of his Academic Bill of Rights, and language related to it was part of the most recent version of the Higher Education Act (H.R. 609) under deliberation by the House of Representatives in fall 2006.

These groups all had ties to the Bush administration.[9] They also all agree with ACTA's claim in *Defending Civilization* that "when a nation's intellectuals are unwilling to defend its civilization, they give comfort to its adversaries."[10] For instance, Horowitz has published widely on the "evils" of a leftist, multicultural professoriate, especially in books like *Unholy Alliance: Radical Islam and the American Left,* where he equates criticism of U.S. empire building with outright support of terrorism.[11] Even though I argue that these attacks all hinge on an intense battle to define "America," it is useful to recognize that they are taking place on three fronts: the preservation of American values and the defense of American civilization, the relationship between the United States and the globe, and the best methods for teaching and researching these two areas. In each of these cases there is a correlation between, on the one hand, legislating a unified vision of America, and, on the other hand, advocating an expanded, deregulated zone of influence on academic work—moves, I argue, that depend on deploying specific linguistic strategies where meaning is simultaneously fluid and fixed.

The War on Terror, according to the logic of the Bush administration, required renewed patriotic vigor and depended on convincing the nation's youth (and their parents) that winning the war was worth losing their lives. Moreover, the War on Terror relied on a public willing to consume the Right's stunning abuse of the representational potential of language. Consequently, those who supported Bush's War on Terror focused attention on the nation's youth and on those who educated them. Because higher education in wartime is expected to prepare students for battle, teaching critical thinking becomes equivalent to treason. There was a direct connection between the Bush administration's ability to deploy linguistic games, a public ill-equipped to engage in productive critique of such games, and the right-wing assault on higher education. For the U.S. public, and especially the nation's youth, to be sufficiently "loyal" to the war effort, it was essential that they uncritically accept statements like "Mission Accomplished," that they allow prisoners of war to be called "enemy combatants," and that they believe that "democracy" has been successfully brought to both Iraq and Afghanistan. Asking questions about such claims is characterized by the Right as an intolerable threat to the state and to the "core values" of American society. According to Lauren Berlant the Bush government depended on an affective public rather than a rational critical public, and, since 9/11, dissent has been linked with amorality and anti-Americanism.[12] The post-9/11 culture of fear depends on minimizing the possibilities of civic engagement and critical citizenship, which has led directly to an assault on our nation's youth and on critical pedagogy.[13]

This assault on higher education has not only targeted the critical thinking advocated by left-leaning faculty, it also has promoted a specific geopolitical ideology. As evidenced by the complementary efforts to police area studies and American studies, the post-9/11 right-wing attacks advance a particular vision of the United States and the globe, one that is a direct outgrowth of Pax Americana, manifest destiny, the Cold War, and neoliberal globalization. Keeping this geopolitical agenda in mind, the analysis that follows focuses on American studies, since so-called American beliefs and values have played a pivotal role in the arguments about the anti-Americanism of university teaching. Unquestionably, the meaning, purpose, and political vision of America are at the center of these assaults, just as they are essential tools in swaying public opinion to favor the Right's policies. For instance, Cheney argues that students need to learn more about the great character of America, and she worries that other cultures are celebrated while the United States is criticized. Before 9/11, she wrote: "As American students learn more about the faults of this country and the virtues of other nations, they will be less and less likely to think the country deserves their special support. They will not respond to calls to use American force."[14] Echoing these sentiments a little over a year after the 9/11 attacks, President Bush gave a speech announcing an educational initiative dedicated to teaching America:

> During the last year, our children have seen that lasting achievement in life comes through sacrifice and service. They've seen that evil is real, but that courage and justice can triumph. They've seen that America is a force for good in the world, bringing hope and freedom to other people. In recent events, our children have witnessed the great character of America. Yet they also need to know the great cause of America. They are seeing Americans fight for our country; they also must know why their country is worth fighting for.[15]

Merging Kurtz, Cheney, and Bush's statements, the Right's attempt to capitalize on the culture of fear by advancing a right-wing educational agenda post-9/11 becomes clear. The state of permanent war requires a vigorous defense of the "core values" of American society and depends on a public disinclined to question the government.

In addition to direct attacks on departments and scholars of American studies, the current assaults, such as those sponsored by Horowitz, have attempted to exploit the nation's hyperpatriotism by using the language of freedom, democracy, tolerance, and plurality. It is no coincidence that the right-wing campaigns to protect "academic freedom" resonate with the nation's fight to protect "freedom." Similarly, the Academic Bill of Rights brings to mind the Bill of Rights and arouses patriotism through labeling. Projects like that of Horowitz's Students for Academic Freedom and ACTA project a romantic version of the nation and recall earlier moments when American studies served the interests of the state. But, most importantly, these assaults on higher education display linguistic strategies similar to those used by the Bush administration. They call for a unified and cohesive defense of "civilization" and American "values," which functions as a traditional call for a return to the master narrative of U.S. identity. They also deploy the language of the Left absent its meaning when they clamor, for instance, for a "diversity" of perspectives to be used in the classroom and for more "representative" faculty hiring policies. Language meant to defend the views of the disenfranchised now argues that creationists should be allowed to advocate their beliefs in biology classes, and affirmative action statements meant to rectify gross inequities in professional opportunities now suggest that all departments should hire token Republicans. Thus, one of my key arguments here is that it is a mistake to focus only on the Right's efforts to distill and unify the meaning of America, because, at the same time, they are engaged in an effort to expand that meaning.[16] In this sense, the effort to legislate the study of America can also be read as an effort to deregulate it. Moreover, the Right is not one monolithic front, and the right-wing attacks on higher education stem from three different camps: the neoconservatives who advocate a return to the traditional values of American society, the fundamentalists who are interested in advancing their religious views in the classroom, and the neoliberals who would like to privatize higher education by defunding all forms of public support and social services. This means that the multiple strategies and tactics used by the Right might require a more complex counteroffensive than generally exists among those of us in American studies who have tended to suggest that hegemony is best challenged by relativism, and that the unified, universalist narrative of America is best answered by a story of diversity.

For the sake of generalization about a vast and varied field of study, let us assume that the dominant critical mode of American studies since the 1960s could be figuratively linked to the idea of deregulation and the loosening of laws of meaning. As Gene Wise explains, American studies since the mid-1960s has focused on dismantling the idea of America as an "integrated whole" and has focused, instead on "a proliferation of subcultural studies."[17] The goal has been to turn the motto on the U.S. seal, _E pluribus unum_ (out of many, one), around to _Ex uno plura_ (out of one, many) in order to account for the multiple and diverse cultures and histories that constitute the United States and that were neglected in favor of describing America as a "melting pot." In other words, the desire has been to deregulate the master narrative of U.S. society into an infinite array of micronarratives. Additionally, the influence of poststructuralist relativism on U.S. critical thought has led to a wariness, if not an outright disavowal, of any foundational ideas or critical groundings. For instance, Bruce Kuklick described his 1972 seminal critique of the myth and symbol school as providing "conclusions" that were "mainly negative."[18] The influence that such a negative position has held on the field is worth revisiting, since, as Masao Miyoshi notes, U.S. scholars share "an undeniable common proclivity . . . to fundamentally reject such totalizing concepts as humanity, civilization, history, and justice, and such subtotalities as a region, a nation, a locality, or even any smallest group."[19] This emphasis on difference without reference ultimately strips criticism of its context. The consequence is that advocates of multiculturalism have often been unwilling to link their claims to an ethical, political grounding. Susan Searls Giroux notes that "The limp endorsement and bland acceptance of principles such as 'nondiscrimination,' 'diversity,' and 'openness' _in the abstract_ enabled the Right's ruthless appropriation of the vision and language of multiculturalism, turning fact and history on their heads."[20] The Left's hesitancy in advocating a political vision has made it easy for the Right to appropriate its language at the service of a rightist agenda.

Consequently, this essay considers the disarticulation of language from its ethical grounds as it has been practiced by _both_ the Left and the Right and argues for an engagement of the concepts of legislation and deregulation, meant both literally and figuratively, as a way to ask how these recent assaults have attempted to both contain and expand the study of America. What I suggest is that the seemingly oppositional concepts of legislation and deregulation have actually been intertwined by the Right, a move that then frustrates a critique of these attacks, since the common response to the hegemonic shaping of American studies has been to call for its dereg-ulation. As Michael Hardt and Antonio Negri note in *Empire,* the forma-tion of power today no longer obeys traditional hierarchies, a fact that calls for a new vision of how best to challenge these power structures:

> The affirmation of hybridities and the free play of differences across boundaries, however, is only liberatory in a context where power poses hierarchy exclusively through essential identities, binary divi-sions, and stable oppositions. The structures and logics of power in the contemporary world are entirely immune to the "liberatory" weapons of the postmodernist politics of difference. In fact, Empire too is bent on doing away with those modern forms of sovereignty and on setting differences to play across boundaries. Despite the best intentions, then, the postmodern politics of difference not only is in-effective against but can even coincide with and support the func-tions and practices of imperial rule.[21]

Thus, while I am critiquing certain features of relativist poststructuralist theory, especially as it is practiced in apolitical, watered-down forms, I want to be clear about the extent of my critique. First, as pointed out by Hardt and Negri, these critical methods require rethinking in the con-temporary landscape of political power and hegemonic practice, which themselves depend on a strategy of difference and multiplicity. In fact, as suggested by the work of Bercovitch and Sollors, American identity and power has always depended on establishing a hegemonic fluidity of mean-ing.[22] Second, I suggest along with Donald Lazere that the celebration of difference and the particular absent the political has meant that many of the original critical groundings of these practices have been abandoned and that this retreat has had conservative consequences:

> although most of the advocates of these theoretical lines consider themselves and their causes as politically liberal or progressive, their insistence on unlimited proliferation of localism and diversity—co-incident with an age of unprecedented concentration of economic ownership, political power, and social control by multinational cor-porations and the right wing in America—has had profoundly con-servative consequences in obstructing the kind of unified opposition that progressive constituencies need to counter-act the right.[23]

By suggesting that the deregulation and legislation of American studies can no longer be understood as functionally oppositional, I propose that any effort to challenge the Right's interest in dominating the field requires a reinvigorated commitment to the ethical and political motives behind the notion of diversifying and deconstructing traditional American studies. It should be emphasized, however, that it is a mistake to seamlessly connect the various critical practices that have commonly been used to challenge monolithic versions of America. There is a difference between the effort to deconstruct the meaning of America, the effort to narrate America as a variety of micronarratives, and the conviction that America can be only understood relatively. Deconstruction, relativism, and an emphasis on the particular are not identical critical moves, and arguably can be seen as contradictory. Nevertheless, as Alice Kessler-Harris explains, debates over multiculturalist perspectives on American studies from both the right and the left during the culture wars often merged these perspectives. She notes that the central theme was the "battle over the idea of America" and the methodological moves revolved around unity/universality/synthesis/cohesion versus fragmentation/plurality/multiculturalism/difference.[24] One question at the center of this essay is whether it remains useful to understand these perspectives as politically oppositional. If, in fact, both positions can serve the interests of hegemonic power, then perhaps it is time to reconsider progressive modes of critiquing the "idea of America."

The following arguments, then, make a number of interrelated points. First, I claim that dominant power has consistently deployed a strategic multiplicity of discursive meaning by suggesting that U.S. hegemony is best understood as a chiasmic relationship between *E pluribus unum* and *Ex uno plura*.[25] The history of the will to power in the United States reveals two twin antinomical gestures of legislating and deregulating the meaning of America. The unified, exceptionalist vision of America exemplified by *E pluribus unum* corresponds to an urge to legislate, by containing and defining, the meaning of America. And yet, this history of legislating unification has also, always, been accompanied by desires for expansion and deregulation—*Ex uno plura*—since such unfettered growth is contingent on an ever-expanding, free-floating, decontrolled meaning of America. As a corollary point, I consider the role of American studies as both an accomplice to this history and as a source of dissent. After briefly tracing the history of the field, I suggest that it currently faces extraordinary challenges most obviously because the right-wing accounts of the failures of higher education are influencing public opinion and affecting legislative initiatives. I argue, though, that much of the academic opposition to these events has been to condemn the idea of legislative interference in higher education. Because the critical tendency of left academics has been to argue for a loosening of traditional categories—a "deregulation" of the universalist "idea of America"—they similarly have responded to the right wing's efforts to control universities by affirming the ideal of free, unregulated academic inquiry. However, this ideal mystifies the actual conditions of intellectual labor and student life, which of course rely upon legislation for funding and protection. This negativist critical tendency has been highly problematic. Not only does it run the risk of advancing the privatization of the university by mirroring the rhetoric of neoliberalism, but it also sabotages the development of a critical vision necessary for progressive pedagogy. Contrary to certain poststructuralist positions that celebrate the free flow of signification, there is no inherent good in deregulation, nor is there an inherent evil in legislation. The free flow of meaning is politically critical when it opposes a fixed and tyrannical legislative agenda, such as the Right's attempt to shape American studies to serve its ideological needs. A defense against the Right's attacks on higher education, however, also requires a collaborative effort to seek legislative support for higher education in the form, for example, of affordable tuition, aid for underfunded areas of study, improved labor conditions for contingent faculty, and the protection of valuable archives. In considering the relationship among American studies, the state, and right-wing ideology as they converge in higher education policy, I hope to suggest that American studies scholars are uniquely positioned to intervene in the assault on U.S. universities. Now that it is clear that the Right has had significant success in pushing its agenda, it is time to reflect on how trends in American studies may have facilitated these attacks. Certainly, these observations apply to scholars in other disciplines, but those teaching American studies have a particularly important role to play. When a nation is at war, those who teach about the nation are on the intellectual front line.[26]

There has been much debate over the official beginnings of American studies, but most scholars concur that in its initial version it was a field of consensus, creating what came to be called the "myth and symbol" school, exemplified by the work of scholars such as Henry Nash Smith, F. O. Matthiessen, Leo Marx, and Perry Miller.[27] This history, interestingly, parallels the history of the founding of the United States, where the most common version stresses the creation of one unified nation out of a diverse plurality. In both cases the dominant narrative has been *E pluribus unum*. Nevertheless, this desire to legislate America, both as state and as field of study, was accompanied from the start by a desire to deregulate it. One especially salient example of these twin impulses at the national level is found in the history of the naming of the United States of America, a history that reveals the linguistic power afforded by using a signifier that can morph into strategic multiple meanings. This history narrates a semantic slippage that I argue parallels the slippage of what "America" has meant to American studies. The nation has been able to capitalize on the loose meaning of the term *America*, since it signifies the most powerful nation in the New World as well as an entire hemisphere. Moreover, the United States of America is one of the few nations in the hemisphere whose name has little connection to the specific territory that it designates. Canada, for instance, comes from the Huron-Iroquois word for "village," Brazil carries the name of its major early export, and Mexico, incidentally also a "United States," is named after the Mexica branch of the Aztecs.

Originating from Martin Waldesmuller's map for South America from 1507, *America* eventually replaced the use of the term *Indias Occidentales,* Columbus's name for the region he had encountered. This effort to rename had a major impact on the ways that the indigenous peoples imagined their connection to the land, for even though they retained their own place-names, the new, imposed names carried with them the weight of colonial power. The use of the term *America* is largely attributed to the efforts of the creole intellectuals of the hemisphere who sought to create linguistic and material distance between the colonies and their colonizers. The etymology of *America,* the feminine, latinized form of *Amerigo,* is carefully parsed by Djelal Kadir who points out that *America* signifies an interesting tension between the "new land" that is "clear," "bright," "shining," "ever young," "ever fair" and "Nowhereland."[28] Hence, the name itself carries a number of key signifiers that were central to the identity of the United States, for the term suggests a sense of constant renewal in conjunction with a spirit that cannot be territorially contained. Even though the term originally designated the southern region of the New World, it later migrated to refer more specifically to the north, appearing with the qualifiers of *Latin, South,* or *Central* when designating the south.

Within the United States it has become so common to associate *America* with the "United States of America" that few pause to reflect on how a term that previously signified all of the New World came to later shift to largely refer to the most "American" part of America. A few months after Thomas Paine's (1776) *Common Sense* stated that "the cause of America is the cause of all mankind," the thirteen colonies signed the Declaration of Independence.[29] While the Declaration of Independence does not formally name the nation-to-be, it hints at its future direction when it refers to the region as "the thirteen united States of America."[30] In the passage from colonies to states the number thirteen loses its capitalization and ceases to function as part of a name, becoming merely an adjective alongside "united." The fact that the number thirteen was dropped from later documents indicates that it was no longer useful to limit the number of states in the confederacy.

Next, the Articles of Confederation, ratified in 1781, gave the territory its first postcolonial name. Ben Franklin's 1775 draft to the final document reveals the deliberations over the new nation's name: "The Name of this Confederacy shall henceforth be the United Colonies of *North* America."[31] However, the final ratified version of the document reads: "The Stile of this Confederacy shall be 'The United States of America.'"[32] Franklin's qualifying "North" no longer remains and his use of "Colonies" is logically abandoned. Most importantly, the name avoids any markers that tie it to a specific part of the hemisphere. Thus, the region is initially named by its first peoples, only to have many of those names forcefully erased by the colonizers. Then, in an effort to indicate the shift from colony to modern state, the creole elites across the region favor the term *America*. Next the word morphs to refer more specifically to only one of the nations of the American hemisphere. The United States was the only nation in the New World to use *America* in its official title, an early sign of how it would be the United States that would alternately use the term to refer to itself, the entire hemisphere, and most importantly to a set of "American" values. The signifying of the United States of America is an example of the intersections of *E pluribus unum* and *Ex uno plura*. The act of defining was also an act of loosening representational fixity, and the designation of the *United* States simultaneously alluded to its diverse zones of influence. Unity was connected to expansion. Legislation was tied to deregulation. Linguistic manipulation was tied to power.[33]

Despite the fact that conservative versions of American history would like to stress what Robert E. Spiller described as the "total and autonomous" nature of American culture, the meaning and physical space attached to the term *America* have always been in flux, and, for the most part, since the Articles of Confederation the flow has been one of U.S. expansion.[34] To a certain extent, the United Sates has increasingly enlarged its sphere of power both territorially and ideologically since it was founded. This fact is acutely visible in the region of the American hemisphere itself where the United States invaded or intervened in the politics of Latin America on eighty-five separate occasions from 1846 to 1996. It has also attempted to control the meaning of the word *America* as well. In one example, the Monroe Doctrine (1823), which served to designate the United States as the main regional power, suggested that *America* referred to the hemisphere but that it was the United States that should control its meaning. The 1840s notion of manifest destiny, which argued that the United States had a divine mission to expand to all sectors of the continent, was shortly followed by the establishment of a new border for the nation via the 1848 Treaty of Guadalupe Hidalgo. Each of these cases illustrates how the concept of America has been simultaneously loose and fixed. In a lesson that indicates the political limits of celebrating linguistic fluidity, the slippage over the meaning of America is not a slippage that reduces power; it is a looseness of language that increases power. The decentered signification of the word *America* has not served to reduce zones of influence, but rather to ensure them. Of course, both the concentrated and the expansionist definitions of America have been contested and critiqued, but none of these challenges has yet to thwart their persistence.

Reconsidering the early work of American studies scholars reveals a similar dual impulse to define and unify while simultaneously expanding into new terrain. In 1979 Wise noted the links between the nation's history and the field of study dedicated to it:

For a movement so critical of the culture around it, American Studies recapitulates America in revealing ways. Both began as revolts against the established order—for America, the Old World, for American Studies, the traditional disciplines. In contesting the old, both have articulated visions of a new and better order; and the insecurity of identifying with an *ought* rather than an *is* has compelled each to continue asking, "Who are we?" and "Where are we heading?" In seeking answers to these questions, neither has been particularly informed by history. Or rather, America has been informed more by fables of its past than by intimate communion with its actual past, and until lately American Studies has had little sense of its own history at all.[35]

The pioneers of American studies were pushing intellectual frontiers, and even though they have been condemned for their seemingly homogenous narrative of American culture, in their day they were radicals.[36] They were radical in their rejection of Europe as the defining source of cultural value and radical in their desire to create interdisciplinary programs that granted graduate degrees for work done in various departments. Wise described these practices as "the obsession to give order, *explanation,* to America's experience, and the will to break through scholarly conventions blocking that quest."[37] Beginning with the work of Vernon Louis Parrington's *Main Currents in American Thought* (1927),[38] scholars have noted that the study of America revealed an "urge to impose form upon experience."[39] In other words, the study of America was linked to a quest for a master narrative and a dominant discourse that could formally signify the nation's cultural history. These early texts of American studies, though, were more interested in developing the myth of America than they were dedicated to elucidating its actual material reality. In seeking a cohesive narrative, these early scholars—in a move that echoed that of the founding fathers—developed a mythical national history that was consistently uniform *and* liberally flexible. It is particularly noteworthy that a number of the foundational texts of American studies deal simultaneously with expanding frontiers and building a unified perspective of the land. Texts spanning American studies from Frederick Jackson Turner's *The Frontier in American History* (1921) to Henry Nash Smith's *Virgin Land* (1950) to Alan Trachtenberg's *Brooklyn Bridge* (1965) repeatedly sought to find that which unified "America" through imaginative narratives of the ways that Americans engaged with the land they lived on.[40]

Understanding the intellectual paradigms of the early Americanists further requires attention to its infrastructure and to its connection with the state. The formal institutional origins of American studies are typically located in the 1950s, with the founding of the American Studies Association in 1951 and the inception of a number of degree-granting programs. During the postwar period American studies began to acquire what Wise has called its "corporate" profile with funding from the Carnegies and Rockefellers.[41] These grants were aimed at "expansion," and Wise notes that they included corporate and government funds. Unquestionably the Cold War played a defining role in shaping American studies by establishing the "state/intelligence/foundation" nexus.[42] Demonstrating the intersections of state interest and American studies, the Congress for Cultural Freedom run by the CIA from 1950 to 1967 promoted the "American way" and supported an international propaganda machine that endeavored to convince Western European intellectuals that communism was antithetical to creativity.[43] In a sign of the state's use of linguistic manipulation, Frances Stonor Saunders notes that when American philanthropic or cultural organizations used the word *free* it inevitably pointed to CIA involvement.[44] Michael Bérubé explains that American studies during the Cold War had a highly ambivalent relationship to the state. It functioned as an ideological motor for exporting American culture abroad and it also capitalized on national investment in American studies because "the establishment of the pax Americana required the funding and nourishment of a non-communist left with high-modernist taste in arts and letters."[45] American studies simultaneously benefited and suffered from these investments. So, in another sign of the intersections of *E pluribus unum* and *Ex uno plura,* the United States dedicated government support toward defining a unified vision of American freedom in order to export it.

The myth and symbol work of American studies, which sought to illustrate the contours of American character and American exceptionalism by imposing "form on experience," helped establish American national identity up to and during the Cold War. Kuklick, author of the seminal 1972 essay that sparked the critique of the myth-symbol school, writes that the early American studies scholars "tried to relate intellectual currents to the culture's zeitgeist and to argue that some symbols and myths dominated all America."[46] There are two main critiques of these early Americanists. First, in terms of content, critics of the myth-symbol school contest the master narrative of national coherence. Second, in terms of method, critics challenge the humanism that had "been the primary theoretical assumption in American Studies."[47]

While the challenging of the myth-symbol school was much deserved, there are pitfalls to the forms these critiques took. First, the eschewal of the master narratives generated by the myth-symbol school apparently suggests a rather simple solution: In order to disengage the representative power of the dominant discourse of *E pluribus unum,* America and its history should be described multiply through attention to the particular. But rather than understand national identity as a static, formal narrative, we should consider how the essentialist discourse of Americanism gained its representative power due to the ease with which it facilitated multiple meanings and interpretations. Think, for instance, of the numerous instantiations of the American Dream that demonstrate both its representative fluidity and its consistency. When Langston Hughes writes of "A

Dream Deferred" or Martin Luther King states "I Have a Dream," they take advantage of the fact that the notion of the American Dream is both meaningful and meaningless, that it defines American identity at the same time that it itself is indefinable.[48] As Bercovitch and Sollors have analyzed, the legislative power of these myths turns precisely on their deregulative nature. For Hughes and King a revised version of the American Dream, one that returns to the democratic and egalitarian ideals that are associated with the United States, is worth rescuing. By reminding Americans that they have yet to live up to the promise of America, they attempt to inspire their audience to actively reform American society by bringing the reality closer to the myth.

This observation leads to the second pitfall: The criticism of the early Americanists' humanism led to a distrust of all critical groundings, a move that deflated the field's political potential. Attention to particularity does not ipso facto lead to the abandonment of a critical foundation from which one speaks. Nor does skepticism of the universalist and hypocritical tendencies of the Enlightenment necessitate an abandonment of all of its ideals. As Miyoshi explains, "a totality is not always a monolithic system for the suppression of all differences and marginalities."[49] The rejection of normalizing, official history does not demand a rejection of history. In fact, without some sense of the historical ground over which we struggle to understand the meaning of America, the notion of American studies makes no sense whatsoever. The assumption made by many of the critics of the myth-symbol school that there are two oppositional ways to view America, as either united, totalized, and exceptional or as multiple, antiessentialist, and particular is methodologically flawed and actually reinforces the types of binaries that were the object of postmodern critique. The tendency to hold to this binary has had significant consequences for those critics dedicated to correcting the dominant paradigms of the early Americanists. As Kessler-Harris explains, "the shift to a new pluralism was accompanied by a simultaneous disavowal of notions of common identity, a fragmentation of any unified meaning to the word 'American.'"[50] She goes on to suggest that emphasizing unity and diversity as oppositional rather than relational has had severe consequences for American studies.[51]

These methodological flaws of oppositional, binary thinking were first set into motion in the 1960s when American studies began a radical critique of the state and its ideological infrastructure. By the 1960s, skepticism of the state and of cultural hierarchies became a dominant critical mode for Americanists. Bérubé suggests that after the height of the Cold

War American studies "aligned itself with an anti-imperialist intellectual tradition in which U.S. history and culture are viewed critically."[52] Assumptions of U.S. cultural superiority and exceptionalism were replaced by theories of hegemony and cultural imperialism. Miyoshi notes that the global student revolts of the period signaled a "newly aroused skepticism about dominant central power."[53] These revolutions eventually led to fundamental ideological shifts in American studies that aimed, first, to reassess the field's complicity with dominant power and, second, to redirect that power to the disenfranchised. Later during the culture wars academics called for postnational or "new" American studies in efforts to distance their work from the perceived ideological bias of their predecessors and in order to rectify the master narrative of U.S. identity through counternarratives of pluralism and diversity. Perhaps ironically, perhaps logically, the internationalist interests of the "new" or postnationalist Americanists coincided with changes in the state that included neoliberalism and increased U.S. imperialism.[54] The key difference between the radical critique of American studies of the midsixties and that of the mid-eighties is largely due to a shift in faith in political change and in the value of building solidarity across different groups. Both moments were equally moments of dissent. But the dissent of the midsixties was "broken down" and "worn out," to use Bercovitch's terminology, by the mid-eighties, and critical questioning often began to serve as an end in itself rather than as a call for change.[55]

In a general, simplified sense, there were two dominant, often interrelated, positions taken by the Americanists of the culture wars, both of which continued to trouble the myth of a unified and cohesive national history. First, Americanists dedicated to the study of marginalized peoples offered alternative micronarratives of American identity that were grounded in identity politics. Second, Americanists influenced by poststructuralism challenged the notions of cultural value and condemned the normalizing tendencies of totalizing concepts, like that of the nation. These positions were forcefully attacked by conservatives who perceived that multiculturalism, relativism, and identity politics sought to shatter the "idea of America."[56] Even though these criticisms did describe the new critical turn in American studies, a new "idea of America" emerged. Replacing the master narrative of unified identity was a new master narrative of diverse identity.[57]

Because many critical Americanists of the culture wars focused on the dangers inherent in projecting a unified vision of America, they often overemphasized diversity as an antidote. The defense of diversity, more-over, was linked with relativism and a reluctance to defend political views, since political activism was often viewed as an effort to "manufacture con-sent." An example of the political paralysis caused by such views is cited by Todd Gitlin who recounts failed efforts to rewrite an elementary school textbook in Oakland, California, that resulted from the inability of pro-gressive multiculturalists to achieve common ground.[58] This reluctance to advocate ethical and political positions in a way that can build politically powerful community has often meant that diversity functions as an end in itself, rather than as a means to rectify a hegemonic narrative of American identity and to rescue specific forms of American diversity that have been historically silenced, ignored, and threatened. Instead, a more productive critical move might have been to focus on the tensions between myth and history and power and ideology, rather than on the opposition of unification versus multiplicity. Of course there is much scholarship of American studies that has bypassed such binaries. Clearly a number of scholars such as Bercovitch, Sollors, Kessler-Harris, and others have sug-gested attention to the role of ideology, to the dialectics between descent and consent, and to identity as a relational concept. Scholars like Nikhil Pal Singh have further argued that the counterposing of "multiculturalism and universalism as principal, opposed terms in the culture wars, simplifies a much more unruly set of issues, involving a series of determinations and mediations of both a local and global kind."[59] The point is that there has been a strong tendency in American studies to get beyond such binary thinking, yet the continual need to argue against such perspectives proves their persistence.

In addition to the problem of the binary of unity versus diversity, the emphasis on ontological critique as the critical grounding for identity pol-itics often overshadowed the political and ethical motives for revolutioniz-ing the "melting pot" view of U.S. culture. The problem lies not with em-phasis on understanding America as diverse or on teaching texts and histories that have been marginalized. The problem has to do with the shape and force of arguments about *why* such practices are important. Since the sixties the political arguments about enfranchising the disen-franchised have waned in favor of arguments that exalt diversity for diver-sity's sake. When diversity becomes an inherent good in itself, it ceases to have political weight as a critical position intricately linked to issues of eq-uity and democracy. Taken to its extreme, for instance, the defense of di-versity absent a political ground has led directly to fundamentalist arguments that academic diversity must include the perspectives of creationists and to neoconservative calls to hire Republicans in literature departments. Moreover, absent a political and ethical ground, identity politics, according to Miyoshi, can "easily be played into the hands of corporate management."[60] In university structure it runs the risk of creating factions that undermine pedagogical solidarity. Similarly, the argument for encouraging a plurality of perspectives on national identity overshadowed the desire to bring those oppositional views into productive dialogue. It would be an oversight to ignore the multiple scholars who have been attentive to the need to approach the study of America from multiple perspectives while simultaneously remaining committed to a consistent, political argument, yet I want to stress that, even though many cases of such scholarship exist, they have been eclipsed by the rhetoric of apolitical relativism. As Kessler-Harris explains: "The search for the particular that had underlined and identified a fully pluralist America had repudiated old certainties of consensus, centrality, and truth without creating anything to replace them."[61] Paul Lauter recognized in 1996 that fellow Americanists needed more vigorous political commitment: "The mixed results of sixties activism, the failure of state socialism, and postmodernist skepticism may have helped put the very idea of 'politics' in bad odor. Still, it seems to me that today's vicious cost-cutting, the efforts to shift higher education toward job training, the deployment of the label 'politically correct' to malign opposition—these and other features of higher education politics create a climate inimical to American Studies."[62]

The post-9/11 right-wing assaults on academic freedom and higher education have built on the arguments of the culture wars and capitalized on the state of fear and sense of vulnerability felt by a nation engaged in a permanent and unbounded war. During the culture wars the right-wing assaults on American studies argued that multiculturalism, identity politics, and political correctness would destroy the nation's core values. They sought to strip public support of arts and humanities funding and launched a "mass-based cultural offensive" against the "so-called evils of political correctness and multiculturalism."[63] But the successes of the Right were tempered in large part because it was generally accepted that the traditional canon and the American ideal needed to be reevaluated to reflect American diversity. While the Right succeeded in reducing public support for the humanities, it arguably lost the debates over the canon and over the traditional image of the United States.[64]

The events of 9/11 and the War on Terror enabled the Right to find a way to turn the losses of the culture wars into gains. The more recent attacks on higher education echo those of the culture wars when they claim that multicultural curricula constitute a threat to the foundation of American civilization, but they have gained persuasive power by adding the post-9/11 caveat that this threat has dire consequences for a nation that must be united in war. However, what is most disturbing is the ease with which the Right has appropriated the critical Americanists' quest for diversity, plurality, and difference. In the transition from the culture wars to the War on Terror, for instance, the call to foster cultural diversity in faculty, students, and curricula has now become a charge to defend conservative views of national history. Rather than argue against multiculturalism, groups like Horowitz's Students for Academic Freedom claim that they are defending the important intellectual values of "pluralism" and "diversity." The fourth point of the Academic Bill of Rights, for instance, states that truth is relative: "Curricula and reading lists in the humanities and social sciences should reflect the uncertainty and unsettled character of all human knowledge in these areas by providing students with dissenting sources and viewpoints where appropriate."[65] These groups claim that because truth is relative and because there should be no hierarchy to knowledge, all viewpoints must be included, especially those of the Right. In another telling example of a progressive pedagogical notion turned on its head, NoIndoctrination.org's mission is to "give a voice to the voiceless."[66] How does it become possible to refer to conservative students as "voiceless" when the nation is currently waging a war with untold Iraqi and Afghan civilian casualties and when U.S. poverty is on the rise? How did the notion of the voiceless become so painfully stripped of its tragic edge?

The Right has been successful in launching such an offensive, in part, because it has dominated the public's definition of America. For instance, Lynn Cheney, whom George Will once described as the "secretary of domestic defense," has capitalized on the public's fear that American values are under siege. A battle-worn culture warrior, Cheney was president of the National Endowment of the Humanities from 1986 to 1993, during which time she consistently attacked multicultural views of America; in 1995, she cofounded ACTA. Since 9/11 she has published two children's books, *America: A Patriotic Primer* (2002) and *When Washington Crossed the Delaware: A Wintertime Story for Young Patriots* (2004). In her introduction to the first, she provides her own spin to Thomas Paine's famous association of America with the world, but, in contrast to Paine, she reads U.S. history as an already accomplished neoliberal success story: "We have benefited from the freedom we have enjoyed, and so has all of humankind."[67] In her book on Washington she further suggests that the United States must be prepared to wage war to protect itself because "our existence as a free and independent nation wasn't always assured."[68] Less than a month after the terrorist attacks, she seized the opportunity to link the study of the nation with the war effort: "At a time of national crisis, I think it is particularly apparent that we need to encourage the study of our past. . . . We need to know, in a war, exactly what is at stake."[69] ACTA, via reports prepared by Martin and Neal, quickly exploited the public panic after 9/11 in order to accuse academia of anti-Americanism, to claim that curricula did not prepare students to defend American values or understand American history, and to suggest that general education has abandoned a "solid" "core" in favor of a "cafeteria style" selection of "odd" topics.[70] But these arguments to more vigorously defend the meaning of America by legislating a more traditional curriculum in order to unite America were also accompanied by a key expansion. In their appropriation of the language of diversity, the Right now argues that teaching a critical view of America is indoctrination and that, in order to foster academic freedom, we must teach students conservative views of their nation's history. For instance, Neal testified before Congress on the intellectual bias of higher education: "Rather than fostering intellectual diversity—the robust exchange of ideas traditionally viewed as the very essence of a college education—our colleges and universities are increasingly bastions of political correctness, hostile to the free exchange of ideas."[71] ACTA argues that all faculty must be united in their defense of American civilization against terrorism, and that students are not presented with sufficient "diversity" of opinions. In a remarkable manipulation of signification, critical thinking equals political correctness which equals indoctrination (or terrorism), and "intellectual diversity" is code for right-wing views.

These contradictions are particularly visible in the presidential initiatives cited earlier that dedicated funding for the study of America via the National Endowment for the Humanities "We the People" grants. These funds represent a clear example of the complexities that flow from criticizing legislation per se. On the one hand, these grants support a variety of academic projects that have the potential to advance our critical awareness of America, through, for example, funds for the preservation of indigenous languages and rare documents and via much-needed public support for the humanities. On the other hand, these grants are marked by a very specific ideological agenda that is fundamentally contrary to academic freedom. In an NEH-sponsored essay contest, "The Idea of America," high school juniors are asked to write about the Cold War while responding to the following questions: "How were the tenets of these totalitarian movements different from the ideals that unite Americans? How did the ideals embodied in the American founding prevail?"[72] Even though students are told to include "all sides of the question," it is clear that essays should not take issue with the premises embedded in the guiding questions. Consequently, these funds foster patriotism rather than critical awareness of U.S. history, and, because they represent significant funding sources for Americanists, it is possible that they will considerably influence the future of American studies. Critical Americanists need to confront this legislation carefully, by first, welcoming federal investment in American studies, and then by forcefully rejecting any intellectual scripting. Arguments must be made that American studies is possibly the field in U.S. institutions most vulnerable to manipulation of academic freedom and that, in the interest of the free pursuit of knowledge, it is essential that academic work critical of the United States be *encouraged*. For American studies to function as a legitimate field of inquiry, it must shed its image as a propaganda tool incapable of generating "new" knowledge.[73]

In yet another remarkable linguistic sleight of meaning, groups like Students for Academic Freedom argue that they are defending academic freedom while attacking it. The Academic Bill of Rights asserts that the premise of academic freedom is that "human knowledge is a never-ending pursuit of the truth."[74] But, in fact, the premise of the American Association of University Professors' 1940 statement is the following: "The common good depends upon the free search for truth and its free exposition."[75] Challenging these right-wing attacks calls for reminding the public of what the Right has tried to erase by shifting the meaning of academic freedom. Why has the Right consistently avoided mention of the "common good" as the foundation for academic freedom? In redefining academic freedom, the Right has stripped it of its progressive charge to link education with democracy, a feat facilitated by intellectual antifoundationalism. What if the arguments to change the "idea of America" from one of unity to one of diversity had been grounded in a polyvalent and dialogic vision of the common good and not on arguments about the relativity of truth claims? Would the Right be enjoying the same success? How did relativism and multiculturalism become mantras rather than strategic challenges to the distorted truths of dominant power?

Americanists' silence on these issues is visible in the American Studies

Association's "Intellectual Freedom in a Time of War," written to condemn the government incursions into academic freedom via the USA PATRIOT Act, the limiting of the Freedom of Information Act, the monitoring of foreign students, and the post-9/11 climate of censorship reminiscent of the McCarthy era. The document's overall stance is to claim that free academic inquiry cannot take place in an atmosphere of vigilance and hostility: "We affirm our commitment to classrooms where ideas are exchanged freely; to libraries where scholars can work free from intimidation for their political beliefs; to laboratories where students and teachers are free from suspicion because of their ethnic affiliations; and to campuses open to the widest range of opinions."[76] Points well taken, to be sure. What is missing, though, is a positive counterargument that highlights the important role that education plays in the construction of civil society. This deregulative position, ironically, ignores the fact that the humanities need state and federal support to survive in a university system that is increasingly privatized and where academic labor is more often piecemeal than secure. Moreover, in the face of the current legislation aimed at monitoring syllabi and curricula, critical thinking about American studies will depend, in part, on legislation that protects academics from government control.

Henry Giroux and Susan Searls Giroux, echoing Simone de Beauvoir, argue that "Critical citizens aren't born, they're made, and unless citizens are critically educated and well-informed, democracy is doomed to failure."[77] Those of us who teach America to Americans are able to reveal how America is simultaneously a story of democracy and imperialism, of one nation and an entire hemisphere, of solidarity and capitalism, of oppression and resistance. We should ask students to consider why the Right has created a synonymous relationship between "America" and "freedom." If America defines freedom for the world and if the United States has brought freedom to Iraq, then how will the Iraqis ever be sovereign? We can teach students to understand how U.S. history led to a problematic association of democracy, justice, rights, and freedom with national identity, and then we can teach them to struggle to resignify those words by linking language and social action. Because discourses of power, like those of the Bush regime, rely on the fluidity of master narratives, it is essential that we teach students to understand the complex ways that national myths are created, disseminated, and legitimated. Attention must also be paid to rectifying the historical repression of many of the other diverse stories of "American" identity, and this must be done not in celebration of diversity for diversity's sake, but in a concerted effort to reshape and simultaneously question the power of dominant ideology. Critical thinking depends on struggling for "social agency," and "educated hope" in the post-9/11 era depends on dismantling right-wing nationalism with vision and critique, engagement and transformation.[78] Then and only then can we respond to Ariel Dorfman's call to teach our leaders the word for "peace."

NOTES

An earlier version of this work originally appeared in *CR: The New Centennial Review* 8.1 (2008) published by Michigan State University Press.

Special thanks to Steven Thomas for comments on this essay.

Ariel Dorfman, "Christopher Columbus Has Words from the Other Side of Death for Captain John Whyte, Who Rebaptized Saddam International Airport as His Troops Rolled Into It," http://www.tomdispatch.com/index.mhtml?pid=590, accessed July 9, 2004.

1. See David Corn, *The Lies of George W. Bush: Mastering the Politics of Deception* (New York: Crown, 2003). Also see Lauren Berlant, "The Epistemology of State Emotion," in *Dissent in Dangerous Times,* ed. Austin Sarat (Ann Arbor: University of Michigan Press, 2005), 46–80.

2. Susan Sontag, "Regarding the Torture of Others: Notes on What Has Been Done—and Why—to Prisoners, by Americans," *New York Times Magazine,* May 23, 2004, 25.

3. Oliver Poole and Alec Russell, "I Am a Survivor, Rumsfeld Tells His Troops," *Telegraph,* May 14, 2004, http://www.telegraph.co.uk/news/main.jhtml?xml=/news/2004/05/14/wirq114.xml&sSheet=/news/2004/05/14/ixnew stop.html, accessed July 9, 2004.

4. Ibid.

5. Sacvan Bercovitch, *The Puritan Origins of the American Self* (New Haven: Yale University Press, 1975), 109.

6. Stanley Kurtz, "Students Fight Back: Introducing NoIndoctrination.org," *National Review Online,* December 2, 2002, http://www.nationalreview.com/kurtz/kurtz120202.asp, accessed July 9, 2004.

7. Vijay Prashad, "An Academic Front of the Right," *Frontline* 22.2 (2005), http://www.frontlineonnet.com/fl2202/stories/20050128000606400.htm, accessed July 9, 2004.

8. American Council of Trustees and Alumni, *Defending Civilization: How Our Universities Are Failing America and What Can Be Done about It* (Washington, D.C.: The Council, 2001), 1.

9. For instance, Karl Rove endorsed Horowitz's *The Art of Political War,* and he has been a guest speaker at ACTA. Pipes was nominated by Bush to serve on the United States Institute of Peace in 2003.

10. American Council of Trustees and Alumni, *Defending Civilization,* 5.

11. David Horowitz, *Unholy Alliance: Radical Islam and the American Left* (Washington, D.C.: Regnery, 2004).

12. Berlant, "Epistemology of State Emotion," 46–47.

13. See Henry Giroux and Susan Searls Giroux, *Take Back Higher Education: Race, Youth, and the Crisis of Democracy in the Post–Civil Rights Era* (New York: Palgrave Macmillan, 2004).

14. Qtd. in Giroux and Giroux, *Take Back Higher Education,* 29.

15. George W. Bush, "President Introduces History & Civic Education Initiatives," September 17, 2002, http://www.whitehouse.gov/news/releases/2002/09/20020917-1.html, accessed July 9, 2004.

16. Sacvan Bercovitch makes a similar reading of John Winthrop's concept of the "city on the hill," arguing that Winthrop crafts consensus through a deliberate use of flexible language. See "A Model of Cultural Transvaluation: Puritanism, Modernity, and New World Rhetoric," in *Early Modern Trans-Atlantic Encounters. England, Spain and the Americas,* 1997 http://web.gc.cuny.edu/dept/renai/conf/Papers/Keynote/Bercovit.htm, accessed June 1, 2007.

17. Gene Wise, "'Paradigm Dramas' in American Studies: A Cultural and Institutional History of the Movement," *American Quarterly* 31 (1979): 314.

18. Bruce Kuklick, "Myth and Symbol in American Studies," in *Locating American Studies: The Evolution of a Discipline,* ed. Lucy Maddox (Baltimore: Johns Hopkins University Press, 1999), 86.

19. Masao Miyoshi, "Ivory Tower in Escrow," in *Learning Places: The Afterlives of Area Studies,* ed. Masao Miyoshi and H. D. Harootunian (Durham, N.C.: Duke University Press, 2002), 41.

20. Susan Searls Giroux, "Playing in the Dark: Racial Repression and the New Campus Crusade for Diversity," *College Literature* 33.4 (2006): 94.

21. Michael Hardt and Antonio Negri, *Empire* (Cambridge: Harvard University Press, 2000), 142.

22. Sollors writes: "The language of consent and descent has been flexibly adapted to the most diverse kinds of ends." Werner Sollors, *Beyond Ethnicity: Consent and Descent in American Culture* (New York: Oxford University Press, 1986), 259. Bercovitch maintains that the Puritans succeeded in "large measure because they so thoroughly committed themselves to the radically unorthodox implications of their rhetoric" (*Puritan Origins,* 109).

23. Donald Lazere, "Postmodern Pluralism and the Retreat from Political Literacy," *JAC* 25.2 (2005): 257.

24. Alice Kessler-Harris, "Cultural Locations: Positioning American Studies in the Great Debate," *American Quarterly* 44.3 (1992): 299–312.

25. I make a related argument about this tendency in an essay on inter-American studies. See Sophia A. McClennen, "Inter-American Studies or Imperial American Studies," *Comparative American Studies* 3 (2005): 393–413.

26. Of course, those scholars who teach the nation's "enemies" in war also occupy the intellectual front line.

27. See Kuklick, "Myth and Symbol."

28. Djelal Kadir, *Columbus and the Ends of the Earth: Europe's Prophetic Rhetoric as Conquering Ideology* (Berkeley and Los Angeles: University of California Press, 1992), 60.

29. Thomas Paine, *Common Sense,* 1776, http://www.constitution.org/civ/comsense.htm, accessed July 9, 2004.

30. Declaration of Independence, July 4, 1776, http://www.law.indiana.edu/uslawdocs/declaration.html, accessed July 9, 2004.

31. Benjamin Franklin, "Franklin's Articles of Confederation," July 21, 1775, http://www.yale.edu/lawweb/avalon/contcong/07-21-75.htm, accessed July 9, 2004; emphasis added.

32. Articles of Confederation, November 15, 1777, http://www.yale.edu/lawweb/avalon/artconf.htm, accessed July 9, 2004.

33. See Bercovitch's *Puritan Origins* for an accounting of this strategy in Puritan rhetoric.

34. Robert E. Spiller, "Unity and Diversity in the Study of American Culture: The American Studies Association in Perspective," *American Quarterly* 25 (1971): 611.

35. Wise, "Paradigm Dramas," 293–94.

36. Spiller, "Unity and Diversity," 612.

37. Wise, "Paradigm Dramas," 303.

38. Vernon Louis Parrington, *Main Currents in American Thought: An Interpretation of American Literature from the Beginnings to 1920* (New York: Harcourt, Brace, 1927).

39. Wise, "Paradigm Dramas," 302.

40. Henry Nash Smith, *Virgin Land: The American West as Symbol and Myth* (Cambridge: Harvard University Press, 1950); Alan Trachtenberg. *Brooklyn Bridge: Fact and Symbol* (New York: Oxford University Press, 1965); Frederick Jackson Turner, *The Frontier in American History* (New York: Holt, Rinehart and Winston, 1962).

41. Wise, "Paradigm Dramas," 308.

42. Bruce Cumings, "Boundary Displacement: Area Studies and International Studies during and after the Cold War," in *Universities and Empire,* ed, Christopher Simpson (New York: New Press, 1998), 173.

43. See Frances Stonor Saunders, *The Cultural Cold War: The CIA and the World of Arts and Letters* (New York: New Press, 2000).

44. Ibid., 135–36.

45. Michael Bérubé, "American Studies without Exceptions," *PMLA* 118.1 (2003): 106.

46. Kuklick, "Myth and Symbol," 79.

47. Jerry Louis Decker, "Dis-Assembling the Machine in the Garden: Antihumanism and the Critique of American Studies," *New Literary History* 23.2 (1992): 282.

48. Langston Hughes, "Let America Be America Again," in *The Collected Poems of Langston Hughes* (New York: Alfred A. Knopf), http://www.poets.org/poems/poems.cfm?prmID=1473, accessed July 9, 2004; Martin Luther King, "I Have a Dream," 1963, http://www.usconstitution.net/dream.html, accessed July 9, 2004.

49. Miyoshi, "Ivory Tower in Escrow," 42–43.

50. Kessler-Harris, "Cultural Locations," 306.

51. Ibid.

52. Michael Bérubé, "The Loyalties of American Studies," *American Quarterly* 56.2 (2004): 226.

53. Miyoshi, "Ivory Tower in Escrow," 40.

54. See Djelal Kadir, "America, the Idea, the Literature," *PMLA* 118.1 (2003): 9–113.

55. Sacvan Bercovitch, *The Rites of Assent: Transformations in the Symbolic Construction of America* (London: Routledge, 1992), 353.

56. Kessler-Harris, "Cultural Locations," 303.

57. This new narrative is described by Bercovitch as the ideology of dissensus, and he points out that such ideologies typically "preclude dialogue" and depend on "programmatic exclusivism." If such ideologies are addressed directly, however, he argues, "the current barbarism of critical debate" could become "a dialogue about common conflicts" (*The Rites of Assent,* 376).

58. Todd Gitlin, *The Twilight of Common Dreams: Why America Is Wracked by Culture Wars* (New York: Henry Holt, 1995).

59. Nikhil Pal Singh, "Culture/Wars: Recoding Empire in an Age of Democracy," *American Quarterly* 50.3 (1998): 470.

60. Miyoshi, "Ivory Tower in Escrow," 46.

61. Kessler-Harris, "Cultural Locations," 343.

62. Paul Lauter, "A Call for (at Least a Little) American Studies Chauvinism," *ASA Newsletter,* 1996, http://www.georgetown.edu/crossroads/AmericanStudiesAssn/newsletter/archive/articles/lauter4.html, accessed July 9, 2004.

63. Henry Giroux, "Post-colonial Ruptures and Democratic Possibilities: Multiculturalism as Anti-racist Pedagogy," *Cultural Critique* 21 (1992): 6.

64. In part, these losses were a consequence of the Right's own ambivalence. Global capital benefits from a public more comfortable with multiculturalism. So the teaching of global cultures served both a Left interested in putting pressure on cultural hegemony and a neoliberal Right that sought to prepare students to fully participate as consumers and workers in a global economy.

65. The Academic Bill of Rights, http://studentsforacademicfreedom.org/, accessed March 3, 2004.

66. NoIndoctrination.org, Mission, http://www.noindoctrination.org/mission.shtml, accessed March 3, 2004.

67. Lynne Cheney, *America: A Patriotic Primer* (New York: Simon and Schuster Children's Publishing, 2002), 1.

68. Lynne Cheney, *When Washington Crossed the Delaware: A Wintertime Story for Young Patriots* (New York: Simon and Schuster Children's Publishing, 2004), 1.

69. Lynne Cheney, "Teaching Our Children about America," Dallas Institute of Humanities and Culture, October 5, 2001, http://www.whitehouse.gov/mrscheney/news/20011005.html, accessed August 8, 2005.

70. Jerry Martin and Anne Neal, 2002. *Restoring America's Legacy: The Challenge of Historical Literacy in the 21st Century,* http://www.goacta.org/publications/Reports/america%27s_legacy.pdf, accessed August 8, 2005.

71. Anne Neal, Testimony before the Senate Health, Education, Labor & Pensions Committee, Hearing on Intellectual Diversity, U.S. House of Representatives, October 29, 2003, http://www.goacta.org/whats_new/Intellectual%20Diversity%20Testimony.htm, accessed August 8, 2005.

72. National Endowment for the Humanities, "Idea of America Essay," http://www.wethepeople.gov/essay/archive/2005/2005question.html, accessed August 8, 2005.

73. See Paul A. Bové, "Can American Studies Be Area Studies?" in Miyoshi and Harootunian, *Learning Places,* 206–30.

74. Academic Bill of Rights.

75. American Association of University Professors, 1940 Statement of Principles on Academic Freedom and Tenure, http://www.aaup.org/statements/Redbook/1940stat.htm, accessed March 3, 2004.

76. American Studies Association, "Intellectual Freedom in a Time of War," March 2003, *ASA Newsletter,* http://www.georgetown.edu/crossroads/American StudiesAssn/newsletter/archive/newsarchive/freedom.htm, accessed March 3, 2004.

77. Giroux and Giroux, *Take Back Higher Education,* 257.

78. These terms are Henry Giroux's and they appear throughout his work, for example in Giroux and Giroux, *Take Back Higher Education.*

ACADEMIC FREEDOM AND THE
CORPORATE UNIVERSITY

OPPRESSIVE PEDAGOGY

Some Reflections on Campus Democracy

Vijay Prashad

A FEW YEARS AGO, AFTER 9/11, my dean called me for a meeting.[1] It was a pleasant enough day, a little chilly and overcast, but nothing dramatic. I walked across the beautiful campus of the private liberal arts college where I teach in Connecticut. Along the way, I greeted and was greeted by students, staff, and other faculty. My geniality felt a little forced, because I was anxious about what awaited me at my walk's end. The dean and I had a fractious relationship, although it was neither personally unpleasant nor professionally threatening. This time, the dean's call had been brief and the summons immediate. His expression was grave. I sat in one of the plush chairs in an office that seemed unusually empty of the books that normally clutter the shelves of an academic room. He was polite, and he asked how I had been. Then he told me that he had received a few letters that accused me of being a communist and an agent of foreign powers. He laid out the facts in the letters, and then, leaned toward me, touched my wrist and asked if the college could do anything to ensure my safety.

I was shocked. Not by the letters, for those are now frequent. My email, answering machine, and mailbox are familiar with the bile of different kinds of hateful political forces. There is even a website that asks for my head. Nothing tops that. What surprised me was the dean's reaction: he could care less about the actual allegations, and was simply worried about my well-being. As I walked back to my office, in a daze, I thought about my position of privilege. The letters that came to the dean were filled with poor English grammar, misspellings, and outrageous accusations. They could not be taken seriously in themselves, particularly when they were being hurled at a tenured professor at a private college. Of course, the same dean, before 9/11, challenged my right to teach a course on Marx, but on this score, he was upright. The braying of the multitude, even if correct, could not assail the comfortable position of the tenured professor. My academic and political freedom trumped their prejudices.

Still, the idea of the "campus radical," the domesticated rabble-rouser who provides the academy with its illusion of ideological diversity, concerned me. As long as the radical is in a minority, as long as the radical is unable to drive campus culture, nothing is threatened. To consider the problem of "academic freedom" and the recent assaults on individual faculty members on the terrain of their right to assert certain opinions, without an analysis of how many of us get away with what we do and say, or even get our views promoted, is insufficient. Shouldn't we at least be asking who gets to even hear our views or can afford to sit in our classes? Campus democracy needs to be understood on a far greater canvas than in the terms of "academic freedom." We have to be alert to the fact that it is this narrowed notion of democracy (academic freedom) that allows our intellectual institutions to get away with a great deal of undemocratic activity.

I recently came upon a survey that helped me widen the way I understand campus democracy. It comes from two up-and-coming social scientists (Harvard University's Neil Goss and George Mason University's Solon Simmons). Their survey of a thousand U.S. residents, conducted for the American Association of University Professors (AAUP), shows that twice the number of those asked have confidence in the U.S. academy than have confidence in the White House.[2] Despite the assaults on the academy by the right wing, the public's faith in the major academic institutions remains. They have not entirely bought the view that higher education is compromised by its liberalism or radicalism. It helps of course that President George W. Bush has such a low standing, so the comparison might not be fair. When asked to name the biggest problem facing higher education, a plurality (42.8 percent) pointed to "the high cost of college tuition," while 17 percent worried about "binge drinking by college students." Only a small number focused on the issue of "political bias in the classroom" (8.2 percent) and "incompetent professors" (5 percent).[3] Add the latter together and you get more people worried about campus larceny and debauchery than about either political indoctrination or incompetence.

The question of affordability of higher education is salient to any discussion of academic freedom. A survey of 850 U.S. residents in the year 2000 found that less than a tenth of adults who enjoy a family income of between $30,000 and $75,000 believe that college education is affordable. Those who make less than $30,000 fear that their children won't be able to go to college, and those who make more than $75,000 also have their misgivings about college costs.[4] A 2005 study by the College Board found that both public and private colleges are increasingly unaffordable to all U.S. residents, but of course among the lowest income earners and wealth holders, the burden is greatest (at public two-year colleges cost of attendance sucks up more than a third of the family income for those in the lowest family income quartile).[5] These high prices come at a time when the buying power of family incomes has declined, and when outright grants given to those who need it have been replaced by merit-driven (public and private) loans. Yet, there seems to be no let up in the desire of young people to go to college (in October 2005, almost 70 percent of high school graduates went to some kind of college).[6]

Campuses, therefore, are now home to students whose families and whose own labor is taxed highly to pay for their education. The increased level of student indebtedness and the pressure to work during college years structures the experiences of students during their college years. A U.S. congressional study found that by the 1990s, when the stock market boomed and the good times rolled for the well-off, college debt spiraled out of control. Between 1992 and 1999, annual borrowing for students at four-year public colleges rose by 65 percent, from $1,800 to $3,000. This meant that the average debt for a four-year cycle rose in this period to $15,000. With this burden, the congressional study noted, "students from low income families are often unable to support loans after graduation."[7]

If this is the case at public schools, it is not dissimilar at private schools (the cutback in federal aid to public schools is now matched by the decline in stock-market held endowments at most private schools). Three-quarters of students work, and most of them do so not to support their excesses, but to get by; the time spent on the job adversely affects their grades.[8] Among working-class students, the problem is acute. A large number (29 percent) work more than thirty-five hours a week, and of them a majority (53 percent) fail to graduate.[9]

College degrees still provide a boost to the earning power of workers. Young people are driven to college by a desire to learn and by the knowledge that today's college degree is worth the price of yesterday's high school diploma. This flow is unchecked, and it is what makes the higher education market inelastic. Prices skyrocket, and the customers continue to throng at the door. There is little choice when the job offerings are fewer. As jobless growth overcomes the economy, and as nontradable services are the only boom sector in the U.S. job market, the anxiety about getting paid after laying out a large investment in the student increases. The pressure on students to curtail their imagination during their college years is immense. Find a major that guarantees a good job, and spend your time on campus doing as many internships as possible to grease your way into the narrowest of doorways that lead to corporate success. For the neoliberal academy, this is the student's stairway to heaven.

The freedom of the student to enjoy the world of ideas and to seek solutions to planetary problems and opportunities is narrowed. Where is the space for the students to enjoy the ideological and intellectual freedom necessary for critical thought and expression? All the talk about a common core curriculum for a liberal student body is anachronistic, and unaware of the neoliberal reality that tears into the students' ability to think outside their indebtedness. This is not to say that our students are always worried about debt, and unable to be creative and bold with their ideas. Rather that the problem of debt in the context of jobless growth inhibits all but the most intellectually driven students, and this debt consciousness contributes to the nihilism felt by many toward our social institutions (the binge drinking is a symptom of the problem, not a problem *sui generis*).

What does all this have to do with academic freedom? The debate over the political commitments and views of the faculty is a red herring. It ignores the academy's main problem with contemporary higher education: the tendency for higher education to become increasingly vocational and less intellectual. This is not the fault of the student or of television or other such cultural shifts alone, but it is the necessary consequence of the way "education" has become one more capital input into the worker-commodity. The freedom of our students to think is not encroached upon by this or that individual faculty member, but by increased costs for higher education, a lack of federal support for these costs, and the fears of joblessness and indebtedness associated with both these high costs and the decreased number of lucrative careers in the offing. Helen Lowery of Boston University put it bluntly, "I really want to work in advocacy law," she told the

Christian Science Monitor, "but from a practical perspective that's not going to happen. I just won't be able to pay back my loans."[10] No wonder the survey found a plurality worried more about college tuition than about the academic freedom of the faculty.

A previous president of my college had the indelicacy to use current corporate jargon when speaking to the faculty. I learned from him the term *blue skying* (thinking outside material constraints), and he once tried to get me to go with him on a fund-raising junket to Europe ("Wheels-up time is 9:00 a.m.," he said in tune with my mumbled demur). He wore corporate blue suits and walked around with a posse of vice presidents, all dressed in corporate livery, each brandishing a folder. They looked like a militia, strolling around the campus, measuring the fat, eagerly, hungrily cutting, cutting, cutting. And yet, spending, spending, spending on noncurricular hardware.

Nothing about this president and his gang is unique. They are now part of the normal fabric of U.S. higher education. Indeed, the campus is no longer an "ivory tower" or a "city on the hill." It more closely resembles that other major culture-creating institution, the U.S. Corporation. Income inequality (between the president and the janitor) is stark, but this is only the most vulgar instance of the convergence of academic and corporate cultures. The assault on campus unions that try to provide a living wage for the workers, on graduate student unions that try to get a wage for indentured teachers, on adjuncts who enjoy no security of tenure, *teach* our students that the corporate free market culture is acceptable and that it is rational. As my Trinity colleague Paul Lauter wrote in 2002, "The free market ideology being taught at U.S. universities has to do with winning the hearts and minds of young Americans to the fantasy that their interests are at one with those of Enron and Worldcom executives. Such lessons are reinforced within the multiplying classrooms devoted to promoting enterprise, marginalizing labor, submerging the realities of social-class disparity, and above all, promoting the underlying ideological tenet of free market capitalism: individualism."[11]

Elsewhere, Lauter argues that what the university *teaches* in its very structure is the culture of the dominant classes: the president is ensured a sweet retirement package, while the faculty is left with bleak options; a university is lauded for its biomedical discoveries, as the population that surrounds it suffers from medical ills untreated for lack of health insurance and an health care infrastructure; a college pays its "adjunct" teaching staff far below a reasonable wage and justifies this based on pleasant sounding terms like *flex-time;* the university extends its dominion over the neighborhood through gentrification and eminent domain.[12] This culture of the dominant class is a culture of hierarchy. Those who are in the right schools are able to aspire to upward mobility, while others can still hope for something better than their origins. Debt becomes the necessary price to pay for the rewards of a system that is already on display on the campus.

Higher education and K–12 are one of the five major sites for the reproduction of U.S. culture (the others being the state, the military, the corporation [including the media] and religious institutions). Because the academy trains young minds when they are at their most vulnerable, the stakes at this site are immense. That such a large section of the U.S. public goes through the higher education system makes management of this site central to the worries of the dominant class. Compounding these objective fears is the nature of the personnel who staff higher education. An unpredictable fragment of the "new class," the professional and managerial sector, staffs the academy. Cultural critic Michael Denning suggests that this fragment of the "new class" betrays ambivalence between the flanks of capital and labor. Such uncertainty by the cultural authors of so powerful an institution makes the stakes of social control "very great indeed."[13]

Since the late nineteenth century, the "new class" within the academy has periodically faced disciplinary pressures from the dominant class. There is a continuous line of suppression that runs from the expulsion of Populist social scientists in the 1890s to the current assault on critical intellectuals. This struggle is over the immense cultural resources of the academy, and how they are deployed for the intellectual and ethical reproduction of the population. Two influential and articulate groups produce in different measures and in separate registers the assault on the "new class." In 1953, the philosopher Sidney Hook called the first group the "cultural vigilantes," among whom he included "political demagogues in *both* political parties, religious fundamentalists in both Catholic and Protestant denominations, and some zealots and marginal types in some patriotic organizations. To these must be added certain lobbyists and advertisers who wish to discount the principles of democratic socialism, the New Deal, the Welfare State. . . . because the economic and social interests they represent would be adversely affected were these principles carried out."[14] Sociologically, Hook's description fits our time, with characters like David Horowitz and his now eponymous center fitting the bill of the "zealots and marginal types," while his enablers, such as Colorado governor Bill Owens (Republican) and Colorado state senator Bob Hagedorn (Democrat) donning the robes of the "political demagogues." The cultural vigilantes draw on a widespread discontent with class hierarchy by painting the institutions of higher education as bastions of elitism; this is their unique ability to draw on mass sentiment and distort popular disgust at hierarchy against this petit bourgeois fragment rather than against bourgeois society and capitalism in general. Many of us intellectuals do ourselves no favors by adopting the mandarin robes of High Culture and setting ourselves apart from the lives and labors of working people. Most of our anxiety about the assault on the "new class" is derived from the populism of the cultural vigilantes, and on their proximity to sections of state power. For politicians, the cry against radicals in the Ivory Tower is a much cheaper way to allay mass concern over the inability to pay for college, than would be actually creating meaningful public policy that opens the doors of higher education to everyone. David Horowitz, for instance, has no plan to address the escalation of costs and tuition. It is far easier for the vigilantes to bemoan elitism and radicalism than actually address the core apprehensions of the public. And because of their ability to influence populist lawmakers who also have no agenda for popular discontent apart from symbolic issues, they are able to make mayhem at public institutions (such as for Ward Churchill at the University of Colorado and Kevin Barrett at the University of Wisconsin). Part of the assault seems calculated with the desire to bash public institutions, and to promote the free-market private model favored by the political demagogues. My liberal New England private college gets a free pass for the time being.

The second group, to upend Sidney Hook, comprises the sanctimonious liberals. These are the guardians of higher education who invoke high-minded principles such as "academic freedom" when it suits them to protect those whom they deem worthy at a certain time. During the McCarthy era, when the vigilantes raised the question of the loyalty of the faculty, it was the liberals who fired them or edged them out on the basis of "academic freedom." An exemplary case comes to us from the University of Washington. On January 22, 1949, the university fired three professors for their relationship with the Communist Party. Dr. Raymond B. Allen, the university's president, defended the action as one that did not abridge the policy of "academic freedom." On the contrary, the removal of the Communists would only strengthen the principle. Communists, Allen wrote a few months later, are not free because they are enslaved "to immutable dogma and to a clandestine organization masquerading as a political party." By joining the legal Communist Party, or being affiliated to it in any way, the teacher has "abdicated control over intellectual life." The classroom, Allen wrote, is a "chapel of democracy," and so, the only teacher who can be allowed into this chapel must be a "free seeker after truth." Indeed, "As the priests of the temple of education, members of the teaching profession have a sacred duty to remove from their ranks the false and robot prophets of Communism or any other doctrine of slavery that seeks to be in, but never of, our traditions of freedom."[15] Hook, who became the leading advocate of anticommunism in the academy, sinisterly wrote of the need for "ethical hygiene" to expunge the profession of Communists.[16]

Allen, and other university presidents, produced a high-minded defense of their assault on certain academics.[17] Their point is simple: to be worthy of the protections of "academic freedom" the faculty member must be an open-minded seeker of the truth and not a dogmatic adherent to received wisdom. Such a principle, of course, immediately excludes anyone who has a religious faith, and whose views are mediated through clerical institutions (such as the Vatican, the Koran, or whatnot). Because the principle appeared so shallow, the philosopher Willis Moore wrote, "Whatever the ostensible goal of the early stages of this restrictive movement, its later intent was the achievement of a settled conservative orthodoxy in the political, economic, and general social opinion of America." The onslaught within the culture industries (including the academy), Moore continued, is designed to undermine "the more humane, idealistic and internationalistic tendencies of the past few decades."[18]

Academic freedom, as Allen bluntly put it, is only to be granted to the intellectual who adopts a solitary pursuit of truth. Anyone who is associated with any organized political change has, by this logic, abdicated his or her intellectual suspicion: the moment you close analysis and act, you have ceased to enjoy the protections of academic freedom. But even this is a selective use of a principle, because it does not apply, as I suggested above, to those who strive for change based on certain theological or even political principles (such as anticommunism). Moore, less enamored by liberal anticommunism, indicates that the crusade on campus was against ideologies and movements that fostered antisystemic change. "Free thinkers" are welcomed if they are gadflies who do not pose a challenge to the system, or if, despite their own political predilections, they worked in the arena of the sciences (where expertise shielded them from the aggression of the political commissars).[19]

Our liberal institutions operate with a general adherence to a concept of academic freedom that is borrowed from John Stuart Mills' 1859 *On Liberty,* where the utilitarian and East India Company official argued that contrary opinions are important, not for themselves, but because they enable society to check its truths, and to ensure that social norms are not in error. We tolerate the campus radical as long as s/he is simply a foil for the correctness of liberal precepts, and as long as s/he does not indulge in any attempt to move a transformative political agenda on the campus culture. This impoverished idea of freedom is valuable for a class society that sees a critique of itself as manageable as its Other, as long as it is constrained. Allen's vulgar statements are not far from the generosity of Mill.

These are not arcane ideas. A majority of those surveyed by the AAUP in 2006 (62.6 percent) said it was acceptable for the university to "dismiss professors who join radical political organizations like the communist party." A small number of people (57 percent) felt that "there's no room in the university for professors who defend the actions of Islamic militants." In this same pool, a majority (61.5 percent) said it was acceptable for a professor to oppose the Iraq War and to "express anti-war views in the classroom."[20] The same dean that worried for my safety challenged my right to teach a Marxist class on *Capital,* because, in his words, "that book is responsible for genocide" (and what about the Bible?).

It is a sign of our times that the academic Left has taken to the principle of academic freedom, not only to defend it against the opportunistic assault of the political Right, but also as a shelter for our opinions. What happened to Ward Churchill and what happens to countless faculty, who, for example, take the side of campus workers or attempt to explain U.S. imperialism's blowback or who fight against the indignity of campus culture for so-called minorities, is to be expected. The academic Left cannot rely upon institutional protection for our adversarial positions; but then again, being embattled and disorganized, this is to be anticipated. When we take positions that challenge the status quo ideology and institutions, particularly in a time of war, we have to find some means to defend our right to those positions. Given the prejudice of academic freedom to protect our individual right to speak, we tend to coast into that safe harbor. This becomes more convenient than defending our right to an opinion based on the social force of the ideas—a defense that is not covered by the institutionally validated horizon of academic freedom. Our political weakness has resulted in agoraphobia. The struggle over "academic freedom," as it is generally constituted, is more than that of a principle, but it is over ideas. The principle is against the creation of the very social force (what the Communist Antonio Gramsci called the ensemble) that would allow our ideas to have cultural valence. That is what makes its defense insufficient.

Alongside a defense of academic freedom, affirmative action, and other such liberal principles, it is imperative that teachers push for a genuine campus democracy. This includes all that we already do, such as give support for the creation of a culture of solidarity over a culture of hierarchy on campus. Unions, collaborative work among students, enriched intellectual debates over contentious issues: all these are fundamental. But none of these are sufficient without the insistence that higher education be a free public good (alongside free preschool). The debate over affirmative action, for instance, is impoverished because all sides accept the neoclassical assumption that educational access is a matter of scarcity and resource allocation. Since there are not enough seats, the colleges have to make some choices of whom to accept. But what if there were enough seats nationwide for all those who wanted to go to college, and what if no one had to compete with anyone else for grants? Colleges would still have to choose their own student body based on a variety of contested factors, but at the very least the applicants would not be barred from entry into campus because of a lack of spaces. In other words, racism and antiracism are not solved by the displacement of neoclassical constraints, but the debate over prejudice will be healthier if it does not occlude the structural problems of scarcity driven by profit-centered and social Darwinist capitalism. If students could come to college on tax money, it would allow them to spend time on ideas and to depart into the world without the albatross of student debt. Their freedom would be greatly enhanced by such a measure.

The call for free higher education is not at all idealistic or utopian. Of the main advanced industrial countries (the 24 OECD states), in only three do public funds cover less than half the costs for college (Japan, South Korea, and the United States). In most of these states, government money accounts for between 70 percent and 90 percent of college costs (Austria, Czech Republic, Denmark, France, Germany, Hungary, Iceland, Ireland, Italy, Mexico, Netherlands, Norway, Portugal, Spain, Sweden, and Turkey). The governments of Australia, Canada, and the United Kingdom contribute between 55 percent and 70 percent of the college bills.[21] As the Labor Institute's Sharon Szymanski found, "the tuition and fees at all public degree granting institutions is approximately $24.7 billion. This is a relatively small amount, equal to approximately 1.3 percent of current federal budgets."[22] A readjustment of military expenditure or corporate tax breaks could easily account for this money. Instead, colleges raise their fees and tuition and make higher education increasingly undemocratic. The campaign for free higher education needs traction, and it needs to be combined with the struggles for affirmative action and for academic freedom.[23] In these scoundrel times, we need more of some things, less of others: more imagination, more resources, more solidarity; less vigilantism, less militarism, less hierarchy.

NOTES

Acknowledgments: Thanks to Malini Johar Schueller and Ashley Dawson for their persistent patience, to Paul Lauter for reading this essay (which draws on many of his ideas), to Amitava Kumar for getting me to think seriously about our profession in the first instance and for a close read of this essay, to Preston Smith for introducing me to the Campaign for Free Higher Education, to the work of Cary Nelson, Evan Watkins, Marc Bousquet, and the people at *Workplace: A Journal for Academic Labor,* on the vocationalization of the university, and to Elisabeth Armstrong for pushing me in directions I didn't even know existed.

1. That dean is now gone, so is the president who appears later in the essay. I now work under a new dean and president, both of whom are aware of the dialectic that constrains and drives academic work in our age.

2. Neil Gross and Solon Simmons, "Americans' Views of Political Bias in the Academy and Academic Freedom," working paper, May 22, 2006, 4. This study was commissioned by the American Association of University Professors and can be downloaded from their website.

3. Ibid., 10–11.

4. S. O. Ikenberry and T. W. Hartle, *Taking Stock: How Americans Judge Quality, Affordability, and Leadership at U. S. Colleges and Universities* (Washington, D. C.: American Council on Education, 2001), 34–35; and Laura W. Perna and Chungyan Li, "College Affordability: Implications for College Opportunity," *NASFAA Journal of Student Financial Aid* 36.1 (2006): 8.

5. The College Board, *Trends in College Pricing* (Washington, D.C.: College Board, 2005), quoted in Perna and Li, "College Affordability," 17.

6. *College Enrollment and Work Activity of High School Graduates* (Washington, D. C.: Bureau of Labor Statistics, 2006).

7. *Empty Promises: The Myth of College Access in America: A Report of the Advisory Committee on Student Financial Assistance* (Washington, D.C.: Advisory Committee on Student Financial Assistance, 2002), 11–13.

8. Ibid., 11; and Tracey King and Ellynne Bannon, *At What Cost? The Price That Working Students Pay for a College Education* (Washington, D.C.: Public Interest Research Group, 2002), 2–3.

9. *Access Denied: Restoring the Nation's Commitment to Equal Educational Opportunity* (Washington, D. C.: Advisory Committee on Student Financial Assistance, 2001), 11.

10. Chris Gaylord, "For Graduates, Student Loans Turn into an Albatross," *Christian Science Monitor,* May 17, 2006. Janet Kidd Stewart covers the parents' point of view in "College's Major Dilemma: for Love or Money," *Chicago Tribune,* November 6, 2005.

11. Paul Lauter, "From Adelphi to Enron," *Academe* 88.6 (2002): 28–32.

12. Paul Lauter, "Content, Culture, Character," *Works and Day* 21, 41–42 (2003): 51–56.

13. Michael Denning, *Culture in the Age of Three Worlds* (London: Verso, 2004), 134.

14. Sidney Hook, *Heresy, Yes, Conspiracy, No* (New York: John Day, 1953), 11.

15. Raymond B. Allen, "Communists Should Not Teach in American Colleges," *Educational Forum* 13.4 (1949), http://www.writing.upenn.edu/, accessed January 5, 2009. The context of the story is well summarized in Ellen W. Schrecker, *No Ivory Tower: McCarthyism and the Universities* (New York: Oxford University Press, 1986), 94–112.

16. Schrecker, *No Ivory Tower,* 107.

17. For a range of view, mostly in favor of curtailment of communists, see Benjamin Fine, "Majority of College Presidents Are Opposed to Keeping Communists on Their Staffs," *New York Times,* January 30, 1949.

18. Willis Moore, "Causal Factors in the Current Attack on Education," *AAUP Bulletin* 41 (1955): 623–24.

19. This is the view of Noam Chomsky, R. C. Lewontin, and Ray Siever, collected in *The Cold War and the University: Toward an Intellectual History of the Postwar Years* (New York: New Press, 1997).

20. Gross and Simmons, "Americans' Views," 14.

21. Sharon Szymanski, "Free for All: Free Tuition at All Public Colleges and Universities for Students Who Meet Admission Standards," Debs-Jones-Douglass Institute Working Paper, Labor Institute and member of PACE, Local 1-149, 2002, 29.

22. Ibid., 29.

23. Information on the campaign is available at http://www.freehighered.org/. For an excellent call for free higher education, see Preston Smith II and Sharon Szymanski, "Why Political Scientists Should Support Free Public Higher Education," *PS: Political Science and Politics,* October 2003, 699–703.

WHOSE RIGHT TO DECIDE?

Union Busting at NYU and the
Future of Campus Governance

Susan Valentine and Michael Palm

IT WOULD BE DIFFICULT, AND PERHAPS even ill-advised, to map a linear history or affiliational boundaries for a unified academic labor movement; nevertheless, one tempting origin story, especially for grad union organizers such as ourselves, is the formation of the Teaching Assistants Association, TAA-AFT/WFT Local 3220, at the University of Wisconsin–Madison in 1970. Since then, graduate students have organized unions at dozens of colleges and universities across the United States and Canada, including the Universities of Michigan and Massachusetts, as well as the entire University of California system. Today tens of thousands of academic workers, full- and part-time faculty as well as grad students, are unionized. As universities increasingly rely on contingent labor for almost every aspect of their operations, academic unions are understood, by organizers and observers alike, as a reaction to commercial pressures and corporate-style university management. Academic employees routinely organize criticism of their employers, institutions, and industry under the pejorative rubric of "corporatization." The term is imprecise, as the corporate world comprises a welter of competing strategies for managing workers and maximizing productivity, but it functions as a kind of gratifying shorthand for the perceived betrayal of collegiate ideals such as shared governance on campus. A long list of scholarly researchers have concluded that these trends and developments within higher education are detrimental to the production and transmission of knowledge, and corrosive of the rights, well-being, and interests of students as well as the academic workforce.[1]

One key element of academic corporatization involves centralized forms of oversight at colleges and universities, whereby top officials assume (or usurp) ultimate responsibility for all significant decisions on campus. More and more deans, provosts, and presidents are becoming CAOs, or "chief academic officers," and making decisions that conventionally have fallen to students and faculty. Recently, federal and private reports on the state of higher education have recommended further consolidation of power on campus, in order to enhance efficiency and ensure that graduates and postdocs are competitive for jobs.[2] Many academic labor activists expose and try to counter administrators who adopt austere and even draconian new methods for valuing and evaluating individuals and departments on campus. Some academic unions and other labor-based organizations on college campuses have been formed directly in response to trends in campus leadership, while other unions and labor groups have redirected their activism to address centralization and abuses of power. The struggles of academic unions and activists to combat these trends has been analyzed in a variety of publications.[3]

Academic labor organizers often find ourselves on the defensive against accusations from university administrators that unions curtail or prevent academic freedom for academic workers. At New York University, the decision to withdraw recognition of GSOC/UAW (Graduate Student Organizing Committee / United Auto Workers) Local 2110 was informed, at least rhetorically, by perceived violations of the university's "academic freedom," namely the right to hire adjunct professors or graduate students from nearby schools and pay them less than half the amount that graduate assistants (GAs) covered by our contract are paid to perform the same work.[4] Faculty as well as graduate student labor activists continue to bolster arguments against these allegations and find innovative ways to debunk them, but academic labor activists can do more than defend unions against charges from management that they encroach upon academic freedom. What if academic labor activists took it upon ourselves to help define academic freedom? What would "academic freedom" mean, or come to look like, if academic unions developed visions of it—and venues for it—alongside the bread-and-butter demands traditionally bargained over, and the progressive politics promoted by some academic unions on and beyond campus?

Contract language to ensure academic freedom should be considered in situations where good-faith negotiations actually happen. But the history of higher education in the United States is replete with principles of academic freedom being invoked or delineated in order to carve out a set of exclusive rights for privileged strata of academic professionals. A labor orientation toward academic freedom need not be limited to contracts and bargaining units, lest we risk promoting further exclusivity and developing an even narrower and more restrictive concept of who on campus might qualify. But academic labor can help expand visions of academic freedom from the individual (or the institutional) to include the collective. Academic unions can do more than accept the given norms and limits of academic freedom and protect eligible members along those lines. Academic labor organizers and activists can challenge our colleagues' as well as our supervisors' assumptions about what it means to be academically free. Academic labor activists should interrogate "academic freedom" while pursuing collective as well as individual autonomy on campus. How can the security of collective bargaining and the ethos of solidarity help us develop a collective concept of academic freedom?

In this chapter we review and analyze some academic freedoms and unfreedoms at NYU, before, during, and after the 2005–6 strike. At various moments during the strike, labor and management each presented academic freedom as the stakes of the conflict, and even a cursory review of the union-busting campaign at NYU reveals why academic labor activists (indeed, all progressive academics) need to stake a claim in fights, discursive or otherwise, over academic freedom. After reviewing the union-busting campaign at NYU, we end by offering two suggestions, in light of the strike at NYU, about how academic labor organizers can help ensure academic freedom for all, by fighting for forms and norms of shared governance whereby all constituencies—from students to staff to faculty to administrators to our neighbors—have a stake and a say in decision making on campus.

UNION BUSTING AT NYU
✦

A 2004 article, "Star Wars," chronicles NYU's transformation from commuter school to "number one dream school," accomplished in no small part through attracting big-name faculty who add to NYU's reputation through remaking departments and running institutes, while leaving the teaching of undergraduates to untenured junior faculty, adjuncts, and graduate students.[5] That article ends on a hopeful note, viewing successful union campaigns by GSOC/UAW Local 2110 and ACT/UAW Local 7902, and the resurrection of NYU's chapter of the AAUP, as opening salvos to mitigate the worst effects of academic labor's increasing casualization at this university.

But that new hope was to be short-lived. Initial victories at NYU have given way to intense struggles simply to retain what was won. Even after the National Labor Relations Board (NRLB) ruled unanimously in October 2000 that GAs at private institutions had a right to form unions, NYU's administration balked at recognizing GSOC/UAW, and was only compelled to the bargaining table by the threat of a strike.[6] Nearly four years later, in summer 2004, an NLRB now dominated by George W. Bush's appointees overturned the precedent of NYU in a review brought by Brown University, splitting along partisan lines.[7] Here we present an analysis of their tactics and a narrative of their campaign as it has unfolded since *Brown*. Classic techniques such as interference from supervisors (faculty, in this case) and the threat—and the fulfillment—of firings come into play, but the most powerful weapons that the university employed were *delay, deflection, and disinformation.*

Before the Strike

The academic year is both short and shifting, its rhythms requiring students and teachers alike to think in increments of weeks and semesters. NYU administrators, on the other hand, consider fund-raising, hiring, and development projects in terms of years and decades. At NYU, the decision to break the union from the safety of the post-*Brown* legal climate was likely made in a handful of high-level meetings of the University Leadership Team (ULT), presided over by John Sexton, a former law professor hand-picked by the board of trustees in 2001 as NYU's next president.[8] The trustees themselves—or the handful of the most powerful trustee-donors—were likely consulted, along with costly advisors on public relations and legal issues. The ULT had thirteen months between *Brown* and the expiration of GSOC's first contract to develop and roll out its plan to withdraw recognition of the union. This year of "deliberations" over whether to negotiate with GSOC, and the two months between the threats of TAs being fired and the execution of firings, are units of time that comfortably fit their long-term plans, but for those subject to the academic year, even a few weeks of uncertainty can feel like a lifetime.

Methods of deflection aided administrators' ability to sustain long periods of delay. For example, shortly after *Brown* the provost asked two governing bodies—the Faculty Advisory Committee on Academic Priorities and a joint committee comprised of the Senate Academic Affairs Committee and the Senate Executive Committee—to consider the issue and report back at the end of academic year 2004–5. The ULT would make the final decision based on this and other "input." This process had the guise of legitimacy and consultation, although it is no leap to assume the ULT already had its plan in place; "consultation" with these governing bodies offered a patina of campus dialogue. GSOC leaders begged for a hearing with both groups (one relented, one refused), after learning that NYU human resources boss Terry Nolan had made presentations to each. Furthermore, these groups absorbed a lot of the anger from GSOC members, faculty, and the outlying community, while sowing confusions about who actually had control over the final decision.[9]

Disinformation, however, was the favored feature of the ULT campaign. Facts were distorted to characterize grievances over equal pay for equal work as "interference in academic affairs," and to make grads' own fight for self-determination into meddling by "Auto Workers."[10] Figures were distorted to make grads' economic situation appear like middle-class comfort, to make the numbers of people at a rally or on strike at a given time appear small, or to minimize the disruption we were causing on campus. Another, more subtle method of disinformation was the university's strategy of dissociating the gains of the contract from the collective bargaining process that had secured them. Hoping to exploit institutional memory gaps, Sexton repeatedly assured graduates in public forums that they could trust the administration to preserve "competitive financial aid packages." This phrase mystified where those "packages" came from: a year of contract negotiations, after five years of organizing. As a result of the contract—and the organizing—pay rose an average of 40 percent and more than doubled in some departments.[11] Sexton and the ULT retermed the money received by graduates "financial aid," articulating the money solely to student status, and not also to teaching and other labor. Further, terming this money "financial aid" created another history for the "competitive" amounts—one that NYU was invested in giving graduates to attract the most competitive candidates, instead of hard-won rises in pay that NYU had fought back on, and would not have increased if the union had not pressured them to do so.[12]

Benefiting from the August 31, 2005 expiration of our contract, the ULT planned to delay a final decision until that summer, betting that the gestures at community input and deliberation would placate the community who returned that fall to a fait accompli. By May, the two internal governance bodies charged with considering the decision recommended against negotiations.[13] Responding to NYU's continued references to the union's "interference in academic affairs," UAW officials decided to call the administration's bluff.[14] At a May 26 meeting, the UAW offered to drop all current grievances and accept new contract language that NYU preferred concerning academic management rights if NYU would sit down and bargain. Members of the ULT who were present said that they would consider this offer, and made no comments to the university community, to GSOC, or to other UAW representatives for nearly a month.

Finally, on June 16, the ULT broke its silence in a memorandum regarding its "proposed decision" not to negotiate with GSOC/UAW. The memo, from executive vice president Lew and provost McLaughlin, explained that the university had always embraced the view stated in *Brown,* placed "reservations" about the impact of grad unionization in the mouths of an unspecified "many in the community," and returned again to those grievances, which they termed a "failure of the union to abide by the original commitment," and which they had determined could not be remedied by new contract language.[15] Lew and McLaughlin asserted the university's desire "to build on the positive impact of unionization," continuing their strategy to disentangle the gains of the first contract from the mechanism by which they were secured. The memo also announced a thirty-day "notice and comment" period, and provided an email address in addition to a town hall on the matter to be hosted by John Sexton on July 12. The constant pressure from GSOC for discussion had finally resulted in an open forum, but just four days before the decision was to be finalized.

July 12 is about as close to the dead of summer as one can get at a university campus, but GSOC members and supporters from all quarters of NYU turned out in full force, filling a large auditorium.[16] While other members of the ULT and the university's government- and media-relations teams hovered in the balcony or in the side aisles, Sexton stood center stage with a handheld microphone. When he indicated two microphones in the aisles, around fifty people lined up to speak. All but one urged him to reconsider. It was clear from Sexton's tone at the event that he was unprepared for the amount of resistance to the ULT's decision. Despite his insistence at the outset that he was there to listen, not to respond, he quickly became angry and urged the crowd to cease talking about whether NYU should negotiate a new contract and instead focus on the suggested "alternatives" that had comprised the June 16 memo.

Rather than announce the final decision after the end of the notice-and-comment period in late July, as promised, the ULT crafted a take-it-or-leave-it "offer" that it sent to UAW executives in Detroit, offering to let the UAW "represent" the unit if it accepted a set financial package as laid out in the letter, as well as two "poison pills"—no third-party arbitration and an open shop.[17] If the UAW could neither support us in negotiations—of which there were to be none—nor in any challenges to the contract through arbitration, exactly what representation would it be providing? The insistence on an open shop seemed a ploy to suggest that the UAW was more interested in GSOC members' paltry dues than our welfare. But an open shop would also ensure that if we were foolish enough to take this "offer," we would have much less ability to organize a resistance to the next attempt to refuse negotiations. The UAW asked again to sit down at the table and negotiate a real agreement, but NYU refused.[18] The next day, Lew and McLaughlin again addressed the university community via email to announce that "the University will not negotiate a new contract with the UAW and . . . we will implement the financial aid benefits and other proposals" as described in the June 16 memo.[19]

Once the semester began (and after a rally for negotiations attracting over a thousand protesters and featuring the arrest of AFL-CIO president John Sweeney and seventy-five others for peaceful civil disobedience), the administration increased its efforts to undermine the union. Supportive faculty let GSOC activists know of oblique references to "consequences" that might befall any grads who participated in a labor action; messages from the administration disseminated through meetings of department chairs and directors of graduate studies (DGS). While this intimidation had to suffice in the majority of departments (where faculty were uncomfortable with NYU's tactics, if not outright supportive of grads' right to fight back), in the few departments where NYU's administration identified faculty allies, more direct threats ensued. Some DGSs sent emails to their whole departments, highlighting the support of the faculty for the administration's decision and warning against participation in any labor action. Some faculty told their advisees, TAs, and RAs of their antiunion position and explicitly warned that participation in a strike would harm their academic relationships. In October, as GSOC began gearing up for a strike vote, an email to all students and a letter to parents worked to activate class prejudices about "Auto Workers," to spread misleading information about grads' economic conditions and to predict failure—all efforts to discourage potential supporters and intimidate the GAs.[20] In the meantime, GSOC worked with Faculty Democracy, a group formed in response to the erosion of faculty governance at NYU, to secure agreements from faculty to remain neutral and refuse to act against GAs.[21]

On October 24, the day GSOC's strike vote began, graduate assistants in the Graduate School of Arts and Sciences (GSAS), by far the largest pool of TAs and RAs, received an email from GSAS dean Catharine Stimpson.[22] While none of the previous missives from the ULT were addressed to the GAs considering whether or not to strike, this was a personal plea asking us to vote "no." The "open letter" began with a dictionary definition of "responsible: 1 liable to be called to account (to a person or for a thing). 2 morally accountable for one's actions; capable of rational conduct." Though prompting mocking responses among many grads, who were shocked to see a respected scholar and member of NYU's English department employing a literary technique most often seen in high school essays, the import of the letter was serious, including both a plea to a higher moral obligation and a threat:

> Graduate assistants or faculty, we are teachers, morally accountable for being with our students in their classrooms and laboratories. A vote for our accountability as teachers must trump a strike vote and a strike. If we are irresponsible, we are liable to be called to account.

Despite, or perhaps because of, this rhetoric, there was a strong turnout for the strike authorization vote, with 85 percent voting yes. The university's tactics had made many angry, but they had also begun to instill fear, especially in departments in which our organizers had not managed one-on-one conversations about our situation. For GAs for whom contact with the union was comprised mainly of emails, GSOC's was just one voice in the midst of a cacophony from the administration. In cases in which departmental faculty was adding a negative or threatening voice, the sheer weight and power of the antiunion rhetoric meant even committed union supporters were hesitant to strike.

During the Strike

Despite a crowd of over a thousand, and an empty main building on the first day of the strike, NYU spokesman John Beckman called disruption "minimal" and suggested that grads taught only 165 out of 2,700 classes at NYU on a given day, marshaling meaningless numbers to misrepresent our strength.[23] 165 classes seems to refer to the classes on a given day in which grads are the sole instructor of record, such as language courses and intro-level classes in other disciplines. Yet Beckman knew well that GAs were re sponsible for recitation sections and grading in hundreds more courses, and for performing research or administrative work for departments, colloquia, or institutes. As part of a long-term strategy, however, this tactic would pay off: although our members recognized these attempts at disinformation for what they were, especially early when energy was high, these lies could easily become reality for undergrads or faculty who were not paying close attention, or for our members who did not come to the picket line or were not in regular contact with other striking GSOC members. The ULT's threats and disinformation and the pressure on faculty supervisors to warn or threaten were creating discomfort in the NYU community, but their next move would prove more disturbing. When faculty discovered on the first day of the strike that university administrators had been added as observers to their virtual classrooms on the Blackboard website, many faculty, at NYU and elsewhere, saw this action as flat-out spying, and an unforgivable blow to the core of academic freedom.[24]

Unlike "Blackboardgate," the ULT's next move received little attention, yet it would prove decisive in breaking the strike. The administration could successfully ignore professors who grudgingly had to do their own grading or work without a research assistant, or undergrads who were not receiving help with papers or the explication of a lecture. The courses in which GAs were the sole instructors—those 165 each day at John Beckman's count—were another story. TA-led courses in the language and literature departments and the Expository Writing Program make up a majority of these grad student-led courses. Here is where NYU was hardest hit; here is where TAs have strong claims against the "mentorship" rhetoric of *Brown*;[25] here is where they would have to break the strike.

On November 16, a memo to department chairs from Deans Catharine Stimpson, Richard Foley, and Matthew Santirocco announced a "policy change" in language and literature departments.[26] The memo was not circulated broadly, and included no reference to the now weeklong strike. The three deans had heard "concerns that the amount and kinds of teaching that graduate students do" in these courses "interferes with their academic progress and the goal of their teaching being an occasion for their development as teachers," and thus would reduce the workload from two courses per semester to one, beginning in spring 2006. The new policy appeared to be a belated attempt to render these jobs more apprentice-like, and perhaps a bribe to reassure these GAs of the administration's goodwill. Not explicitly stated in the memo, however, was the directive to give the GAs who had been teaching two courses in the fall a "free" semester in the spring, in which NYU would pay roughly the same without demanding teaching in return. This seemed to be the carrot before the stick, but it would prove to be both at once.

We expected the other shoe to drop on November 23, the Wednesday before Thanksgiving. When it had not, many of us welcomed the holiday, exhausted from picketing and the intense pressure of the campaign. Returning the next Monday, we heard it drop loud and clear. Buried in a three-thousand-word email missive from President Sexton were the "consequences": we would not lose our pay for the three weeks that we had been on strike, as we might expect, but instead would be fired for all of next semester if we did not return to work in the next week.[27] The email included a threat of firing for the following fall to boot if we dared come back now and strike again in the spring. As more than five thousand academics from around the world would quickly affirm through an Internet sign-on letter, this ultimatum was not simply punishment for our three-week absence from our work, but retaliation and coercion.[28]

Our first membership meeting that week demonstrated that the ULT had successfully deflected pressure back onto the union, as the fears of hundreds of people resulted in mistrust in every direction. At meetings later that week, however, many agreed with the organizing committee's assessment that we should call NYU's bluff. To discover who was on strike and who was not would be nearly impossible for the administration, as would forcing departments to deny those workers spring appointments, especially in light of faculty neutrality agreements and relative autonomy in hiring. The deluge of letters attacking NYU for these outsized penalties provided additional resolve. But the FAS "policy change" and a new bit of deflection by the ULT would serve to compound our troubles.

The TAs teaching stand-alone courses in the affected departments faced a terrible dilemma—return to work, and enjoy a spring semester free of teaching, with time to devote to neglected dissertations, or stay on strike, and lose their pay when they had been preemptively replaced. As ads seeking temporary "Instructors" to teach three courses of Italian per semester appeared in the *Chronicle of Higher Education,* we realized that NYU was hiring replacement workers without scrutiny, while convincing our members that their sacrifice would be meaningless. Many of the TAs in language courses are international students whose visa status disallows them from work outside the university yet demands that they prove adequate financial support to live here. Despite assurances from the university that no one's visa status would be at risk, many international students felt too vulnerable, with the Bush administration's stance on immigration, to remain on strike. Others took the risk, and around one hundred international students wrote a letter to the university asserting their continued commitment to the cause of unionization and their disappointment in NYU's actions regardless of whether they remained on strike.[29]

In the face of all of this pressure, hundreds of grads prepared to remain on strike past the December 5 deadline. Knowing that this was likely, the ULT took advantage of a new opportunity for delay and deflection. At 4:00 p.m. on Sunday, December 4, as we were planning picketing and fielding phone calls from the press about our plans for the next day, an email from Brian Levine and Rodney Washington of the Graduate Affairs Committee (GAC) appeared via NYU-Direct, the email system restricted to administrators.[30] They asked that the university extend the deadline until Wednesday to let both parties consider a proposal from the GAC, a "compromise" solution resembling a more fully formed version of plans to build on the "positive elements of unionization" from the ULT's July 16 memo. The GAC had never contacted GSOC, and must have had the administration's approval, or it would not have been able to use NYU-Direct. The intended target of the email could only be the NYU community. A few hours later, Sexton and McLaughlin agreed via NYU-Direct, switching the new "deadline" to December 7.

Some undergrads, unclear about the relationship of the GAC to the striking GAs, thought that we had called off the strike. The massive show of resolve planned for Monday's picket line, ripe for media coverage, was suddenly undercut as reporters called asking whether Wednesday was now the "new deadline." Striking GAs had two more days to persevere. Members of the community who were already afraid for the GAs started to consider whether a "third way" was a possibility. By Wednesday the seventh, a group of faculty had adapted Washington and Levine's proposal and presented their refined version of a company union to the community via NYU-Direct, and introduced a resolution in a Faculty of Arts and Science meeting that called for an end to the strike and the removal of the threats. Faculty met with their union-supportive grad students to sell them on the idea, openly in some departments and privately in others, prompting fissures where union support had run high.

Publicly, NYU spokespeople returned to minimizing the disruption that we were causing, and directed press attention toward these proposals as the reason they hesitated to act on their outsized threats. Privately, administrators encouraged more concerned faculty, worried about their grad students and about the labor of their departments come spring, to try to broker "compromises," all of which traded our union, which we had gone on strike to fight for, for the booby prize of no firings and some variation on a company union, bringing us no further than where we started. More than a few teaching assistants faced down their department chairs, their advisors, and respected scholars in their field, as these professors pushed one "deal" or another. On December 7, NYU spokesman Josh Taylor had told the *Washington Square News* that three-quarters of TAs were back at work, perhaps the most egregious piece of disinformation of the whole campaign, at least in public statements, but by the end of the break, it was probably true.[31]

Winter break provided a welcome reprieve, but it also meant we were away from the support of one another, which had helped us immensely in the face of so much pressure. Organizers had little energy to work the phones and urge people to strike in the spring. Over the break many GAs received emails—some innocent, some less so—from the professors to whom they were assigned in the spring, asking if they would be working. (These communications would have been illegal if GAs were covered under the NLRA.) One dean called for a meeting of all the GAs in her school, another instance of management interference, and discussed a separate company union just for them. TAs were moved off of teaching rosters and into fellowship semesters against their will.

Among those who began the semester on strike, very few would return to work. Some sections were simply canceled by professors, preventing administrators from discovering whether their TAs were striking. Although the administration maintained that disruption was minimal and the strike all but over, they followed through with their threats in a few cases, perhaps to scare a few more back to work, or to prevent a resurgence later in the semester. In late January, a few stand-alone instructors received letters that they were losing their spring pay. Clearly these were the easiest targets—if a few students reported that classes were not being met, the administration could act. Directors of graduate studies, undergraduate studies, and department chairs were receiving emails phrased in the negative: "We have heard that So-and-So is not working. Please let us know if this is incorrect information." Other TAs were not assigned spring jobs at all. Overall, twenty-three individuals lost their pay for the entire spring semester. If the firings were intended to scare others back to work, they had the opposite effect: one's returning to work or GSOC's calling off the strike in February would not have restored our colleagues' salaries, as they were fired for the whole semester. But the international outcry that had come when many were threatened did not return when just a few were harmed.

At a town hall meeting on February 8 called by the Graduate Student Council, hundreds of GSOCers filled the room. Only three had been fired at this point, and one of these TAs asked Provost McLaughlin why only three had been fired: did he think there were only three people on strike? McLaughlin explained the policy: a report that a TA was not teaching began a process of investigation that could result in firing. If anyone in the room wanted to tell him that they were not working, he coldly stated, he would be happy to start the process.

We continued to pressure the administration by showing up at trustee meetings and public appearances by Sexton and other university leaders. When circumstances demanded, they reacted to our actions by painting us as a few misguided troublemakers, contrasting us with the majority that had returned back to work, neglecting to mention the coercive actions that forced them there. The misrepresentation of our support reached absurd levels. Speaking at the UN, to an audience including about fifteen GSOCers, with more demonstrating outside, Sexton reacted to our questions by explaining to the assembled that the issue of grad unionization at NYU had been decided "democratically" and "the only people who disagree with that decision are in this room." After spring break, we worked to counter these statements by once again demonstrating majority support among NYU's graduate assistants. In just a few weeks, GSOC organizers scoured the campus, collecting signatures for a petition stating that, regardless of whether GAs had returned to work or stayed on strike, they still wanted a union contract. Before this petition drive was public, another town hall with Sexton at the microphone demonstrated that the ULT would simply switch rhetoric rather than respect the GAs. He told a room full of GSOC supporters that it did not matter if every GA wanted a union contract, the issue had been decided.

After the Strike

Although our strike ended with the academic year, GSOC is still struggling against the university's antiunion campaign. For one, we have grappled with what the university probably hoped would be the final piece of the campaign—replacing the union with an in-house body, derived from that original GAC proposal, itself clearly an echo of the ULT's original July 16 memo. In another instance of improbably coincident timing, the GAC released its final proposal to the *Washington Square News* on April 27, the day GSOC announced majority support for the union (no small feat six months into a now-minority strike) and staged a second mass arrest in protest of NYU's refusal to recognize the union.[32]

Understanding that the ULT would proceed with elections to this "House of Delegates" with or without the consent of the GAs, GSOC members decided to run for seats on this body. Furthering the ULT's attempt to conflate wages for our labors with funding and financial aid, the GAC proposal called for the conclusion of all "fully-funded" graduate students, creating a membership about twice the size of the GSOC bargaining unit, meaning that in some cases whole departments that had not been in the union could both run and vote in the election. Despite these efforts at gerrymandering, GSOC candidates took thirty-seven out of forty-seven seats in the December election.[33] As the democratically elected representatives of a majority of grads at NYU, we will continue to fight for the rights and benefits of our members through this channel as we do through others.

FROM ACADEMIC FREEDOM TO CAMPUS DEMOCRACY
♣

Judith Butler, among others, has written that the "original efforts to secure academic freedom were . . . efforts to clarify and institutionalize a set of employer-employee relationships in an academic setting."[34] In this volume and elsewhere historians have charted a number of political and conceptual debates throughout the twentieth century that inform contemporary understandings of academic freedom. While conceptions of academic freedom may have lurched and shifted over the years, today, according to Ellen Schrecker, "above all, academic freedom is a professional attribute."[35] Although few grad and faculty unions (unlike the AAUP) identify the issue as central to members' concerns, such a thoroughly professionalized history for academic freedom suggests there is a central role for academic labor to play in shaping how we understand and enshrine it. While an academic union (and the AAUP) will defend a member who feels her academic freedom has been denied, academic labor runs the risk of ceding to management the terms of academic freedom.

At NYU our employer continues to insist that academic freedom is outside of our union's purview or jurisdiction. One lesson that academic organizers can take away from the NYU strike: don't let your employer drive a wedge (in either propaganda or contract language) between "academic" and "economic" matters. While the NYU strike was obviously a unique situation, it is reasonable for academic organizers to anticipate administrators at other campus adopting similar antiunion rhetoric and strategies. The experience of GSOC at NYU suggests that academic unions must do more than sharpen defenses against accusations of encroachment upon academic freedom. Before, during, and since the strike, attacking the union as a threat to academic freedom is a fundamental antiunion tactic of NYU administrators and spokespeople. The centrality of this particular tactic in this particular academic labor struggle indicates to us that academic labor activists should begin explicitly including academic freedom among The Things We Are Fighting For. We believe academic organizers can build power by including discussions about academic freedom in conversations with colleagues, and we think academic unions can find ways to account for it in negotiations. Can academic labor, understood more broadly as a professional movement or a personal orientation, develop a new approach to academic freedom? How can academic labor organizers approach issues of academic freedom, orient them toward our own and our colleagues' actual working lives, and expand rather than limit the people on campus who qualify for academic freedom? Here are two ideas we hope will help academic labor activists address these questions.

Academic freedom is collective as well as individual or institutional. One significant debate about academic freedom involves "conflicting claims" and questions of whether and how academic freedoms accrue to individuals and institutions.[36] For example, college and university administrators invoke academic freedom when claiming the right to admit students, hire faculty, and set curriculum without interference. Occasionally these claims conflict with the individual rights of students and faculty, usually their First Amendment free speech rights. Historically academic freedom in the institutional sense involves freedom from "outside forces," namely government. Relationships between universities, the state, and other "outside forces" are beyond the scope of this chapter, but we can note here one pernicious twist, characteristic of "the corporate university": university administrators have begun to invoke institutional academic freedom to insulate themselves from inside forces as well, including students, faculty, and staff. Probably the most relentless talking point in the union-busting campaign at NYU has been to "third-party" the union and portray the UAW as a corrosive external influence. Of course our members would prefer to be recognized as UAW members ourselves ("We are the union"), but the broader point here is that union members, or graduate students more broadly, are not the only affected constituency being systematically excluded from significant decisions on campus.

Supreme Court justice John Paul Stevens has written that "academic freedom thrives not only on the independent and uninhibited exchange of ideas among teachers and students . . . but also, and somewhat inconsistently, on autonomous decision-making by the academy itself."[37] No doubt institutional autonomy was exercised by "the academy" when recognition of GSOC was withdrawn at NYU, but it was exercised by a handful of people, who were appointed (by an even smaller group of people) rather than empowered by consensus or an identifiable majority. Meanwhile literally thousands of students, faculty, and staff at NYU felt utterly shut out of the process. If academic labor were to embrace academic freedom rather than bracket it, then we see two ways organizers and activists can help redefine the relationship between academic freedom and institutional autonomy, which might help prevent such systematic exclusions elsewhere. On the one hand, the mission and spirit of academic unions, academic labor organizing itself, and even the act of self-identifying as an academic worker all help build what Vijay Prashad in this volume calls "the creation of a culture of solidarity over a culture of hierarchy on campus." On the other hand, unions can help systematically include interested parties in significant decisions, rather than systematically exclude them. Here we are referring not only to contracts and bargaining units, but more immediately to coalition building among campus unions and other groups and organizations on campus and in the surrounding communities.

Campus democracy entails academic freedom for all. The principle of self-determination coupled with GSOC's continual ability to maintain majority support among eligible members should be all we need for recognition from our employer. But our members are not the only people with a stake in our union, or in whether or not NYU's administrators recognize our union, or with a stake in how that decision is reached. While support for GSOC at NYU runs high, it was clear last year that disapproval of the decision-making process leading to the withdrawal of recognition ran higher. In other words, many people at NYU support GSOC, more people support graduate students' right to unionize if we democratically choose to do so, and still more people disapprove of how the "decision" to withdraw recognition of GSOC was reached. "Faculty Democracy" at NYU, for example, was formed less in support of GSOC and more in response to faculty's exclusion from the decision in the first place. The group's most powerful statements (as well as most popular in terms of signatures) were those that criticized John Sexton and other administrators directly, not those that offered support for GSOC or that defended the rights of graduate students.

Academic unions already help protect the academic freedom of individual members. In suggesting here that academic labor embrace academic freedom as a labor issue, we are not merely trying to add it to the list of issues that unions advocate for and negotiate over. We encourage academic labor activists to reconsider academic freedom in terms of collective autonomy and campus democracy, principles that should already be central to any academic union's mission. Above and beyond (as well as prior to) pursuing and protecting academic freedom for union members, academic labor can follow Vijay Prashad, who insists in this volume that "campus democracy needs to be understood on a far greater canvas than in the terms of 'academic freedom.'" Prashad reminds us "to be alert to the fact that it is this narrowed notion of democracy (academic freedom) that allows our intellectual institutions to get away with a great deal of undemocratic activity."

The professionalized history of academic freedom gives academic labor license on the term, but it is up to us to claim it. The union-busting campaign at NYU is but one example of why academic labor can no longer afford to let management set the terms of this debate. Academic workers should be free to unionize, and we should not hesitate to identify instances where we are not thus free — not only as violations of the right to unionize, or an "unfreedom of association," but also as instances of specifically *academic* unfreedom. These unfreedoms belong not only to potential union members, but also to all students, faculty, and staff on campuses like NYU. If academic labor can reconceive academic freedom in terms of campus democracy rather than as a set of exclusive, professional rights, then it may be easier for undergraduates and faculty (let alone grad students) to stake a claim in decisions like whether or not certain academics should be free to unionize. By striving to redefine academic freedom as campus democracy, academic labor can help expand the pool of people eligible for it and invested in it far beyond our bargaining units.

NOTES

1. Sheila Slaughter and Larry Leslie, *Academic Capitalism: Politics, Policies, and the Entrepreneurial University* (Baltimore: Johns Hopkins University Press, 1997); Sheila Slaughter and Gary Rhoades, *Academic Capitalism and the New Economy* (Baltimore: Johns Hopkins University Press, 2004); Stanley Aronowitz, *The Knowledge Factory: Dismantling the Corporate University and Creating True Higher Learning* (Boston: Beacon Press, 2001); Marc Bousquet, *How the University Works: Higher Education and the Low-Wage Nation* (New York: New York University Press, 2007); Cary Nelson and Stephen Watt, *Academic Keywords: A Devil's Dictionary for Higher Education* (New York: Routledge, 1999); David Kirp, *Shakespeare, Einstein, and the Bottom Line: The Marketing of Higher Education* (Cambridge: Harvard University Press, 2004); Sheldon Krimsky, *Science in the Private Interest: Has the Lure of Profits Corrupted Biomedical Research?* (Lanham, Md.: Rowman and Littlefield, 2003); Christopher Newfield, *Ivy and Industry: Business and the Making of the American University, 1880–1980* (Durham, N.C.: Duke University Press, 2004); Gigi Roggero, *Intelligenze Fuggitive: Movimenti Contro LUniversita Azienda* (Rome: Manifestolibri, 2005).

2. *A Test of Leadership: Charting the Future of U.S. Higher Education,* a report of the commission appointed by Secretary of Education Margaret Spellings, 2006, http://www.ed.gov/, accessed December 13, 2008; *The Responsive Ph.D.: Innovations in U.S. Doctoral Education,* the Woodrow Wilson National Fellowship Foundation, 2005, http://www.woodrow.org/, accessed December 13, 2008.

3. Cary Nelson, ed. *Will Teach for Food: Academic Labor in Crisis* (Minneapolis: University of Minnesota Press, 1997); Patrick Kavanagh and Kevin Mattson, eds., *Steal This University: The Rise of the Corporate University and the Academic Labor Movement* (New York: Routledge, 2003); Jim Downs and Jennifer Manion, eds., *Taking Back the Academy! History of Activism, History as Activism* (New York: Routledge, 2004); Randy Martin, ed., *Chalk Lines: The Politics of Work in the Managed University* (Durham, N.C.: Duke University Press, 1999); Marc Bousquet, Tony Scott, and Leo Parascondola, eds., *Tenured Bosses and Disposable Teachers: Writing Instruction in the Managed University* (Carbondale: Southern Illinois University Press, 2004); Gary Rhoades, *Managed Professionals: Unionized Faculty and Restructuring Academic Labor* (Albany: SUNY Press, 1998); Judith Wagner DeCew, *Unionization in the Academy: Visions and Realities* (Lanham, Md.: Rowman and Littlefield, 2003): Joe Berry, *Reclaiming the Ivory Tower: Organizing Adjuncts to Change Higher Education* (New York: Monthly Review Press, 2005). *Workplace: A Journal of Academic Labor* (online at http://www.cust.educ.ubc.ca/workplace) is an indispensable source of

commentary on academic labor (the Spring 2007 number is a special issue on the NYU strike). InsideHigherEd (at http://www.insidehighered.com) has also provided a good deal of coverage and commentary. Print journals that have consistently published articles on academic labor include *Social Text, Radical Teacher, Minnesota Review, Works and Days,* and *Academe,* the monthly publication of the AAUP.

4. For a detailed discussion of the administration's accusations, see Alan Sokal, "Some Thoughts on the Unionization of Graduate Students," http://faculty democracy.org/somethoughts.html, accessed December 13, 2008. See also "Article XXII: Management and Academic Rights" of the GSOC-NU contract, http://www.2110uaw.org/gsoc, accessed December 13, 2008.

5. Jonathan Van Antwerpen, "Star Wars: NYU," in Kirp, *Shakespeare, Einstein.*

6. National Labor Relations Board, "New York University and International Union, United Automobile, Aerospace and Agricultural Implement Workers of America, AFL–CIO, Petitioner. Case 2–RC–22082," October 31, 2000.

7. National Labor Relations Board, "Brown University and International Union, United Automobile, Aerospace and Agricultural Implement Workers of America, UAW AFL-CIO, Petitioner. Case 1-RC-21368," July 13, 2004. The board's two Democrats wrote a vehement dissent, noting that the reversal was based on no new evidence, but a redefinition of the term *employee* to satisfy a policy decision, and that the reversal would disenfranchise a group of workers currently enjoying the benefits of a union contract. See also Steven Greenhouse and Karen W. Arenson, "Labor Board Says Graduate Students at Private Universities Have No Right to Unionize," *New York Times,* July 16, 2004.

8. During the union-busting campaign, key members of the ULT were VPs Cheryl Mills, Jack Lew, and Robert Berne, and provost David McLaughlin. NYU announced formation of Sexton's team upon his becoming president: "The New University Leadership Team," *NYU Today,* November 19, 2002, http://www.nyu .edu/nyutoday/archives/16/03/Stories/LeadershipTeam.html. Today's ULT: http:// www.nyu.edu/public.affairs/leadership/.

9. In late March 2005, senior VP Cheryl Mills and director of labor relations Terrence Nolan sent an email claiming, "Ultimately, the University leadership will make a determination about whether to renegotiate with the UAW after listening to the thoughts, views, and recommendations of the community." Cheryl Mills and Terrence Nolan, "University Review Process Regarding Unionization of GA/TAs," March 31, 2005, http://www.nyu.edu/provost/communications/ga/communica tions-033105.html.

10. All of the official university communications on the issue remain on NYU's website in a section on the Provost's pages called "GA/TA issues": http://www .nyu.edu/provost/communications/ga/ga.html.

11. In response to the union drive, NYU announced that all entering Ph.D. candidates in the Graduate School of Arts and Science would receive MacCracken Fellowships, which governed not only the years in which students worked as GAs, but also awarded Ph.D. students fellowship years of funding at the same rate as assistantships, grouping both categories into "stipends." Other private universities, including Columbia, raised their own wages and funding to match, hoping to quell organizing drives on their own campuses.

12. Private universities like NYU have succeeded in some part in shaping a nar-

rative that a competitive market, rather than academic labor organizing, has driven up wages for GAs. See, for example, Scott Jaschik, "Upping the Ante in Graduate Stipends," *Inside Higher Ed,* February 8, 2007, http://insidehighered.com/news/2007/02/08/chicago.

13. "Recommendation from the Faculty Advisory Committee on Academic Priorities," dated April 26, 2005, and "Final Report from the Senate Academic Affairs Committee and the Senate Executive Committee," May 2, 2005, http://www.nyu.edu/provost/communications/ga/ga.html.

14. Though future university communications would refer to this meeting and subsequent letters and calls between the two parties as "negotiations," this was not the case: the university had not decided whether to negotiate or not at this point, and never agreed to sit down with GSOC's bargaining committee.

15. http://www.nyu.edu/provost/communications/ga/communications-061605.html.

16. Audio recorded at the town hall, along with a selective selection of email comments received during the notice and comment period, is available at http://www.nyu.edu/provost/communications/ga/noticeandcomment.html. See also Barbara Leonard, "Three Days before the Final Decision, Hundreds Rally for Grad Union," *Washington Square News,* July 15, 2005.

17. "Contract Proposal to the UAW," August 2, 2005, available at http://www.nyu.edu/provost/communications/ga/ga.html. The chair of NYU's board of trustees, Martin Lipton, is credited as the inventor of the "poison pill" as a defense to fend off mergers and acquisitions.

18. "Letter from UAW to NYU," August 4, 2005, available at http://www.nyu.edu/provost/communications/ga/ga.html.

19. Jacob Lew and David McLaughlin, "Final Decision Regarding Our Graduate Assistants," August 5, 2005, http://www.nyu.edu/provost/communications/ga/communications-080505.html.

20. "By now many of you are aware that the United Auto Workers is publicly discussing a job action involving graduate assistants (GAs) at NYU in the near future. In our opinion, the Auto Workers union is embarking on a regrettable and unfortunate course: regrettable because it fails to respect the significance of your efforts to pursue your education, and unfortunate because such an action will not result in recognition of the UAW to represent our graduate assistants." John Sexton and David McLaughlin, "Memo to Students from Sexton and McLaughlin," October 20, 2005, http://www.nyu.edu/provost/communications/ga/communications-102005.html.

21. Faculty Democracy's website maintains a listing of these resolutions: http://www.facultydemocracy.org/departmental.html.

22. This communication, which does not derive from the ULT, is not collected with the others on the provost's website. For Stimpson's email *in toto* as well as a reply and analysis, see Emily Wilbourne, "The Future of Academia Is on the Line: Protest, Pedagogy, Picketing, Performativity," *Workplace: A Journal for Academic Labor* 14 (May 2007): 9–30, http:www.cust.educ.ubc.ca/workplace/issue7p2/index.html, accessed December 13, 2008.

23. Beckman used these figures on several occasions, for example: http://www.insidehighered.com/news/2005/11/10/strike.

24. David Epstein, "Digging In," *Inside Higher Ed,* November 11, 2005, http://in

sidehighered.com/news/2005/11/11/strike; Barbara Leonard, "Blackboard Access Infuriates Profs," *Washington Square News,* November 14, 2005. President Sexton's response: "A Letter to the NYU Community," November 14. 2005, http://www.nyu .edu/provost/communications/ga/communications-111405.html.

25. Language instruction is not training for being a professor of French litera-ture. Instructors in EWP compete with other grads and outside instructors in an application process to secure their jobs.

26. Catharine R. Stimpson, Richard Foley, and Matthew Santirocco, Memo to FAS Chairs, "Re: A New Arts and Science Policy about Teaching Assistants and Stand-Alone Courses," November 16, 2005.

27. Sexton referred to the time until the December 5 deadline as a period of "amnesty," which "represents a balance between our respect for the principled posi-tions of those choosing to strike and our obligation to undergraduates," John Sex-ton, "A Letter to NYU Graduate Assistants," November 28, 2005, http://www.nyu .edu/provost/communications/ga/communications 112805.html.

28. The petition, begun by renowned gender scholar Judith Butler, remains on-line, and ultimately garnered more than seven thousand signatures: http://new.peti-tiononline.com/tosexton/petition.html.

29. The blog on which this letter was hosted is no longer online. The letter is referenced here: David Epstein, "Conflicting Claims on NYU Strike," *Inside Higher Ed,* December 12, 2005, http://insidehighered.com/news/2005/12/12/nyu.

30. The Graduate Affairs Committee is a subcommittee of the University Committee on Student Life, itself a subcommittee of the Student Senators Coun-cil, comprised of fifteen senators elected through one of the notoriously undersub-scribed NYU student government elections, plus seven who are appointed by the Executive Committee of the University Senate, comprised of one student, one ad-ministrator, one faculty member, and one dean. Brian Levine was then a student at the medical school, and Rodney Washington was an M.A. student at the Wagner School for Public Affairs. http://www.nyu.edu/pages/stugov/about.html.

31. Shayne Barr and Adam Playford, "Univ: 3/4 of TAs at Work," *Washington Square News,* December 8, 2005. The supposed count of 150–200 classrooms com-pleted by the Office of the Provost on Wednesday, December 7, would produce a meaningless result: only a minority of our jobs would have actually required our presence in classrooms on Wednesday. Many classes meet on a Tuesday-Thursday schedule, and Friday teaching is largely made up of TA-led recitations and labs. Even when TAs had returned to work, or did not strike in the first place, some taught off-campus.

32. On the arrests, see Steven Greenhouse, "51 Teaching Assistants Arrested at N.Y.U. Sit-in for Union Rights," *New York Times,* April 28, 2006; on the House of Delegates, see Brett Ackerman and Paige Glotzer, "Senate Group Expands Grad Rep Proposal," *Washington Square News,* April 28, 2006.

33. Demonstrating the general lack of interest and faith in this proposed body, six seats out of a proposed fifty-three had no candidates. By contrast, GSOC's ac-tive participation in the election in GSAS led to more than 40 percent turnout for the vote—usual turnout in student government elections at NYU is well below 10 percent. See Sergio Hernandez, "New Graduate Delegation Dominated by GSOC," *Washington Square News,* January 16, 2007.

34. Judith Butler, "Academic Norms, Contemporary Challenges: A Reply to

Robert Post on Academic Freedom," in *Academic Freedom after September 11,* ed. Beshara Doumani (New York: Zone Books, 2006), 107.

35. Ellen Schrecker, "Academic Freedom in the Age of Casualization," in *The University against Itself: The NYU Strike and the Future of the Academic Workplace,* ed. Monika Krause, Mary Nolan, Andrew Ross, and Michael Palm (Philadelphia: Temple University Press, 2008), 31.

36. David Rabban, "Academic Freedom, Individual or Institutional?" *Academe,* November–December 2001, 3.

37. Stevens, quoted in ibid. Here Stevens is using "the academy" to refer to one institution of higher learning, not as the elitist moniker for higher ed as an industry.

REFLECTIONS ON ACADEMIC FREEDOM AND UNIVERSITY, INC.

An Interview by Ashley Dawson and Malini Johar Schueller

Andrew Ross

Ashley Dawson & Malini Johar Schueller: How would you evaluate the strengths and limitations of academic freedom as a guarantor of the perquisites of intellectual life in the United States today? The ongoing NYU graduate employee/student struggle for a contract, for example, underlines the increasingly large percentage of those working in the academy who do not enjoy academic freedom. How useful is academic freedom as an organizing tool given the downsizing of academia?

Andrew Ross: Academic freedom has to be a bedrock principle, and the institution of tenure, which is its guarantor, remains a key battleground. In the UK, for example, where tenure was abolished by Thatcher in exchange for the state's legal protection for academic freedom, the indirect result has been quietly catastrophic. Casualization has flourished almost as rapidly in some sectors as it has here, and the state's rigid quotas for research assessment mean that most British academics spend their time churning out superfluous publications for journals that no one reads. The disinterested pursuit of knowledge—a precondition of academic freedom—no longer really exists there as a matter of practice, either for fulltimers, or the growing ranks of contingent faculty.

We also know, however, that the tenured academic is an endangered species in the United States, and that the de facto erosion of tenure here has been steady and systematic—the latest AAUP figures show over two-thirds of the profession is now off the tenure track. Consequently, the majoritarian experience of academic teachers is not marked in any way by access to or contact with the promised land of security and freedoms. This experience is entirely out of synch with traditional academic culture, which takes such things for granted, and which continues to assume that the professional identity of academics is bound up in exercising these rights. The AAUP's foundational 1940 Statement of Principles on Academic Freedom and Tenure, for example, sees these two concepts as interdependent, almost indivisible. But what does it mean today when most academic professionals are unlikely to see much of either? Solutions have to go beyond increasing sensitivity to the rights of contingent faculty. In practice, the academic labor movement is taking its lead from contingent faculty and graduate teacher organizations, just as the experience of their members is becoming a norm, and a moral ground for all future action.

It would be dangerous, however, to conclude that these key AAUP principles should be sidelined because they are out of reach for most university teachers. The same might be said of "shared governance"—the other AAUP pillar. Most faculty governance systems make no provision for representing the rights and interests of part-timers or full-timers on limited contracts (the biggest growth sector in academic labor). In this area, at least, reforms are well overdue. University governance should be expanded beyond tenure track faculty and senior administrators to include contingent faculty and, for that matter, managerial professionals, whose expertise is crucial to matters of governance and who have an equally legitimate stake in the system.

AD & MJS: The culture wars returned with a vengeance after 9/11. Indeed, writers such as David Cole have compared the current moment to the McCarthy era. What similarities, if any, do you see with such earlier periods of dissent squelching? What are the limitations of such comparisons? What is particularly novel about the current moment?

AR: If the global geopolitical map was indeed redrawn by 9/11, then certain fields became hotspots, Middle Eastern studies most prominently, while other area studies disciplines, like East Asian, Slavic, and Latin American studies, which had been rigorously surveilled and policed during the Cold War, got some relief. The concerted pressure on Middle Eastern studies scholars by right-wing attack groups has been as noxious as anything seen since the McCarthy era; smear campaigns, threats on funding, demands on universities to withhold recruitment, outside pressure on tenure and publication decisions. And to some degree, the repression extends to anyone who departs from the very narrow spectrum of opinion that U.S. society permits on Israel/Palestine. The successful yanking of the play *My Name Is Rachel Corrie* from its New York run was a real eye-opener, as was the campaign against Ward Churchill for a stray reference to Eichmann, but you can take your pick on any day of the week from the available evidence. The moratorium on criticism of Israel extends back to the early 1970s, but it has been amplified since 9/11, especially since evangelicals fell zealously into line, and it has become an acid test in the United States (though nowhere else) for the new kinds of cultural warrior.

Yet few disciplines are immune. Because of the renewed interest in patriotism (both among boomer liberals as well as conservatives), my field, American studies, has been beset in all sorts of ways by charges of anti-Americanism. Not long after 9/11 (and during the anthrax scare) I remember receiving letters at NYU addressed to the "Department of Anti-American Studies." Around about the same time, Thomas Friedman recommended that Saudi Arabia establish more American studies programs in their universities, unconsciously invoking the sorry history of the field's Cold War manipulation by the state. Though I have no explicit evidence of this, I would imagine that overseas American studies programs are likely to be feeling some pressure from consulates and embassies to do their bit and support the State Department's flat-footed campaign to combat the worldwide rise of anti-Americanism.

Whether the lobbying activities of groups like American Council of Trustees and Alumni or the efforts of David Horowitz to push his Academic Bill of Rights legislation will result in a blanket silencing of voices (or alignment with state power) as was the case in the 1950s remains to be seen. I am skeptical that self-censorship on that scale will materialize, but institutional intellectuals, for all their vaunted job security, do not have to look far for reasons to bite their tongues. The rewards for self-restraint may be relatively small—favors from your dean or provost, grant renewals from your funding source, or recognition from the state—but, in our world, they are all too eagerly acknowledged. So, too, academic institutions today are arguably more vulnerable to political pressure because of their commercial ties than in the postwar heyday of the public university beholden to the state. The race to consolidate intellectual property (IP) claims and rights has significantly reduced the freedoms of academics involved in commercially viable research. Whether through nondisclosure agreements with corporate funders, or because universities themselves impose material transfer agreements (MTAs) on academics that are almost as rigid as the corporate restrictions, faculty voices are circumscribed. Most academic inventions are licensed on an exclusive basis, and the so the open pathways for exchange of academic knowledge are closed off at their source upstream. Much of this stuff is nonrivalrous research (like DNA sequences, medical procedures, or even mathematical formulae), funded by taxpayers, but the gold rush to propertize renders all these as private products. Faculty who don't play along, or who violate the IP agreements in order to exercise their academic freedoms, are penalized accordingly. During the Cold War, the military-industrial complex sought out academic freedom as a convenient cloak with which to obscure the dodgy status of all that Cold War research funding. While the laundering may still apply in the case of industry paying for "objective" research to be done in science departments, the nature of the freedoms is now ever more complicated by the growing claims on IP, including those of universities themselves.

So the short answer to your question is that, politically speaking, the furniture has merely been rearranged, with some seats hotter, and others colder, but economically speaking, the rush to propertize knowledge may be changing the landscape more appreciably.

AD & MJS: The latest round of culture wars is concentrated, as was true in the past, in the humanities and social sciences. But what of the natural sciences? How has corporatization of the university affected the norms of free inquiry in ways that the mainstream media have tended to ignore?

AR: Good question. There was much attention to the Bush administration's willful selectivity when it comes to taking the advice of scientists. The trail of junk science ranged from big picture topics like climate change to virtually any science-based criticism of the administration's corporate paymasters. But that kind of conduct in and of itself is not a novelty, nor is it necessarily a threat to the everyday practices espoused by research scientists. In many ways, the real threat to "the norms of free inquiry" has been the long-term impact of the Bayh-Dole Act (1980), which was introduced as a response to the national deficiency in high-tech innovation vis-à-vis East Asia, and was written with a view to capturing IP-rich opportunities through intimate university-industry partnerships. Bayh-Dole encouraged universities to give priority to commercially relevant research in the applied sciences. Of course, faculty had to be converted to this way of thinking by including them in a profit-oriented, stakeholding role. Applied science and entrepreneurial sciences aimed at technology transfer became the frontline for funding as universities began to invest in start-ups, real estate holdings, and opportunities that would enable their ownership of intellectual property (copyrights, patents, trademarks). Today, U.S. universities now hold most of the patents on DNA sequences, and most research scientists in IP-rich fields either sit on the boards of corporations or have close ties with such firms. Indeed, there are few research departments of this sort where faculty do not such ties.

Inevitably, nonprofit institutions have taken on the character of for-profits, and well-established trends confirm that the research university (with science faculty in the lead) is behaving more and more like an adjunct to private industry; the steady concentration of power upward into managerial bureaucracies, the abdication of research and productivity assessment to external assessors and funders, the pursuit of intimate partnerships with industrial corporations, the pressure to adopt an entrepreneurial career mentality, and the erosion of tenure through the galloping casualization of the workforce. From the perspective of increasingly managed academic employees, the result is systematic deprofessionalization; the value of a doctoral degree has been degraded. For most graduate students, the attainment of a degree is not the beginning, but the end of their teaching career; they are not a product, but, as Marc Bousquet has put it, a by-product or waste product, of graduate education; their degree holding is not a credential to practice, rather it presents a disqualification from practice, while new divisions of labor have emerged that are corrosive to any notion of job security or peer loyalty.

As Clark Kerr once prophesied, academics are now more like "tenants" than "owners" of their university institutions, but today's university is not quite the "knowledge factory" that he, and his critics, described. The research academy is undoubtedly a conduit for capitalizing and transmitting knowledge to the marketplace, but it is also an all-important guardian of the public domain. Indeed, the academic workplace is characterized by a tension that lies at the heart of knowledge capitalism. As the academy increasingly hosts property formation and incorporates the customs of the marketplace, ever greater care must go into maintaining its function as a guarantor of truth and unreservable knowledge. This is not just window-dressing, or money-laundering. Without an information commons to freely exploit, knowledge capitalism would lose its primary long-term means of reducing transaction costs. Nor, if all knowledge were proper-tized, could faculty entrepreneurs poach on the community model of aca-demic exchange to advance their own autonomy and status as knowledge owners. Consequently, the traditional academic ethos of disinterested freedom of inquiry is all the more necessary not just to preserve the sym-bolic prestige of the institution but also to safeguard commonly available resources as free economic inputs, in much the same way as manufacturing, extractive, and biomedical industries all depend on the common ecological storehouse for free sources of new product.

AD & MJS: Thus far, most of the debates about academic freedom have focused on universities even though public schoolteachers are most likely to be overwhelmingly affected by restrictions on the ways they teach. For instance, in early June 2006, Jeb Bush approved a law barring "revisionist history" in Florida public schools. Florida's Education Omnibus Bill states, "The history of the United States shall be taught as genuine history and shall not follow the revisionist or postmodernist viewpoints of relative truth." To what extent would it be useful to shift the debates on academic freedom to other arenas such as public schools? Does academic freedom take on a different resonance in this arena?

AR: Yes and no. One of the reasons that so many of the revisionist methodologies developed in the last few decades have been aimed at de-mystification is because the state of knowledge that university educators "inherit" from the secondary tier is so systematically corrupt. Freshmen bring with them a head full of national mythologies, and it has been our task, as we experience it, to reeducate students' minds, by overturning most of the presumptions that are established in the course of the average sec-ondary education. This has been an entirely necessary task, and easier to accomplish in a milieu that is defined as *in loco parentis*. But the American public school system elicits the participation of parents, and, combined with the role of local school boards, is all too susceptible to outside pres-sure on curricular decisions. The Christian Right has long taken advantage of this vulnerability. Back in the late 1980s, Ralph Reed pronounced the Christian Coalition's goal of taking over school boards: "I would rather have a thousand school board members than one president and no school board members." There are few public schoolteachers who have not had to deal with the bitter result of this effort to take over. In many instances, the boards have a direct line to state legislatures, while most schools have felt the impact in the form of challenges to the professional autonomy of teachers. Those who resist strongly get burned out easily, and the pressure to make compromises, especially if you live within the community, is immense. The potential of alliances with higher education professionals to resist the outside pressure is enormous, but actual networks are few and far between. The ASA has initiated a program of University/Secondary School Collaborations in California and Massachusetts, but the challenge of the "red states" is more formidable.

So while knowledge production originates within the elite research universities, the transmission flow down through the schools is all too often hijacked. Accordingly, while academic freedoms can be more easily secured at the top, the outcome of those freedoms doesn't travel very far if the same freedoms are being denied in the public schools.

AD & MJS: Knowledge production in U.S. universities has often been geared to the needs of empire. The directives of Operation Camelot were perhaps the clearest in recent history about the political requirements of research, but fields like American studies have also arguably emerged as arms of U.S. imperialism. Is it possible for knowledge production disengage itself from the aims of U.S. imperialism and if so, how?

AR: As for American studies, the initial formation of the discipline was a wartime project—it was considered useful for the officer class to know something about the values of American Civilization (the original name for the field) that they were fighting to defend. Appreciation of these values, soaked in the ideology of American exceptionalism that pervaded the discipline, also buttressed Washington's fitness as a global overlord in the postwar years. The international establishment of programs fell under the purview of the State Department, and, like the other areas studies fields, American studies abroad was heavily shaped by the needs of Cold War policymakers. Once quite accurate as a map of power relations, their geographical scope is now largely anachronistic

After 9/11, I consulted the ASA listings for international programs, institutes, centers, and addresses, and found, in response to Thomas Friedman's proposal, that there were indeed precious few entries in predominantly Muslim countries. So far, the State Department has chosen not to invest in establishing new programs, after the Cold War model. This may have something to do with the political orientation of the field. In the majority of U.S. locations where it is taught, American studies has a distinctly anti-imperialist leaning, and this has been true for the best part of two decades. Instead, Bush administration appointees, like Charlotte Beers and Karen Hughes, have tried to use the government's, and the military's, own charm schools to propagate Americanism in Middle Eastern countries, usually with farcical results.

But perhaps it's only a matter of time (and, predictably, under a Democrat administration) before efforts are made to induct academic Americanists, by one means or another. Certainly, there are no fields where intellectuals are immune to the blandishments of power. Even so, it will be difficult, for example, to replicate the extensive network of CIA recruiters, and CIA research programs, many in the most elite Ivy locations, that once existed on campuses around the country. The truth of the matter is that intellectual legitimation can be gotten outside the academy these days. The establishment of the private, right-wing institutes and think tanks, which did not exist (RAND and the Hudson Institute notwithstanding) as a pervasive force in the Cold War, has made available a hireling class of experts, and a ready source of "expert" knowledge and opinion tailored to domestic and foreign policy needs. There is no longer any need for policymakers to draw on credentialed academic voices and research for backing.

The more likely path for faculty is that academic complicity with imperial adventures will be secured through commercial avenues, when institutional pressure to raise revenue puts our colleagues' salaries, rather than their patriotism, on the line.

AD & MJS: What might a discussion of academic freedom on a global plane look like? What points of connection, if any, do you see between concerns about academic freedom in the United States and, say, the Indian government's decision to purge history textbooks of references to Hindu extremism?

AR: Although there are networks like Scholars at Risk (hosted at NYU), there is no high-profile academic equivalent of PEN, unfortunately, and, of necessity, Amnesty International tends to focus on the more extreme cases of repression. The AAUP, American Federation of Teachers, and National Education Association have limited international ties (mostly through Education International), and like any American NGO, have to operate in a context where any pressure from a U.S. advocacy group is received overseas with skepticism, if not hostility. There is no high ground available in that context. The willy-nilly use of rhetoric about "freedom" as a weapon of U.S. foreign policy has corrupted all such claims to the point of moral bankruptcy. This is unfortunate because strong public passions can be usefully mobilized against overt intellectual fascism of the sort evinced by the Hindu nationalist example that you cite. Widespread protests ensued in China and Korea in 2005 when officially approved textbooks in Japan (*Atarashii Rekishi Kyokasho*, or "new history textbook") whitewashed the Imperial Army's wartime atrocities in East Asia. There's no question that such efforts to hijack history can trigger mass sentiment. But it's largely because of the potential strength of populist sentiment that the Left has had to learn to be wary of what happens when the shoe is on the other foot. This is the lesson of civic liberties, which a democratic Left has had to fight to absorb.

That said, fears about disturbing the free exchange of ideas among academics can sometimes pose an obstacle to other kinds of political action. The much debated recent efforts of the British academic unions, AUT and NATFHE (now merged as the University and College Union), to back the broad-based Palestinian Campaign for the Academic and Cultural Boycott is a case in point. The AUT's initial vote of support was repealed after a massive campaign of pressure orchestrated primarily from the United States. Rather than presume that the academic freedoms of Israeli academics can and should be a priority, we might ask why the exercise of Israeli academic freedoms has not resulted in the censure of any institutions and individuals colluding with the occupation regime, whether as advisers or knowledge providers. As Omar Barghouti, one of the Palestinian boycott organizers, put it:

> But can they or should they be able to enjoy these freedoms (which sound more like privileges to us) without any regard to what is going on outside the walls of the academy, to the role of their institutions in the perpetuation of colonial rule? We are faced here again with the problem of Israelis seeing the world from their vantage point, and assuming—and demanding—that others do the same. Why does the world owe it to Israel's academics to help them perpetuate their privileged position? (http://www.zmag.org/content/showarticle.cfm?ItemID=7640)

In the United States of course, any such boycott is not even remotely likely. Indeed, it is shot down on grounds of curtailing Israeli academic freedom almost as quickly as criticism of Israel is marginalized in the sphere of public opinion. In an intellectual environment where Edward Said's basic formulations about Orientalism have been readily absorbed, it is much more rare for American academics to respond to his call to see "Zionism from the standpoint of its victims."

The result has colored the entire question of boycotts. The AAUP leadership has tied itself in knots over whether boycotts can be considered legitimate under any circumstances. It is not the first time that fundamentalism regarding academic freedom has stood in the way of other kinds of political action. Historically, the AAUP had a hard time accepting that it had a role to play in academic labor organizing, in part because of fears that it would interfere with the organization's commitment to protecting academic freedom. During the NYU strike, we discussed whether it would be possible to distinguish between an economic and an academic boycott— we were looking for a means for non-NYU faculty to put additional pressure on the administration. The sticking point among many of our colleagues was whether any such call for action would be perceived, disastrously, from the perspective of public relations, as a threat to academic freedoms.

It seems to me that there has to be a better way of balancing priorities and goals, especially in instances when the freedoms one might be striving to protect are being exercised to oppress others.

AD & MJS: Assaults on individual professors such as those in David Horowitz's *The Professors: The 101 Most Dangerous Academics in America* tend to obscure another dimension of the attack on academic freedom: the erosion of faculty sovereignty as a whole. The name of the NYU group with which you have been involved—"Faculty Democracy"—seems to recognize precisely such erosion. How has your group tried to address this situation? What are some of the principal strategic lessons of the battles at NYU?

AR: The erosion of faculty governance is a nationwide phenomenon, whether in public universities dependent on increasingly fickle state legislatures, or in private colleges where the faculty governance system was granted powers, after the 1980 *Yeshiva* decision, to compensate for having their unionization efforts legally blocked. The latter was the case at NYU, whose antiunion campaign against adjuncts in the late 1970s was in fact the prototype for the *Yeshiva* defense. NYU has been typical of the private university experience, but its sharp upwardly mobile path over the last decade means that nationwide trends have been magnified here; the concentration and centralization of power in the upper administration has been more pronounced, and especially so since the appointment of John Sexton (achieved by our trustees without any faculty consultation whatsoever) in 2001.

When Sexton came into office (and recruited many members of the outgoing Clinton administration as his leadership team), the legal battle to stop the accreditation of GSOC was largely lost. NYU's zealous nouveau riche bid for acceptance by the Ivy League had suffered a setback (a true ruling-class institution would have known how to hold the line), and the pressure on Sexton from Yale, Brown, Penn, and Columbia (all facing down organizing drives that were spurred on by the success of GSOC) was intense. Under these circumstances, it was hardly surprising that an effort would be made to break the union after its first contract had run its course, but the means by which the campaign was waged came as an affront to a broad slice of the NYU community. Even NYU antiunion faculty had found little to complain about during the three years of the initial contract. The administration made little to no effort to "consult" with faculty over its decision to break the union, and, when pushed to solicit a wider circle of opinion, resorted to tactics that were little short of manipulation. Reports in favor of the union-busting position were elicited from select (i.e., co-opted) committees within the faculty senate, none of which polled the general faculty on the question. Faculty requests for information were denied or stonewalled. By the end of the academic year 2004–5, it was clear to most of us that no volume of faculty opinion would make any difference, and it was at that point we formed Faculty Democracy (FD) as a pressure group independent of the governance system.

A group of us had been laboring in the vineyards with the AAUP chapter for several years, finding it difficult to rouse a typically apathetic faculty body. The mercurial rise of FD, to a membership of 230, over the course of the next few months was immensely gratifying. The group, which existed primarily as an e-list, but which met monthly as a plenary, clearly benefited from its spontaneous, nonorganizational nature, and it developed as a quicksilver vehicle for sharp critiques of the administration's mode of governance. As a result, FD was able to mobilize a large and influential member base in opposition to the administration's policies. Not all of our FD colleagues supported GSOC—the majority were comfortable with advocating neutrality and some were vocally antiunion. Unity came through a broadly shared perception that faculty prerogatives were being overridden or circumvented.

Of course, this perception cut both ways, and, if anything, it was the first lesson we learned about the path of solidarity. To mobilize full-time faculty (in an upwardly mobile private university) it is strategic to appeal to their sense of eroded privileges. Nothing animates full-timers more than the perception that their entitlements are being ignored. However, you have to be careful what you wish for. The reassertion of these entitlements will likely come at the expense of those outside the guild. We certainly saw some of this occur in the course of the NYU strike, which began in November 2005. Faculty who expected a speedy resolution were unprepared for a prolonged action that might disrupt their schedules, and their initial willingness to play a supporting role wore thin after it became clear that the administration was digging in. Frustration gave way to paternalism, and the "we know best" attitude that pervades the academic relationship between faculty and graduate students took its toll on the strike. Several "third way" efforts were made by faculty to resolve the standoff. None of these involved consultation with the GSOC membership, and the result sowed seeds of distrust in many departments. While a faculty core (fifty to eighty) remained firm in their support of the union, many FD members drifted away from their initial public positions, advised students to leave the picket line, and some even turned antagonistic toward students who would not heed their freedom to offer paternal advice.

A strike is about learning solidarity, and the libertarian spirit of academic freedom does not always sit well with the labor culture of solidarity. There were few of us involved in the strike, regardless of our leanings, who did not feel the tension between these traditions. Nor, it is fair to say, was the tension absent from the GSOC membership, some of whom found it difficult to sustain the discipline demanded by UAW/GSOC leadership. Some part of this difficulty was a direct result of academic habits of criticism—how much can a union meeting afford to resemble a graduate seminar where free critique is valued above all? How do you distinguish between the custom-bound critique of the academy and the kinds of self-criticism that every union needs and should encourage as a matter of healthy renewal? When you are under the pressure of strike conditions, it is not so easy to make that kind of judgment.

Academic freedom has to be a prime component of labor organizing in the academe, if only because the denial of the right to organize is a violation of that freedom. But it can just as easily be an obstacle or a recipe for inaction when it is invoked as an a priori principle. The likelihood of the latter only increases under circumstances where only a privileged few enjoy the securities that are envisaged as part of the academic ideal. For example, while FD was open to all, it was widely perceived to be voice of full-timers, especially those empowered by tenure, and who had most to lose in terms of their privileges.

AD & MJS: The recent strikes in New York by the Transit Workers Union and UAW-affiliated graduate student employees at NYU have generated little meaningful support from the labor movement as a whole. What tactics might we adopt to forge common consciousness and action?

AR: This was another instructive lesson from the NYU strike. GSOC members voted to go out in the understanding that the broader labor movement would make their struggle into a top-level priority. The UAW made it known that the AFL-CIO's big guns and deep pockets would be made available, and John Sweeney and other top brass made a point of coming to participate in a high-profile rally and CD arrests. As the first and only TA union at a private university, the GSOC cause was already a front-line struggle for academic labor, but it was understood that this could and would be turned into a test case struggle for the labor movement as a whole. As for the UAW itself, the integrity of its much-prized white-collar New York local (2110—which also includes Museum of Modern Art, the *Village Voice,* Barnard, and New School members) was on the line. So there was every cause for optimism, every reason to expect the best kind of high-profile corporate campaign. After the strike began, a series of rallies featured national union presidents—from the UAW, the Teamsters, AFT, the steelworkers, transit workers, etc.—alongside regional bigwigs, and a host of local politicians and celebrities. All of them promised the world to our students, and so you can appreciate that this attention was very flattering to graduate students. Last but not least, it was difficult to believe that a visibly liberal institution like NYU could actually succeed in busting a union in the heart of New York City.

As the strike wore on, the GSOC rank and file were hard pressed to see the resources promised by the UAW and others. It took several months, for example, to get the Teamsters to refuse to pick up NYU trash. Many of the members grew cynical, and some concluded that the rallies had been more in the way of photo-ops, the rhetoric little more than union boilerplate. By the time the UAW took over control of the campaign from the local's leadership and pumped in resources (in April 2006), the strike had lost a good deal of member solidarity. Lack of follow-through from the big guns who spoke at the rallies had not only undermined expectations, it had weakened the perception that the union belonged to its membership and that the rank and file could play a substantial role. The effort to resuscitate grassroots support was hugely successful but came late in the semester as the summer recess beckoned.

On another equally relevant note, the combination of traditional union discipline with the strategy of a single, long strike did not always sit well with members who had alternative, less orthodox, ideas about political action, or who had cut their teeth on social justice activism. Inevitably, there was an involved, and protracted, debate about whether the conventional strike tactics and the union's culture of hierarchy were the best fit for an academic milieu. The principle of academic freedom played some role in this debate, but perhaps more influential were the traditions of autonomous action that were more familiar to GSOC members who had cut their teeth on social movement activism. For others, the romance of being involved in a "real" labor strike remained quite potent, and the freedom to organize was held up as the paramount interpretation of academic freedom.

On the administration's side, its claim (which was the chief legal argument for breaking the union) that GSOC had meddled with its right to adjudicate "academic affairs" was never substantiated, and the flimsy evidence put forth in its support was repeatedly exposed as such. President Sexton's line about the union violating traditional academic rights got little traction, even among faculty sympathetic to his antiunion position. However, insofar as it formed the core of the legal attack on the union, it seems clear that, if the administration proves successful, this will play a persistent role in academic antiunionism for some time to come.

Faculty and student unions at public universities have shown that unions can coexist very happily with governance structures like faculty senates that are empowered to regulate academic affairs and safeguard freedoms. But it's probably fair to say that this kind of environment—where the largely self-directed work life of employees is an integral part of their identity as knowledge producers—is not well understood within the labor movement. After the successes in organizing in public education in the 1960s and 1970s, the failure to make headway in high-skill private sectors of the knowledge industries has been a lost opportunity. It's important, I think, to see the issue of academic freedom within this broader context, because it reminds us of the continuity between our labor and those of our counterparts in other knowledge industries that have fashioned a culture of free, open speech in direct emulation of the academic ethos, albeit in the cause of corporate profit.

But if the labor movement has not gotten very far in understanding our kind of workplace, neither have academic unions proved to be particularly innovative. For the most part, they are only active around issues relating to the contract, and play little or no role in educational or intellectual activities. If the labor movement is to reinvent the spirit of a different kind of unionism (1930s social unionism, say, versus the business unionism of the postwar compact, for example), then it seems to me that academic unions are in a position to offer some new models. To do so, they clearly have to transcend the two-tier system of labor that is already well established within academe, the upper tier tied to the security still afforded to the tenure system, and for which the traditional cause of academic freedom is taken for granted; and the lower tier tied to conditions of contingency, sharing with other precarious workforces the kinds of priorities that have more to do with basic workplace rights of access to fair labor.

Academic unionism has yet to face its "CIO moment," when unions acquire the will to include all members of the workforce—full-time faculty, staff, contract teachers, adjuncts, and TAs. As the research universities are more fully integrated into the corporate circuits, it will make more and more sense to see all those who work within them as a unitary workforce rather than as a full-time professional core, surrounded by preprofessional teachers, and white-collar and blue-collar support staff. If class divisions within the university workplace are to be properly confronted, then fully inclusive unions are the models to strive for, even for knowledge industries, which are basically structured along similar lines. The goal would be to stem deprofessionalization, on the one hand, which is shared by such disparate groups as medical professionals (struggling with HMOs) and high-tech engineers (Taylorized by global managers), and to erode the guildlike mentality of full-timers.

AD & MJS: Your recent work has dealt with the increasingly precarious character of contemporary knowledge work in the United States and in developing countries like China and India. What connections do you see between the struggles around academic freedom and labor today and the issues that arise in the broader world of contingent labor? How might we productively refine our understandings of intellectual labor to forge solidarity across professions and geographical spaces?

AR: While researching my book, *Fast Boat to China,* I hung out a lot at the American Chamber of Commerce in Shanghai—it was a wonderful search site because every profiteer eventually passes through there looking to make a fast buck. Over the course of my year in the field, I lost count of the American university reps who also showed up there, basically in pursuit of the same revenue-chasing, cost-cutting goals as the corporations. There are few colleges today not in the business of actively promoting their brand internationally or setting up shop in these offshore locations, and it is not always easy to distinguish the fiscal side of their operations from those of your average corporate outsourcer. In global study-abroad sites, teaching, drawn from a local, contingent labor pool, is infinitely cheaper (remember that the academy is intensely labor-intensive) while the college can still collect top-dollar tuition fees. NYU, always in the forefront of such tendencies, already has eight such global sites—in Paris, London, Madrid, Prague, Florence, Accra, Shanghai, and Buenos Aires—and has agreed to build a new branch campus in Abu Dhabi. In some colleges, routine scientific research is already being outsourced to cheaper offshore sites, directly located, as in Dubai and Qatar, inside free trade zones built to host global corporations. As the global networks get more established, and the pursuit of revenue more desperate, more and more colleges will find it fiscally prudent to transfer other kinds of operations overseas, and this will undoubtedly include instructional costs. To put this in perspective of international trade policy, education and training is the fifth largest services export in the United States (bringing over $12 billion in 2004) and figures prominently in the WTO's efforts at services trade liberalization all over the world. No surprise that the U.S. Commercial Service, run by the Commerce Department, actively advises universities on how to exploit the emerging market for foreign educational service providers. As more and more overseas operations come online, in countries where academic freedom is a fiction, the transfer of teaching overseas will inevitably involve the sacrifice of traditional securities and freedoms, and the escalation of downward wage pressure on domestic salaries.

The prototype for these overseas transfers exists in the historical record of casualization over the last two decades. Just as corporate offshore outsourcing was preceded by domestic subcontracting, so too, in the academy, we are now likely to see a similar move from contingent teaching onshore to even cheaper labor offshore. It's difficult for us to imagine right now what this dispersal will look like. After all, didn't the online education crusade of the late 1990s fail? Actually, it didn't—private, for-profit, online institutions like the University of Phoenix, Walden University, Kaplan University, Westwood College, and DeVry University are the biggest growth sector in academe, and their corporate parents—Apollo Group, Laureate Education Inc., Kaplan Inc., and the Career Education Corporation—are already huge investors in global distance learning. The Laureate group owns higher education institutions all over South America and Europe, often in de facto violation of a country's laws prohibiting the establishment of for-profit private universities.

But, really, the move offshore is happening in all of the other professions, making the world of livelihoods a more precarious place by the minute. There's no question that "knowledge transfer"—the corporate euphemism for high-skill outsourcing—will become familiar to us too. And when it does, it won't necessarily come in the form of a transfer from one employee to another one offshore. Corporations have developed workflow platforms and other business process technologies to slice up knowledge operations and disperse them to various global sites only to be gathered, coordinated, and reintegrated. These technologies, and the modular units of information that they move around, are designed to minimize IP leakage or theft. Patent-rich universities will likely follow a similar path, and when the knowledge is dispersed in this disembodied manner, you will stand to lose the capacity of a single legal person to exercise traditional academic freedoms in and around the knowledge field. That kind of scenario—much more than the traditional profile of the McCarthyist crackdown on individual voices—is the more potent threat to academic freedom on the horizon.

COLUMBIA VERSUS AMERICA

Area Studies, Academic Freedom, and Contingent
Labor in the Contemporary Academy

Ashley Dawson

NEW YORK HAS ALWAYS HAD ITS SHARE of pest problems, but
in spring 2005 a new species of vermin began setting up camp in front of
some of the city's most august institutions. Like something from a nuclear-
age horror movie, these grubby rodents were alarmingly large, often tower-
ing over fifteen feet tall when standing erect on their hind legs. Although
New Yorkers have grown used to seeing these monstrous figures outside
restaurants and building sites in recent years, the juxtaposition of one such
grotesque, scab-encrusted rat with the serene sculptural figures in front of
Columbia University's gates was nevertheless more than a little jarring.
Planted firmly next to "Letters," the classically proportioned granite statue
of a woman with an open book who greets visitors to the university's campus, the huge inflated plastic rat figure was part of a weeklong strike by Columbia University's graduate student employees demanding collective bargaining rights. Although the giant rat of Morningside Heights was placed
in front of the university gates to support a specific campaign, it was a
symptom of contradictions and conflicts that run deep in academia today.

In the spring of 2005, a cascade of apparently disconnected disruptions
that included searing accusations of anti-Semitism and the first coordinated strike by graduate student employees at Ivy League institutions

roiled Columbia University. Although they followed hard on one another's heels, commentators seldom linked these disruptions to one another, and never addressed their common cause. Instead, sensational talk of a leftist putsch, of tenured radicals commandeering the ivory tower and purging right-thinking students, dominated the media and came to define the terms of public debate over higher education in state and national legislative forums. The concept of "academic freedom" became a keyword and battleground in the controversy over Columbia's Middle East studies program that unfolded on campus and in the media during 2005.[1] This much-misunderstood term refers to the set of practices such as tenure and faculty governance that allow academics to generate new knowledge in an unfettered manner and to disseminate that knowledge using pedagogic practices that inspire critical thinking among students.[2] With this freedom comes responsibility: scholars must conform to the mores of their disciplines, and their behavior is monitored through a network of institutions that enforce such professional conduct. The point of academic freedom, in other words, is to ensure the autonomous self-governance of higher education and, in so doing, to defend the production of original knowledge for the greater public good. Of course, over the last half-century in the United States such notions of independence and public interest have been at best half-truths given the dependence of the humanities and social sciences on funds derived ultimately from the Cold War military-industrial complex. Nonetheless, key articulations of academic freedom such as the American Association of University Professors' 1940 Statement of Principles on Academic Freedom and Tenure, produced in response to politically motivated attempts to control research and teaching, elaborated a code of professional conduct that has shielded scholars from outside meddling with some success and that has thereby contributed significantly to the dynamism of higher education in the United States.

While critical thinking on campus has been embattled since at least the period of campus reaction and counterreaction during the Vietnam War, following the attacks of September 11 the teaching and scholarship of professors, particularly those working in controversial fields such as area studies, came under attack in a manner unparalleled since the McCarthy era. Waged largely by well-funded private advocacy groups rather than by legislative inquisition, these neoconservative attacks gained traction not simply because of the broader national climate of anxiety over terrorism. In addition, the autonomy of scholars and the institutions in which they work has been weakened by the quiet but nonetheless dramatic transformation of academia over the last three decades by neoliberal government policies and corporate power. As a result, not only is the university increasingly subject to external influence from big business and corporate-sponsored pressure groups, but academia itself has come to operate increasingly like a lean-and-mean American firm. As the events at Columbia demonstrate, it is all too easy for groups hostile to academic freedom to play to Americans' perennial antagonism toward what they view as the coddled world of the professoriate, in the process steamrollering over the weak defenses of university administrators whose eyes are increasingly on the financial bottom line, and thereby exacerbating the deep contradictions in contemporary academia. In what follows, I discuss the crisis at Columbia, linking the potency of the neoconservative attack on the university's Middle East studies program to the creeping corporatization of the university and to the most visible manifestation of academic capitalism: the creation of a mass of contingent instructors whose lack of protection by the protocols of academic freedom hobbles the autonomy and the integrity of the university.

In the spring of 2002, the state of Israel had a serious public relations problem on its hands. Following a wave of deadly suicide bombings by Palestinian factions that culminated in the "Passover Massacre," Ariel Sharon's government unleashed Operation Defensive Shield to "catch and arrest terrorists" and to "expose and destroy terrorist facilities and explosives."[3] Within a week, the Israeli Defense Force (IDF) was carrying out major military operations in virtually every Palestinian city. During these operations, strict curfews were enforced, leading to complaints by human rights groups that needy Palestinian civilians were being denied water and medical attention and that Israel was practicing collective punishment, behavior that is prohibited by the Fourth Geneva Convention. Allegations of a slaughter of Palestinian civilians surfaced after the IDF began using heavily armored bulldozers built by the Caterpillar corporation to destroy houses in the Jenin refugee camp, where a protracted battle between Israeli forces and Palestinian militants raged for a week in early April. Rumors circulated for weeks in the world press that hundreds of Palestinian noncombatants had been crushed during the house demolitions. Although human rights organizations such as Amnesty International and Human Rights Watch ultimately found these rumors to be unfounded, their reports concluded that the IDF had "committed violations of international law during the course of military operations in Jenin and Nablus, including war crimes, for which they must be held responsible."[4] Controversy over the events was stoked when the Israeli government insisted that its troops be granted immunity from prosecution for potential violations of international law before agreeing to a United Nations fact-finding commission. The U.N. mission was ultimately scuttled in the face of Israeli intransigence, leaving many vexing questions unresolved.

The events in Jenin galvanized pro-Palestinian activists on U.S. campuses into circulating divestment petitions. Despite the fact that the petitions *specifically* targeted U.S. firms such as Caterpillar that were providing military support to Israel, antidivestment forces outnumbered prodivestment ones by large margins on most campuses.[5] Nonetheless, the divestment movement generated intense concern among pro-Israeli groups within the United States. That same spring, a group of national Jewish organizations—including the American Israel Public Affairs Committee (AIPAC), the Anti-Defamation League of B'nai B'rith (ADL), and the Zionist Organization of America—banded together to form the Israel on Campus Coalition (ICC). Backed by a $1,050,000 grant from the oil- and banking-based riches of the Charles and Lynn Schusterman Family Foundation, the ICC drew, according to a Jewish Telegraphic Agency article, on the pro bono services of a powerful Washington consulting firm, who drafted a plan to "'take back the campus' by influencing public opinion through lectures, the Internet, and coalitions."[6] Within six months, a student group at Columbia, cleverly calling itself Columbians for Academic Freedom (CAF), had begun work on a film documenting the intimidation allegedly experienced by pro-Israeli students on campus. At the center of their accusations were specific professors in Columbia's Department of Middle East and Asian Languages and Cultures (MEALAC).

Although the Israel on Campus Coalition's tactics sent Columbia administrators reeling, they were hardly novel. Back in 1974, representatives of AIPAC, the American Jewish Committee, and the ADL created a "truth squad" to challenge the supposed growth of pro-Arab propaganda, which they felt threatened Israel's "special relationship" with the United States. According to Robert Friedman, the organizations that created the truth squad "turned into a kind of Jewish thought police" in their zeal to protect what they perceived as Israel's interests.[7] Using committed college students as well as sources with access to classified documents, the ADL and AIPAC opened files on journalists, politicians, scholars, and community activists who were critical of Israel. In addition to monitoring critics' writings, speeches, and professional activities, the groups often also smeared such critics with charges of anti-Semitism or with the pernicious label of self-hating Jew. As Friedman puts it, "the intention was to stifle debate on the Middle East within the Jewish community, the media, and academia, for fear that criticism of any kind would weaken the Jewish state." Similar tactics were in evidence more recently during the firestorm over John Mearsheimer and Stephen Walt's article on the Israel lobby and U.S. foreign policy.[8]

Sitting at a dorm-room table whose crinkly aluminum foil covering lingers from recent Passover celebrations is Ariel Beery, a twenty-five-year-old senior, president of Columbia's School of General Studies, and one of the prime movers of Columbians for Academic Freedom. His shoulder-length curly brown hair and small oval glasses dramatize his public pose as a nonconformist intellectual. Beery's self-description seems calculated to undermine expectations of thought police-like behavior. He is, he says, a proud product of the New York public school system, having grown up in the city after his parents left Israel following the election of the nation's first Likud government. They did not, Beery says, want their children to grow up in such a political climate. Since age eight he has been an active member in a Socialist Zionist youth movement, and, after completing high school, he went to the Gaza Strip as a peace activist. Although he has served in the IDF, he states explicitly that he's against the occupation and the policies of the Sharon regime. Beery tells me he joined the army after meeting Palestinian youths who were "putting their lives on the line and saying, 'Look, I'm only here because I'm willing to defend my people.'" He says this made him ask, "What the hell right do I have to come and try to negotiate for the Zionist side or represent the Israelis if I'm not willing to even serve in the army?"[9]

This kind of statement seems typical of Beery, who professes a strong desire to puncture established dogma at every turn, even if it involves serving in the army in order to gain firsthand knowledge of what it means to be "on the other side." When I ask him to talk about what he learned from his experience of being in the IDF, he replies, "I truly still believe that there needs to be two narratives known before you can make peace. What was upsetting me a lot when I was in the youth movement here and in Israel was that people did not understand the Zionist narrative, they did not understand the *nakba* [the Arabic term for the "catastrophe" of Israel's creation], they do not understand the human element of the occupation. The majority of people just see the Palestinians as a blob that they can't really deal with, and when I came here I was like, 'Holy shit, nobody understands the Israeli side.'"[10]

It is this emphasis on knowing both sides, on negotiating one's way toward some sort of mutual understanding and accommodation, that is at the bottom of Beery's complaints against certain MEALAC professors at Columbia. Beery believes ardently in his right as a student to interrogate and challenge his teachers. He tells me that established precepts of academic freedom support this right: "Academic freedom in the beginning was conceptualized in two cases: it was conceptualized as the student's right to learn and to learn whatever the student feels in the way that the student feels is correct; and the professor's right to teach in the professor's area of specialty."[11] Beery is, strictly speaking, incorrect on this score. Academic freedom was originally elaborated in order to protect the faculty *as a whole* from the capricious power of their employers, who tended to react harshly when scholars punctured national pieties.[12] This origin of the term has, however, been largely forgotten as a culture of rights has developed over the last half-century, leading to the association of academic freedom with First Amendment rights to free expression. Of course, all "citizens of a free society" possess such entitlement to unregulated expression, a fact that helps explain Beery's argument that he has just as much right to academic freedom as his professors.

Beery identifies two central problems in the teaching of certain MEALAC professors that he feels infringe on students' academic freedom: first, these professors focus too heavily on the Israeli-Palestinian conflict in their classes, to the exclusion of other important issues in the Middle East; and second, these professors construct their courses and run their classes in a manner that squelches dissent. The latter point seems to be the real crux of CAF's argument, an issue Beery returns to again and again, driven by a sense that he has been silenced not simply in the classroom but at Columbia in general as a result of CAF's criticism of MEALAC. Professors who claim to have access to the absolute truth make their students passive, Beery argues, and by doing so perpetuate an orthodoxy that is anathema to the students' right to free speech and intellectual disputation. Beery concludes our discussion on a note that stresses the importance of this perspective for progressives today: "My hope is that we can create a norm of dissidence. If you hold people to a certain responsibility of dissidence where they allow for dissent to exist in the classroom but also in the writings that they present, and the content that they present, then you create an academic culture that can withstand the shifting winds of ideological change."[13]

Beery and his CAF comrades gained support in their efforts to challenge MEALAC from the David Project, a Boston-based organization founded in 2003 by longtime pro-Israeli activist Charles Jacobs. As the ICC's sole "affiliate" organization, the David Project and its regional offices stand to benefit from a significant portion of the Schusterman Foundation's substantial largesse. David Project head Charles Jacobs, who writes frequently in the Columbia student paper and appeared on campus during the MEALAC controversy, is hardly a dispassionate analyst of Middle Eastern affairs. In the past, he has written pro-Likud speeches, as well as editorials in favor of the annexation of Palestinian land by Israel in the name of security.[14] In the late 1980s, Jacobs worked as the deputy director of CAMERA, a strenuously pro-Israeli media watchdog organization that in at least one instance assigned reporters to dig into the personal lives of journalists who questioned Israel's policies during the invasion of southern Lebanon.[15] Notwithstanding his involvement with organizations that have sought to stifle legitimate debate on the Middle East, Jacobs habitually couches his work and that of his organizations in the language of objectivity. Indeed, the David Project website states, "we believe that the values of tolerance, pluralism, and civil society are prerequisites for achieving genuine peace for all people of the Middle East."[16] This stance is an extension of the one adopted by CAMERA, which cannily deploys peculiarly American notions of journalistic "objectivity" in order to ensure that pro-Likud perspectives get adequate coverage in reporting on the Middle East. The resemblance between the group's pressure tactics to maintain journalistic "balance" in U.S. newspapers and the efforts of Beery and CAF to promote "objectivity" at Columbia is surely more than a passing one.

The ICC's economic investment and political savvy bore fruit quickly after the summer of 2002. Beginning in October 2003, CAF and the David Project organized screenings of *Columbia Unbecoming,* the constantly reedited film documenting alleged student intimidation, for a highly select group of sympathetic Columbia faculty and for right-wing newspapers such as the *New York Sun* and the *Daily News,* generating a firestorm of public controversy. Even the *New York Times* eventually jumped on the bandwagon, publishing an editorial that blasted vaguely defined "anti-Israeli bias on the part of several professors" at Columbia.[17] In response, a member of Congress wrote to Columbia president Lee Bollinger demanding the firing of faculty members impugned by the film. MEALAC faculty members such as Joseph Massad and George Saliba were subjected to barrages of harassing email messages and telephone calls, and Professor Rashid Khalidi's job as advisor to a New York City public school program on Middle Eastern affairs came under intense scrutiny. Each of these professors, it should be noted, speaks to a transnational academic and political audience; their targeting, therefore, was no accident and was sure to have ramifications far beyond the walls that surround Columbia's Morningside Heights campus. After months of silence, President Bollinger eventually reacted to the external attacks by appointing an ad hoc commission to investigate the charges against MEALAC professors and to evaluate the adequacy of student grievance procedures.

Rather than defending his faculty members' freedom to teach the materials they see fit, in other words, Bollinger decided to investigate the charges of a group of students, most of whom had not studied with the professors in question and none of whom had pursued established university grievance procedures against their teachers. The ad hoc committee reported back in March 2005 that there was absolutely no evidence of anti-Semitic behavior on campus or of unfair treatment (such as biased grading) of pro-Zionist students in MEALAC courses. Although the committee did censure Joseph Massad, a then untenured assistant professor in MEALAC, for one instance in which they felt a student's testimony of his overly heated response during a classroom exchange was "credible," they also noted that Massad had endured a remorseless campaign of heckling and harassment during his three-year teaching career at Columbia. The David Project and CAF attacked the ad hoc committee as soon as it published its report, claiming that it had engaged in a biased whitewash.[18]

Gil Anidjar is a young professor recently hired by MEALAC. We meet in his book-lined office in a building whose dark hallways feel eerily quiet: the building housing MEALAC stands across a small green courtyard from Edward Said's former office, which was firebombed in 1985. A certain sense of menace hangs in the air given recent events, and I'm surprised to find no security guards patrolling the halls. Seated in his office, Anidjar speaks quickly, with a beguiling accent that reflects his years of study in France and Israel, some of which were spent working with Jacques Derrida. Despite this esoteric apprenticeship, Anidjar's response to me when I ask him about CAF's charge of a lack of dissent in MEALAC courses is completely pragmatic. For Anidjar, claims of bias in Joseph Massad's classes are hypocritical since they ignore the fact that he is a member of a political minority.[19] Here Anidjar alludes not simply to the relative weakness of advocates for the Palestinian cause on the national stage in the United States, but to equality in representation of views that challenge Zionist narratives at Columbia specifically. If we are going to discuss "balance," he says, we need to be talking about it at the level of the department and the university. Columbia's Center for Israel and Jewish Studies (CIJS), Anidjar notes, has seven endowed chairs, as well as fourteen faculty affiliates. MEALAC, by contrast, has one endowed chair and twenty faculty members, three of whom are CIJS affiliates. More than parity exists, in other words, between faculty devoting themselves to Israel and Jewish studies and those focusing not simply on North Africa and the Middle East, but also on South Asian countries such as India, Pakistan, and Bangladesh. In addition, Anidjar points out, several blocks north of where we're sitting is the Jewish Theological Seminary, a Columbia affiliate and one of the foremost institutions of Jewish studies in the world. Barnard College, just across the road from Columbia, also has an endowed chair of Jewish studies. Of course, there's nothing to say that faculty members at CJIS will adopt a pro-Israeli perspective, but, Anidjar points out, the fact that Columbia faculty have chosen to associate Jewishness and Israeli identity in the title of their center says something about their general political orientation.

Interested in curricular offerings, I later check the course catalog and find that MEALAC offers eight courses in explicitly Israeli or Jewish culture, including Zionism: A Cultural Perspective, Readings in Hebrew Texts, and Post-Zionist/Post-Modern Hebrew Prose. Conversely, the department offers only eight courses with explicitly Arabic (*not* Palestinian) content, such as Islam in Modern Arabic Literature, Survey of Islamic Science, and Culture and Power in Iraqi Literature. Anidjar's conclusion resonates: the situation is one that "to any sane person would be recognizable as one of minimally utter dissymmetry between pro-Israeli or Zionist views and non-Zionist views."[20] By insisting on the introduction of dissenting viewpoints into the courses offered by one professor from a minority perspective and glossing over the many courses taught from an antithetical viewpoint, in other words, Beery and the other members of CAF are ironically working to entrench this very dissymmetry and thereby to diminish precisely the "norms of dissidence" they claim to espouse.

But the question of students' right to dissent in the classroom still gnaws at me. When I ask him about this, Anidjar begins by acknowledging that all teachers grapple with pedagogy: "That many of us make mistakes, that's not in doubt," he says, "but I'm not convinced that mistakes were made here." "Remember," Anidjar urges me, "that there is no institutional trace of any damage to students' rights in this case: no bad grades, no expulsions, no damning letters of recommendation."[21] Even the allegation by one student that Massad spoke to her in an excessively heated fashion has been challenged in a letter signed by twenty-three students who participated in the same class.[22] Yet, he claims, in a Derridean moment, "a certain violence, which is part of what pedagogy is, has to exercise itself."[23] This apparently startling admission is based on a facet of classroom life that has come to appear inescapable: there seems to be an inherent conflict between the student's freedom to hear views of their own choosing and the teacher's freedom to teach the subject as he or she understands it. Unless the professor ceases to be a teacher, that is, he or she will always be in a position of power over the student. Simply to put together a syllabus is to engage in a gesture of authority, as was made abundantly evident during the canon wars of the 1990s. Indeed, contrary to Ariel Beery's assertion, the American Association of University Professors' definition of academic freedom is predicated on recognizing the teacher's—*not* the student's—right to define the field of knowledge in the classroom. While the AAUP's 1940 statement enjoins teachers to respect students' opinions and to avoid introducing issues unrelated to the class topic, it unequivocally states that teachers are "entitled to freedom in the classroom in discussing their subject."[24]

Of course, such freedom, which is a kind of power, should be exercised in a professional, sensitive, and nurturing manner, establishing relations of cooperation between teacher and student. In today's increasingly polarized national environment, however, such ideals of mutuality are becoming difficult to achieve. But for a teacher to abdicate this position of authority would be an act of great irresponsibility. After all, the point of research and teaching is to discover and communicate the truth, unless one assumes that there is no truth and that it's simply a matter of balancing different, mutually exclusive opinions against one another.[25] Admittedly, there is a distinction between advocacy, which characterizes all great scholarship, and indoctrination. Yet one person's blatant bias is another person's judicious overview, as the heated debates over MEALAC suggest.

Who is to judge in controversial cases? Should it be the responsibility of university administrators? Should students be able to take their professors to court if they disagree with their research? Do we want politicians and powerful lobbying groups adjudicating academic research and classroom teaching? Over the last century, academics in both the sciences and the liberal arts developed a self-regulating system based on peer review, falsifiability, and standards of evidence precisely in order to guarantee the accuracy of research and to hive it off as far as possible from overt political manipulation. As the AAUP states, "the line between indoctrination and proper pedagogical authority is to be judged by reference to scholarly and professional standards, as interpreted and applied by the faculty itself."[26] It is precisely this right to self-governance and expert, impartial review by one's peers that is endangered by recent developments.

As the controversy over MEALAC continued to heat up, I decided to attend a high-profile conference organized by a group called Scholars for Peace in the Middle East, hoping that it might offer a forum for establishing dialogue and healing the wounds opened over the last year at Columbia. In order to get into the conference, however, I had to run the gauntlet of an airport-grade battery of metal detectors, x-ray machines, and body searches that made the organizers' title seem rather wishful. When I eventually found a seat in the well appointed but jam-packed auditorium at Columbia's business school, a wiry man in a suit was standing at the podium, denouncing the ad hoc panel appointed by President Bollinger to investigate MEALAC. He was, a woman in a surprising combination of cowboy boots and a brown wig informed me, a U.S. congressman. I had missed most of his presentation, but the general tenor of the conference became unmistakably clear when Laurie Zoloth, a professor of religion and bioethics at Northwestern University, stepped up to the microphone to offer us greetings from "the West Bank of Lake Michigan." While affirming the duty of academics to govern themselves and the problem of commenting on events at Columbia from afar, Zoloth opined that the academic Left had become a hotbed of anti-Semitism. In addition, human rights organizations were helping perpetuate this new form of racism. According to Zoloth, photographs of Palestinian children killed by the Israeli security forces have reawakened a species of blood libel. Where once Jews were held responsible for the killing of Christ, she argued, they are now seen as a source of sin in the world because of the suffering they are inflicting on the Arab world. According to Zoloth, postmodern philosophical relativists who dismantle ideas of truth are reproducing the views of early modern anti-Semites who helped foster pogroms and the Inquisition in Europe. The presentation concluded with Zoloth calling for the "reconstruction" of the academy in order to stamp out this rising tide of anti-Semitism, an injunction that was greeted with thunderous applause.

The atmosphere in the room grew increasingly electric as speaker after speaker rose to denounce the new anti-Semitism. Natan Sharansky, an ex-Soviet dissident who resigned from Israeli prime minister Sharon's cabinet to protest his plan to dismantle settlements in the Gaza Strip, described the atmosphere at Columbia as "like a ghetto," since Zionist activists suffered unpopularity on campus. Rachel Arenfeld, director of the American Center for Democracy, argued that Middle East studies programs are part of a "Saudi fifth column" in U.S. universities. Things proceeded smoothly in this vein until a young man interrupted Dr. Phyllis Chesler's account of the nihilistic romanticization of terrorism that has infected academia. Chesler had been arguing that leftists view suicide bombers as doing the work that the Soviet Union failed to do to bring capitalism down, and that human rights observers are regularly taken in by fake massacres performed by Palestinian actors, when a man in his midtwenties spoke up, saying that he personally had been tortured with electric shocks by Israeli security forces. Someone in the audience yelled back, "They shoulda killed you." Cacophony ensued, until the conference MC, a business school professor, stood up and admonished the audience by saying, "This is precisely what *they* want to happen." Calm restored, a beefy guy with a shaved head and a T-shirt with "security" written on the back got up from a seat near me and sat down in the aisle next to the electrocuted heckler. He didn't seem to be trying to make the young man feel more at home. The unflappable Chesler wound up her presentation, without further interruptions, by explaining that the feminist academy has become "Palestinianized" out of a desire to atone for European racism. We must fight back and not appease the terrorists, she concluded, by which she meant students and scholars critical of Israel.

The conference reached a kind of crescendo with an appearance by Martin Kramer, who was piped in live by a satellite feed from Tel Aviv. Kramer edits *Middle East Quarterly,* a journal published by the Middle East Forum under the leadership of Daniel Pipes, one of the founders of Campus Watch, an organization that blacklists scholars who challenge U.S. and Israeli policy in the Middle East. Kramer's *Ivory Towers on Sand,* published by a conservative Washington think tank that has supported prominent neocons such as Paul Wolfowitz, attacks Edward Said's *Orientalism* and the movement to criticize scholars' complicity with imperial power of which Said's work was a part.[27] Kramer's book provided the ammunition for key testimony by Stanley Kurtz, also of Campus Watch, during the Congressional hearings for H.R. 3077, the International Studies in Higher Education Act, in fall 2003. This amendment to Title VI of the Higher Education Act of 1965 provides government oversight of funds disbursed for international education and area studies programs. Such government supervision would take the form not of peer review, as has traditionally been the practice, but of an International Advisory Board composed in part of nonacademics invested in national security. The amendment explicitly shifts Title VI funds from knowledge production and teaching to advancement of "Homeland Security and effective U.S. engagement abroad." Department of Homeland Security funding has perhaps rendered H.R. 3077 unnecessary by initiating the creation of a new national security cadre, completely bypassing existing area studies programs.[28] In his appearance at the Scholars for Peace conference, Martin Kramer built on his previous work by attacking Columbia for lobbying against passage of H.R. 3077 when it reached the Senate. In order to underline the urgency of measures such as H.R. 3077, Kramer described MEALAC and similar area studies programs around the country as "ticking away like time bombs." His message to student activists at Columbia, however, was that they are the turning point. "9/11," Kramer concluded with a flourish, "means we have the wind at our backs and it won't take too long to unravel the appointments of the last two decades."

The strategic acumen and confident tone on display at the Scholars for Peace in the Middle East conference is a product of decades of organizing to uproot the opening of the humanities and social sciences to the social movements of the 1960s. In fields such as English, for example, which purposely cultivated its marginality during the Cold War in the name of an insular anticapitalist aesthetic, challenges to the elitist character of the canon led to the opening up of departments to literature written by African Americans, women, Latinos, gays and lesbians, and non-Westerners, among others.[29] In addition, programs created explicitly to serve U.S. national interest during the Cold War such as area studies were shaken when student activists attacked the complicity of academics with initiatives like Project Camelot, a program created by the U.S. Army's Special Operations Research Office in 1963 to develop psy-ops techniques to manage the national liberation movements of the era.[30] As the Vietnam War turned into an increasingly bloody quagmire, many area studies scholars were driven to challenge the motives and outcome of U.S. behavior in their region of specialization. Having gained control of most of the public sphere, right-wing activists now seek to exirpate the residues of post-1960 liberation movements from the academy using politically motivated litmus tests for hiring and tenure decisions. Of course, they don't admit to this. Instead, they claim that they are acting *in the name* of academic freedom. In the forefront of this campaign is Students for Academic Freedom (SAF), one of the many groups founded by lapsed Trotskyite David Horowitz. SAF operates out of Horowitz's Center for the Study of Popular Culture, an organization that has received over $13,895,000 from arch-conservative donors such as the Olin, Bradley, and Sarah Scaife Foundations alone over the last decade.[31] Horowitz set up his organization after having an epiphany during the first Reagan administration, and it has since grown into a miniempire incorporating a publishing imprint, multiple websites, a weekly policy-oriented lecture series, and multiple offshoot organizations, including the Committee on Media Integrity, the group behind the recent campaign to defund public television. Given the knee-jerk antistatist ideology that drives much of Horowitz's activism, it is rather ironic that he has now begun pleading for a form of state-mandated affirmative action for conservatives, but contemporary cultural warriors tend to be caught up in such contradictions. While posing as the saviors of critical thinking and humanistic education, Horowitz and company are bankrolled by the corporate interests responsible for the bulk of our culture's philistinism and subscribe to the Manichaean sound-bite strategies that characterize the worst contemporary political demagogues.[32]

Some initiatives undertaken by Students for Academic Freedom seem to live up to the group's name. For instance, SAF counsels students on methods for investigating and obtaining parity of funding for right-wing campus organizations. Other tactics encouraged by the organization, however, cross over into distinctly neofascist territory: for example, the group runs a website where students are apprised of the ins and outs of informing on their professors.[33] Students are encouraged to record classes clandestinely and to log complaints on the website as a prelude to seeking redress in the courts or the local legislature. But by far the most ominous initiative launched by SAF is the "Academic Bill of Rights" (ABOR). Authored by Horowitz, ABOR appropriates and slyly undermines language from the AAUP's landmark 1940 statement of academic freedom to produce a set of standards that would enforce political "balance" in classrooms. Where the AAUP cautions professors not to introduce tendentious subject matter into classrooms, for example, ABOR makes it illegal to discuss material not directly pertinent to the course. In contrast to the AAUP's injunction to teachers to exercise professional judgment when selecting course materials, ABOR mandates standards of diversity in teaching, hiring, and scholarship that are measured in purely political terms. While it is unlikely that chemistry departments will be forced to hire alchemists any time soon, in states such as Florida Christian conservatives have already begun to make noises about legislating equal time for "intelligent design."[34] Who will adjudicate diversity? Not scholars. In the version of ABOR advanced by advocates in

Colorado, for example, responsibility for student evaluations is transferred into the hands of administrators or the legislature based on the principle of the "uncertainty of knowledge," an intellectually nihilistic position that ignores the search for truth that is academia's cardinal value. Versions of ABOR have been moved for consideration in thirty state legislatures and in a bill introduced by congressional Republicans to reauthorize the federal Higher Education Act. Uniting these disparate efforts is one central principle: the move to demolish faculty autonomy and self-governance. As the AAUP puts it, "The Academic Bill of Rights threatens to impose administrative and legislative oversight on the professional judgment of faculty, to deprive professors of the authority necessary for teaching, and to prohibit academic institutions from making the decisions that are necessary for the advancement of knowledge."[35]

Even if organizations like the AAUP succeed in beating back Students for Academic Freedom, the fight will consume precious, scarce resources. In addition, Horowitz's drive to "empower" students and promote "balance" is helping to foster a climate of witch hunting that is inimical to free inquiry and discussion. As Steve Leberstein, a historian who has written on the purges of progressive professors at City College in New York during the 1940s, and contributes a chapter to this collection, put it to me: "Many people feel that there's a Damocles sword hanging over their heads. There's been no equivalent to the House Un-American Activities Committee hearings, not that there has to be. . . . The real threat here is that people will simply censor themselves. I think that's already happening. That's obviously the purpose here — to impose a kind of political orthodoxy on the country."[36]

Contrary to popular stereotypes, the majority of red baiting during the McCarthy period was not conducted by governmental panels, but by private organizations such as Allan Zoll's National Council for American Education, which deluged local school districts with pamphlets with inflammatory titles like "How Red Are the Schools?" and "They Want Your Child."[37] Terrifying parents with lurid warnings about schools infiltrated by subversive teachers, Zoll's group and its many local front organizations attacked public funding of education as a concession to collectivist ideology and pushed campaigns for lower taxes that were quietly bankrolled by corporate business interests. Ironically, it was during precisely this era that the New York Board of Education fired David Horowitz's father when he refused, on First Amendment grounds, to testify before a local commission of inquiry into his political affiliations. But it seems that a salary of over

$300,000 dollars a year and the perks that come with an insider's ties to powerful conservative politicians have inspired a certain strategic historical dementia in David Horowitz.[38]

Maida Rosenstein is standing next to the United Auto Workers' giant rat, telling me about what she calls one of Columbia's biggest dirty secrets. Next to her, graduate students bundled up against the chill that's still in the air of this spring morning file past, holding handwritten signs saying "Colmart," "We are the Union," and "Will Teach for Food." Now president of UAW Local 2110, Rosenstein gained her first union experience as a Columbia clerical worker, fighting in the 1980s for the right to collective bargaining with the university. But currently she's marching back and forth in front of Columbia's gates with graduate employees, young people in their twenties and thirties who are struggling to persuade the university to recognize their vote to join the UAW. Columbia is one of the richest universities in the world; it has an endowment of $4.5 billion, a figure larger than the gross national product of 95 countries around the globe. It is one of New York City's largest landholders, and, as a nonprofit institution, it does not pay real estate taxes. Its president, Lee Bollinger, makes over $650,000 a year.[39] And yet Columbia's graduate employees make only $18,000 a year—"at least half of which we have to pay back to the university as rent and health insurance," a passing grad student chips in. And guess what, Rosenstein says. These graduate students milling round in circles on the picket line teach *over half* of Columbia's classes. Graduate student employees are particularly vulnerable to attacks on academic freedom, Rosenstein tells me, since they have no right to security of employment, let alone to the protections afforded by the AAUP guidelines. Shortly after I discuss these issues with Maida, Gil Anidjar speaks at a rally organized by the union, underlining the links between the contingent character of graduate employees at Columbia and precarious status of dissident scholars in MEALAC.

Columbia is not the only institution where vulnerable and ill-paid graduate students and adjunct instructors do most of the teaching. According to recent Department of Education statistics, 44.5 percent of all faculty members in U.S. higher education are employed part-time today.[40] In 1969, only 3 percent of faculty held non-tenure track appointments; today, 60 percent have no chance of gaining tenure and the protection for critical inquiry it was designed to afford. How could the university have been transformed so quickly? During the Cold War, the government pumped money into universities, which functioned as an integral research arm of

the military-industrial complex.[41] This infusion of government funds sub-
sidized a massive expansion of higher education, a transformation that
benefited the liberal arts as well as defense-oriented scientific research.
During the 1970s, the fiscal crises of federal and state governments choked
off this flow of funds. As neoliberal economic dogma began to take hold
and taxes were cut, education was refigured from a public good to a private
investment. Student loans, for example, were developed under the Nixon
administration in order to encourage students to think of their education
in precisely those terms. Faced with their own fiscal constraints and the
siren call of corporate ideology, university administrators began casting
about for ways to save money. The primary measure that universities have
adopted since the 1980s to cut expenditures has been the systematic replacement of tenured and tenure-track faculty members with casualized
temporary workers. As a result, academic employees are now divided into
core and peripheral populations, the former enjoying many of the perks of
popular stereotype and the latter grappling with exploitative conditions
typical of the nether reaches of the service economy.

Although university administrators don't talk about and may not even
be aware of this, the casualization of the academic labor force is part of a
systematic attack on tenure and on academic freedom more broadly. As the
ranks of tenured professors dwindle, so the university as a whole becomes
more divided and, consequently, unable to manage its own affairs. The faculty's ability to regulate its own affairs diminishes, making higher education more vulnerable to corporate pressure and the profit ethic. Power lost
by faculty flows directly into the hands of administrators, who today behave far more like corporate CEOs than like intellectuals dedicated to the
pursuit of knowledge for the public good. Increasingly, the only moral imperative that binds them is that of satisfying the trustees, most of whom
are corporate lawyers or bankers, by squeezing steeper profits out of the
university.[42] This also leaves the university increasingly susceptible to well-
funded pressure groups such as the David Project and Students for Academic Freedom, which have become adept at bringing economic and media pressure to bear.

The rise of academic capitalism is changing the university beyond
recognition. University funding has shifted out of liberal arts fields that
are "unproductive" according to corporate ideology, and into areas such as
biotech, where professors also tend to be CEOs of start-up firms flush with
venture capital. Faced with an uphill battle for well-paid employment, students are flocking to forms of vocational and professional education that

they see as increasing their luster as job candidates, further gutting funding for fields designed to promote critical thinking and active citizenship. In addition, the deteriorating working conditions of graduate students and adjuncts militate against quality teaching.[43] The implicit message sent by cost-cutting administrators to students is that teachers and the life of the mind they seek to cultivate are not the real concern of the university. And, as Jennifer Washburn explains in *University, Inc.,* since the passage of the Bayh-Dole Act in 1980s, professors and the universities where they belong increasingly vie for patent rights for government-subsidized research, leading to a creeping privatization of the knowledge commons.[44] Research, once undertaken in the name of the public good, is now all too frequently framed and pursued in terms of private gain.

Faculty in the liberal arts and sciences, home to critical inquiry and greatest victims of the contemporary downsizing of academia, are the logical opponents of this transformation of academia. Yet they have been remarkably silent in the face of this sea change. This is partially a result of the fragmentation of the university. Professors in the humanities and social sciences often fail to see beyond the pale of their own disciplines. In addition, however, some liberal arts faculty members also choose complicity with university bureaucrats consciously, seduced by the promise of lighter teaching loads as the grunt work of undergraduate instruction is shifted onto the backs of grad students and adjuncts. But these opportunists, more numerous than one would suspect, are shortsighted in the extreme, for by abetting the division of the faculty they hasten the eclipse of their own privileges. As Maida Rosenstein put it, a resigned expression on her face, "The whole setup of the university has evolved. The real action goes on at the medical school and biomed labs. It's a completely different track. I don't know if liberal arts faculty get this. But I think they're so irrelevant to most of what goes on at the university. They're in their own little shrinking world, you know."

While most of the privileged professoriate hunkers down behind the embattled walls of their disciplines, the movement for unionization among graduate student employees is highlighting the destructive impact of academic capitalism on core values of the university, including academic freedom. When I arrived at the picket line one afternoon during the five-day coordinated strike of Yale and Columbia students, I found people gathered in tight knots of agitated conversation. Since 2001, a solid majority of teaching and research assistants at Columbia have expressed support for establishing a union. Columbia's administration has obstinately refused to recognize this majority and negotiate a fair contract, instead joining with other elite universities such as Yale and Brown to fight collective bargaining rights by reversing a landmark National Labor Relations Board ruling. Now, the text of a memo by Columbia provost Alan Brinkley had just been made public. Professor Brinkley is a celebrated liberal labor historian who has lamented the decline of unionization in the United States as a blow to democracy and has stated that "students are free to join or advocate a union, and even to strike, without retribution."[45] Yet in his official capacity as provost, Brinkley penned a memo alerting departments of the sanctions they could impose on graduate student employees should the strike be prolonged. In his memo, Brinkley suggested requiring department chairs to report teaching fellows who honored the strike and warned that disciplinary steps against such students could include loss of eligibility for summer stipends and other special awards as well as blackballing from further instructional assignments.[46] These measures would be illegal if graduate student employees were covered under the National Labor Relations Act. As one angry grad student explained, "Union busting is perfectly normal, you know. You can be the most liberal, progressive intellectual institution, but you can behave like a Walmart manager and that's fine. I just don't understand it."[47] The goal of preserving academic freedom—not to mention respecting democracy—evaporates all too quickly, it seems, when the interests of the corporate university are at stake.

These battles over the right of graduate employees to collective representation became even more bitter during the 2005–6 academic year, when New York University took advantage of the regressive NLRB ruling to try to destroy the school's graduate employee union. NYU, which has engineered a meteoric rise to academic prominence by hiring scads of academic stars while quietly staffing its undergraduate service courses with graduate and part-time employees, triggered a protracted and painful strike by offering a new contract replete with union-busting clauses to the graduate employee union. Despite the fact that the NYU administration is filled with prominent refugees from the Clinton administration, under whose sway the NLRB had ruled in favor of the NYU grad employees union, President John Sexton, in order to delegitimate the union, now cited the Bush NLRB decision that graduate students teaching at private universities are essentially apprentices rather than workers. If academic freedom was originally developed to curb the arbitrary power of dismissal wielded by university administrators, it became clear in the course of the NYU strike that contingent faculty today are sorely in need to such protection. Yet, in a supremely cynical move that demonstrated the extent to which the term has been perverted away from its original intention, NYU claimed that the graduate employees' attempt to secure a fair contract was inhibiting their control of the university's resources and was, consequently, an infringement of administrators' academic freedom.

From the time of Socrates' execution for misleading the youth of Athens, teachers have always been under suspicion for disloyalty to the interests of the powerful. Over the past half-century, attacks on teachers have come with incremental frequency if not severity: the witch hunts of the McCarthy era, backlash against critics of the Vietnam War, the culture wars, and now, the assault on academic freedom. Given the increasingly crucial role of higher education in reproducing a social order that has grown manifestly more unjust in recent decades, it should not be so surprising that academia should be coming under such concerted attack. Pundits from across the political spectrum incessantly drum home the importance of university education for individual economic mobility and for the nation as a whole. We live, the line goes, in a knowledge economy, a world of cutthroat Darwinian competition in which only those individuals and nations with the most up-to-date and flexible forms of learning will be able to compete successfully.[48] Middle- and working-class Americans have reacted to this information by scrimping and saving to send their children—and themselves—to college. The United States currently has the highest rate of college attendance in the industrialized world. Yet, although they frequently gripe about the spiraling cost of education, parents seldom recognize that the schools to which they send their kids increasingly resemble Walmart stores rather than ivory towers.

Today, the questions posed by the great British historian E. P. Thompson during a university struggle in the 1960s weigh more heavily than ever on our society: "Is it inevitable that the university will be reduced to the function of providing, with increasingly authoritarian efficiency, prepackaged intellectual commodities which meet the requirements of management? Or can we by our efforts transform it into a center for free discussion and action, tolerating and even encouraging 'subversive' thought and activity, for a dynamic renewal of the whole society within which it operates?"[49] Thompson's hopes for the university seem very far away today, his fears all too prescient. The recent spate of attacks on academia by powerful, corporate-funded groups such as the David Project and Students for Academic Freedom has made the intimate connection between the corporatization of the university and the decline of academic freedom that

Thompson described several decades ago particularly vivid. As the internal structure of academia has changed, so its autonomy has declined and the impact of external political pressure has grown. All too often, educators have allowed those outside the university to define the terms of debate around these issues by adopting a purely defensive posture. It is certainly important to defend academic freedom, tenure, and the values of independent inquiry more broadly. Faced with assaults by powerful corporate interests, educators have begun to strike back by emphasizing that it is they who are the true conservatives, intent on preserving access to higher learning by resisting tuition hikes, budget cuts, tax giveaways to the rich, and the assault on critical thought by neocon activists backed by wealthy private foundations.

Ultimately, however, the only way to reassert the university's public role is to challenge what French sociologist Pierre Bourdieu called the *doxa* or common sense of neoliberalism: that every sphere of social life should be subjected to the ruthless calculus of market-based efficiency.[50] After all, the university does not simply offer individual students the possibility of class mobility. Scholarship should not be pursued for private profit alone. Instead, as the founders of the modern university system in the United States recognized, education builds community and prepares students to be engaged, responsible citizens in a democracy. Similarly, research must ultimately be conducted for the public good, or else the basic foundations for building the edifice of scientific knowledge will crumble. The scientific research and critical thinking produced by U.S. universities over the last century are a vital part of our collective patrimony. Faced with a daunting new set of challenges, educators and their allies need to open a public debate about the shape and future role of the university in our culture. The university and the values of skeptical inquiry and academic freedom that it harbors are public goods, after all, and their enduring health should be seen as a fundamental element of our democracy.

NOTES

1. In fact, the group of Columbia students behind attacks on the university's Middle East studies department called themselves Students for Academic Freedom.

2. For extended discussion of the history and definition of academic freedom, see Robert Post, "The Structure of Academic Freedom," and Judith Butler, "Academic Norms, Contemporary Challenges: A Reply to Robert Post on Academic

Freedom," both in *Academic Freedom after September 11,* ed. Beshara Doumani (New York: Zone, 2006).

3. http://en.wikipedia.org/wiki/Operation_Defensive_Shield, accessed November 19, 2008.

4. http://web.amnesty.org/library/Index/ENGMDE151432002, accessed November 19, 2008.

5. The ratio of anti- to prodivestment signatures was twenty to one at Columbia University. Gil Anidjar, personal interview, May 13, 2005.

6. Scott Sherman, "The Mideast Comes to Columbia," *The Nation,* April 4, 2005, 22. On the sources of the Schusterman Foundation's wealth, see Bob Feldman, "The Israel on Campus Coalition and the David Project: Sponsored by U.S Oil and Israeli Bank Profits," *Electronic Intifada,* April 25, 2005, http://electronicintifada.net/v2/article3795.shtml, accessed November 19, 2008.

7. Robert Friedman, "PACmen," *The Nation,* June 6, 1987, 770–73.

8. John J. Mearsheimer and Stephen Walt, "The Israel Lobby and U.S. Foreign Policy," ksgnotes1.Harvard.edu/Research/wpaper.nsf/rwp/RWP06-011, accessed November 19, 2008.

9. Ariel Beery, personal interview, April 28, 2005.

10. Ibid.

11. Ibid.

12. Post, "Structure of Academic Freedom," 62.

13. Beery, personal interview, April 28, 2005.

14. Yohai Ben-Nun and Charles Jacobs, "Mideast Parley: Israel Should Annex Land Now," *Atlanta Journal and Constitution,* December 8, 1991, C7.

15. Friedman, "PACmen," 773.

16. http://www.davidproject.org.

17. *New York Times* editorial, April 7, 2005.

18. See Charles Jacobs's statement on the David Project website.

19. Anidjar, personal interview, May 13, 2005.

20. Ibid.

21. Ibid.

22. See http://www.monabaker.com/, accessed December 13, 2008.

23. Anidjar, personal interview, May 13, 2005.

24. 1940 Statement of Principles on Academic Freedom and Tenure, http://aaup.org/AAUP/pubsres/policydocs/contents/1940statement.htm.

25. See Stanley Fish, "'Intellectual Diversity': The Trojan Horse of a Dark Design," *Chronicle of Higher Education,* February 13, 2004, http://chronicle.com/free/v50/i23/23b01301.htm, accessed November 19, 2009.

26. Committee on Academic Freedom and Tenure, "Statement on the Academic Bill of Rights" (2003), http://www.aaup.org/AAUP/comm/rep/a/abor.htm, accessed December 11, 2008.

27. Naomi Paik, "Education and Empire, Old and New," http://www.yale.edu/amstud/wkgrp_essays.html, accessed November 19, 2008.

28. William Martin, "Manufacturing the Homeland Security Campus and Cadre," *ZNet* (April 8, 2005), http://www.zmag.org, accessed December 11, 2008.

29. Richard Ohmann, "English and the Cold War," in *The Cold War and the Uni-*

versity: Toward an Intellectual History of the Postwar Years, ed. André Schiffrin (New York: New Press, 1997), 73–107.

30. Christopher Simpson, "Universities, Empire, and the Production of Knowledge: An Introduction," in *Universities and Empire: Money and Politics in the Social Sciences during the Cold War,* ed. Christopher Simpson (New York: New Press, 1998), xi–xxxiv.

31. http://www.mediatransparency.org/recipientgrants.php?recipientID=63, accessed November 19, 2008.

32. Donald Lazere, "The Contradictions of Cultural Conservativism in the Assault on American Colleges," *Cultural Studies* 19.4 (2005): 421.

33. I'm referring here to the Nazi practice of encouraging students to inform on professors who didn't support the party, a practice that led to the decimation of Germany's famous university system in the 1930s. Of course, this persecution of intellectuals ultimately provided a major boost to higher education in the United States, where many of Germany's exiled academics fled.

34. Tom Auxter, "Faculty and Students Defeat 'Academic Bill of Rights' Legislation in Florida," email letter, June 1, 2005.

35. Committee on Academic Freedom and Tenure, "Statement on the Academic Bill of Rights" (2003), http://www.aaup.org/AAUP/comm/rep/a/abor.htm, accessed December 11, 2008.

36. Stephen Leberstein, personal interview, May 9, 2005.

37. Stuart J. Foster, *Red Alert! Educators Confront the Red Scare in American Public Schools, 1947–1954* (New York: Peter Lang, 2000), 63. See also Ellen Schrecker, *No Ivory Tower: McCarthyism and the Universities* (New York: Oxford University Press, 1986).

38. For Horowitz's financial data, see http://www.mediatransparency.org.

39. Columbia teaching research assistants *On Strike* brochure.

40. Jennifer Washburn, *University, Inc.: The Corporate Corruption of American Higher Education* (New York : Basic Books, 2005), 202.

41. For a very useful historical overview of the role of higher education during the post-1945 period, see Michael Denning, "Lineaments and Contradictions of the Neo-liberal University System," http://www.yale.edu/amstud/wkgrp_essays .html, accessed November 19, 2008.

42. Columbia University's board of trustees, for example, is composed of eight corporate CEOs, four lawyers, six investment bankers, one doctor, and three academics (counting President Bollinger himself).

43. According to Ana Marie Cox, 75 percent of part-time faculty members are paid less than $3,000 per course taught. See Ana Marie Cox, "None of Your Business: The Rise of the University of Phoenix and for-Profit Education—and Why It Will Fail Us All," in *Steal This University: The Rise of the Corporate University and the Academic Labor Movement,* ed. Benjamin Johnson, Patrick Kavanagh, and Kevin Mattson (New York: Routledge, 2003), 22.

44. Washburn, *University, Inc.,* 59–71.

45. Jennifer Washburn, "Columbia Unbecoming," *The Nation* online, April 25, 2005, http://www.thenation.com/doc/20050509/washburn, accessed December 11, 2008.

46. Alan Brinkley memo, cited in Washburn, "Columbia Unbecoming."

47. Sudhir Mahadevan, personal interview, April 28, 2005.

48. See, for instance, Thomas Friedman, *The World Is Flat: A Brief History of the Twenty-first Century* (New York: Farrar, Straus and Giroux, 2005), 275.

49. E. P. Thompson, *Warwick University Ltd.* (London: Penguin), 165–66.

50. Pierre Bourdieu, *Firing Back: Against the Tyranny of the Market 2* (New York: Verso, 2003), 80.

CASE STUDIES

THE MYTH OF ACADEMIC FREEDOM

Personal Experiences of Liberal Principle in a
Neoconservative Era (Sketches from a Work in Progress)

Ward Churchill

> . . . "academic freedom" is defined as the freedom to inquire,
> discover, publish and teach truth as the faculty member sees it,
> subject to no control or authority save the control and author-
> ity of the rational methods by which truth is established.
> Within the bounds of this definition, academic freedom
> means that members of the faculty must have complete free-
> dom to study, to learn, to do research, and to communicate the
> results of these pursuits to others. . . . The fullest exposure to
> conflicting opinions is the best insurance against error . . . All
> members of the academic community have a responsibility to
> protect the university as a forum for the free expression of
> ideas.
> —Laws of the Regents of the University of Colorado, Article
> 5, Part D: Principles of Academic Freedom

IT WOULD BE DIFFICULT to improve upon the articulation of principle
just quoted,[1] especially since the statement goes on in the following subsec-
tion to state that "Faculty members have a responsibility to . . . exert themselves to the limit of their intellectual capacities in scholarship, research,
writing, and speaking" and that "While they fulfill this responsibility, their
efforts should not be subjected to direct or indirect pressures or interference from within the university, and the university will resist to the utmost

such pressures or interference when exerted from without."[2] In sum, "the appointment, reappointment, promotion, and tenure of faculty members . . . should not be influenced by such extrinsic considerations as political, social, or religious views. . . . A disciplinary action against a faculty member . . . should not be influenced by such extrinsic consideration."[3]

The elegance with which words are deployed in these passages is undeniable, but, unmatched by performance, such verbiage is meaningless. More likely, some active form of subterfuge is involved. As a rule, exploration of the gulf separating rhetoric from reality stands to shed considerable light upon the actualities of institutional character. The matters addressed in this essay mainly involve how officials at the University of Colorado at Boulder (UCB or "CU") comported themselves the first time their willingness to defend academic freedom was subjected to a serious test, how the situation at UCB fits into a broader pattern of intellectual/scholarly repression currently evident in the United States, and the implications of this situation for the academy as a whole. But first, a bit of contextualization seems in order.

THE LIBERAL DIMENSION OF LIBERAL ARTS

   ᐁ

On July 2, 2004, I was contacted by Nancy Rabinowitz, director of the Kirkland Project for the Study of Gender, Society and Culture at Hamilton College, to deliver a public lecture on that campus sometime during the academic year. It was agreed that I would do so on February 3, 2005, in conjunction with Susan Rosenberg, a former political prisoner whose sentence had been commuted by Bill Clinton and who'd been contracted by the Project to teach a course on memoir-writing during the spring semester. At the time I entered into the arrangement I was unaware that the Kirkland Project—a left-leaning enterprise situated in an especially "conservative" area of upstate New York—had been targeted for elimination by a small circle of reactionary faculty members working in concert with off-campus organizations like David Horowitz's Scaife/Olin/Bradley-funded Center for the Study of Popular Culture (a subpart of which is Students for Academic Freedom) and Lynne Cheney's American Council of Trustees and Alumni (ACTA).

In October 2004, a well-coordinated campaign was launched against the Project's plan to employ Rosenberg. Spokespersons for the offensive contended that Rosenberg had "no right to teach the youth of our county" because of her supposed record as a "terrorist" and "cop-killer." Both labels referred to her alleged "complicity" in a 1981 Brinks truck robbery in Nyack, New York, during which two policemen were shot to death, although she'd never been prosecuted on any charge related the incident.[4] The publicity attending the campaign was sufficient to cause Rosenberg, who was then on parole, to withdraw from her contract in early December. Professor Rabinowitz contacted me, inquiring as to whether I, too, wished to cancel. Infuriated by what had already transpired, I declined unless specifically requested to do so by the Project. We agreed that in addition to my public lecture I would make a joint presentation, along with Georgia State University law professor Natsu Taylor Saito,[5] on the theme of ideological repression in the academy.[6] At that point, I myself was "taken under investigation" by the same clique who'd orchestrated the anti-Rosenberg initiative. By mid-January, a political science professor named Theodore Eismeier had come up with a three-year-old op-ed piece on the website of an electronic journal, *Dark Night field notes,* wherein I'd described the investment bankers, stockbrokers, and other finance technicians killed in the World Trade Center on September 11, 2001, as "little Eichmanns."[7]

The "story" first appeared in the Hamilton student newspaper on January 21, 2005. On January 28, my analogy was the topic of an editorial in the *Wall Street Journal* and was featured that evening on the Fox News Channel's *O'Reilly Factor.* For three straight nights, O'Reilly provided Hamilton president Joan Hinde Stewart's email address to his viewers, suggesting that they "let her know how [they] felt" about my scheduled appearance. That very night, death threats against me began to pour in. By then George Pataki had entered the fray, publicly demanding that Hamilton rescind its invitation. President Stewart responded with a statement to the effect that the college would "never compromise" its commitment to defending the principle of academic freedom. The campus police thereupon initiated regular contact with me to coordinate security arrangements, and, as of January 31, I was still receiving assurances that everything would go as planned.

Hours before Saito and I were slated to board our aircraft, Stewart abruptly pulled the plug, stating that she'd been left with no alternative because the number of credible death threats received by her office indicated that public safety could no longer be ensured. I was initially inclined to accept her explanation, even while disagreeing with her decision. That same evening, however, an exultant Bill O'Reilly suggested that my appearance was canceled because Stewart must have realized that "donations to the college would plummet, and so would her job security. The truth is that Hamilton is home to radical professors, and is a troubled college."[8] Far more convincing support to O'Reilly's primary thesis would soon be provided by Hamilton's avowedly liberal president herself, however. On February 2, Rabinowitz inquired whether I'd be willing to appear at some later date or deliver my lecture by videoconferencing. I agreed to do whichever she preferred. It was decided that she would consult with the faculty and students, meanwhile sending my honorarium (standard practice when an institution unilaterally cancels an engagement, especially at the last moment). This she did on February 3, and I deposited the check on the tenth. On the eleventh, I received an urgent phone call from Rabinowitz, informing me that she'd been removed from her position directing the Kirkland Project—which she'd cofounded—and that Stewart had ordered a stop payment on my check.

On February 12, I phoned President Stewart seeking an explanation. She dissembled, saying that she "understood [my] position," and had "no intention of not paying" me, but, because the Project had been "taken under review," she herself was obliged to "exercise due diligence" in the matter. She said she'd "be in touch within thirty days" concerning the status of my check. That was the last I ever heard from Joan Stewart. Not only did she herself never contact me or delegate the task to a subordinate, she remained perpetually "unavailable" to take my calls. It was not until September, amid a court-ordered mediation process, that Stewart finally conceded that Hamilton's obligation to make good on its debt entailed no reciprocal obligation on my part by remaining silent on the matter to help her maintain the pretense that Hamilton hadn't made good on its obligation.

Now, years later, the Kirkland Project remains in receivership and, although it carries a rather more "conservative" signature than in the past, it has never regained its full operational capacity. Nancy Rabinowitz took a year's sabbatical, and no effort was ever made to reschedule my appearance. The small clique of right-wing faculty who were the primary instigators of the "controversy" have prevailed. What of Hamilton's staunchly liberal president? Obviously, she was placed in an exceedingly difficult position by a confluence of circumstances largely beyond her control. The price paid, however, has been the principle of academic freedom, which Stewart claimed she would never compromise. In its stead, she has substituted a realpolitik wherein neocons waving checkbooks dictate what must, and what cannot, be said on campus.

ON THE HOME FRONT
↷

Following the right-wing media offensive, UCB interim chancellor Philip DiStefano immediately issued a statement denouncing my analysis of 9/11—which he'd apparently not bothered to read—as being "abhorrent," "repugnant," and "hurtful to everyone effected." Within twenty-hours, several members of the board of regents had also weighed in, recording their collective "ire" that I had expressed the "truth as [I] see it." At least one of them went on to imply that my tenure should be revoked. It is important to emphasize that these positions were taken, not in response to substantive pressure from the Right, but purely in *anticipation* of it. The interim chancellor's statement was released even before Colorado's arch-reactionary Republican representative, Bob Beauprez, became the first member of Congress to demand my resignation; three days before Governor Bill Owens demanded that I resign; and five days before both chambers the Colorado legislature passed resolutions condemning me and commenced a round of threats about withholding some portion of the university's annual budget unless I was "removed" from the faculty.

Faced with such bluster, the regents convened in an emergency session on February 3 to consider what might be done about a senior professor bold enough to have taken at face value their own guarantee of academic freedom. DiStefano asked that the board defer action for thirty days while he and an "ad hoc investigating committee" determine whether I might have published or voiced other views that "crossed" some undefined "line," and would therefore bolster the case for my termination on speech grounds alone. This proposal was quickly accepted, whereupon the regents proceeded to ante up yet another official resolution purporting to apologize to the entire nation for my analysis of 9/11 and pronounce the meeting adjourned. At that point, Shareef Aleem, a nonstudent Denver resident who'd attended the meeting in order to make a statement, and who'd sat quietly through the proceedings, inquired from the floor as to when, exactly, the board planned to hear public commentary. Several cops immediately converged on him, but Aleem was having none of it. When the police sought to lay hands on him, a sharp scuffle ensued. Charged with felony assault on a police officer, Aleem faced up to sixteen years in prison—he was tried twice and acquitted each time—mainly for displaying the temerity of insisting that exercise of a citizen's First Amendment right to petition the government is in no sense contingent upon the receipt of official permission to do so.[9]

The thirty-day grace period obtained by DiStefano on February 3 seems to have been intended to afford the administration time to work out a "resolution" of the issue without really addressing it. There were negotiations to buy out my tenure, an approach to which administrators apparently believed I might be receptive because of the willingness I'd displayed in relinquishing my position as chair of UCB's Department of Ethnic Studies at the very outset of the "controversy." It undoubtedly came as an unpleasant surprise when they discovered that, while I was willing to consider early retirement in exchange for truly nominal compensation, my quid pro quo was that the regents formally—and publicly—affirm the validity of the standard peer review process by which the quality of my scholarship had been vetted during each stage of my career, and—equally publicly—reaffirm their commitment to the principles of academic freedom articulated in their own laws.

Tellingly, it was the last point that proved to be a deal-breaker. Although a majority of the board members were prepared to ante up even more money than the agreed-to amount, they were unwilling to take any public position defending academic freedom. Rather, they announced their intent to subject the entire system of tenure to a comprehensive review.[10] Meanwhile, on March 3, President Elizabeth Hoffman, addressing an emergency session of the Boulder Faculty Assembly, warned that "a new McCarthyism" was afoot, pointing out that there was "no question that there's a real danger that the group of people [who] went after Churchill now feel empowered." Although Hoffman sought to "balance" her warning with the assertion of a suddenly discovered "institutional need" to investigate my academic record on other than speech grounds, few of the faculty were convinced. Already, on February 25, nearly two hundred tenured UCB faculty members had taken out a full-page ad in Boulder's *Daily Camera* demanding that school officials halt their investigation of Ward Churchill's work.

By March, Hoffman, under heavy fire from the Right for her observations on the resurgence of McCarthyism, and having hardly endeared herself to the Left by appearing to collaborate with it, had resigned her presidency. Although mine was by no means the only issue on the table, her demise was undoubtedly catalyzed by a veritable blitzkrieg of hostile coverage of me/my "case" in the local media. In short order, all manner of no-doubt academically relevant information about me was being published as "news." Coupled to this nonstop Westbrook Pegler–style smear campaign was a concerted effort by the press to find some basis upon which to discredit me in scholarly terms.[11] The latter charade was begun on February 8 by the decidedly undistinguished UCB law professor Paul Campos when he not only took issue with my ethnic identity, but aired disagreements posted by two obscure "scholars" concerning a total of three conclusions I'd drawn at various points in my work. Campos went on to observe—falsely—that one of the pair, University of New Mexico law professor John LaVelle, had accused me of plagiarism. From there, the media's "critical scrutiny" of my scholarship quickly gained momentum.

Hence, although the allegations thus drummed up were ludicrous, and evidence that I was solidly supported by both faculty and students at UCB was overwhelming, DiStefano announced on March 24 that while his ad hoc committee had concluded that no disciplinary action could be taken against me on the basis of my writing and other "speech activities," it had, nonetheless discovered several instances in which it appeared that I'd transgressed various rules of scholarly comportment. These allegations, he said, would be forwarded to the faculty's Standing Committee on Research Misconduct (SCRM) for purposes of further review. In the event a SCRM subcommittee determined that a full investigation was warranted, a process would be initiated that could ultimately result in my being terminated for "cause."

The subterfuge extended even to the claim that DiStefano and his ad hoc committee had themselves "discovered" the instances of supposed research misconduct he'd forwarded to the SCRM. In fact, most of them were known, or should have been known, to the university for years, and none had been considered credible from a normal institutional/scholarly standpoint. In a classic example of "Trial by News Media," only those matters that had been heavily reported were referred as allegations to the committee—this, despite the fact that I'd been exonerated by the university when faced with the very same allegation in 1994, included the charge that I'd engaged in "ethnic fraud" by identifying myself as an American Indian.

On June 15, after Rudy Giuliani had taken time during a campus appearance to opine that an exemplary firing might still be a good idea,[12] DiStefano pushed his own travesty further still. He forwarded as "new allegations" some fifty-nine downloaded pages of text accruing from a week-long series run as "The Churchill Files" in the *Rocky Mountain News*. Thus was the university's standard procedure jettisoned, placing me in the peculiar position of having to defend myself in academic terms against accusations made in the viciously partisan local media. In an effort to ensure that the expected lynching would be carried out smoothly, moreover, the press also undertook to discredit, and thereby to precipitate the removal of, any member of the SCRM suspected of harboring the least doubts that I stood guilty as charged. On this "fair and balanced" basis, the process entered its next phase, that of having the integrity of my work subjected to "scholarly assessment by my peers."[13]

THE CHARGES
ᴄᴬᴼ

In its original form, DiStefano's charge sheet accused me of having (1) "fabricated an historical incident" by falsely and repeatedly stating that in 1837 the U.S. Army had deliberately infected Mandan Indians at Fort Clark, on the upper Missouri River, with smallpox, unleashing a pandemic that claimed the lives of more than 100,000 Native people before running its course;[14] (2) falsely and repeatedly asserted that a half-blood quantum standard was applied for purposes of identifying Indians during the government's compilation of tribal rolls under provision of the 1887 General Allotment Act;[15] (3) falsely asserted that, under provision of the 1990 Act for the Protection of American Indian Arts and Crafts, a quarter-blood quantum is required of those artists and artisans identifying themselves as being of Native descent;[16] (4) engaged in plagiarism in three separate instances;[17] and (5) identified myself as being of American Indian descent as a means of enhancing my academic credibility.[18]

In August, DiStefano sought to add yet another set of charges by forwarding a complaint submitted by the sister of my late wife that I'd committed "academic fraud" by (1) getting the name of the hospital at which my wife died wrong in a biographical preface I'd written to accompany a posthumously published collection of her writings;[19] (2) getting the name of the residential school attended by her father wrong in the same piece;[20] (3) falsely stating that my wife had been diagnosed as suffering Borderline Personality Disorder;[21] (4) falsely asserting that the entire family suffers from what is referred to in the clinical literature as "Residential School Syndrome";[22] and (5) falsely stating that Ojibwes, my wife's people, were traditionally matrilineal in their kinship organization.[23]

With more than a dozen allegations on the table, there can be little question but that the administration was using the time-honored prosecutor's tactic of "shotgunning" me with charges in hopes that something might "stick." DiStefano's attempt to palm off my sister-in-law's accusations as "research issues" proved to be a bit too much even for the SCRM to swallow, however, and they rejected this one on its face.[24] Of the remaining charges, several more—the allegation that I'd engaged in "ethnic fraud," and all three of the supposed copyright violations—were dismissed as unsustainable when the SCRM subcommittee of inquiry reported its preliminary findings on August 19, 2005.[25]

There are serious questions as to why most of the rest were not also simply dropped.[26] Regarding one of the three allegations of plagiarism, for example, it was conceded in the preliminary findings that I myself appeared to have written the material I supposedly plagiarized.[27] Nor is it possible to follow the subcommittee's reasoning in deciding that my single and carefully qualified reference to "circumstantial evidence" concerning the "John Smith smallpox incident"— the source of which I'd cited—might in any defensible sense be cast in terms of "fabricating" it.[28] There were only two allegations ambiguous enough to have warranted any further examination: those concerning my interpretations of (1) the 1837 smallpox pandemic, and (2) the 1887 General Allotment Act. There were, as was later concluded by a review panel drawn from the faculty senate's Committee on Privilege and Tenure (P&T), significant problems with these as well, but there were at least a few factual issues to look at in each instance—and thus at least a theoretical possibility that *some* form of research misconduct might actually be revealed. Nonetheless, a seven-count "indictment" was returned by the SCRM's subcommittee of inquiry in its August 19 report.[29] On these, DiStefano solemnly announced to the press, it would be necessary to proceed to a full investigation.

ABOUT THAT "PANEL OF MY PEERS"

According to the rules governing such procedures in the CU system, the investigation of my work was to be conducted by a small panel of impartial scholars, preferably senior in rank and experience, and endowed with demonstrated competencies in the topics at issue. From the outset, however, the SCRM held that all two hundred UCB faculty members who'd signed the academic freedom petition in February, would be ineligible to participate.[30] In response, I argued that *no* University of Colorado faculty members should be considered unbiased, and that the panel should therefore be composed entirely of "outside experts."[31]

This rather common expedient was quickly rejected by the SCRM. I then moved that insofar as UCB faculty members would be appointed, none of the members of the panel—given its relatively small size, combined with the clearly negative roles already played by two of its more influential members, Getches and Campos—should be selected from the law faculty.[32] Yet, unbeknownst to me, the SCRM was even then arranging for a UCB law professor, Marianne Wesson, to head the investigation. Also unbeknownst to me at the time, Wesson had written about me in personal correspondence in February 2005 that she was "mystified by the variety of people this unpleasant (to say the least) individual has been able to enlist to defend him. . . . [T]he rallying around Churchill reminds me unhappily of the rallying around OJ Simpson and Bill Clinton."[33]

When confronted with a copy of this missive during the subsequent P&T hearings, the SCRM's chairperson, business professor Joseph Rosse, found that the email reflected no bias on Wesson's part and he therefore felt no particular obligation to notify me of its existence.[34] The next selections were Marjory K. McIntosh, specializing in medieval English women's history, and Michael Radelet, chair of UCB's sociology department and a specialist in the death penalty. To this mix were added a pair of "outsiders": Bruce Johansen, a well-respected professor of journalism and American Indian Studies at the University of Nebraska, and Robert A. Williams, Jr., a professor at the University of Arizona and an expert on the evolution of Indian law.[35]

Although Williams was the only Indian—indeed, the sole person of color—on the panel, it was my sense that his involvement, together with Johansen's, would be sufficient to counteract the near-total ignorance displayed by the three UCB panelists, both of my discipline, American Indian studies, and the matters addressed in my work. I was therefore prepared to accept the panel as it was then constituted. Wesson and Rosse apparently were not, however, and set about correcting the situation. On November 1, 2005, the names of the panelists were released to the press.[36]

Within hours, the panel was declared a "fraud" because I'd once blurbed a book by Johansen—at the request of the publisher, not Johansen himself—and Williams had issued a statement asserting my right to academic freedom several months previously. Both men were also pronounced guilty of having occasionally cited my work.[37] The university maintained a silence in the face of the onslaught, and themselves precluded from mounting a defense by the university's gag order, both Johansen and Williams resigned from the panel. Several worthy candidates, including Michael Yellow Bird, an associate professor of Indigenous Nations studies at the University of Kansas and probably the most knowledgeable scholar in the country with regard to indigenous understandings of the 1837 events at Fort Clark, and Richard Delgado, the acknowledged founder of Critical Race Theory, who both expressed willingness to serve on the panel, were each passed over. The panel's new composition included no American Indians, only a single person of color, nobody grounded in the relevant areas/methods of history, and nobody with a demonstrated competency in American Indian or even ethnic studies—but Rosse informed me that the matter was "settled."[38]

ASSESSING THE VERDICT
❧

The investigative panel never *did* meet its obligation to cite the "clearly established standards" it claimed I violated. In its report, it says only that it used "the 'Statement on Standards of Professional Conduct' prepared by the American Historical Association as a general point of reference," but that they had "made no decisions based solely upon it."[39] What *else* the panelists might have relied upon was left unstated, although it was later demonstrated that they'd misrepresented what is said even in the university's own general formulation of standards.[40] It was also claimed that I'd "concurred" in this nebulous approach,[41] a matter easily disproven during lengthy P&T hearings conducted in January 2007 to review the investigative findings.

Unlike the investigative process, in which I was not allowed to examine even my own witnesses directly—everything had to be filtered through Wesson—the P&T review procedure afforded my attorney and me an opportunity to question anyone who gave testimony. The P&T proceedings were far less rushed than those of its predecessor, moreover, with twice the number of days allotted to hearing witnesses and the reviewers allowing themselves a further ninety days in which to weigh the evidence and arrive at their conclusions. The result was an appreciably different set of findings than those produced by the investigative panel concerning my interpretations of law and historical events.

On the main points in both of these substantive areas, the P&T reviewers concluded that the investigative panel had failed to meet the burden of proof necessary to sustain its "verdict" that I'd engaged in either falsification or, less still, "fabrication" in my depictions.[42] As concerns several secondary points of my analysis of the 1837 smallpox pandemic, however, they blinked clear evidence to arrive at the opposite conclusion. By and large, they also turned a blind eye to the implications attending equally clear evidence that, to make its case, Wesson's panel had engaged rather massively in the very sorts of fraudulent scholarship of which I'd been accused.

While limitations on the length of the present essay preclude detailed discussion of the merits and demerits of the P&T reviewers' findings—in-depth analyses will be presented elsewhere—it seems appropriate to offer relatively brief summaries.

On Matters of Legal Interpretation

Regarding my contentions that both the 1887 General Allotment Act and the 1990 Indian Arts and Crafts Act define "Indians" in terms of blood quantum requirements, the P&T reviewers held that, at worst, I'd conflated the acts with the manner in which they were implemented, and that "failure to be precise about this distinction [does not fall] below minimum standards of professional integrity."[43]

On Matters of Historical Interpretation

With respect to the investigative panel's findings that I was guilty of fabrication by contending that there is circumstantial evidence indicating that John Smith may have deliberately infected the Wampanoags with smallpox at some point shortly before the landing of the Plymouth colonists in 1620, that the U.S. Army deliberately infected the Mandans and other peoples of the upper Missouri in 1837, and that vaccine was available but withheld from the Indians once the latter outbreak was under way, the P&T reviewers once again concluded that there was no "clear and convincing evidence for the conduct alleged."[44] Indeed, the panelists found that in her zeal to *dis*prove my contentions, McIntosh, who wrote both sections of the *Investigative Report* at issue here, had repeatedly "exceeded [her] charge."[45]

On the other hand, they concurred with McIntosh's findings that I was guilty of fabrication in stating that the items with which the infection was spread were taken from a smallpox infirmary in St. Louis,[46] and that "post surgeons" subsequently instructed Indians who'd been exposed to the pox to "scatter," thereby infecting healthy communities.[47] The reviewers also concurred that I'd misrepresented the work of UCLA anthropologist Russell Thornton by once observing that he'd suggested that the resulting death toll "might have" run as high as 400,000.[48] There are, to be sure, significant problems with each of these findings, summaries of which once again seem in order.

- On the question of whether items were collected from a military infirmary in St. Louis, I acknowledge that I probably erred—additional evidence has now convinced me that the items were more likely brought from Maryland[49]—but find the proposition that I "fabricated" the St. Louis idea rather strained, given that one of McIntosh's own expert witnesses, Michael Timbrook, testified that he, too, has always suspected—and is still "digging into" the prospect—that the source of the infection was the army infirmary at the Jefferson Barracks, in St. Louis.[50]
- The issue of my using the term "post surgeon" was/is mainly semantic—I, along with many others, consider it entirely appropriate when referring to medical personnel assigned to facilities designated "forts."
- As to infected Indians being told to scatter, there are multiple accounts in literature referenced by McIntosh in the *Investigative Report*. These concern Charles Larpenteur, a fur company employee who filled in as post surgeon at Fort Union while Denig (a company employee with medical training who functioned as post surgeon) was recovering from a very mild case of the pox.[51]
- The claim that I misrepresented Thornton's material—whether advanced by the interim chancellor's ad hoc committee, the SCRM investigators, or Thornton himself[52]—is simply false. While Thornton for the most part correlates no estimated numbers of fatalities to his list of peoples ravaged by the pandemic, he *does* provide a handy reference for readers interested in such things: "(. . . Stearn and Stearn, 1945: 94)."[53] Turning to page 94 of the Stearn's seminal study, as McIntosh claims she did, *all* one finds is a chart offering very much the same list of peoples as Thornton, but also providing estimated death tolls. For north-central California alone, the estimates given by the source to which Thornton refers his readers run as high as 300,000 dead; the total exceeds 350,000. Adding the standard estimate for western Canada brings it to over 370,000.[54] Including the other "missing" peoples produces a figure well within range of the 400,000 I said Thornton offered as a "maybe."

With the exception of a single reference, *all* of the information deployed in the preceding four bullet-points was in the record available to the P&T reviewers when they began their deliberations on January 21, 2007. There is thus little excuse, notwithstanding the sheer scale of the record, for the reviewers to have missed the obvious in these matters. Of course, it's always possible that, to borrow a phrase from their report, "something more than just sloppy research" was involved.[55] Unfortunately, their performance with regard to the issue of "accepted practices" in authorial attribution lends at least some credence to such suspicions.

While the investigators held that I'd violated "clearly established practices of author attribution" in certain of my writings on law, Langer ruled testimony about authorship practices common in legal scholarship out of bounds.[56] The reviewers were, he declared, going to "stick to evidence about practices accepted in A&S."[57] When questions concerning the prevalence of ghostwriting in political science became uncomfortable, however, he declared that irrelevant as well.[58] So, too, history, and then communications—the discipline in which I myself was trained at both the undergraduate and graduate levels—when it was shown that ghostwriting is actually considered a professional competency by ranking communications scholars.

In the end, although somewhat more qualified in their assertions, the P&T reviewers joined their investigative predecessors in masking the realities of how authorship is *commonly* attributed in academia behind a vacuous assertion that ghostwriting and similar practices are condemned by "an overwhelming consensus" of scholars.[59] The earlier verdict that I'd "failed to comply with established standards on the use of author names on publications" was upheld on three counts (two on plagiarism, one on ghostwriting).[60]

Plagiarism

The first finding on plagiarism concerned the 1972 *Dam the Dams* pamphlet, which all parties agreed I'd been asked by a purported representative of the group to rework for publication in 1987.[61] All parties also agreed that when I included the resulting essay in an edited volume a year later, it was done with appropriate credit to *Dam the Dams,*[62] and, grudgingly, that when still another version of the material was published as a *Z Magazine* article in 1991, an editorial decision was made to remove the group's coauthorial credit from the byline without my knowledge. None of this, including the last fiasco, was deemed by either the investigative panelists or their P&T successors to constitute plagiarism.[63]

Where my supposed plagiary comes in is that when I incorporated material from *Dam the Dams* into a pair of subsequent essays, I cited the 1988 book chapter rather than the original pamphlet.[64] It was also argued that I should have cited *Dam the Dams* at the end of each sentence in which its material was paraphrased rather than at the end of paragraphs in which such paraphrases appeared.[65] Most conclusively, according to the P&T reviewers, was the fact that while I claim to have disavowed the Z article because of its inaccurate attribution of authorship, I "continued to cite" it in the later essays.

The last assertion is false. I have *never* cited the Z article, *only* the 1988 book chapter.[66] As to whether I should have cited *Dam the Dams* at the end of every sentence rather than the end of every paragraph in which the group's material is paraphrased, it may once again be true that I was in some sense "obliged" to do so. If my failure to adhere quite *that* strictly to certain conventions of scholarly citation constitutes plagiarism, however, then academia is truly littered with comparable offenders. As Marc Cogan, chair of the AAUP Committee on Professional Ethics wrote, "the whole point of plagiarism is to pretend that you wrote something somebody else wrote."[67] It follows that "As a general rule, if the sources are given, and given clearly enough so they can be seen, so [that readers] can go back and spot it, then plagiarism doesn't come in . . . because clearly there was no intent to hide" the fact that use has been made of someone else's material.[68] Imperfect though my citational practices may have been in this instance, they nonetheless comport with this "general rule" of the academic community.

Plagiarism (Round 2)

The second plagiarism finding upheld by the P&T reviewers concerned the incorporation of material written by professor Fay Cohen into an essay attributed to the Institute for Natural Progress (INP), including *The State of Native America,* a 1992 book edited by my ex-wife, M. Annette Jaimes, now a member of the Women Studies faculty at San Francisco State University. While I readily acknowledged having performed copyediting/ rewrite functions on the INP piece at Jaimes's request,[69] and that I'd suggested crediting the essay to the by-then defunct INP as a way of keeping her name from "showing up too many times" in the book,[70] the evidence was uncontradicted that the manuscript I'd "tuned up" had actually been written by Jaimes and others.[71] While the reviewers asserted in their report that the "Legal Counsel at Dalhousie University has provided a 'well-documented conclusion' that Professor Churchill plagiarized Professor Cohen,"[72] this is a gross misrepresentation of what is said in the Dalhousie document; it concludes only that Cohen's material was plagiarized, *not* that I plagiarized it.[73] The reviewers, moreover, failed to address the obvious question of why, assuming Dalhousie's legal counsel had actually concluded that I was the guilty party, the University of Colorado was not notified for nearly a decade.[74] Still more problematically, they avoided all mention of the fact that Cohen herself has never contended that I was responsible for the plagiarism of her material, declining even an open invitation to do so during the investigative process.

While Cohen's answers to the investigative panel's and my interrogatories did nothing to prove my supposed plagiarism, they were highly revealing in other respects. In response to a question about how contact between Cohen and UCB was initiated, for instance, she stated that "Contact with the University of Colorado was initiated in February 2005 by Dean David Getches, through John LaVelle."[75]

The P&T reviewers ultimately advanced the rather oxymoronic proposition that they'd found "clear and convincing evidence" of my being "somehow . . . involved" in plagiarizing Cohen—as in, "we don't know what it was you did, but we can prove you did it"—and affirmed the investigative panel's no less vacuous finding that I was "at least an accomplice."[76] The most—indeed, *only*—substantive bit of evidence wielded by either panel was that the offending essay was listed in my annual report of professional activities for 1991.[77] Although I explained that I'd always left it to my assistants to fill out such forms, both panels contended that my signing of the 1991 report conclusively demonstrated my culpability.

Ghostwriting

The P&T reviewers followed the investigative panel in absolving me of allegations that I'd plagiarized portions of an essay attributed to former Arizona State University professor Rebecca Robbins—and, as a subtext, several essays attributed to Annette Jaimes—in accordance with the time-honored dictum that "one cannot plagiarize oneself," that is, I'd ghostwritten *all* of the material at issue.[78] That accomplished, the reviewers turned to the question of ghostwriting and, once again echoing the *Investigative Report,* asserted that my engagement in it constituted another of my supposed failures to comply with established standards regarding author names on publications, and thereby was "conduct fall[ing] below minimum standards of professional integrity."[79] The basis upon which the reviewers reached such conclusions, or felt they might ultimately be defended against judicial challenge, is a bit mysterious since, to a far greater degree than the investigative panel, they openly "acknowledge[d] the difficulty in finding specific guidelines related to ghostwriting" (which is to say, they could find none at all).[80]

Moreover, as the reviewers were informed, three noted experts on the question—the AAUP's Marc Cogan, are all on record in connection with my case as describing the treatment of ghostwriting as a violation of ethical standards to be a "curveball" for which they are aware of no precedent.[81] It would be reasonable to expect that, in order to demonstrate significant deviation on my part, the panel would have cited considerable evidence that the practice of ghostwriting is *not* accepted in the various research communities relevant to an interdisciplinary scholar such as I. Indeed, to uphold a "guilty" verdict, they were ethically/legally obliged to do so.

However, apart from a bald assertion that "no credible evidence [has been] provided that [ghostwriting] is an accepted practice for academic research in Communications and/or Ethnic Studies Departments, the reviewers made no effort to do so. Since the investigative panel's claim that ghostwriting is a practice proscribed by an "overwhelming consensus" among academics could not substantiated,[82] it was impossible for me to have "departed from accepted practices" in this regard.

Self-Citation of Ghostwritten Material

At issue here is the question of whether my citation of what the investigative panel described in their report as "two *apparently independent third-party* sources [emphasis in the original]"—that is, material I myself had ghostwritten—constitutes a "form of evidentiary fabrication" that was "part of a deliberate research stratagem to create the appearance of independent verifiable claims that could not be supported through existing primary and secondary sources."[83] Elsewhere in the report, the panelists elaborated further, claiming that such citations allowed me "to create the false appearance that [certain of my] claims are supported by other scholars when, in fact, [I am] the only source for such claims" as were involved in my interpretations of the General Allotment Act and the Indian Arts and Crafts Act.[84]

While the P&T reviewers addressed this matter only collaterally, observing that it "contributed" to the supposed failure to comply with established standards regarding author names on publications involved in my ghostwriting of the Robbins and Jaimes essays, they did state that my practice in this regard "seems inherently deceptive" and at odds with "what *we take to be* accepted standards by *large components* of the *academic world* [emphasis added]."[85] Once again, the conflation of "established standards"—which, as was shown in the preceding section, do not exist—with "accepted practices" is obvious. A gross distortion is readily apparent in the investigative panel's above-quoted assertion that no "independent third parties" were at issue when I cited material I'd ghostwritten.[86] To make this rather peculiar proposition seem at least superficially plausible, it was necessary for the panelists to deliberately blur the distinction separating ghostwritten material from that published under pseudonyms, to the point of coining a new term—"pseudo-authorship"—in furtherance of their pretense that the two types of material are rightly viewed as interchangeable.[87]

This is sheer nonsense, of course. While it is true that no third parties exist when a writer publishes under pseudonyms, the exact opposite pertains to ghostwriting, where material is, by definition, written *for* a third party. And, unless she is somehow coerced into accepting attribution of authorship for something she didn't write, the third party is *always* independent, that is, inherently empowered to revise or specify revisions to anything in the text incompatible with her own thinking, or to simply reject the material.[88] Professor Craig Smith observes that, once ghostwritten material is published under the name of the third party for whom it was ghostwritten, she "takes responsibility for it," that is, embracing the ideas/information set forth therein by publicly "owning" them.[89] He is by no means alone in this view.

It follows that ghostwriters are under no obligation, ethical or otherwise, to attribute authorship to *themselves* when quoting/citing material they've ghostwritten in their own subsequent scholarship. Relatedly, scholars routinely attribute authorship to those for whom they *know* it was ghostwritten, and often by whom. While the identities of the ghostwriters are well known in each case, which scholar is it who attributes Kennedy's *Profiles in Courage* to Ted Sorenson,[90] or Hillary Clinton's *It Takes a Village* and *Living History* to Barbara Feinman Todd?

This is so because, once the person for whom material is ghostwritten "takes responsibility for it" by publishing it under her own name, the material's "authorship is wholly unimportant." "What *is* important is what is said" therein.[91] Hence, when asked during the P&T review hearings whether he viewed the fact that I'd ghostwritten the essay by Rebecca Robbins I cited when interpreting the General Allotment Act as diminishing the integrity of my scholarship, Robert Williams replied, "Absolutely not. I mean, it says what it says [and] it's absolutely true, and it doesn't matter if Mickey Mouse wrote it."[92]

Consequently, the investigative panel's assertion that my "self-citation" of material I'd ghostwritten "creat[ed] the false appearance that my claims are supported by other scholars" was itself false. So, too, its pretense that I was ever "the only source for such claims." As was thoroughly demonstrated during the P&T hearings, a number of other scholars have arrived quite independently—that is, citing neither the Robbins/Jaimes material nor work published under my own name—at conclusions virtually identical to mine. Accordingly, the P&T reviewers overturned the investigative panel's findings that I'd engaged in "falsification" with regard to both the 1887 Allotment Act and 1990 Arts and Crafts Act (see the section titled "On Matters of Legal Interpretation," above).

Little Matters of Citational Convention

Although the P&T reviewers failed to address the matter one way or the other, the investigative panelists also found that what they termed the "unconventional referencing style frequently employed by Professor Churchill"[93]—that is, providing reference signals like "Overall, see . . ." or "See generally . . ." when citing sources "*in their entirety* [emphasis in the original]"[94]—constituted a "form of research misconduct."[95] Specifically, they held that such "referencing of a lengthy source without pinpoint page or chapter citation . . . creates the appearance of support without providing a reader the tools to rapidly check [my] authority," and is thus "part of a pattern and consistent research stratagem to cloak extreme, unsupportable, propaganda-like claims of fact."[96]

This astonishing rhetorical barrage set the stage for yet another illuminating exchange during the review hearings. On January 9, when a reviewer asked Clinton, who had written the purplish prose just quoted, whether he was "aware that the style manual of the American Psychological Association does not provide for the listing of page numbers when citing whole books unless a direct quotation is involved," and, since "hundreds of thousands of social scientists use that style manual, wouldn't that render Professor Churchill's failure to provide page numbers just common practice?"[97]

Clinton replied, "No. I think not," and thereupon launched into a lecture on why the APA conventions were inapplicable because psychology has become increasingly experimental, making reference to "the literature

[ever] less significant." "In history, by contrast, and in law," he continued, "pinpoint citations are critical [whenever] you're making a pinpoint point."[98] The parade of ever-shifting standards and conventions continued. The following morning, after she'd gone on at considerable length about the supposed problems with my footnotes, I had a chance to ask McIntosh how it was that if my referencing style was really so unconventional, she herself had cited entire books on 92 occasions and entire articles or book chapters no fewer than 388 times in her *Working Women in English Society*.[99] Her initial answer was that "With respect to citing articles or essays . . . unless it's a direct quotation, one is not expected to give the particular page reference." I simply followed McIntosh's lead, observing that since those of my citations to which she'd objected were not tied to direct quotes, I was confused as to what she found problematic about them.[100]

As I later summed up the exchange to my daughter, it was a classic example of the "rules for thee but not for me syndrome" that was a defining feature the process from start to finish. Given the overall circumstances described herein, the P&T reviewers' finding that the university had not "engaged in selective enforcement of its rules concerning Research Misconduct" in my case was a travesty, pure and simple.[101] No less so their conclusion—despite their straightforward acknowledgment that "but for his exercise of his First Amendment rights, Professor Churchill would not have been subjected to the Research Misconduct and Enforcement Process or received [DiStefano's] Notice to Dismiss"[102]—that the process had not been "so fundamentally flawed as to deny [my] right to Due Process."[103] Such are the liberal "protections" accorded radical scholars and scholarship in the face of reactionary aggression.

Aftermath

The P&T reviewers submitted their final report to Hank Brown, a former Republican senator and ACTA cofounder brought in to replace Elizabeth Hoffman as president of the university, on May 8, 2007. On May 25, Brown submitted a letter to the board of regents in which, although he has no discernable competence in matters of federal Indian law, he overruled not only the reviewers but the expert witnesses, reinstating the investigative panel's findings that I had misrepresented both the 1887 and 1990 acts, and recommending that the board vote to revoke my tenure and fire me for cause on the earliest practical date. This was done by an eight-to-one count at a meeting already scheduled for July 24.[104] David Lane filed suit on my behalf the following morning.

In truth, the counterattack had commenced well before Brown received the P&T report. By late March, Eric Cheyfitz, a noted professor of American Studies at Cornell University, and others had begun to comment upon some of the misrepresentations of fact littering the *Investigative Report*.[105] In early April, apparently unnerved by the growing scrutiny of the report both within and without the university, Wesson admitted that the investigative panel had "misunderstood" what was said in one of the sources I'd cited and consequently "erred" with regard to certain "facts" presented in their finding on the John Smith / smallpox question.[106] She claimed that the panel would "soon take steps to ensure that the error is corrected for the scholarly record." Eighteen months later, no such corrections have been made, that is, no revisions have been made to the *Investigative Report*, which remains posted on the university website under the guise of a "scholarly work product," while neither Wesson nor any other panelist has said another word on the matter (plainly suggesting that, in the wake of her initial—and undoubtedly unsanctioned—foray into the realm of public "truth-telling," she/they were quickly muzzled by the administration).

By then, similar misrepresentations of fact had been detected on virtually every page of the *Investigative Report*, and more were cropping up every day. On April 23, seven members of the UCB faculty, joined by Eric Cheyfitz and Yellow Bird, published an open letter citing "a pattern of violations . . . of standard scholarly practice so serious that [they were] considering the additional step of filing charges of research misconduct" against the panelists.[107] When Michael Poliakoff—an ACTA veteran hired as Brown's assistant in early 2006—refused their demand, the group, joined by two additional members of the Boulder faculty, filed a formal complaint with the SCRM.[108]

Meanwhile, on July 10, a P&T panel convened to consider a collateral grievance I'd filed *nearly two years* previously,[109] finally returned its verdict, finding that the administration had clearly and repeatedly violated my right to confidentiality, as specified in the university rules pertaining to personnel matters, and that such violations had had "a prejudicial or detrimental effect on [my] reputation."[110] The grievance panel also concluded that while the lengthy "delay to hear [my] grievance compounded the damage to [my] reputation given the continuous media coverage," the source of the delay was the P&T committee itself—i.e., the faculty senate—rather than the administration.[111] Nonetheless, it recommended that there be "a public statement, i.e., press release and/or website posting acknowledging the breaches of the SCRM rules by the University against Professor Churchill."[112] Unsurprisingly, the recommendation was rejected by G. P "Bud" Peterson,[113] yet another ACTA notable "brought aboard" by Brown, in this case to replace DiStefano as chancellor of the Boulder campus.[114]

Then, on July 18, I received a letter from Rosse, informing me that the SCRM would "not be reviewing [my] allegations regarding the report of the investigating committee, nor any future allegations regarding the report."[115] The reasons, as reported in the *Silver & Gold Record* a few days later were that

> complaints of scientific misconduct lodged against the committee which investigated Professor Churchill do not fall within the purview of the Standing Committee because the activities of [investigative panel] did not constitute research[;] rather, they were an administrative investigation and are therefore not scientific misconduct.[116]

While the SCRM's defensive ploy was clearly intended to immunize the panelists against the consequences of their fraud, this was by no means the only implication. As I explained at the time, "President Brown claims that I should be fired to preserve 'academic integrity.' Yet he relies on a report which the University refuses to investigate against credible and well-documented charges of falsifications, fabrications and plagiarism. The University cannot have it both ways. If the investigative [panel's] report is scholarship, it must be held to the same standards to which it claims to be holding me accountable. If not, President Brown's recommendation is based on no credible evidence at all" (or at least none that could withstand scholarly scrutiny).[117]

The great bulk of the information set forth in this section had been provided to the regents prior to their meeting on July 24.[118] That the motive underlying their vote had little, if anything, to do with academic concerns is evidenced by the fact that Brown had already prepared a missive to donors and alumni—posted to a university list-serve the moment the results were official—informing them of my firing and that they should therefore proceed with whatever financial contributions they'd been withholding.[119] To all appearances, his efforts cemented a record-breaking influx of contributions to the university foundation.[120]

Mission accomplished, Brown announced his retirement, effective as soon as a "suitable replacement" could be hired. Here, the wages of liberal accommodation to the reactionary Right were finally visited, full-force, on the CU faculty. Brown's choice, and the *only* name presented to the regents, was Bruce Benson, a man whose "qualifications" include a B.A. in geology, a career spent as an oil company executive, and considerable experience as a Republican activist, including the founding of a 527 organization called the Trailhead Group (à la the "Swift Boat Veterans for Truth").[121] On February 20, 2008, Benson became the president of the University of Colorado, and his first major initiative was to establish an endowed professorship of "conservative political philosophy."[122]

In the interim, the university attempted, unsuccessfully, to have my lawsuit dismissed.[123] The case is currently scheduled for trial on March 9, 2009. While one can never predict the outcome of such proceedings, it can be said with certainty that the rules will be very different from those prevailing in the university's tortured version of "due process." Perhaps the extent to which I'm deserving of David Horowitz's flattering designation as the proverbial benchmark by which other "dangerous professors" should be measured will be clarified in the judicial arena.[124]

A MATTER OF SCHOLARLY STANDARDS?

∂

Despite the many irregularities that I have detailed in these pages, the university was ultimately successful in its attempt to fire me. That it was, is an index of the ease with which the procedural rules intended to protect the academic freedom of faculty members can be circumvented when political appearances and fear call for such measures. It should be said that while my own case is no doubt by far the most sensational—or sensationalized—I am by no means the only University of Colorado faculty member to have been targeted for elimination in recent years because of our politics.[125] Indeed, UCB availed itself of the opportunity presented by the initial furor over my Eichmann analogy, to rid itself of Adrienne Anderson, a highly rated instructor shared by Environmental and Ethnic Studies whose superlative research on military/corporate pollution in the Denver area had long been the bane of Lockheed-Martin, Coors, and other major contributors to the university. Documents disclosed under Colorado's Open Records Act have subsequently revealed that the corporations, in concert with the governor and several Republican legislators, had brought considerable and sustained pressure on the administration to eliminate Anderson precisely because she was so effective, both in exposing their often illegal activities and in teaching students how to do so. The courses she was teaching have at this point been replaced by offerings on "environmental management" taught by the UCB School of Business.[126]

Such developments are by no means unique to the Colorado context. Even as Bill O'Reilly was launching his nightly blitz against me, Shahid Alam, a professor of economics at Northeastern University, was targeted for comparable defamation by Daniel Pipes. At Columbia University, Joseph Massad, George Saliba, and Hamid Dabashi, all faculty members of Department of Middle East and Asian Languages and Cultures (MEALAC), were accused of "anti-Semitism" by students belonging to the "David Project," a Horowitz-affiliated "Zionist youth organization."[127]

That researchers in the hard sciences are not immune to such politically motivated abuse is also demonstrated by the experience of University of Virginia climatologist Michael Mann, Raymond Bradley of the University of Massachusetts, and the University of Arizona's Malcolm Hughes, who, together, had authored a seminal paper on "the hockey stick effect" of fossil fuel emissions in producing global warming.[128] In June 2005, Republican congressman Joe Barton, Exxon/Mobil-backed chair of the House Committee on Energy and Commerce, issued a demand that the trio cough up a lengthy list of materials supporting the conclusions drawn from every study for which they'd ever received even partial federal funding, including specialized computer programs they'd written for purposes of modeling various climatic processes, all within three weeks.[129] As in my own case, the "necessity" for such sweeping and intensive scrutiny is said to result from claims of "research fraud" advanced by a pair of obscure and self-evidently reactionary "scholars."[130]

This technique of seeking to discredit the content of dissident scholarship by questioning the integrity of method employed by those producing it has been honed to an exceedingly fine edge by the Right over the past quarter-century. To appreciate the implications in their full impact, it is necessary to consider the record of consequences suffered by right-wing academics revealed to have engaged in often quite extravagant violations of the rules of scholarship applied with such rigidity to those on the left. A useful comparison is between the penalty imposed upon Michael Bellesiles for supposedly falsifying a minor amount of data providing marginal support to his thesis, and that suffered by the NRA's favorite "independent scholar," John R. Lott, when it was revealed that he'd simply fabricated the survey data anchoring the entire argument he presented in his acclaimed *More Guns, Less Crime* (aka, "the Bible of the Gun Lobby").

To launch his vociferous polemic in behalf of gun ownership, Lott claims that "98 per cent of the time that people use guns defensively, they merely have to brandish a weapon to break off an attack."[131] He based this on "national surveys."[132] When this assertion was challenged in *The Criminologist*,[133] however, Lott abruptly switched his reference to a previously unmentioned "national survey [he himself had] conducted."[134] Lott could not defend this version of reality either. First, he claimed that he'd lost all data on the 2,424 "respondents" surveyed in a computer crash, then he couldn't provide information as to where he'd acquired the list from which the sample was supposedly taken. When asked who'd placed the thousands of calls required to have gleaned more than 2,400 responses, he claimed that the work had been done by "undergraduate student volunteers." He could provide neither the names of these students nor phone records, however.[135] Lott, to be sure, did have his defenders, the staunchest of whom turned out to be Lott himself, writing under the pseudonym "Mary Rosh." This, rather than the magnitude of the research fraud he'd perpetrated, briefly caught the attention of the national media.[136] In other words, unlike Bellesiles, Lott was given an all but complete pass by the press.

Also conspicuously absent is James Lindgren, the Northwestern University law professor and active member of the right-wing Federalist Society described above as a "ubiquitous" presence in the media campaign against Bellesiles. Having conducted the preliminary investigation revealing the fraudulence of Lott's "survey," Lindgren suddenly announced that he had "no research interests in this subfield," that the inquiry "distract[ed] from [his] other scholarly efforts," and that he was therefore dropping the matter.[137] Only a few months later, he reversed himself completely, suddenly displaying an all but obsessive "research interest" in the very same "subfield" through his relentless effort to destroy Bellesiles.

By any reasonable estimation, it was the different intensities with which they were pursued rather than any greater degree of egregiousness embodied in the offenses of which Bellesiles was accused that account for the fact that he suffered a far harsher penalty than Lott. True, Lott could not be subjected to formal academic sanction since he occupied no academic position (rather, he was funded by the right-wing Olin Foundation at the time he wrote *More Guns, Less Crime,* and has since moved into a berth with the equally reactionary American Enterprise Institute, where he is paid to emit much the same spew).[138] This, however, does not explain why, although the plainly fraudulent data upon which its argument depends remains very much intact, the University of Chicago Press continues to promote Lott's book on its website, complete with glowing endorsements from the *Wall Street Journal, Business Week,* and "Goth U's" (the University of Chicago's) own icon of "free market" economics, Milton Friedman.[139] Plainly, the rigor with which the academy's vaunted "standards of scholarly integrity" are enforced is rather situational.

There is much more that should be said with regard to how the duplicitous use of "academic misconduct" charges has come to be a primary tactic employed by the Right in its campaign to purge what it sees as key voices from the academy (and thereby to nullify critical discourse more generally), how the liberal Left has been increasingly complicit in this process, what it portends not only for the notion of academic freedom but for the function of higher education in its entirety, and how my own case may be used as a lens through which to examine this broader reality. Suffice it here to note that these and related matters are addressed in substantially greater depth in a longer—that is, near-book-length—version of the present essay.

NOTES

1. The language quoted accrues from the Laws of the Regents of the University of Colorado as amended on October 10, 2002, at 5.D.1. I have deleted the original formatting for reasons of space and readability.

2. Ibid., 5.D.2.

3. Ibid.

4. For details concerning October 20, 1981, incident and Rosenberg's ostensible background role in it, see John Castellucci, *The Big Dance: The Untold Story of Weather-Man Kathy Boudin and the Terrorist Family That Committed the Brinks Robbery Murders* (New York: Dodd, Mead, 1986).

5. Saito was on leave from Georgia State at the time, having accepted a tenured position with the Department of Ethnic Studies at the University of Colorado–Boulder. She will shortly be returning to her position at Georgia State. Candor requires that I disclose the fact that we were married in July 2005.

6. As my appearance at the college became increasingly "controversial" during late January, Hamilton president Joan Hinde Stewart prevailed upon Professor Rabinowitz to add a third speaker—an avowedly pacifist resident philosophy professor named Richard Werner—to my and Saito's "panel," and to change the focus of our collective presentation to "The Limits of Dissent."

7. My op-ed, titled "Some People Push Back: On the Justice of Roosting Chickens," was written during the afternoon and evening of 9/11, and posted on the *Dark Night* website on September 12, 2005. The virulence of the response it has

evoked is in some ways peculiar, given that my "Nazi analogy" follows closely upon Hannah Arendt's reasoning in her *Eichmann in Jerusalem: A Report on the Banality of Evil,* 2nd ed. (New York: Viking, 1964). Similar metaphors have been employed many times by activists like David Dellinger, as well as Noam Chomsky and other dissident scholars; on Dellinger, see his *More Power Than We Know* (New York: Anchor Press/Doubleday, 1975), 51; for examples from Chomsky (occasionally quoting other scholars), see his *American Power and the New Mandarins* (New York: Pantheon, 1967), 8–9, 14–15, 165–69, 213 n. 37, 308, 323–24, 337, 363 n. 64; *The Culture of Terrorism* (Boston: South End Press, 1988), 255–56; *Rogue States: The Rule of Force in International Affairs* (Cambridge, Mass.: South End Press, 2000), 45, 85, 162–64; *Hegemony or Survival: America's Quest for Global Dominance* (New York: Metropolitan Books, 2003), 13, 68–69, 189, 191. Even such mainstreamer politicos as George McGovern and Illinois senator Dick Durbin have made such comparisons; Mc Govern quoted in Fred Turner, *Echoes of Combat: The Vietnam War in American Memory* (New York: Anchor Books, 1996), 50, and Eric Zorn, "What Dick Durbin *Should* Have Said," *Chicago Tribune,* June 23, 2005.

8. "Taking Points: Hamilton College Folds," *O'Reilly Factor Flash,* www.billoreilly.com/show?action= viewTVshow&showed=17, February 1, 2005.

9. See "Support Shareef Aleem," *Rocky Mountain Resister* (Denver), October 25, 2006.

10. See Elizabeth Mattern Clark, "CU Tenure Attacked after Spat: Professor's Essay Sparks Calls to End Protective System," *Daily Camera,* February 6, 2005; Colleen Slevin, "It's Baaaaack: Academic Freedom Bill Has Provision on Tenure," *Colorado Daily,* February 11, 2005.

11. For a sample of the editorial cant, see Victor Davis Hanson, "A Case against University Tenure," May 13, 2005, http://m.dailycamera.com/news/2005/may/13/hanson-a-case-against-university-tenure/, accessed January 5, 2009; Mike Rosen, "Just the Tip of the Iceberg," *Rocky Mountain News,* February 11, 2005; Andrew Cohen, "Churchill's Work Needs Close Look," *Denver Post,* February 13, 2005; Scott Heiser, "What about Churchill's Honor Code?" *Colorado Daily,* February 17, 2005.

12. Casey Freeman, "Giuliani Speaks to CU: Former NYC Mayor Talks about Churchill, Leadership," *Colorado Daily,* April 4, 2005.

13. Those appointed to the SCRM Subcommittee of Inquiry were professors Cort Pierpont (biochemistry), Russell Moore (physiology), and Bella Mody (journalism). There was also a graduate student. *None* of these individuals professed—or exhibited—the least professional familiarity with my own or related fields. Rosse later acknowledged that this lack of disciplinary heterogeneity may have been problematic in terms of affording me a fair hearing at the inquiry stage; *P&T Hearing Transcript,* January 20, 2007, 1880, 1967–68.

14. Philip P. DiStefano to Prof. Joe Rosse, "Referral to the Standing Committee on Research Misconduct, University of Colorado at Boulder; Professor Ward Churchill," March 29, 2005, 3 (copy on file). This document is hereinafter cited as *DiStefano Referral.* The references are to "Bringing the Law Back Home: Application of the Genocide Convention to the United States," in my *Indians Are Us? Culture and Genocide in Native North America* (Monroe, Maine: Common Courage Press, 1993), 11, 35; and my *A Little Matter of Genocide: Holocaust and Denial in the Americas, 1492 through the Present* (San Francisco: City Lights, 1997), 155–56.

15. *DiStefano Referral,* 1–2. The references are to the essay "Perversions of Jus-

tice: Examining the Doctrine of U.S. Rights to Occupancy in North America," in my *Struggle for the Land: Indigenous Resistance to Genocide, Ecocide, and Expropriation in Contemporary North America* (Monroe, Maine: Common Courage Press, 1993), 49; and "Like Sand in the Wind: The Making of an American Indian Diaspora in the United States," in the revised and expanded second edition of the same book, *Struggle for the Land: Native North American Resistance to Genocide, Ecocide, and Colonization* (San Francisco: City Lights, 2002), 341.

16. *DiStefano Referral, 2.* The reference is to the essay "Nobody's Pet Poodle: Jimmie Durham, an Artist for Native North America," in my *Indians Are Us?* 89, 92.

17. *DiStefano Referral, 4.* The first such allegation is to language appearing from an article published under the byline of Rebecca L. Robbins that is incorporated verbatim and without attribution into my essay "Perversions of Justice," 93; and again in the same essay as it appears in my *Perversions of Justice: Indigenous Peoples and Angloamerican Law* (San Francisco: City Lights, 2003), 14. The second allegation concerns language duplicating, with partial or insufficient attribution, that contained in an article by Fay G. Cohen included in one of my anthologies. Curiously, the apparent plagiarism occurs in an essay that was *not* authored by me; see Institute for Natural Progress, "In Usual and Accustomed Places: Contemporary American Indian Fishing Rights Struggles," in *The State of Native America: Genocide, Colonization, and Resistance,* ed. M. Annette Jaimes (Boston: South End Press, 1992), 217–40.

18. "The question of Professor Churchill's Indian status with respect to research misconduct is whether he attempted to gain a scholarly voice, credibility, and an audience for his scholarship by wrongfully asserting that he is an American Indian. . . . The committee should inquire as to whether Professor Churchill can assert a reasonable basis for clarifying such identity"; *DiStefano Referral, 5.*

19. I referred to the hospital as "St. Joseph's" although it was actually St. Anthony's. See my "Kizhiibaabinesik: A Bright Star Burning Briefly," in Leah Renae Kelly, *In My Own Voice: Explorations in the Sociopolitical Context of Art and Cinema* (Winnipeg: Arbiter Ring, 2001), 49.

20. I stated that both of my wife's parents attended residential schools; ibid., 27. In actuality, although the facility she attended accommodated residential students—and was thus a residential school—my former mother-in-law was a day student there. It was further asserted that I erred with regard to the name of the school attended by my late father-in-law, although I took the information directly from his CV (copy on file).

21. A few months before her death, my wife—a severe alcoholic—was diagnosed by Centennial Peaks clinicians as suffering from Borderline Personality Disorder (paperwork on file). On the ugly and intractable nature of this malady, see Judith Herman, *Trauma and Recovery: The Aftermath of Violence—from Domestic Abuse to Political Terror,* 2nd ed. (New York: Basic Books, 1997), esp. 123–26, 136–39, 147.

22. My late father-in-law openly acknowledged that his own acute alcoholism derived from his residential school experience and that his resulting behavior traumatized all six of his children, of whom my late wife was the youngest. One of my wife's brothers has suffered acute alcoholism and other symptoms of childhood trauma for well over a decade; a second brother recently suffered the breakup of his family as a result of his own losing battle with alcohol, while the third brother and

a sister—both in their forties—live what amounts to lives devoid of romantic relationships while continuing to reside in their mother's basement. The eldest sister, who raised the complaint against me, spent years attending Adult Children of Alcoholics meetings while getting her own drinking problem under control, and remains one of the most empathy-impaired people I've ever encountered. These patterns are directly indicative of "Residential School Syndrome," as is—in some ways even more prominently—a pathological compulsion to deny that the patterns exist. See Herman, *Trauma and Recovery*, 1–2, 9, 28–29, 87, 101, 180–81; Donald L. Nathanson, "Denial, Projection and the Empathic Wall," and Michael H. Stone, "Denial in Borderlines," both in *Denial: A Clarification of Concepts and Research*, ed. E. L. Edelstein, Donald L. Nathanson, and Andrew M. Stone (New York: Plenum Press, 1989), 37–60, 203–18; William H. Crisman, *The Opposite of Everything Is True: Reflections on Denial in Alcoholic Families* (New York: Quill, 1991). With regard to the Residential School Syndrome itself, see Assembly of First Nations, *Breaking the Silence: An Interpretive Study of Residential School Impact and Healing as Illustrated by the Stories of First Nations Individuals* (Ottawa: Assembly of First Nations, 1994).

23. This was mentioned in a single sentence in one of 257 footnotes. I don't dispute the error. It's worth mentioning, however, that Rhonda Kelly, who raised the issue, very much considers her own children to be Ojibwe—as do the rest of the family—despite the fact that their father is a "full-blood" Croat. This is hardly suggestive of adherence to a patrilineal tradition.

24. "I have concluded that these allegations, even if true, do not represent research misconduct"; letter, Rosse to DiStefano, August 30, 2005 (copy on file). Also see Associated Press, "3 Allegations about Churchill Not Misconduct: CU Panel Tells Distefano It Is Not Committee's Job to Judge Inaccuracies," *Boulder Daily Camera*, September 8, 2005.

25. "Report to the Standing Committee on Research Misconduct from the Inquiry Subcommittee Appointed to Consider Allegations of Research Misconduct Against Professor Ward Churchill," August 19, 2005 (copy on file); Jennifer Brown, "Tentative 'Victory' for Prof: Churchill Report Supports Dropping of Ethnicity Issue," *Denver Post*, August 23, 2005; Amy Herdy, "CU Panel Drops Three Allegations against Churchill," *Denver Post*, September 7, 2005.

26. "Churchill Asks Cu Panel to Discontinue Its Inquiry," *Denver Post*, September 2, 2005; P. Solomon Banda (AP), "Churchill Investigation Moving Forward: New Committee to Research Seven Allegations," *Boulder Daily Camera*, September 10, 2005; Arthur Kane, "Prof Decries CU Statement: Churchill Accuses CU of 'Shoddy' Handling of Case," *Denver Post*, September 13, 2005.

27. As the subcommittee put it at p. 10 of its findings, "A comparison shows that Ward Churchill's style and the writing style of the so-called 'Robbins' chapter are similar, leading us to believe that Ward Churchill's claim that he wrote the chapter and gave Robbins authorship may have merit. . . . [T]here has been complete silence from Robbins in the face of Churchill's supposed misuse over the last dozen years, lending credence to Churchill's account." Also see Jim Hughes and Amy Herdy, "Churchill Says He's Ghostwriter: CU Prof Denies Plagiarism," *Denver Post*, May 26, 2005; Berny Morson, "1993 Essay Also Raises Questions: Churchill Says Pieces Credited to Others Are Actually His Work," *Rocky Mountain News*, June 7, 2005.

28. This allegation was based entirely upon a single sentence in the edited transcription of a public lecture I delivered at the Brecht Center in 1998, published under the title "An American Holocaust? The Structure of Denial," *Socialism and Democracy* 17.2 (2003): 25–75. Appearing on p. 54, it reads: "There's some pretty strong circumstantial evidence that Smith introduced smallpox among the Wampanoags as a means of clearing the way for the invaders." In support, I cited Neal Salisbury's *Manitou and Providence: Indians, Europeans, and the Making of New England, 1500–1643* (New York: Oxford University Press, 1982), 96–101. I should probably have extended the page-span through p. 109. I could also have cited additional sources. Such points are mooted by the fact that Salisbury refers to the Wampanoags as "Pokanokets," and it appears that none of the subcommittee members—not one of whom were trained in a relevant discipline (indeed, all but one are tenured in the hard sciences)—were equipped to realize that both names refer to the same people.

29. These consisted of (1) my alleged misrepresentation of the 1887 act, (2) similar misrepresentation of the 1990 act, (3) my supposed fabrication of the John Smith / smallpox connection, circa 1614, (4) a similar fabrication of the U.S. Army / smallpox connection in 1837, (5) plagiarizing *Dam the Dams,* (6) plagiarizing Fay Cohen, and (7) plagiarizing Rebecca Robbins, an independent scholar; University of Colorado at Boulder, Office of Research Integrity, August 19, 2005 (copy on file).

30. Email, Ward Churchill to Joseph G. Rosse, October 12, 2005, Subject: RE: exclusions; quoting email dated October 11, Rosse to Churchill, on the same topic (copy on file). During the subsequent P&T review, Rosse claimed that the SCRM later abandoned this criterion for disqualification. He was unable to produce a memorandum or any other form of corroborating evidence, however, and was unable to recall *when* this decision was supposedly made.

31. Ibid. Also see email, Churchill to Rosse, October 8, 2005, Subject: Re: Possible members of the SCRM Investigative Committee (copy on file).

32. "I must express strong concern regarding the inclusion of anyone from the law faculty, given the poisonous atmosphere instigated there by David Getches, Paul Campos, and several others over the past few months"; email, Churchill to Rosse, October 8, 2005, Subject: Re: Possible members of the SCRM Investigative Committee (copy on file).

33. Email, Marianne (Mimi) Wesson to [name withheld at the request of the recipient], February 28, 2005, Subject: SUSPECT: Re: [SALT] Letter Supporting Ward Churchill (copy on file). The missive was sent from Wesson's university address. The acronym "SALT" refers to the Society of American Law Teachers.

34. Wesson testified that she turned copies of all offending emails over to Rosse, in his capacity as chair of the SCRM, with the expectation that he, in turn, would provide copies to me, and professed "surprise" that he'd not done so; *P&T Hearing Transcript,* January 8, 2007, 147–48, 154–55. Rosse, for his part, stated repeatedly that he did not recall her doing so; *P&T Hearing Transcript,* January 20, 2007, 1938–40. In any case, copies have never been divulged by the university, despite its obligation under the Colorado Open Records Act to do so upon request.

35. Williams holds a joint appointment in the law school and the American Indian Studies program at Arizona. He also serves as a tribal judge for both the Pascua Yaqui and Tohono O'odam, as well as a legal consultant for the Navajo Nation; *P&T Hearing Transcript,* January 11, 2007, 1298–99.

36. Jim Kirksey, "CU Names Five Investigating Churchill," *Denver Post*, November 2, 2005; AP, "Churchill Panel Members Named: CU Identifies Committee Members," *Colorado Daily*, November 3, 2005. The press release itself is dated November 1, 2005.

37. See, e.g., Caplis and Silverman, "Is the Churchill Review Committee Compromised?" (audio archive, http://www.khow.com/hosts/caplis-silverman.html), accessed November 25, 2005.

38. Email, Churchill to Rosse, December 21, 2005, Subject: RE: committee (copy on file).

39. Marianne Wesson, Robert N. Clinton, José E. Limón, Marjorie McIntosh, and Michael Radelet, *Report of the Investigative Committee of the Standing Committee on Research Misconduct at the University of Colorado at Boulder concerning Allegations of Academic Misconduct against Professor Ward Churchill* (May 10, 2006), 10, http://www.wardchurchill.net; hereafter cited as *Investigative Report*.

40. It is, for example, argued at p. 89 of the *Investigative Report* that "the publication of one's own scholarly work (as distinct from creative work or fiction) under another name" constitutes a "failure to comply with established standards regarding author names on publications" under both the SCRM rules and the CU system's "Statement on Misconduct in Research and Authorship." Neither formulation contains language exempting "creative work and fiction" published by faculty members, however. This, in all likelihood is due to the fact that—as several one-time SCRM members have pointed out—the rules were never intended to proscribe the practices at issue in my case. Rather, they were written to prohibit faculty members from engaging in the widespread practice of appropriating the work of / denying authorial credit to student research assistants. On the scope of the latter problem, see generally, Bill L. Williamson, "(Ab)Using Students: The Ethics of Faculty Use of a Student's Work Product," *Arizona State Law* 26 (Winter 1994): 1029–73.

41. *Investigative Report*, 10.

42. Interestingly, the SCRM rules provide that a "preponderance of the evidence" is sufficient to establish guilt, while the P&T requires that evidence be "clear and convincing." It is the latter standard that the investigative panel failed to meet. Although research misconduct proceedings are the academic equivalent of a criminal prosecution, the "reasonable doubt" standard is not applied at any level, at least by the University of Colorado.

43. *Investigative Report*, 38, 42.

44. University of Colorado, Faculty Senate Committee on Privilege and Tenure, *Panel Report regarding Dismissal for Cause of Ward Churchill and the Issue of Selective Enforcement* (April 11, 2007), 48, 52; hereafter cited as *P&T Report*, http://www.wardchurchill.net.

45. Ibid., 52, 53.

46. Ibid., 49.

47. Ibid., 51.

48. Ibid., 54.

49. Bernard Pratte, Jr., captain of the *St. Peter's*—the boat on which the infected items were transported upriver—stated in interview some thirty years after the fact that they were brought to St. Louis from Baltimore by an unnamed fur company employee who I've been able to identify as William May. Pratte says May placed the

items aboard the *St. Peter's* itself. An independent source both identifies the infected items as having been blankets, and says that they were towed upriver in a pair of Mackinaw boats. It is confirmed that the *St. Peter's* was towing such boats. I have also been able to confirm that smallpox was present in Baltimore in late 1836, reaching epidemic proportions in 1837. Citations regarding these matters are being withheld, pending publication of an essay fully devoted to the topic.

50. *Investigative Transcript,* February 18, 2006, 107, 109.

51. While Barbour says that the job "fell to Larpenteur" because Denig was "incapacitated" by his illness, this would seem to be something of an overstatement. As Robertson and others have observed, Denig recovered rather quickly; by August he and Larpenteur were "work[ing] together" in administering "the white world's medical remedies." See Barton H. Barbour, *Fort Union and the Upper Missouri Fur Trade* (Norman: University of Oklahoma, 2001); R. G. Robertson, *Rotting Face: Smallpox and the American Indian* (Caldwall, Idaho: Canton Press, 2001), 175–76; testimony of Michael J. Timbrook, *Investigative Transcript,* February 18, 2006, 116.

52. As was pointed out by Getches to the P&T panel, Thornton has been quoted in the press as making this claim; *P&T Hearing Transcript,* January 20, 2007, 1867. For Thornton's statements, see David Kelly, "Colorado Professor Faces Claims of Academic Fraud," *Los Angeles Times,* February 12, 2005.

53. Russell Thornton, *American Indian Holocaust and Survival: A Population History since 1492* (Norman: University of Oklahoma Press, 1987), 94–95; cite on p. 95. Providing such a reference rather than attempting to offer estimates in his own text was probably a wise choice on Thornton's part, given his inability to keep his numbers straight. On p. 95 he states that the 1837 epidemic claimed "virtually all of several thousand Mandan," while in a chart at the top of p. 96 he indicates that the Mandan population numbered only "1600–2000" in 1836. This is only one of many such examples.

54. Robert Boyd, *The Coming of the Spirit of Pestilence: Introduced Infectious Diseases and Population Decline among Northwest Coast Indians* (Vancouver: University of British Columbia Press, 2000), 136.

55. *P&T Report,* 54.

56. When, for example, in response to my attorney's attempt to question Wesson about the practices prevailing in legal scholarship, the university counsel heatedly objected, "This isn't law," Langer instructed my attorney, "Please stick to the question of whether this is question of history or sociology or ethnics [*sic*]." A few minutes later, when Lane attempted to return to the topic, the university counsel again objected. Langer sustained the objection, stating, "We'll stay out of law." Later, when Lane attempted to question expert witness McCabe about Harvard law professor Richard Ogletree's admitted reliance on student ghostwriters, Langer's response was, "Again, let's stay away from law"; *P&T Hearing Transcript,* January 8, 2007, 243, 249, 370.

57. Langer's exact framing was that legal scholarship is "not the Arts and Sciences, so please let's leave the law example alone"; *P&T Hearing Transcript,* January 8, 2007, 365.

58. In this connection, I observed that the people "hired by political science departments have often been "primarily engaged in what amounts to ghostwriting, formulating policy statements and so forth. Those go out under the senator's name or the president's name. Who do we cite?" Langer, in a complete logical tangle, cut

off this line of questioning, saying that such issues are not "within the university framework" because "Under scholarship. If you cite so-and-so, you assume they have written it, and if they haven't written it, within the academic community, that's a problem"; *P&T Hearing Transcript,* January 8, 2007, 389–91.

59. *Investigative Report,* 90. McCabe, also offering no supporting evidence, made an all but identical assertion: "Broadly, I think there's a common understanding across the academic community with the need to appropriately cite the source of materials"; *P&T Hearing Transcript,* January 8, 2007, 394. For their part, the P&T panelists, "acknowledg[ing] the difficulty in finding specific guidelines related to ghostwriting" nonetheless went on to speak of "*what we take to be* accepted standards by large components of the academic world"; *P&T Report,* 66; emphasis added.

60. *P&T Report,* 66.

61. My recounting is quoted at length in the *P&T Report* at p. 57. As the P&T panelists observe on the same page, John Hummel, the individual who requested my assistance, has been quoted "in a manner generally consistent with Professor Churchill's testimony."

62. The volume was *Critical Issues in Native North America,* ed. Ward Churchill (Copenhagen: IWGIA, [1989]).

63. Even if they had, the university's "jurisdiction" in the matter would have been questionable at best, given that the material was published prior to my joining the UCB faculty. The 1988 version of the material was never included in my CV, and thus played no role in my hiring or promotion. The *Z Magazine* article, moreover, was neither a scholarly publication nor ever claimed as such. That DiStefano—following the *Rocky Mountain News*—advanced allegations on these matters in the first place, that the SCRM opted to treat them as falling within its purview, and that both the investigative and the P&T panels followed suit, speaks volumes to the nature of the process.

64. *Investigative Report,* 84, 87; *P&T Report,* 55, 56, 59.

65. As Wesson frames the matter at p. 87 of the *Investigative Report,* my "footnotes . . . are not associated with . . . near-verbatim language from the 1989 [*sic,* 1988] essay" appearing in the paragraphs to which the note numbers are attached. In other words, they do not appear in *direct* conjunction with the passages paraphrased.

66. At issue are the version of the "Water Plot" included in the 1993 edition of my *Struggle for the Land,* and its greatly expanded successor, and in the 2002 edition of *Struggle* (both eds. cited in note 15) at pp. 329–74 and 292–329, respectively. In the earlier version, the 1988 book chapter crediting *Dam the Dams* as first author is cited five times—in notes 16, 91, 94, 106, 114—while the *Z Magazine* article is unmentioned. In the later version, the book chapter is once again cited five times—in notes 16, 91, 94, 110, 137—while the article remains unmentioned.

67. Quoted in Morson, "1993 Essay Also Raises Questions."

68. Prof. Stephen Cahn, a specialist in academic ethics at the CUNY Graduate Center, quoted in Morson, "1993 Essay Also Raises Questions."

69. "[T]here is no refutation of Professor Churchill's claim that others were responsible for the alleged plagiarism"; *Investigative Report,* 68, as paraphrased in *P&T Report,* 68.

70. The INP was a "think tank."

71. Even Jaimes, who refused through her attorney to speak with the investigative panel—the P&T panel did not attempt to contact her—has been quoted in the press as at least partially corroborating my own description of my role, stating that, as she recalled, what I'd gone over was "a preliminary or pilot paper." For obvious reasons, she also professed *not* to recall who'd been involved in writing it; quoted in Laura Frank, "Prof Accused of Plagarism: Nova Scotia School Sends CU a Report on Churchill Essay," *Rocky Mountain News,* March 11, 2005. On Jaimes's refusal to speak to the investigative panel, see *Investigative Report,* 92; *P&T Report,* 68.

72. *P&T Report,* 67; citing *"Investigative Report,* p. 91" as well as Dalhousie document itself. As is clearly stated at p. 91 of the *Investigative Report,* however, the "well-documented conclusion" reached by legal counsel at Dalhousie was that the passages plagiarized from Cohen appeared in an essay she'd written for the second volume of *Critical Issues in Native North America,* which I'd edited, and which was published fully a year before the Jaimes book. The Dalhousie document reaches no "conclusion that [Churchill] was responsible for the plagiarism of Cohen in *State of Native America,"* and the investigative panel nowhere claims that it does.

73. The document at issue assumes the form of a letter: Brian C. Crocker, Q.C., University Secretary and Legal Counsel, Dalhousie University, to Social Sciences and Humanities Research Council of Canada, Re: Plagiarism, February 9, 1997 (copy on file).

74. In a written response to my question as to why she'd waited "approximately 13 years to complain to the University of Colorado about any role I may have had" in plagiarizing her material, Cohen stated that she "did not 'complain' at *any* point in time" and had provided a copy of Crocker's letter *"only when requested [to do so by] University of Colorado officials."* Fay G. Cohen to Eric Elliff, Re: Professor Ward Churchill, April 11, 2006 (copy on file); emphases added.

75. Cohen to Elliff, April 11, 2006, 3.

76. *P&T Report,* 70; *Investigative Report,* 93.

77. Much was also made of my being credited, in the volume's "About the Contributors" section, with having "assumed the lead role in preparing the INP contribution" to *The State of Native America.* It was demonstrated during the investigation, however, that the entries had been written by the volume editor, Jaimes, rather than the individual contributors. It is worth mentioning, moreover, that had she said that I'd "assumed the lead role in *finalizing* the INP contribution," the entry would have been quite accurate. As I explained to Wesson during an exchange on the matter, it is my impression that Jaimes may have felt she was thanking me for my assistance by framing the entry as she did. In the alternative, of course, she may have been trying to disguise her own plagiarism. See *Investigative Transcript,* April 1, 2006, 122, 127; *Investigative Report,* 92.

78. *P&T Report,* 61; *Investigative Report,* 88. The essays primarily at issue were Robbins's "Self-Determination and Subordination: The Past, Present, and Future of American Indian Self-Governance," and Jaimes's "Federal Indian Identification Policy: A Usurpation of Indigenous Sovereignty in North America," both in Jaimes, *State of Native America,* at 87–122 and 123–38 respectively.

79. *P&T Report,* 64, 66.

80. Ibid., 66. To their credit, the panelists seem to have simply ignored—or at least declined to rely upon—Clinton's tortured attempt to gloss the issue by arguing that the standards at issue are "established," not in black letter form, but within

a sort of "academic common law"; *P&T Hearing Transcripts,* January 9, 2007, 577–80.

81. All three are quoted in Morson, "1993 Essay Also Raises Questions."

82. "[A] single counterexample, no matter how distinguished, cannot nullify an overwhelming consensus about established practices"; *Investigative Report,* 90. The reference to "a single counterexample" concerns the fact that when asked by the investigative panel whether I could name a scholar known to have published under names other than his/her own and not been censured as a result. My immediate response—although I subsequently provided a number of other examples—was "C.L.R. James."

83. *Investigative Report,* 23, 24, 31.

84. Ibid., 90.

85. *P&T Report,* 66.

86. *Investigative Report,* 23, 24, 31, 90.

87. Ibid., 90.

88. There is no shortage of readily-available manuals on this, produced both for those desiring to ghostwrite and for those—including scholars—desiring their services. See, e.g., Eva Shaw, Ph.D., *Ghostwriting for Fun and Profit* (Carlsbad, CA: Writeriffic, 2004).

89. Ibid.

90. Sorenson ghostwrote numerous articles for Kennedy, as well as his *Profiles in Courage* (New York: Harper Bros., 1956). For details, see Sorenson's memoir, *Counselor: A Life at the Edge of History* (New York: Harper, 2008) 142–52, 259–60.

91. "In traditional Indian practices, "authorship has no importance whatsoever," at least in this respect; testimony of Prof. Eric Cheyfitz, *P&T Hearing Transcript,* January 12, 2007, 1606. At p. 1607, Cheyfitz goes on to link such concepts to "some pretty sophisticated literary theory [like that set forth in] Foucault's famous essay, 'What is an Author?'" The essay in question is included in Paul Raninow, ed., *The Foucault Reader* (New York: Pantheon, 1984), 101–20.

92. Testimony of Prof. Robert A. Williams, Jr., *P&T Hearing Transcript,* January 11, 2007, 1335–36. At pp. 1339–41, when confronted with the same question in connection with the Jaimes essay, Williams replied, "It doesn't matter. . . . [A]s far as I'm concerned, it's clearly, clearly within the accepted realm of discursive stances of [an] Indian studies scholar." Williams also links my citational practice in this regard to "Homi Bhabha's notion [of] plasticity and double identity and posing," observing that "anybody who reads anything in postcolonial theory knows that the idea of the pose is absolutely necessary for the minority scholar to say certain things."

93. *Investigative Report,* 23. Also see Prof. Clinton's testimony in *P&T Hearing Transcript,* January 12, 2007, 1614–18.

94. *Investigative Report,* 23, 25, 73.

95. Ibid., 25.

96. Ibid., 24, 23.

97. *P&T Hearing Transcript,* January 9, 2007, 692.

98. Ibid., 692–93.

99. *P&T Hearing Transcript,* January 10, 2007, 937. The book in question is Marjorie Keniston McIntosh, *Working Women in English Society, 1300–1620* (Cambridge: Cambridge University Press, 2005).

100. Ibid., 938.

101. *P&T Report,* ii.

102. Ibid., 6.

103. Ibid., ii.

104. Allison Sherry and Tom McGee, "Regents Ax Prof; Battle Not Yet Set-tled," *Denver Post,* July 25, 2007; Berny Morson, "Churchill Fired; Next Shot in Court," *Rocky Mountain News,* July 25, 2007; Brittany Anas, "Churchill Dismissed: Controversial CU Prof Vows to Fight Back with Lawsuit," *Daily Camera,* July 25, 2007; Paula Plant and Nicole Danna, "Churchill Fired: Tenured Professor Dismissed from CU for Academic Misconduct by a Vote of 8–1," *Colorado Daily,* July 25, 2007.

105. Cheyfitzis quoted extensively in Jefferson Dodge, "Debate over Churchill Case Persists: P&T Report to Go to President Brown next Week," *Silver and Gold Record,* March 29, 2007.

106. Mimi Wesson, "An Error in Report on Churchill Needs Correction," *Silver & Gold Record,* April 12, 2007. Although "writing in [her] capacity as chair of the in-vestigative committee," Wesson purported speaks only for herself ("It is not possi-ble at this juncture for me to speak in behalf of the entire committee"). The book in question is Neal Salisbury, *Manitou and Providence: Europeans, Indians, and the Making of New England, 1500–1643* (New York: Oxford University Press, 1982).

107. Professors Eric Cheyfitz, Elisa Facio, Vijay Gupta, Margaret LeCompte, Paul Levitt, Tom Mayer, Emma Perez, Martin Walter, and Michael Yellow Bird, "Open Letter from Faculty Calling for Churchill Report Retraction," *Silver & Gold Record,* April 23, 2007.

108. Professors Vijay Gupta, Margaret LeCompte, Paul Levitt, Thomas Mayer, Emma Perez, Michael Yellow Bird, Eric Cheyfitz, Elisa Facio, Martin Walter, Leonard Baca, and Brenda Romero, "A Filing of Research Misconduct Charges against the Churchill Investigating Committee," submitted to the SCRM on May 10, 2007 (available at http://wardchurchill.net). For background, see Jefferson Dodge, "Group: Look into Churchill Committee," *Silver & Gold Record,* May 17, 2007.

109. My original grievance concerning the administration's continuous breaches of confidentiality was filed in June 2005. As of August 2006, the only ac-tion taken by the P&T Committee was to request that I combine it with a griev-ance I'd filed on the matter of selective enforcement in November 2005, and re-submit. See letter, Churchill to Lodwick (chair of the P&T Committee), Re: Attached Consolidated Grievance, August 16, 2006 (copy on file).

110. Professors Lynda Dickson (chair), Jana Everett, Laurie Gaspar, and Joe Juhasz, "Level 2 Panel Report: Grievance on Breaches of Confidentiality against Professor Ward Churchill," July 10, 2007 (copy on file), 3.

111. Ibid., 3.

112. Ibid., 4.

113. Peterson to Weldon A. Lodwick, Privilege and Tenure Chair, September 18, 2007 (copy on file).

114. DiStefano—who undoubtedly thought his services in my case would be more suitably rewarded—was thereupon forced to reclaim his permanent position as provost, displacing Susan Avery, who then returned to the faculty. Such is often the lot of liberals who collaborate in the fulfillment of reactionary agendas.

115. Letter, Rosse to Churchill, Re: Allegations of Research Misconduct, July 18, 2007 (copy on file).

116. Jefferson Dodge, "Churchill, Others Had Filed Claims against Committee," *Silver & Gold Record,* July 26, 2007.

117. Quoted in ibid. I also pointed out that if the investigation had been "administrative," there was no need for the university to have made such a well-publicized point of recruiting only "senior scholars" to serve on the panel when the services of the director of the campus rec center were more cheaply and conveniently available.

118. "Submission of Professor Ward Churchill to the Board of Regents of the University of Colorado," July 12, 2007 (copy on file).

119. "An important letter from CU President Brown forwarded to CU alumni," July 24, 2007 (distributed by CU Boulder Alumni Association [cobadmin@coloradoalum.org] under the heading "Breaking news re: CU professor Churchill"). For background and analysis, see Allison Sherry, "Donors Applaud Churchill Decision: A CU Spokesman Says Money Wasn't a Factor in Firing the Prof, but There's No Denying Higher Ed Is in a Squeeze," *Denver Post,* July 26, 2007.

120. The potential payoff from my firing had already been calculated; see Berny Morson, "Fundraising Record of $125 Million in CU's Sights," *Rocky Mountain News,* June 7, 2007. Brown attributed such largesse on the part of right-wing donors to "renewed confidence" in the university's leadership.

121. There were other candidates, but their names—and credentials—were withheld even from the regents on grounds of "confidentiality." On Benson's background, see "Bruce Benson Biography," *Daily Camera,* February 21, 2008.

122. See, e.g., Stephanie Simon, "Help Wanted: Lefty College Seeks Right-Wing Prof; CU-Boulder Bid to Endow a 'Conservative' Chair Leaves Both Sides Uneasy," *Wall Street Journal,* May 13, 2008.

123. "University Seeks Suit Dismissal: Fired Professor Alleges Regents Violated His First Amendment Rights," *Colorado Daily,* September 6, 2007.

124. See David Horowitz, *The Professors: The 101 Most Dangerous Academics in America* (Washington, D.C.: Regnery, 2006), ix–xxxvii.

125. John C. Ensslin, "Free Speech Can Cost Profs: Outspoken Faculty Have Paid Price in Loss of Jobs, Tenure," *Rocky Mountain News,* February 12, 2005; David Olinger, "Churchill Isn't Alone, Profs Say: Faculty at Other Colorado Campuses Say Discipline Came Quickly for Their Words," *Denver Post,* March 29, 2005.

126. Matt Williams, "Anderson Files Grievance," *Colorado Daily,* August 29, 2005. Also see quotes from Anderson in Elizabeth Mattern Clark, "Churchill Criticizes CU's Use of Donors: 'If you can't make waves, you can't do your job,'" *Boulder Daily Camera,* October 28, 2005.

127. See "War and Peace at Columbia," *Inside Higher Ed,* April 1, 2005, http://insidehighered.com/ news/2005/04/01/columbia; Madiha R. Tahir, "Columbia Undone: The Anatomy of a Controversy," *Ghadar,* April 2005; on the JDL, once described by the FBI as a terrorist organization, see Janet L. Dolgan, *Jewish Identity and the JDL* (Princeton, N.J.: Princeton University Press, 1977), esp. 33–49; Yair Kottler, *Heil Kahane* (New York: Adama Books, 1986), esp. 46–61.

128. M. E. Mann, R. S. Bradley, and M. K. Hughes, "Northern Hemisphere Temperature Patterns during the Past Millennium: Inferences, Uncertainties, and Limitations," *Geophysical Research Letters,* no. 26 (1999).

129. Barton received $523,099 from ExxonMobil and other such "energy and natural resource interests" during his 2004 reelection campaign; David Ignatius, "A Bid to Chill Thinking: Behind Joe Barton's Assault on Climate Scientists," *Washington Post,* July 22, 2005. For an example of objections accruing from the scientific community, see Union of Concerned Scientists, "Last-Gasp Attempt to Undermine Climate Science? Rep. Joe Barton's Misguided Congressional Investigation," June 23, 2005, http://www.ucsusa.org/global_warming/solutions/Barton-Investiga tion.html, accessed September 9, 2005.

130. "Barton began investigating Mann and his colleagues late last month asking that they justify their work with documents from hundreds of studies. . . . Noting that two Canadian researchers had questioned their findings, Barton wrote that he had opened 'this review because the dispute surrounding your studies bears directly on important questions about federally funded work upon which climate studies rely'"; Juliet Eilperin, "Global-Warming Debate Heats up between Legislators," *Washington Post,* July 18, 2005.

131. John R. Lott, Jr., *More Guns, Less Crime* (Chicago: University of Chicago Press, 1998), 3.

132. Jon Wiener, *Historians in Trouble: Plagiarism, Fraud, and Politics in the Ivory Tower* (New York: New Press, distributed by Norton, 2005), 137, citing, among other things, John R. Lott, Jr., "Packing Protection," *Chicago Sun-Times,* April 30, 1997; John R. Lott, Jr., "Unraveling Some Brady Law Falsehoods," *Los Angeles Times,* July 2, 1997; John R. Lott, Jr., "Childproof Gun Locks: Bound to Misfire," *Wall Street Journal,* July 16, 1997. Also see Lott's testimony before the House Judiciary Committee, "Gun Regulations Can Cost Lives," May 27, 1999, http://www.house .gov/judiciary/lott.pdf, accessed September 13, 2005.

133. The surveys cited said nothing resembling what Lott attributed to them; Otis Dudley Duncan, "Gun Use Surveys: In Numbers We Trust?" *The Criminologist* 25.1 (2000), 1–7.

134. John R. Lott, Jr., *More Guns, Less Crime,* 2nd Q ed. (Chicago: University of Chicago Press, 2000), 3.

135. James Lindgren, "Comments on Questions about John R. Lott's Claims Regarding a 1997 Survey," http://.cse.unsw.edu.au/-lambert/guns/lindgren.html, accessed September 13, 2005. Also see Wiener, *Historians in Trouble,* 138–40.

136. See, as examples, Richard Morin, "Scholar Invents Fan to Answer His Critics," *Washington Post,* February 1, 2003; Claudia Dean and Richard Morin, "A Fabricated Fan and Many Doubts," *Washington Post,* February 11, 2003; David Glenn, "Scholar's Most Vigorous Defender Turns Out to be Himself, Pseudonymously," *Chronicle of Higher Education,* February 14, 2003; Martin Stamasky, "BOOX: Pity the Poor Gun," *New York Times Book Review,* March 2, 2003.

137. Wiener, *Historians in Trouble,* 249 n. 28.

138. See, as examples, John R. Lott, Jr., "Baghdad's Murder Rate Irresponsibly Distorted," *Investor's Business Daily,* December 12, 2003; John R. Lott, Jr., "The Spin on Gun Control," *Washington Times,* November 14, 2003; John R. Lott, Jr., "Many Experts Agree: Concealed Guns Cut Crime," *Madison Capital Times,* September 8, 2003; John R. Lott, Jr., *The Bias against Guns: Why Almost Everything You've Heard about Gun Control Is Wrong* (Chicago: Regnery, 2003).

139. Wiener, *Historians in Trouble,* 147.

ACADEMIC FREEDOM ON THE ROCK

Robert Jensen

THREATS TO ACADEMIC FREEDOM—direct and indirect, subtle and not so subtle—come from a variety of sources: Politicians, the general public, news media, administrators, corporations, and students. In my academic career, I have been criticized from all of those quarters. Though these attacks have been relatively easy to fend off in my particular case, the threats are real and should trouble us; they require of us sharper analysis and a strategic plan to fend off attempts to constrain inquiry. But, even with that understanding of the seriousness of these external threats, I will argue that the most important aspect of the current controversies is how they mark the complacency and timidity of faculty members themselves.

I will focus on two specific incidents in my career—one involving administrators and the other students—that illustrate these threats. From there, I will examine the responses of faculty members on my campus to the events, and offer suggestions for analysis and action. Throughout I will remain rooted in my own experience at the University of Texas at Austin. While Texas may in some ways be idiosyncratic, I do not believe my experience at that university is radically different from others around the United States.

My concern with this issue is not rooted in optimism for the short term. While I would like to see U.S. academics, as a class, take a leading role in movements to assert radical humanistic values that have the possibility of transforming society, I don't believe it is likely, or even possible in the near future. In fact, I assume that in the short term there is very little progressive political change likely in the United States, with or without the assistance of university-based academics. But we should work to hold onto what protections for academic freedom do exist in order to provide some space for critical thinking in an otherwise paved-over intellectual culture, with an eye on the long term. Toward that goal, I will suggest ways to approach these threats to academic freedom and attempt to assess realistically the conditions under which such defenses go forward.

HISTORY AND CONTEXT
⚭

Although threats to academic freedom, and freedom of expression more generally, can come rooted in many political projects, it is in times of war and national crisis (real or manufactured) that such threats intensify and have the potential to undermine democracy most severely. Such is the case in the post-9/11 world. In this sense, the "war on terrorism" serves a function similar to the Cold War as a way to both obscure the fundamental motivations behind U.S. foreign policy (to extend and deepen U.S. domination over the strategically crucial areas of the world through a combination of diplomatic, military, and economic control mechanisms) and focus public attention on threats that, while not completely illusory, are overdramatized. In each case, politicians also hype the threat to make it easier to marginalize any domestic dissent to the project of control and domination. One can see echoes of the late 1940s and the 1950s in the post-9/11 United States. In such situations, dissident intellectuals and their academic freedom become easy targets.

Despite these similarities, it is crucial to recognize that the repression of the Cold War dwarfs anything we've seen in recent years. The Supreme Court upheld the criminalization of political discourse in what became known as the Communist conspiracy cases prosecuted under the Smith Act of 1940.[1] The law made it a crime to discuss the "duty, necessity, desirability, or propriety of overthrowing or destroying the government," an odd statute in a country created by a revolution against the legal government of that day. It was not until 1957 that the Supreme Court reversed the trend in those cases, overturning convictions under the act.[2] In that repressive social climate, principles of academic freedom and administrative protections around tenure meant little, as universities routinely ignored both principles and rules, with no objection from the courts.[3]

Both the general public and academics live with far more expansive freedoms today, primarily as a result of the popular movements of the 1960s and 1970s, which pressured elites to expand free speech and association rights. We should recognize that since 9/11, for example, many people critical of U.S. foreign and military policy have written and spoken in ways that would have without question landed them in jail in previous eras (and would land them in jail, or worse, in many other nations today). Of course, it is crucial to note that such protection is still incomplete and is most available to those who are from the dominant sectors of society. I am white and American-born, with a "normal" sounding American name (meaning, one that indicates northern European roots), and while I have been the target of much hostility, I have never felt that my safety or job were threatened in any serious way. The hostility toward some faculty members has not stayed within such civil boundaries, most notably toward Sami Al-Arian, the tenured Palestinian computer science professor at the University of South Florida who was vilified in the mass media and fired in December 2001 for his political views, and then subjected to federal prosecution/persecution.[4] Being a white boy with tenure offers added protection.

So, much of the discussion about academic freedom these days is not about direct attempts to remove or punish faculty members for their ideas—with some notable exceptions, such as Ward Churchill (a tenured ethnic-studies professor fired in 2007 from the University of Colorado at Boulder after intense public controversy concerning critical comments he made on U.S. foreign policy after 9/11) and Nadia Abu El-Haj (an anthropology professor at Barnard College whose 2007 bid for tenure was challenged, unsuccessfully, by pro-Israeli groups and individuals who objected to her research). Instead, typically we are struggling with issues about the climate on campus and in society more generally. These questions are no less important, but we should keep in mind the relative level of the threat as we strategize.

FROM ADMINISTRATORS: "AN UNDILUTED FOUNTAIN OF FOOLISHNESS"

❧

About midafternoon on September 11, 2001, I began writing an essay that argued the United States should not use the attacks to justify aggressive war, one of several pieces that would circulate in Left/progressive circles. At the end of the evening, I sent it to Common Dreams and other such polit-

ical websites under the headline "Stop the insanity here."[5] Just as I was
shutting down the computer for the evening, on a whim I decided also to
send the piece to several Texas newspapers for which I had occasionally
written, though I did not expect that any would publish it given the emo-
tional/political realities right after the attacks. Surprisingly, the *Houston
Chronicle* ran the piece at the end of the week, under the headline "U.S. Just
as Guilty of Committing Own Violent Acts."[6] By midmorning, right-wing
talk show hosts in Houston had read the piece on the air and encouraged
people to call and write University of Texas officials to demand my firing.
The deluge of mail, to me and my various bosses, continued for weeks. On
September 18, UT president Larry Faulkner began circulating an official
response, which was published the next day in the *Chronicle*:[7]

> In his Sept. 14 Outlook article "U.S. just as guilty of committing own
> violent acts," Robert Jensen was identified as holding a faculty ap-
> pointment at the University of Texas at Austin. Jensen made his re-
> marks entirely in his capacity as a free citizen of the United States,
> writing and speaking under the protection of the First Amendment
> of the U.S. Constitution. No aspect of his remarks is supported,
> condoned or officially recognized by The University of Texas at
> Austin. He does not speak in the University's name and may not
> speak in its name. Using the same liberty, I convey my personal judg-
> ment that Jensen is not only misguided, but has become a fountain
> of undiluted foolishness on issues of public policy. Students must
> learn that there is a good deal of foolish opinion in the popular me-
> dia and they must become skilled at recognizing and discounting it.
> I, too, was disgusted by Jensen's article, but I also must defend his
> freedom to state his opinion. The First Amendment is the bedrock
> of American liberty.

This was the first time in anyone's memory that a high-ranking university
official had publicly condemned a faculty member by name for political or
intellectual beliefs. In addition to this public rebuke, some other administrators circulated notes privately with similar views. For example, UT
provost Sheldon Ekland-Olson wrote, in a note he copied to me: "What
came to my mind when reading his column was a statement, at the moment I do not recall who said it, that the price of freedom of speech and
the press is that we must put up with a good deal of offensive rubbish. For
me, Professor Jensen's comments fall deeply into this category."

I had previously crossed paths with Faulkner and the UT administration during campus organizing efforts around affirmative action and the wages/working conditions for nonteaching staff. I had met Faulkner once during the former campaign, and I was aware that I was not on his list of favorite faculty members. But at the time of this incident I assumed (and nothing since then has changed my assumption) that his letter denouncing me had little or nothing to do with me and was simply a reaction to pressure from various key constituencies: alumni, donors, legislators, and the general public. I didn't take Faulkner's rebuke personally, because it clearly wasn't about me.

For some weeks after that, I was asked how I felt about Faulkner's statement and what effect it had on my behavior. I stated repeatedly in public that I didn't *feel* anything in particular; administrators' opinions about my writing had never been of great importance to me. Nor was I affected by the denunciation; I continued my political work without interruption and taught my classes as I would have if there had been no controversy. When people asked me if I thought my academic freedom had been compromised, I was tempted to laugh. I am a tenured professor at a moment in history in which tenure is honored in all but a handful of extremely controversial cases. My academic freedom was, at that moment, not in jeopardy. But I did critique Faulkner for his comments, on two points.

First, Faulkner's statement modeled bad intellectual practice. He engaged in an ad hominem attack, condemning me for my views without attempting to explain what substantive disagreements he had with my position. As far as I know, he has never made such an explanation in a public forum, though I know of one case in which he turned down the chance to engage me directly (on an NPR radio show). While refusing such an engagement was strategically sensible given his objectives, it was intellectually and morally cowardly.

More important, of course, was the possible chilling effect of Faulkner's broadside on others, especially junior professors and students. Whatever Faulkner's strategy—whether he was simply trying to placate important constituencies or actually intended to create a climate on campus hostile to dissent—I heard directly from one untenured professor and several graduate students that they had modified or ended political activities when they read the statement. I assume many others made similar choices.

Was any of this an attack on academic freedom? Not in direct fashion; no one's rights were abridged. But it was not the kind of practice one would hope for from the leader of a major university.

FROM STUDENTS: "THE GUISE OF TEACHING
POTENTIAL JOURNALISTS TO 'THINK'"

⚭

In 2004 a conservative student group at the University of Texas published a "professor watch list" of instructors who "push an ideological viewpoint on their students through oftentimes subtle but sometimes abrasive methods of indoctrination."[8] After a lifetime of being second-rate, I was proud to finally be number one in something, albeit a list of allegedly deficient professors.

I have long held that one of the most serious problems on my campus—which is among the largest in the country, with 50,000 students—has been that the student body is largely depoliticized. Given that lack of political engagement, I am grateful for anything that gets students talking about politics, especially the role of politics in the university. So, when my name ended up on this list of the alleged indoctrinators (with no clear indication whether I am subtle or abrasive), I wasn't upset, even though the group's description of my introductory journalism course didn't quite square with my experience in the classroom:

> In a survey course about Journalism, one might expect to learn about the industry, some basics about reporting and layout, the history of journalism, the values of a free press and what careers make the news machine function. Instead, Jensen introduces the unsuspecting student to a crash course in socialism, white privilege, the "truth" about the Persian Gulf War and the role of America as the world's prominent sponsor of terrorism. Jensen half-heartedly attempts to tie his rants to "critical issues" in journalism, insisting his lessons are valid under the guise of teaching potential journalists to "think" about the world around them. Jensen is also renowned for using class time when he teaches Media Law and Ethics to "come out" and analogize gay rights with the civil rights movement.[9] Ostensibly, this relates somehow to his course material.[10]

It's possible that this watch-list strategy sprang fresh from the minds of the Young Conservatives of Texas, but it's more likely they were influenced by the national group Students for Academic Freedom[11] and leftist-turned-right-wing-activist David Horowitz.[12] Their strategy is simple: Rather than attack specific professors for holding views critical of the dominant culture and its institutions, better to claim that the universities are dominated by these kinds of critical intellectuals who crowd out other perspectives. Instead of calling for the firing of lefties, the group calls for promoting greater balance, out of its dedication to "restoring academic freedom and educational values to America's institutions of higher learning" through pursuit of four key goals:

1. To promote intellectual diversity on campus
2. To defend the right of students to be treated with respect by faculty and administrators, regardless of their political or religious beliefs
3. To promote fairness, civility and inclusion in student affairs
4. To secure the adoption of the "Academic Bill of Rights" as official university policy[13]

Especially brilliant is the co-optation of the concept of diversity to argue that conservative forces (forget, for a moment, that conservatives, and fairly reactionary conservatives at that, just happen to run most of the world these days) are barely surviving under the jackboot of Stalinist intellectuals.[14] The strategy of the Right[15] seems fairly clear: To avoid looking fascistic, these groups cloak themselves in an odd combination of core Enlightenment values (the importance of the university as an open intellectual space) and a caricatured postmodern relativism (everybody's truth is valid, so the goal is simply balance because no definitive judgments are possible).

In such a world, it seems to me that one of the main tasks is to challenge a key assumption of the right-wing project: Professors can, and should, eliminate their own politics from the classroom. For example, the UT professor watch list valorizes one professor who "so well hides his own beliefs from the classroom that one is forced to wonder if he has any political leaning at all." These illusions of neutrality only confuse students about the nature of inquiry into human society and behavior.

All teaching—especially in the humanities and the social sciences—has a political dimension, and we shouldn't fear that. The question isn't whether professors should leave their politics at the door (they can't) but whether professors are responsible in the way they present their politics and can defend their pedagogical decisions. It's clear that every decision a professor makes—choice of topics, textbook selection, how material is presented—has an underlying politics. If the professor's views are safely within the conventional wisdom of the dominant sectors of society, it might appear the class is apolitical. Only when professors challenge that conventional wisdom do we hear talk about "politicized" classrooms.

But just because the classroom always is politicized in courses that deal with how we organize ourselves politically, economically, and socially, we should not suggest that it's all just politics. Because there's a politics to teaching doesn't mean teaching is nothing but politics; indeed, professors shouldn't proselytize for their positions in the classroom. Instead, when it's appropriate—and in the courses I teach, it often is—professors should highlight the inevitable political judgments that underlie teaching. Students—especially those who disagree with a professor's views—will come to see that the professor has opinions, which is a good thing. Professors should be modeling how to present and defend an argument with evidence and logic.

For example, in both my Critical Issues in Journalism and Media Law and Ethics classes, I offer a critique of corporations in capitalism. For most students, corporations and capitalism have been naturalized, accepted as the only possible way to organize an economy. I suggest to them a fairly obvious point: The modern corporation—a fairly recent invention—should be examined critically, not taken as a naturally occurring object. Given the phenomenal power of corporations, including media corporations, in contemporary America, how could one teach about journalism and law without a critical examination of not only the occasional high-profile corporate scandals but the core nature of the institution?

The conservative group claimed its goal is "a fair and balanced delivery of information" in the classroom. If that really were their concern, of course, the first place they would train their attention is the business school. (I've heard reports that some faculty members there teach courses in marketing, management, finance, and accounting that rarely, if ever, raise fundamental questions about capitalism.) Highlighting the selective way in which accusations of politicized classrooms are identified and faculty are targeted for sanction is crucial.

FACULTY RESPONSES TO THE WATCH LIST: CHICKEN LITTLE
ᴄᴀ

Rather than focus on the threats posed by administrator condemnations or student campaigns aimed at Left/liberal biases, I want to focus on the responses I have seen and heard from faculty members on my campus. Again, I don't pretend that the University of Texas is representative.

Rather than claim this is the way most faculty in the United States act, I want to highlight what I consider to be the problems in some faculty members' reactions where I work. I'll begin with the watch list.

In informal conversations as these political campaigns have gained prominence, I have heard far too many of what I believed to be overly dramatic responses, including references to these student efforts as McCarthyism or a suppression of academic freedom. Yes, these student initiatives are part of a broader goal of shutting down some of the remaining institutional spaces left for critical, independent inquiry. But it is inaccurate and counterproductive to compare a student-initiated endeavor (even if the inspiration for it comes from right-wing political operatives) to the use of state power to fire professors and destroy people's lives on a large scale. Could we someday return to the suppression of the two major Red Scares of the twentieth century? Of course it's possible, but it's not happening now. And to talk in those terms is to invite being labeled by the public as overreactive, whiny, self-indulgent intellectuals cut off from the day-to-day reality of most people's struggles in the employment world, where job protection on the order of academic tenure is the stuff of dreams. The public is quick to label us that way, in part because it is so often an apt description of so many faculty members. Professorial rhetoric that bolsters the perception is not strategically helpful.

For example, one of my UT colleagues said in a television news story about the watch list: "I feel like they [students observing his class for potential inclusion on the watch list] were put there to watch me. And this watch list or my position on this watch list is a result of that. So, do I feel like I'm under surveillance? I am under surveillance."

First, is it accurate and/or strategic to describe the presence of a student in your class, even one there to keep tabs on any hint of professional failure, as being under surveillance, given that the term carries a connotation of being shadowed by law enforcement? Second, why is it a bad thing for students to be paying close attention to our teaching? In my large classes, where there is physical space available for visitors and their presence would not disrupt the flow of the class, I invite anyone to sit in. In fact, I would be happy to have a team of right-wing ideologues sit through my classes, for two simple reasons. One is that knowing they were present likely would make me strive to be even more precise in my use of language; knowing someone from a dissenting position is in the audience tends to make me more conscious of what I'm saying, which is good. Another is that I am confident that I can defend the content of my course and my teaching methods, and I would invite a debate in which I could defend myself.

In short: The sky is not falling because of a student-generated professor watch list. Yes, we are in a period of backlash and reactionary right-wing domination of all the society's major institutions. Yes, we struggle to cope with how to handle students in a modern liberal university who are often resistant to considering any critique that goes against their preconceived notions of the political and moral order. There are more than enough serious issues to grapple with, and taken together these concerns suggest this society is on a dangerous course. But we should talk about the danger in that context, not episodically and overly dramatically. The sky is clouding but it is not falling.

FACULTY RESPONSES TO ADMINISTRATION CONDEMNATIONS: LITTLE CHICKENS
ঞ

After sixteen years in academic life, I have concluded that the vast majority of faculty members are like the vast majority of any comfortable professionals in a corporate capitalist empire: Morally lazy, usually cowardly, and unwilling and/or unable to engage with critics. I say that with no sense of superiority; I can look at my own life and see examples of such laziness and cowardice. Perhaps because of that, I am willing to name it in our profession.

Let me offer an anecdote to illustrate. During fall semester 2005, I was leaving a meeting of the University of Texas's faculty Committee of Counsel on Academic Freedom and Responsibility. By some fluke, I had been elected to this university-wide committee, which is charged by the Faculty Council with the task of monitoring these issues on campus. (All of this is window dressing; at the University of Texas, there is no faculty governance and all committees are merely consultative.)[16]

As a fellow committee member and I walked back to our offices, he asked what action this committee took in 2001, after Faulkner had condemned me. (That's an indication of the importance of the committee and its pronouncements; virtually no one remembers what it says, or even that it exists.) I told him that the committee had passed a weak resolution that reasserted the basics of academic freedom and asked people to be nice to each other, but made no reference to the controversy and rendered no judgment about the UT president's actions. The resolution is as follows:

RESOLUTION FROM THE COMMITTEE OF COUNSEL ON ACADEMIC FREEDOM AND RESPONSIBILITY

Given current national and global events and the importance of members of the University community discussing these matters on campus and extramurally, the Committee of Counsel on Academic Freedom and Responsibility submits the following Resolution. Resolved:

1) That all members of the University community—students, faculty, staff, and administrators—be reminded of the principles involving Academic Freedom and Responsibility as stated by the American Association of University Professors in the 1940 Statement of Principles on Academic Freedom and Tenure, including:

    a) "The common good depends upon the free search for truth and its free exposition."

    b) "College and university teachers are citizens, members of a learned profession, and officers of an educational institution. When they speak and write as citizens, they should be free from institutional censorship or discipline, but their special position in the community imposes special obligations. As scholars and educational officers, they should remember that the public may judge their profession and their institution by their utterances. Hence they should at all times be accurate, should exercise appropriate restraint, should show respect for the opinions of others, and should make every effort to indicate that they are not speaking for the institution."

2) That these principles of Academic Freedom and Responsibility be widely disseminated to the University community via e-mail and in the Daily Texan [campus student newspaper] so that all students, faculty, staff, and administrators have these statements as guiding principles for discourse on campus and extramurally.

3) That the members of the academic community treat one another with dignity in both their words and actions during the days ahead.[17]

Shortly after that resolution was passed, I asked the chair of that committee why something more forceful wasn't presented to the Faculty Council—something that at least raised the actual question instead of reproducing boilerplate. The chair explained that any resolution of that kind would not have received support from the committee. The implication was that there was no significant support for me, my political position, or the notion that a faculty member with such positions should be defended on principle.

I reported this to my faculty colleague on the current committee, and he expressed outrage. How could the committee not have taken a more forceful position? Whatever the disagreements with my politics, didn't they see the issue about creating a supportive climate for free expression and scholarship? he asked. I offered no judgment of the committee, but instead asked this colleague what action he had taken at the time if he felt so strongly about the principle? He hesitated. I pressed: We are faculty members in the same department. Did anyone in our department circulate a letter of support? Did anyone on the faculty generate a petition critical of the president? He froze and didn't respond, but the answer is, no. I know of only one UT professor who, in a letter to the campus paper, publicly criticized the president's actions. On a progressive listserv there was discussion of a petition drive that never materialized. I was busy in those weeks and may have missed it, but to the best of my knowledge there was no public faculty action to rebuke a university president who had singled out a faculty member for ridicule in the largest newspaper in the state. Some professors told me later that they weighed in privately with the president, but such private interventions clearly were not going to result in any change in the president's public stance and, hence, were politically irrelevant. Beyond that, such private action did nothing to resist the narrowing of discussion in public.

So, on one of the largest university campuses in the United States with about 2,500 faculty members, the committee charged with protecting academic freedom was silent on the most prominent attack on a faculty member for political reasons in recent memory. But, more striking, a faculty member who had done nothing to support academic freedom in that crucial moment seemed to have rewritten history in his own mind to forget that he, like virtually all the others, had remained silent in public.

It is one thing for members of a privileged class to decide they will avoid confrontations with power in order to protect there privilege. Depending on the context, we may deem that to be cowardly or expedient. But for such people to then twist reality to allow them to valorize themselves is, in any context, pathetic. It shows the degree to which some (perhaps a majority) of faculty are ill-equipped to assess threats to academic freedom or present an effective defense.

WHAT I AM NOT SAYING, POLITELY
❧

I am not arguing that all faculty members must commit themselves to my politics or my style of public political engagement.

I am not bitter. Given the contemporary political landscape, I do not expect support from faculty members for my political activities.

I am not disappointed. As a class, faculty members act in ways that one would expect a privileged class to act.

I am not overly optimistic that these conditions—either in the political culture generally or in academia specifically—will change in the short term. The struggle is best understood as a long-term effort on all fronts.

I am not spending a lot of time worrying about this, given the myriad other ways I can spend my time and energy in political engagement in the world. Academic freedom matters, but not to the exclusion of other pressing issues.

And, I am not trying to paint with too broad a brush. I am aware that throughout the United States there are faculty members who take academic freedom seriously and are diligent in defending it.

WHAT I AM SAYING, BLUNTLY
❧

The AAUP's 1915 Declaration of Principles—freedom of (1) inquiry and research, (2) teaching within the university, and (3) extramural utterance or action—is worth defending, but not because most faculty members can be expected to make serious use of these privileges to challenge power, and not because at this moment in history the university is a space where most faculty members pursue truly critical, independent inquiry. I find much of the university with which I am familiar (the humanities and the social sciences) to be populated with self-important and self-indulgent caricatures. Much of the intellectual work is trivial, irrelevant, and/or flabby. Most components of the contemporary U.S. university have been bought off, and bought off fairly cheaply. As a result, in the words of my late friend Abe Osheroff, the institution is generally "a fucking dead rock."

Osheroff, a lifelong radical activist who died in 2008 at the age of ninety-two,[18] exemplified an organic intellectual. In a 2005 interview with him about contemporary intellectual and political issues, I asked Osheroff about universities and faculty members:

You can take this as a criticism, an indictment, of your profession, but most academics aren't worth shit as activists. You're overpaid, and you still all complain about the workload. I was lucky. I got out of the academic game early. What saved my ass was becoming a carpenter. . . . The fact is that I have contempt for most of academia. Not just criticism, but contempt for it as an institution. I know there are some wonderful teachers here and there, but to me the universities are mostly fucking dead rocks. There are some diamonds and some gold that you can discover, but basically it's a fucking dead rock. I have a professor friend who tells me about his investment in his career. Yea, well while academics are doing their thing, some guys were down in a hole in the ground digging coal and making concrete and building your houses. Let's think about those people. Don't talk to me about your fucking investment. Academia was not too difficult a road. There are things worse than having to sit up at night and read books. Try 'em. Go out and dig a hole in the ground every fucking day, eight hours a day, and then you come back and we'll talk about it. I'm a little extreme, I must admit, but just the word academia makes me growl.[19]

Those of us who have the privilege of making a living as academics would do well to take Osheroff's words to heart. Perhaps he was a bit harsh in his condemnation, but can one blame a lifelong radical activist who has taken serious risks in his life for such an assessment of a privileged group that takes so few risks? The spirit of his remarks seem fair to me. It is a reminder that we all—even those of us who try to commit significant amounts of our time and energy to our obligations as citizens and human beings, and who attempt to leverage some of our institutional resources for progressive public activity—should always be asking a simple question: Are we doing enough? I know no one, including myself, for whom the answer is a definitive yes.

The impetus to protect academic freedom should be seen in this context, as part of a long-term strategy of protecting a saving remnant of intellectual integrity that at some point in the future *may* provide the core of a politically activated group that can be part of a meaningful shift in values in this society. There are no guarantees. But we can be reasonably sure that the common faculty reactions today—(1) duck-and-cover when things get edgy, or (2) whine when there really is little at stake—guarantee failure.

NOTES

1. *Dennis v. United States,* 341 U.S. 494 (1951).

2. *Yates v. United States,* 354 U.S. 298 (1957).

3. Noam Chomsky et al., *The Cold War and the University: Toward an Intellectual History of the Postwar Years* (New York: New Press, 1997).

4. Al-Arian was indicted in 2003 by the U.S. government on charges that he used an academic think-tank at USF and an Islamic charity as fronts to raise money for the Palestinian Islamic Jihad. He eventually was acquitted on eight charges, with the jury deadlocked on the remaining nine counts. Al-Arian agreed in 2006 to plead guilty to one count of conspiring to aid the PIJ and was sentenced to fifty-seven months, most of which he had served awaiting trial, to be followed by deportation. Al-Arian was then subpoenaed to testify before a new grand jury, which he refused to do, and as of June 2008 he remained imprisoned under civil contempt citations. For details, see the documentary film *USA vs Al-Arian,* dir. Line Halvorsen (2007), http://www.usavsalarian.com/, accessed November 23, 2008.

5. Robert Jensen, "Stop the Insanity Here," Common Dreams News Center, September 12, 2001, http://www.commondreams.org/views01/0912-08.htm, accessed November 23, 2008.

6. Robert Jensen, "U.S. Just as Guilty of Committing Own Violent Acts," *Houston Chronicle,* September 14, 2001, A33, http://www.chron.com/cs/CDA/story.hts/editorial/1047072, accessed November 23, 2008.

7. Larry R. Faulkner, "Jensen's Words His Own," *Houston Chronicle,* September 19, 2001, A39, http://www.chron.com/cs/CDA/story.hts/editorial/1053207#jensen, accessed November 23, 2008.

8. http://studentorgs.utexas.edu/yct/events/watchlist/, accessed November 23, 2008.

9. At one point I did publicly identify as gay. I am today most accurately categorized as bisexual. For details, see Robert Jensen, "Homecoming: The Relevance of Radical Feminism for Gay Men," *Journal of Homosexuality* 47.3–4 (2004): 75–81. Reprinted in Todd G. Morrison, ed., *Eclectic Views on Gay Male Pornography: Pornucopia* (Binghamton, N.Y.: Harrington Park Press, 2004).

10. http://studentorgs.utexas.edu/yct/events/watchlist/.

11. http://www.studentsforacademicfreedom.org/.

12. http://www.frontpagemag.com/.

13. http://www.studentsforacademicfreedom.org/documents/1917/pamphlet.html, accessed November 23, 2008.

14. For an analysis of the limits of diversity talk, see "Against Diversity, For Politics" in Robert Jensen, *The Heart of Whiteness: Confronting Race, Racism, and White Privilege* (San Francisco: City Lights, 2005), 77–87.

15. For an assessment of Horowitz's and SAF's tactics and honesty, see Molly Riordan, "Academic Freedom Takes a Step to the Right," *PR Watch,* 2005, http://www.prwatch.org/prwissues/2005Q3/saf.html, accessed November 23, 2008.

16. To be fair, this is perhaps not completely accurate. When I made this point in a committee meeting, a faculty member objected, saying he had been on the Parking Committee, which had the ability to set policy. To date, I have not taken the time to find out if, in fact, the faculty members on the Parking Committee have this power.

17. http://www.utexas.edu/faculty/council/2001-2002/legislation/ccafr.html, accessed November 23, 2008.

18. Robert Jensen, "The End of Osheroff's Dance: Lessons from a Life of Resistance and Love," Monthly Review Zine, April 9, 2008, http://mrzine.monthlyreview.org/jenseno90408.html, accessed November 23, 2008.

19. Robert Jensen, "Abe Osheroff: On the Joys and Risks of Living Authentically in the Empire," October 2005, http://thirdcoastactivist.org/abe-osheroff.pdf, accessed November 23, 2008.

CONTRIBUTORS

Ward Churchill (Keetoowah Band Cherokee) formerly was Chair of the Department of Ethnic Studies at the University of Colorado at Boulder. He is the author, most recently, of *Pacifism as Pathology: Reflections on the Role of Armed Struggle in North America,* with Mike Ryan and with an introduction by Derrick Jensen (AK Press, 2007) and the forthcoming *To Disrupt, Discredit and Destroy: The FBI's Secret War against the Black Panther Party* (2010). Five of his more than twenty books have received human rights writing awards, while a sixth was a runner- up for the Colorado Book Award for nonfiction writing in 1996. Among the many honors he has received at the University of Colorado are the President's University Service Award (1987), the Robert L. Stearns Alumni Award for Service (1988), the Thomas Jefferson Award (1990), the College of Arts and Sciences Award for Best Writing in the Social Sciences (1992), the Boulder Faculty Assembly Award for Excellence in Teaching (1994), and the Herd Award for Best Undergraduate Teacher (2005).

Ashley Dawson is Associate Professor of English at the Graduate Center, City University of New York, where he specializes in postcolonial studies. He is the author of *Mongrel Nation: Diasporic Culture and the Making of Postcolonial Britain* (University of Michigan Press, 2007) and coeditor of two essay collections: *Democracy, States, and the Struggle for Global Justice,* coedited with Heather Gautney et al. (Routledge, 2009); and *Exceptional State: Contemporary U.S. Culture and the New Imperialism,* coedited with Malini Johar Schueller (Duke University Press, 2007).

Robert Jensen is Associate Professor in the School of Journalism and director of the Senior Fellows Honors Program of the College of Communication at the University of Texas at Austin. Jensen is the author of *All My Bones Shake: Seeking a Progressive Path to the Prophetic Voice* (Soft Skull Press,

2009); *Getting Off: Pornography and the End of Masculinity* (South End Press, 2007); *The Heart of Whiteness: Confronting Race, Racism, and White Privilege* (City Lights, 2005); *Citizens of the Empire: The Struggle to Claim Our Humanity* (City Lights, 2004); and *Writing Dissent: Taking Radical Ideas from the Margins to the Mainstream* (Peter Lang, 2002); coauthor with Gail Dines and Ann Russo *of Pornography: The Production and Consumption of Inequality* (Routledge, 1998); and coeditor with David S. Allen of *Freeing the First Amendment: Critical Perspectives on Freedom of Expression* (New York University Press, 1995).

Stephen Leberstein was the longtime Executive Director of the Center for Worker Education at City College, which he helped found and where he taught history. He now teaches part-time on race, labor, radicalism, and abolitionism at the Brooklyn College Graduate Center for Worker Education. He is a member of the editorial board of *WorkingUSA: The Journal of Labor and Society.* He has written on French syndicalism at the turn of the twentieth century and on political repression of the labor Left in the United States, a project that he is pursuing this year as the Frederic Ewen Academic Freedom Fellow at the Tamiment Library of New York University. He has been active in his union, the Professional Staff Congress, as Chair of its chapter at City College, as Chair of its Academic Freedom Committee, and as delegate and grievance counselor. Leberstein earned a Ph.D. in European history from the University of Wisconsin at Madison.

Sophia McClennen is Associate Professor of Comparative Literature, Spanish, and Women's Studies at Pennsylvania State University, University Park, where she directs the graduate program in Comparative Literature. Her books include *The Dialectics of Exile: Nation, Time, Language, and Space in Hispanic Literatures* (Purdue University Press, 2004); *Comparative Cultural Studies and Latin America,* coedited with Earl E. Fitz (Purdue University Press, 2004); *Ariel Dorfman: An Aesthetics of Hope* (forthcoming, Duke University Press, 2009); and a volume entitled *Representing Humanity in an Age of Terror,* coedited with Henry James Morello (forthcoming, Purdue University Press, 2009). She has published a series of articles on the assaults on higher education in journals such as *Comparative American Studies, College Literature, Counterpunch, Works and Days,* and *Radical Teacher.*

Bill V. Mullen is Professor of English and Director of American Studies at Purdue University. He is the author or editor of several books, including

Afro-Orientalism (University of Minnesota Press, 2004); and *Afro Asia: Revolutionary Political and Cultural Connections between African Americans and Asian Americans,* coedited with Fred Ho (Duke University Press, 2008).

Cary Nelson is Professor of English at the University of Illinois, Urbana-Champaign, and president of the American Association of University Professors. He has coauthored the Association's Redbook statements on graduate students and on academic professionals. His twenty-five authored or edited books include *The Incarnate Word: Literature as Verbal Space* (University of Illinois Press, 1973); *Our Last First Poets: Vision and History in Contemporary American Poetry* (University of Illinois Press, 1981); *Marxism and the Interpretation of Culture,* coedited with Lawrence Grossberg (University of Illinois Press, 1987); *Cultural Studies,* coedited with Lawrence Grossberg, Paula A. Treichler, et al. (Routledge, 1992); *Higher Education under Fire: Politics, Economics, and the Crisis of the Humanities,* coedited with Michael Bérubé (Routledge, 1994); *Will Teach for Food: Academic Labor in Crisis* (edited volume) (University of Minnesota Press, 1997); *Academic Keywords: A Devil's Dictionary for Higher Education,* with coauthor Stephen Watt (Routledge, 1999); *Revolutionary Memory: Recovering the Poetry of the American Left* (Routledge, 2001); and *Office Hours: Activism and Change in the Academy,* with coauthor Stephen Watt (Routledge, 2004). He is the author of over a hundred essays, including a number published in *Academe, The Chronicle of Higher Education,* and *Inside Higher Education.*

Robert M. O'Neil continues to teach a First Amendment Clinic at the University of Virginia School of Law, though he retired in the summer of 2007 from full-time teaching. In the spring semester of 2009 he will be teaching Constitutional Law of Church and State at the University of Texas Law School. Formerly President of the University of Wisconsin System (1979–85) and of the University of Virginia (1985–90), as well as serving in other senior administrative posts at the University of Cincinnati and Indiana University—Bloomington, he has taught constitutional law at each institution. He is Founding Director of the Thomas Jefferson Center for the Protection of Free Expression and Director of the Ford Foundation's Difficult Dialogues Initiative. He has held several roles in the American Association of University Professors—twice as General Counsel, seven years as Chair of Committee A on Academic Freedom and Tenure, and currently as Chair of the Special Committee on Academic Freedom and National Security in Time of Crisis. His writings include many law review articles and comments in higher education journals. His most recent book is *Academic Freedom in the Wired World: Political Extremism, Corporate Power, and the University* (Harvard University Press, 2008).

Michael Palm is Assistant Professor of Media and Cultural Studies in the Communication Studies Department at the University of North Carolina at Chapel Hill. He served as bargaining unit chairperson for GSOC/UAW Local 2110, the union for graduate students employed by New York University, from 2004 to 2007. He is a coeditor of *The University against Itself: The NYU Strike and the Future of the Academic Workplace,* coedited with Monika Krause et al. (Temple University Press, 2008), and the editor of a special 2007 issue of *Workplace: A Journal of Academic Labor* devoted to the New York University strike. He is currently writing a book based on his dissertation, provisionally titled "Phoning It In: Self-Service, Telecommunications and New Consumer Labor."

Vijay Prashad is the George and Martha Kellner Chair of South Asian History and Director of International Studies at Trinity College. His most recent book is *The Darker Nations: A People's History of the Third World* (New Press, 2007).

R. Radhakrishnan is Professor of English and Comparative Literature at the University of California, Irvine. He is the author of *Diasporic Mediations: Between Home and Location* (University of Minnesota Press, 1996), *Theory in an Uneven World* (Blackwell, 2003), *Between Identity and Location: The Cultural Politics of Theory* (Orient Longman, India, 2007), and *History, the Human, and the World Between* (Duke, 2008). He is completing *Edward Said: A Contrapuntal Dictionary* (Blackwell, 2010) and a collection of essays *When Is the Political?* He is also coeditor of *Theory as Variation* (Pencraft, India, 2007), coeditor with Susan Koshy of *Transnational South Asians: The Making of a Neo-diaspora* (Oxford University Press, 2008), and coeditor with Kailash Baral of *Theory after Derrida: Essays in Critical Praxis* (Routledge, 2009). His essays and articles have appeared in a wide range of national and international journals and collections. Author of a volume of poems in Tamil, he is also a translator of contemporary Tamil fiction into English.

Andrew Ross is Professor and Chair of the Department of Social and Cultural Analysis at New York University. He is the author of several books, including *Nice Work if You Can Get It: Life and Labor in Precarious Times* (New York University Press, 2009), *Fast Boat to China: Corporate Flight and the Consequences of Free Trade—Lessons from Shanghai* (Pantheon, 2006), *Low Pay, High Profile: The Global Push for Fair Labor* (New Press, 2004), *No-Collar: The Humane Workplace and Its Hidden Costs* (Basic Books, 2003), and *The Celebration Chronicles: Life, Liberty and the Pursuit of Property Value in Disney's New Town* (Ballantine, 1999). He has also edited several books, including *No Sweat: Fashion, Free Trade, and the Rights of Garment Workers* (Verso, 1997), *Anti Americanism,* coedited with Kristin Ross (New York University Press, 2004); and *The University against Itself: The NYU Strike and the Future of the Academic Workplace,* coedited with Monika Krause et al. (Temple University Press, 2008).

Malini Johar Schueller is Professor of English at the University of Florida. She is the author of *The Politics of Voice: Liberalism and Social Criticism from Franklin to Kingston* (State University of New York Press, 1992), *U.S. Orientalisms: Race, Nation, and Gender in Literature 1790–1890* (University of Michigan Press, 1998), and *Locating Race: Global Sites of Post-Colonial Citizenship* (State University of New York Press, 2009). She has also coedited *Messy Beginnings: Postcoloniality and Early American Studies,* coedited with Edward Watts (Rutgers University Press, 2003); and *Exceptional State: Contemporary U.S. Culture and the New Imperialism,* coedited with Ashley Dawson (Duke University Press, 2007). Her essays have appeared in journals such as *American Literature, SIGNS, Cultural Critique, Social Text,* and *Counterpunch.*

Susan Valentine is a Ph.D. candidate in Medieval History at New York University and a staff organizer with Unite Here. She was an organizer and press spokesperson during GSOC/UAW strike in 2005–6.

INDEX